La Nouvelle Agence
7, rue Corneille
75006 Paris

Bach in Berlin

Mendelssohn's instrumentation (music for the first violin) of the 1829 performance of the *St. Matthew Passion*: Evangelist's recitative, "Und siehe da, der Vorhang im Tempel zerriss in zwei Stück" [And behold, the veil of the temple was rent in two]. From *200 Jahre Sing-Akademie zu Berlin: "Ein Kunstverein für die heilige Musik,"* by Gottfried Eberle (Berlin, 1991), by permission of the Preussische Kulturbesitz.

Bach in

Berlin

Nation and Culture in
Mendelssohn's Revival of the
St. Matthew Passion

CELIA APPLEGATE

CORNELL UNIVERSITY PRESS   ITHACA AND LONDON

First published 2005 by Cornell University Press

Printed in the United States of America

Library of Congress Cataloging-in-Publication Data

Applegate, Celia.
    Bach in Berlin : nation and culture in Mendelssohn's revival of the St. Matthew
Passion / Celia Applegate.
        p. cm.
    Includes bibliographical references and index.
    ISBN-13: 978-0-8014-4389-3 (cloth : alk. paper)
    ISBN-10: 0-8014-4389-X (cloth : alk. paper)
    1. Bach, Johann Sebastian, 1685–1750. Matthäuspassion.   2. Bach, Johann
Sebastian, 1685–1750—Appreciation.   3. Mendelssohn-Bartholdy, Felix, 1809–1847.
4. Music—Social aspects—Germany.   5. Music—Germany—19th century—
History and criticism.   I. Title.
    ML410.B13A7 2005
    780'.943'09034—dc22   2005013205

Cloth printing   10 9 8 7 6 5 4 3 2 1

To my mother

CONTENTS

ACKNOWLEDGMENTS

This book has taken shape over a number of years, in the course of which I have benefited beyond measure from the generosity of music historians in opening up their field to such an outsider as myself. My greatest debts are to Ralph Locke and Pamela Potter, who must be counted two of the finest ambassadors of musicology. Their work has exemplified for me the interdisciplinary study of music; their friendship has fed and sustained my enthusiasm for this field of research. Colleagues in both musicology and German studies have provided encouragement and opportunities for me to cross these music-historical disciplinary borders; I would like particularly to thank Michael Beckerman, James Retallack, Michael Kater, Albrecht Riethmüller, Geoff Eley, Jan Palmowski, Philippe Ther, Kerala Snyder, Peter Hohendahl, David Barclay, Jonathan Sperber, and David Blackbourn. My graduate adviser, Paul Robinson, showed me many years ago how music might be made part of our study of European history. I have been following his example ever since. Support, in the form of fellowships, leaves, and publication subsidies, from the National Endowment for the Humanities, the Stanford Humanities Center, the Office of the Dean at the

University of Rochester, and the Department of History at the University of Rochester, made it possible to complete this book. Thanks also to John Ackerman and Ange Romeo-Hall of Cornell University Press, to the two readers, and to John LeRoy, each of whom brought more clarity to this work.

Beyond scholarship are music and life. Beginning with the former, my appreciation for the work of Felix Mendelssohn, Carl Friedrich Zelter, and the members of the Berlin Singakademie, who in the spring of 1829 were scrambling to learn a lot of notes in a very short time, comes from many rewarding experiences in similar organizations, all heirs to the tradition the Singakademie began. I express particular thanks to the California Bach Society, to which I belonged in 1995–96, the first year I spent researching this book. Participating in its performance of the Bach motets *Komm, Jesus, Komm* and *Singet dem Herrn ein neues Lied* under the baton of guest conductor John Butt, musician and Bach scholar extraordinaire, taught me much. I owe another debt of gratitude to the Rochester Bach Festival Chorus and its director, Thomas Folan, whose work in bringing Bach's cantatas to a broader public would have impressed both Mendelssohn and Adolf Bernhard Marx. To Celia and Henry Weaver go thanks for distractions, comedy, and wondrous love and to Stewart Weaver for that and more. I dedicate this book to my mother, Joan Strait Applegate, musician, musicologist, and humanist, who makes music intelligible and beautiful.

ABBREVIATIONS

AMZ	*Allgemeine Musikalische Zeitung* (Leipzig)
BAMZ	*Berliner Allgemeine Musikalische Zeitung*
BMZ	*Berliner Musikalische Zeitung*
Charlton	Charlton, David, ed. *E. T. A. Hoffmann's Musical Writings: Kreisleriana, The Poet and the Composer, Music Criticism.* Trans. Martyn Clarke. Cambridge, 1989.
Coleridge	Coleridge, A. D., ed. and trans. *Goethe's Letters to Zelter, with extracts from those of Zelter to Goethe.* London, 1892.
Forkel-Hoffmeister	Stauffer, George B., ed. *The Forkel-Hoffmeister and Kühnel Correspondence: A Document of the Early 19th-Century Bach Revival.* Trans. Arthur Mendel and George B. Stauffer. New York, 1990.
Geck	Geck, Martin. *Die Wiederentdeckung der Matthäuspassion im 19. Jahrhundert: Die zeitgenössische Dokumente und ihre ideengeschichtliche Deutung.* Regensburg, 1967.

Hensel	Hensel, Sebastian. *Die Familie Mendelssohn 1729–1847.* 1879. Reprint, Frankfurt am Main, 1995.
New Bach Reader	David, Hans T., and Arthur Mendel, eds. *The New Bach Reader: A Life of Johann Sebastian Bach in Letters and Documents.* Rev. ed. enlarged by Christoph Wolff. New York, 1998.
Schröder	Schröder, Cornelia. *Carl Friedrich Zelter und die Akademie: Dokumente und Briefe zur Entstehung der Musik-Sektion in der Preussischer Akademie der Künste.* Berlin, 1959.

Bach in Berlin

Introduction

What used to appear to all of us against the background of these times as a possibility that could only be dreamed about, has now become real: the Passion has been given to the public, and has become the property of all.

—Fanny Mendelssohn to Karl Klingemann, March 22, 1829

On February 21, 1829, a prominent notice in the leading musical journal of Berlin, the *Berliner Allgemeine Musikalische Zeitung*, invited readers to "an important and happy event," a performance of "The Passion According to St. Matthew by Johann Sebastian Bach" under the "direction of Herr Felix Mendelssohn-Bartholdy." The notice, written by the editor, Adolf Bernhard Marx, and reprinted with additional commentary over the next few weeks, described the *Passion* as the "greatest and holiest work of the great composer." The performance, Marx wrote, "would open the gates of a temple long shut down." "We are called," he continued, "not to a festival of art, but to a most solemn religious celebration."[1] And Berliners answered the call. On March 11, 1829, the date of the first performance, the hall of the Berlin Singakademie was filled; close to a thousand people were turned away. Many prominent Berliners came, from King and Court to Hegel and Schleiermacher. Goethe, unable to travel all the way from Weimar, still

[1] Adolf Bernhard Marx, "Bekanntmachung," *Berliner Allgemeine Musikalische Zeitung* 6, no. 8 (21 Feb. 1829): 57; hereafter *BAMZ*.

commented on the event in his correspondence with Carl Friedrich Zelter, director of the Singakademie, the amateur group that provided singers for the *Passion*'s double chorus. In the next months, more performances took place in Berlin and Frankfurt. In the next years, the score was published for the first time, and groups in Breslau, Stettin, Königsberg, Cassel, and Dresden performed it. Revivals and publications of Bach's other large-scale vocal works—notably the B-minor Mass—followed. By 1850 and the founding of the Bach Gesellschaft, an association dedicated to producing a collected edition of Bach's complete works, the revival of Johann Sebastian Bach had become a defining feature of the musical landscape of both Europe and the United States, shaping private and public performances, establishing music associations and publications, influencing composers, inspiring teachers and students, and reaching broad segments of the music-loving public. Mendelssohn's revival, more than any other single event, laid the foundation stone for the "imaginary museum" of musical works of the past and made music, Bach's music, *German* music, as essential to what it meant to be German as the language itself.[2]

The book that follows does not, however, trace the aftermath of the 1829 performance through the nineteenth century and into our own times, fascinating though such a journey would be. Instead, it places the performance at the end, not at the beginning, of a historical evolution, understanding it as the convergence of cultural and social developments, all of which made possible a performance of such contemporary resonance and long-lasting influence. The years before 1829 brought into existence an array of institutions, both state and private, and attitudes, some abstract and intellectualized, others more everyday and assumed. Together they defined a singular space for music among the creations of what Germans understood to be their nation, and thus together defined what national culture was and what it took to sustain it. Describing how the 1829 performance of the *St. Matthew Passion* happened offers an opportunity to examine the range of historical practices that make up what we call a national culture. "Culture," wrote Max Weber, "is a finite excerpt from the meaningless infinity of events in the world, endowed with meaning by human beings" and accessible to those "who are people of culture, with the capacity and the will deliberately to adopt an *attitude* towards the world and to bestow *meaning* upon it."[3] This is a book about how a group of people, narrow in their range of social backgrounds but broad and various in their views of the world

[2] Lydia Goehr, *The Imaginary Museum of Musical Works: An Essay in the Philosophy of Music* (Oxford, 1992).

[3] Cited in Wolfgang J. Mommsen, *Imperial Germany, 1867–1918: Politics, Culture, and Society in an Authoritarian State*, trans. Richard Deveson (London, 1995), 137.

around them, "bestowed meaning" on Bach, on his vocal works, on listening to and making music altogether.

The metaphor that describes such an examination is not, then, one of peeling back the layers of something to find its essence but rather one of taking apart the pieces of a well-integrated whole, so that one can see how they came together. The 1829 performance was about many things and reflected many aspects of life in Berlin and central Europe, but what emerged in the course of the performance was not a random mixture. It was a moment of consolidation, perhaps even of transformation, in collective life, and for many listeners a moment of self-realization, which encompassed all that their philosophers and writers had been saying of the relationship between individuality, spirituality, nationality, and the aesthetic life. Its lasting effect was to suggest the possibility that such moments came more readily, perhaps only, through musical performance and through the peculiar alchemy of sound, time, player, and listener. Thomas Mann devoted his last great novel, *Doktor Faustus*, to accounting for the terrible consequences of such an attachment to music among Germans, how it led them to neglect practical virtues in pursuit of some ineffable spiritual fulfillment and left them susceptible to the "political and moral regression" that Nazism embodied.[4] This book will, in more pedestrian fashion, try to account for the origins of this attachment.

The *St. Matthew Passion* of 1829 remains one of the most famous performances in German music history.[5] Carl Dahlhaus believed that only the première of Wagner's *Parsifal* in 1882 compared in importance as a single musical event with both great contemporary resonance and lasting significance. Others have called it a "milestone in the concert life of Germany, indeed of the world," an epochal moment reflecting "the brilliant genius of an individual" and carrying a "meaning for the music history of the nineteenth century" that cannot be overestimated.[6] The most enthusiastic ac-

---

[4] Hans Vaget, "National and Universal: Thomas Mann and the Paradox of 'German' Music," in *Music and German National Identity*, ed. Celia Applegate and Pamela Potter (Chicago, 2002), 156.

[5] Information about the performance is, therefore, abundant. Martin Geck has assembled a collection of the "contemporary documents" surrounding it; it has served as a "musical case study" in an Open University foundation course in the humanities; it wins mention in every survey history of music in the nineteenth century; it features in the many biographies, both popular and scholarly, of Felix Mendelssohn. For German readers, the definitive account is still Geck's *Die Wiederentdeckung der Matthäuspassion im 19. Jahrhundert* (Regensburg, 1967); hereafter Geck; also brief and useful is Gottfried Eberle, *200 Jahre Sing-Akademie zu Berlin: "Ein Kunstverein für die Heilige Musik"* (Berlin, 1991), 87–99. English readers may wish to consult Gerald Hendrie, ed., *Mendelssohn's Rediscovery of Bach: A Humanities Foundation Course* (Bletchley, UK, 1971).

[6] Hugo Riemann, *Geschichte der Musik seit Beethoven, 1800–1900* (Berlin, 1901), 251; Susanna Grossmann-Vendrey, *Felix Mendelssohn Bartholdy und die Musik der Vergangenheit* (Regensburg, 1969), 28; Geck, 5.

counts, like that of the eminent musicologist Friedrich Blume, reckon it something of a miracle. From the music-historical perspective that has shaped such judgments, the performance brought the choral and church music of Bach back into circulation, affecting compositional practice, musical instruction, historical research, performance, and taste. It consolidated the nineteenth-century movement to revive old music, which (again in Blume's estimation) "has engulfed in waves the whole musical activity of the nineteenth and twentieth centuries."[7] The *St. Matthew Passion* became, in Christoph Wolff's view, the first musical "classic in the repertoire," indeed "perhaps *the* classic of our Western music repertoire." Mendelssohn's performance of it established that historical, not contemporary, music would be regarded as "the weighty part of our contemporary musical life."[8]

As for the performance itself, Martin Geck's documentary study of 1967 gathered a definitive collection of the relevant archival and printed sources, accompanied by an admirable, if brief, analysis. Only a few new discoveries have been made since the book's publication, none of which has significantly altered his judgments on such musicological issues as the score Mendelssohn used, his instrumentation and tempos, the size of the chorus, and so on. In this book I explore instead the pathways, some straight and wide, others meandering, that converged to make the performance both possible and comprehensible. Barbara Herrnstein Smith has written that any act of literary or artistic evaluation, such as that by which the Berlin public of 1829 judged Bach's *St. Matthew Passion* a work of transcendent beauty and profundity, involves "articulating an estimate of how well that work will serve implicitly defined functions for a specific implicitly defined audience, who are conceived of as experiencing the work under certain implicitly defined conditions."[9] The following chapters will attempt to make explicit just such aspects of the historical condition of north Germans in the first decades of the nineteenth century—why they thought making music was important, who they were, and how they made music.

The first chapter provides an account of the performance itself, viewed mainly from the perspective of Felix Mendelssohn's first twenty years. Mendelssohn has been the focus of considerable renewed attention since Geck published his study of the "rediscovery" of the *St. Matthew Passion*. This new scholarship, combined with my own interpretation of letters and

---

[7] Friedrich Blume, "Bach in the Romantic Era," *Musical Quarterly* 50 (1964): 290.

[8] Christoph Wolff, "The Saint Matthew Passion" (lecture, Bethlehem Bach Festival 1999, Bethlehem, PA, 14 May 1999).

[9] Barbara Herrnstein Smith, *Contingencies of Value: Alternative Perspectives for Critical Theory* (Cambridge, MA, 1988), 13.

biographical information, enriches a story that will be already familiar to those versed in nineteenth-century music history. The opening account of the general circumstances of the performance and its place in Felix Mendelssohn's career also serves as the foundation for the chapters that follow. In them, I move backward from the performance in order to explore its intellectual and social contexts.

The intellectual background to nineteenth-century music reception forms the substance of chapter 2, "Toward a Music Aesthetics of the Nation." Mendelssohn and his circle were heirs to a highly developed way of thinking about the place of art in collective life, and their attitudes toward music reflected this tradition's ambivalence about where music fitted into a hierarchy of art, ideas, creativity, and taste. Particularly in his cultivation of Bach, Mendelssohn represented what the historian John Toews has called "a revisionist generational appropriation" of "a vision of the public ethical function of music."[10] This chapter goes back to the eighteenth century to recover the beginnings of a literary discussion of music's significance and the patriotic importance of rescuing music from the dominance of Italian and French music in the princely courts. It follows the progress—repetition and stagnation describes the situation more accurately—of music aesthetics from Johann Mattheson to Immanuel Kant and its transformation under the influence of first-generation romantics like Ludwig Tieck and Wilhelm Heinrich Wackenroder.

The chapter then juxtaposes this familiar story of intellectual history, with one thinker influencing another in a progression of texts, to the changing circumstances of working musicians and their efforts to join the emerging mainstream of national cultural life. Thinking again of Max Weber's definition of culture, we might call this the attempt of musicians themselves, especially those among them who understood the increasing importance of a newly formed public sphere, to bestow meaning on their own work and assert its aesthetic value. An earlier Weber, the composer Carl Maria von Weber, began his never-finished novel of 1809, *Tonkünstlers Leben* (A Musician's Life), with the exhortation to his young hero, "Out into the world with you, for the world is the artist's true sphere! What good does it do you to live with a petty clique and to earn the gracious applause

---

[10] John Toews, "Memory and Gender in the Remaking of Fanny Mendelssohn's Musical Identity: The Chorale in *Das Jahr*," *Musical Quarterly* 77 (1993): 735. Toews's fuller consideration of Mendelssohn's "generation of ethical community from the spirit of music" may be found in his *Becoming Historical: Cultural Reformation and Public Memory in Early-Nineteenth-Century Berlin* (Cambridge, 2004). This just-published work came out too recently to integrate its perspectives more fully into this book.

of a patron. . . . Out! A man's spirit must find itself in the spirits of his fellow creatures."[11] This understanding of the role of the musician reflected a sea change in cultural life in German Europe. It resulted in an ever closer union between music making and German literary culture, the enduring product of which was a broader, musically inclusive understanding of the German nation—in Schiller's words, that "moral greatness" which "lives in the culture and in the character of the nation, independent of its political fate."[12] This chapter, then, explores both how music became national and how the nation itself took shape in now-obscure writings about music.

The third chapter, "Music Journalism and the Formation of Judgment," continues the story chronologically and thematically. Beginning with the establishment in 1798 of the long-lived and widely influential *Allgemeine Musikalische Zeitung* (General Musical Newspaper), this chapter explores the ways that new kinds of intellectuals—people who wrote about musical performances, newly published music, and the genres and forms of music in general—tried to develop the public's ability to make sense of music, to judge its worth and its broader significance. These intellectuals sought also to define high standards for music and to turn both performance and composition into activities important in the life of the nation, not mere amusements. Music journalism of the intellectually ambitious sort represented by the *Allgemeine Musikalische Zeitung* was not an unprecedented phenomenon in 1798, but the geographical reach and the longevity of this particular journal made it something new. Its founding editor, Friedrich Rochlitz, and his gifted stable of writers, including the great romantic writer E. T. A. Hoffmann, established a way of writing and thinking about music that proved to be of enduring significance. They clarified and elaborated previously vague distinctions between serious and frivolous music, between music of lasting value and music of transient, "entertainment" value, between "classical" and popular music. In the process, they contributed immeasurably to the formation of what we usually call bourgeois musical culture, to distinguish it in its formality and unprecedented self-consciousness from the previous musical cultures of court, church, and village square. The most important contemporary imitator of Rochlitz's journal was the *Berliner Allgemeine Musikalische Zeitung*, which began publication in Berlin in 1824 under the editorship of Adolf Bernhard Marx. Marx's advocacy of the *St. Matthew Passion* in 1829 formed a key element in the impact and

---

[11] Carl Maria von Weber, *Writings on Music*, ed. John Warrack, trans. Martin Cooper (New York, 1981), 318–19.

[12] Schiller quoted in James J. Sheehan, *German History, 1770–1866* (New York, 1989), 373.

eventual influence of the performance, and the chapter culminates in an account of Marx's promotion of this musical event.

The fourth chapter, "Musical Amateurism and the Exercise of Taste," considers the same period, roughly the first three decades of the nineteenth century, from the perspective of making music rather than writing about it. The historian Hagen Schulze has characterized the process of consolidating a national culture in German Europe as a matter of achieving a "unity of taste and judgment which transcended territorial boundaries."[13] Whereas the preceding chapter shows how music journalists tried to foster common ways of judging musical value, this chapter illustrates how the lively participation of music lovers, dilettantes, and pedagogues established a taste for music as a measure of a fully cultivated life. The contribution of amateurs to Germany's reputation as the "people of music," established already by midcentury, is neither well understood nor, as a result, adequately appreciated. Amateurs, arguably more than any other group of musicians, created the environment in which the 1829 performance was possible, and their activism carried forward the intellectual and institutional trends described in earlier chapters. Interspersing discussions of women in music, Prussian state involvement with music, and music education, this chapter tells of the growth of the Berlin Singakademie, the prototype of all amateur choral societies in Germany, and the work of its longtime director, Carl Friedrich Zelter. Like the previous chapter, this one culminates in an account of the 1829 performance of the *St. Matthew Passion*, this time from the perspective of the amateur musicians of the Singakademie.

The fifth chapter, "The *St. Matthew Passion* in Concert: Protestantism, Historicism, and Sacred Music," restores Johann Sebastian Bach to the narrative of cultural preparation that previous chapters pieced together. Understanding the vigor with which Mendelssohn and his contemporaries chased down Bach manuscripts, studied Bach counterpoint, and ultimately attempted a large-scale performance of Bach's great *Passion* requires, of course, more than a consideration of aesthetic philosophers, journalists, and amateurs. The story of the 1829 *St. Matthew Passion* takes us, in this chapter, into the crisis and renewal of German Protestantism of the early nineteenth century—a process that made people once again receptive to Bach as the greatest composer of Protestant church music and, ironically, unable to listen to his music in actual churches. Over the years it has been easy to characterize a historical development by which the "greatest of all Christian

---

[13] Hagen Schulze, *The Course of German Nationalism, from Frederick the Great to Bismarck, 1763–1867,* trans. Sarah Hanbury-Tenison (Cambridge, 1991), 46.

works" reappeared in a public hall in a weekday concert for music lovers as one simply of secularization.[14] But the term secularization is hardly simple and straightforward. In reality, it characterizes—inadequately, one might add—a complex process of historical transformation. It also carries with it unwarranted assumptions, about loss of religious belief and rise of secular ideologies and institutions, that one must confront individually in order to assess.

This chapter, then, takes apart the pieces of the secularization story of the 1829 performance of the *St. Matthew Passion*. It looks first at how the Protestant church union of 1817 exacerbated an existing crisis of church music in Protestant Germany, rendering the institutions that had sustained Bach during his life useless in his revival. It turns then to how romanticism and historicism made it increasingly likely after 1800 that one would hear sacred music not in churches but outside them, in concert halls and private salons. Finally, this chapter considers the remarkable story of the reception of J. S. Bach's musical works after his death in 1750—a familiar story, to be sure, but one that bears retelling from the perspective of German cultural developments as a whole. A comparative consideration of Bach's two main rivals in the area of public performances of sacred works—George Frederick Handel and Carl Heinrich Graun—leads at the last to an assessment of responses in 1829 to the *St. Matthew Passion*, the work that Marx believed would bring the "sun of a new day into the fog of our times."[15] The 1829 performance presents us with the paradox, rich in cultural meaning, of a work of art that was once considered antiquated beyond recovery suddenly acquiring all the resonance of the newly created. In the responses of 1829, moreover, we can recognize our own reception of this music and of great music of the past in general, for we remain indebted to the nineteenth-century work of modern reinterpretation.

A sixth and final chapter recounts the subsequent careers of the main participants in the 1829 *St. Matthew Passion* performances in order to emphasize the extent to which this single experience continued to resonate in their later musical and cultural work. All of these people, from Fanny and Felix Mendelssohn to their friends Eduard Devrient and Johann Gustav Droysen to old Bach himself, contributed to the shaping of German cultural consciousness in the nineteenth century, sometimes purposefully and

---

[14] The phrase "greatest of all Christian works" is from the memoirs of Eduard Devrient, Felix Mendelssohn's friend and the man who sang the part of Jesus in the 1829 performance: see his *Dramatische und Dramaturgische Schriften, Bd. 10: Erinnerungen an Felix Mendelssohn Bartholdy* (Leipzig, 1869), 35. Unless otherwise noted, all translations from the German are my own.

[15] Adolf Bernhard Marx, "Vierter Bericht über die 'Passionsmusik nach dem Evangelium Matthäi' von Johann Sebastian Bach," *BAMZ* 6, no. 13 (27 March 1829): 97.

sometimes, as of course in the case of Bach, inadvertently. The range of their activities and the complexity of the reception of Bach after 1829 attest to the capaciousness of a term like national culture, a slippery concept with uncertain points of reference in actual historical experience. National culture can include practically anything, yet despite the almost insurmountable vagueness of both terms in the phrase, it still continues to serve on most lists of what constitutes a nation, producing one of those circularities—a nation is that which has a national culture, a national culture is the culture of a nation—that so plague our study of the history of nations. The only way out of this circularity is to look at national culture as a set of practices by which a group of people achieve consensus, even if temporary, about the significance of what its ancestors have produced. When people begin to refer to their literature, their art, and their music as national, as an expression of their national character, then we can see national culture in the making and speak of nationalizing tendencies in cultural life.

This final chapter gathers together what previous ones suggest about the ways that the appreciation of Bach reinforced the integration of the many strands of German cultural experience into a coherent, unified national culture. People who wrote about music in the early nineteenth century came to focus on Bach in particular as the embodiment of German character and German achievement. The 1829 performance of the *St. Matthew Passion* drew on decades of Bach discussion and added something new as well, something contained in the experience of performance itself and the collective life it enacted. Difficult though it may be to pin down the dimensions of a nationalizing culture, the study of a single event provides an opportunity to avoid generalizations and to identify how a group of people at a particular moment decide that a work of art has special significance for them *as* a people. That this moment proved to be literally unforgettable tells us even more about the renewal of a national culture over time. If we can understand better how and why people define themselves as members of a common nation by giving meaning to aspects of their world—its social arrangements, its law and politics, its art, its music—then we will also learn something of the integrative power of national cultures.

Great Expectations

Mendelssohn and the *St. Matthew Passion*

This momentous event, the rediscovery, preparation, and performance of Bach's incomparable masterpiece, seems to have had an almost accidental genesis. We could say that it began with Abraham and Lea Mendelssohn's decision, in 1819, to have Carl Friedrich Zelter instruct their two elder children, Fanny and Felix, in music theory. The decision was a wise one, characteristic both of Lea's musical intelligence and of her and her husband's careful management of their children's lives. It tells us, first, about the Mendelssohn family, which had emerged from the poverty of grandfather Moses Mendelssohn's lifetime into a position of wealth and status.[1] This change in turn reflected two intertwined social developments at the turn of the eighteenth and nineteenth centuries. The first was the emergence of a class of people whose identity came from the possession of property and

---

[1] For a definitive account of Felix Mendelssohn's life, including extensive discussion of his parents' and grandparents' generations, we have now R. Larry Todd's new biography, *Mendelssohn: A Life in Music* (New York, 2003).

knowledge rather than privilege and place, and the second, fatally linked to it, was the emancipation of European Jews.

THE MENDELSSOHNS OF BERLIN

As is well known, when Moses Mendelssohn arrived in Berlin in 1743 to continue his studies with his former teacher David Fränkel, now the new chief rabbi of Berlin, he had none of the markers of social position, old regime or new, except for the beginnings of an education. Indeed, as an unprotected foreign Jew, coming from Dessau in the small principality of Anhalt-Dessau, he entered the Prussian capital only with the permission of Jewish gatekeepers, who were appointed by the elders of the Berlin Jewish community to keep the numbers of Berlin Jews within the strict bounds of an edict of 1737.[2] Nearly three-quarters of a century later, in 1812, Friedrich Wilhelm of Prussia passed the edict of emancipation, which at least briefly gave "the same rights and freedoms of citizenship as for Christians" to all Jews living in Prussia.[3] Shortly thereafter, Moses's son Abraham, by then a prosperous banker living in a fine house close to the Gendarmenmarkt, was elected to the city parliament. The juxtaposition of these dates suggests progress and frames the rise to public prominence and commercial fortune in the family of Moses of Dessau.

At the same time, these dates frame a narrative of loss—a loss of religious and cultural identity and to some extent also of family ties. Through his unremitting intellectual labor, the first Mendelssohn became a legend in his time and thereafter as a leader of the German Enlightenment, as "*the* Jewish thinker of modern times" and as the "first modern German Jew" altogether.[4] But for his children, the beginnings of a mutual recognition between German Christian and German Jewish culture seemed to die an untimely death. Four of them—Abraham, Henriette, Dorothea (born Brendel), and Nathan—converted to Christianity, an act that denied all that Moses Mendelssohn had struggled for in his lifetime and would certainly have pained him deeply had he lived to witness it.[5] Henriette never mar-

---

[2] Alexander Altmann, *Moses Mendelssohn: A Biographical Study* (Birmingham, AL, 1973), 16–17.

[3] Julius H. Schoeps, "1786–1871: Ringen um Reform und Emanzipation," in *Juden in Berlin, 1671–1945: Ein Lesebuch,* ed. Annegret Ehmann (Berlin, 1988), 81.

[4] David Sorkin, *Moses Mendelssohn and the Religious Enlightenment* (Berkeley and Los Angeles, 1996), xvii.

[5] Henriette and Dorothea both converted to Roman Catholicism (the latter after first converting to Protestantism), Abraham and his family to Lutheran Protestantism. Dorothea married the Berlin businessman Simon Veit, had two children, and then, in one of the great scandals of the time, left him to marry the young writer Friedrich Schlegel. The conversions of Moses Mendels-

ried, lived in Paris much of her adult life, and remained isolated in her religious life even from Abraham and Lea. Dorothea's estrangement was more marked and deliberate, deepening as she moved ever further into the Christian-romantic enthusiasms of her second husband, Friedrich Schlegel, and his intimates. Likewise, Abraham's wife Lea had a brother Jacob, who converted to Protestantism, changed his name to the Christian-sounding Bartholdy, broke off all contact with his observant Jewish parents, and lived in Rome, where his house became the meeting place for the Christian-romantic painters known as the Nazarenes. This same Jacob persuaded Abraham some years later to add the name Bartholdy to the unmistakably Jewish Mendelssohn.[6] Far from being a natural step in the path to enlightenment—as Lavater had tried unsuccessfully to prove to Moses in their exchanges in the 1770s—conversion brought disruption, dislocation, alienation, and no assured acceptance.

Given all this, Abraham's conversion seems the least likely. Not subject to the emotional turbulence that marked Dorothea's flight into the nineteenth century, Abraham had joined his elder brother Joseph's bank in Berlin—a bank that prospered until 1933—and married the granddaughter of Daniel Itzig, revered leader of Berlin's Jewish community and financial genius of Friedrich II's Prussia. Together they had four children, each of whom were named with exquisite attention to the claims of family and Christian society: Fanny, for instance, born in 1805, was given the more Christian-sounding name of her great-aunt on the Itzig side, Fanny von Arnstein (at her conversion in 1816, her parents added the even more Christian Cäcilia to her name, after great-aunt Cäcilia Zipporah von Eskeles); Paul, born in 1813, was given a significantly modified version of Saul, the brother of Moses Mendelssohn.[7] Abraham had by all accounts a complex and demanding personality, shaped by a profoundly ambivalent relationship to his father and what he symbolized. On the one hand, no Mendelssohn was more conscious of the claims of family and tradition: this is the consciousness, after all, that lay behind his ironic quip that "earlier I was the son of a father and now I am the father of a son."[8] It accounts also for the tortured logic

---

sohn's children have generated a historiography of their own. See Steven M. Lowenstein, *The Berlin Jewish Community: Enlightenment, Family, and Crisis, 1770–1830* (New York, 1994); see also Todd, *Mendelssohn*, 13–23.

[6] The oft-quoted letter only exists in Sebastian Hensel's version in *Familie Mendelssohn* (Hensel, 114–15). Felix Mendelssohn's biographer, Eric Werner, regards Hensel's versions of family letters as unreliable, but Hensel does not seem to have actually invented any letters, just edited them with an eye to his audience in imperial Germany.

[7] Eric Werner, *Mendelssohn: Leben und Werk in neuer Sicht* (Zurich, 1980), 30–31.

[8] Ibid., 28.

behind his at times belligerent insistence that Felix append Bartholdy to his name, especially in public. "A Christian Mendelssohn is an impossibility," as he wrote to Felix in London in 1829. "Nor should there be a Christian Mendelssohn; for my father himself did not want to be one. . . . If Mendelssohn is your name, you are *ipso facto* a Jew."[9]

On the other hand, as the conversion narrative itself starkly reveals, Abraham did not regard Judaism as a viable tradition but rather as an "antiquated, corrupt, contradictory" religion. A rationalist deist himself, Abraham believed the forms of religious life were arbitrary masks that obscured the single truth of "one God, one virtue, one truth, one happiness."[10] But reason in its practical guise of self-interest demanded that one attend to the social mores of one's times. Moreover, in 1816, a Prussian State Council interpretation of the 1812 edict of emancipation reneged on its promise of legal equality for Jews, throwing up yet another obstacle on the grudgingly built road to full inclusion in German society. On March 22, 1816, Abraham had his children baptized in a private ceremony in his home, performed by the minister Johann Jakob Stegemann. Six years later, in 1822, he and his wife converted, once again privately, in Frankfurt. Not until 1825 and the death of Lea's observant mother did the family go public with the conversion and the name change to Mendelssohn Bartholdy, though long before that, many Berliners at least knew of the children's conversion. As John Toews has observed, confessional identities in the family of Abraham Mendelssohn were "thus quite confused, and often secretive and hidden."[11]

BACH AMONG THE MENDELSSOHNS

Never hidden was Abraham and Lea Mendelssohn's determination to participate fully in the cultivated circles of Berlin society, a participation to which their own family background, education, and achievement gave them title, even as Jews. The Berlin salons of Jewish women were, after all, a famously vital part of Berlin life, and this second generation of Mendelssohns established their own, to which the leading writers, intellectuals, and leaders of Berlin all came. As the female patronage of salon life waned, the scope of the Mendelssohns' connections expanded.[12] From the start, this kind of cul-

---

[9] Abraham Mendelssohn to Felix Mendelssohn, 8 July 1829, reprinted in full in Werner, *Mendelssohn*, 59–61.

[10] Abraham Mendelssohn to Fanny Mendelssohn, 5 April 1819, in Hensel, 117–18.

[11] Toews, "Memory and Gender," 730.

[12] On the decline of Jewish women's salons, see Deborah Hertz, *Jewish High Society in Old Regime Berlin* (New Haven, 1988), 251–85.

tivation through association with like-minded men and women formed the necessary backdrop to the formal education of the Mendelssohn children— an education that took place largely at home, under the tutelage first of the parents and then of an array of remarkable private teachers. From the start as well, music formed an integral part of this education, to such an extent that the Mendelssohn children became, in a sense, the living models for music's claim to participation in the great humanistic project of the German Enlightenment. Their parents sought out the elite among the city's instrumental instructors for their children. They secured Ludwig Berger, himself a former piano virtuoso and student of Clementi, as their piano teacher, and (to return to where we began) Carl Friedrich Zelter, the central representative in Berlin of serious, non-operatic music, became their instructor in music theory and composition.

Of course, to receive musical training does not always lead, now or then, to an interest in the compositions of Johann Sebastian Bach. As the nineteenth century began, the music of Sebastian Bach—as he was widely called in order to distinguish him from his more famous sons—was not so much unknown as obscure, the object of esoteric rather than general interest, of a specializing rather than a universalizing musical education. Berlin happened to be the main center for such esoteric knowledge, and through their family connections, the Mendelssohn parents had an unusually broad exposure to the elder Bach's work.[13] All the daughters of Daniel Itzig, including Lea Mendelssohn's mother Bella (Babette), had contact with court musicians, among them Carl Philipp Emanuel Bach, through their father's position as a leading court Jew. According to Adolf Weissman, "at the Itzig house, a veritable cult of Sebastian and Philipp Emanuel Bach was in operation."[14] Lea's aunt, Sara Itzig Levy, studied harpsichord with Bach's eldest son, Wilhelm Friedemann Bach, during his decade in Berlin and was an important patron of Carl Philipp Emanuel Bach. Sara Levy became the leading collector in central Europe of music of the early eighteenth century, especially members of the Bach family. Such collecting was all the more important given the paucity of Bach's works available in print in the eighteenth century; even the *Well-Tempered Clavier*, his best-known work, circulated only in manuscript form before 1801. Sara Levy also began a musical salon, in the

---

[13] By the late eighteenth century, Berlin, not Leipzig, had become what Heine would later call it—the "capital city of Sebastian Bach" (Heinrich Heine, *Sämtliche Werke*, ed. Oskar Walzel, [Leipzig, 1913], 8:106).

[14] Adolf Weissmann, *Berlin als Musikstadt: Geschichte der Oper und des Konzerts von 1740 bis 1911* (Berlin, 1911), 36.

decade in which most salons were devoted to philosophizing and flirtation, and through its ambitious performances she became an influential exponent of Baroque musical aesthetics.[15] Her sisters also played the harpsichord, though not as brilliantly as Sara Levy. Her sister Fanny studied with Johann Philipp Kirnberger, J. S. Bach's student and a key figure in the Berlin circle of Bach disciples; her niece Lea regularly performed pieces from the *Well-Tempered Clavier*. Little wonder, then, that when Lea's first child was born, she exclaimed that the girl had "fingers for Bach fugues."[16]

In the small world of privileged Berlin, Christian and Jewish, social, familial, and professional connections crossed and overlapped; moreover, coming together on the basis of common interests provides as good a definition of Enlightenment sociability as any.[17] Musical interests, as we shall see, did not develop as a matter of course among the educated elite of the late eighteenth century, though they were not peculiar. Still, to care about music, especially Bach's music, placed one in a small circle within the educated elite. It is therefore not surprising to find Sara Levy as an early member of a new musical organization in Berlin called the Singakademie. Carl Friedrich Fasch founded the amateur singing group in 1791. Its formal existence evolved out of an informal gathering of women, most of them wives of government officials and minor Prussian nobility, to sing religious choral works. Fasch's involvement in this circle reflected the waning of musical activity at the Prussian court, where the days were long gone when Friedrich II had piped his way through flute concerti with his long-suffering harpsichord accompanists C. P. E. Bach and, apparently more patiently, Fasch himself.[18]

Frustration with the court and the need to find supplemental income took Fasch the short but significant distance from Potsdam to Berlin, from court culture into the growing world of urban enlightened sociability. The Singakademie, so called because in 1793 the group secured permission to move out of the living rooms of members and into a room of the Royal

---

[15] Peter Wollny has reconstructed the contents of this collection, which after her death was dispersed. The largest part of it went to the library of the Berlin Singakademie, which disappeared in 1945 and was recently rediscovered. See Wollny, "Sara Levy and the Making of Musical Taste in Berlin," *Musical Quarterly* 77 (1993): 650–68; and Christoph Wolff, "Recovered in Kiev: Bach et al. A Preliminary Report on the Music Collection of the Berlin Sing-Akademie," *Notes: Quarterly Journal of the Music Library Association* 58 (December 2001): 259–71.

[16] Hensel, 110.

[17] See especially, Richard van Dülmen, *The Society of the Enlightenment: The Rise of the Middle Class and Enlightenment Culture in Germany*, trans. Anthony Williams (New York, 1992).

[18] Carl Freiherr von Ledebur, *Tonkünstler Lexicon Berlins* (Berlin, 1861), 145.

Academy of Arts, never in its early years performed publicly. Nevertheless, its amateur members, soon of both sexes, practiced and collected with increasing seriousness the works of J. S. Bach, Graun, Handel, and others.[19] With Fasch's health failing, the group acquired an assistant director in the person of Carl Friedrich Zelter, a former composition student of Fasch, tenor, fledgling composer, and master mason. By one of the more piquant coincidences that marked the life of a small city like Berlin, Zelter's first masonry project had been to renovate one of the Berlin houses of Daniel Itzig in 1783.[20] We do not know whether the young mason, who was pursuing his musical interests clandestinely in the 1780s, had any contact with the Bach-loving Itzig daughters. He certainly came to know an Itzig intimate, Abraham Mendelssohn, and in 1796 persuaded him to join the Singakademie. Moreover, by the 1790s, Zelter had begun to fashion himself into a leading expert on the elder Bach, and in 1800, upon Fasch's death, he became director of the Singakademie, now 147 members strong, and began to rehearse the Bach motets.

From this point on, the cultivation of J. S. Bach among Sara Levy and her circle intertwined closely with that of Zelter and the Singakademie, with performances, manuscript acquisition and copying, and instruction all forming a mutually reinforcing, expansive appreciation of his work. Fanny and Felix Mendelssohn were the heirs to all this, a legacy as expressive in its own way of the German-Jewish cultural symbiosis as that of their paternal grandfather. Their instruction in musical composition at Zelter's hands reflected the same line of Bach inheritance in which Sara Levy was so crucially involved, from J. S. Bach to C. P. E. Bach and J. S. Kirnberger, to Fasch, and then to Zelter. Zelter based his teaching on Kirnberger's treatise *The Art of Pure Composition in Music*, which assembled Bach's harmonic and contrapuntal methods into a formal system, and he led his pupils accordingly from the study of figured bass "through chorale, invertible counterpoint, canon and fugue."[21] The children both joined the Singakademie in 1820, where the study of Bach's choral writing, often from scores donated to the Singakademie library by Sara Levy, was a regular part of the weekly rehearsals. And Felix began to study the organ with August Wilhelm Bach, no close relation to the composer but an important performer of his organ works. At the same time, Bach was coming at the Mendelssohn children through family sources independent of Zelter, from the concerts at Sara

---

[19] Gottfried Eberle, *200 Jahre Sing-Akademie zu Berlin: "Ein Kunstverein für die Heilige Musik"* (Berlin, 1991), 23–39.

[20] Ledebur, *Tonkünstler Lexikon*, 663.

[21] R. Larry Todd, *Mendelssohn's Musical Education: A Study and Edition of His Exercises in Composition* (Cambridge, 1983), ix.

Levy's house, which they attended, to Lea's encouraging them to memorize twenty-four preludes from Bach's *Well-Tempered Clavier*, a feat that Fanny accomplished first.[22] Finally, Lea's mother, Bella Salomon, presented her grandson Felix with a transcription of the full score of the *St. Matthew Passion* in 1824.[23]

This intertwining of Bach cultivation among the teachers and family of Felix Mendelssohn has generated controversy over the years. At stake is the question of who should get credit for the 1829 performance of the *St. Matthew Passion*, and ultimately of course, of whether Jews can be acknowledged to have a place in the genealogy of German culture. The choice has always come down (despite the angling for recognition by various bit players) to either Zelter or Mendelssohn, either the teacher or the pupil, the crusty old music man or the daring young prodigy, the German or the Jew. Only three years after the performance, Zelter died and sank quickly into obscurity, whereas Mendelssohn went on to a brilliant musical career: the "Unforgettable," Schumann called him, naming his sixth child Felix. It was a career that put him at the creative center of musical performance, composition, and institutions in Europe. During this time, an aura began to surround the 1829 performance, particularly given Mendelssohn's leading role in many subsequent aspects of Bach revival. In the first decades after his death in 1847, the legend of his rescue of the *Passion* from utter obscurity only grew. A series of admiring memoirs from friends and associates—Eduard Devrient, A. B. Marx, Ferdinand Hiller, Ignaz Moscheles, Johann Gustav Droysen, and the celebrated Mendelssohn family history by his nephew Sebastian Hensel—all dwelt on his early years. Within the unfolding story of one prodigious accomplishment after another, the 1829 performance, in all its solemnity and drama, served as the perfect capstone, the culminating moment in the dazzling first act in the life of a musical genius.

But Mendelssohn's posthumous reputation soon plummeted, a victim not only of the growing anti-Semitism of late-nineteenth-century Europe but also of a sea change in taste and with it an ill-considered characterization of Mendelssohn's work as expressive only of smug middle-class complacency.[24] Still, even such dismissive attitudes allowed for recognition at least of Mendelssohn's historicism, if not his creative genius. Only with the growing domination of right-wing nationalism in German musicology

---

[22] Arnd Richter, *Mendelssohn: Leben, Werke, Dokumente* (Mainz, 1994), 68.

[23] Todd, *Mendelssohn: A Life*, 122–23.

[24] Leon Botstein, "The Aesthetics of Assimilation and Affirmation: Reconstructing the Career of Felix Mendelssohn," in *Mendelssohn and His World*, ed. R. Larry Todd (Princeton, 1991), 5–42.

after the First World War did the notion that Zelter might have master-minded the performance begin to gain adherents; the process culminated in the erasure of Mendelssohn as a German musical figure during the Nazi years.[25] Musicologists like Georg Schünemann wrote of Zelter's long-standing mastery of the Bach repertory and went so far as to speculate, all evidence to the contrary notwithstanding, that he alone came up with the idea for the performance, giving the conductor's baton to a pampered young Felix only under pressure from his wealthy and influential parents.[26] For the nationalists of the interwar era, Zelter shared a racial bond with Bach—both north German Aryans, both men of the *Volk*. Given the temper of the times, the reality of such bonding precluded the possibility that so effete and inauthentic a person as Mendelssohn, false even to his Judaism, should have led the revival. This portrait of Zelter as an "absolutely authentic and plain-spoken Berliner" enjoyed a final ironic popularity in the people's state of the German Democratic Republic. Once again the primacy of the social over the aesthetic meant that Zelter's working-class status (never mind that his father was a profit-minded entrepreneur and employer of dozens of brickmakers and construction workers) made him a more appropriate hero in this musical drama than the capitalist financier's son (and Jew).

But the reality has always been the intertwining and coalescence of many parts into the whole that was the *St. Matthew Passion* of 1829. We cannot assign priority to one part over any other, any more than one could have brought the work to performance without the chorus or sung without the score or held it together without the conductor. Most recent accounts of the event acknowledge the roles of all the players—Zelter, Mendelssohn, and a host of others. Given that, it is perhaps not entirely arbitrary to have begun with Zelter's tutelage of young Mendelssohn, for in practical terms, the institutions of the former provided the setting for the projects of the latter, and, the 1829 performance of the *St. Matthew Passion* was, if nothing else, Felix Mendelssohn's project.

[25] For a full account of German musicology in the twentieth century, see Pamela M. Potter, *Most German of the Arts: Musicology and Society from the Weimar Republic to the End of Hitler's Reich* (New Haven, 1998).

[26] Georg Schünemann, "Die Bachpflege der Berliner Singakademie," *Bach-Jahrbuch* 25 (1928): 148–51; Schünemann, *Carl Friedrich Zelter: Der Mensch und sein Werk* (Berlin, 1937); Schünemann, *Die Singakademie zu Berlin 1791–1941* (Regensburg, 1941); Oswald Schrenk, *Berlin und die Musik: Zweihundert Jahre Musikleben einer Stadt, 1740–1940* (Berlin, 1940), 91–94. Martin Geck also refers to the "popular notion in the National Socialism period" that Justus Thibaut gave Mendelssohn the idea to perform the *St. Matthew Passion* (Geck, 21)—a highly implausible notion, as discussed in chapter 5.

FELIX MENDELSSOHN ON THE ROAD TO THE
ST. MATTHEW PASSION

He did not, of course, come up with it immediately on acquaintance with Bach's figured bass, for he was a boy with many projects, chiefly his own composing. By age fourteen, he had written more than one hundred compositions. Nor were even these early works, begun probably in 1819 when he was ten years old, at all negligible. Charles Rosen wrote that "Mendelssohn was the greatest child prodigy the history of Western music has ever known." "Not even Mozart or Chopin before the age of nineteen," he explained, showed such talent "for lyrical melodic lines and delicate, transparent textures," and his "control of large-scale structure" was "unsurpassed by any composer of his generation." Nor was Bach, again in Rosen's view, the model that Mendelssohn imitated and made his own, despite Zelter's tutelage; it was rather Beethoven, and more unexpected yet, the demanding, difficult Beethoven of the late sonatas and quartets.[27] At the same time, Mendelssohn began to appear occasionally in public as a pianist and composer and in semipublic, at the Sunday concerts in the Mendelssohn home, as a composer, conductor, and even producer of his own small-scale operas. He was following a modern pattern of musical development, pursuing innovation based on incorporation of and reaction against the most daring of contemporary models. His best early compositions—the Piano Quartet in B Minor, the Octet for Strings, the overture to the *Midsummer Night's Dream*—neither recycled his teacher's instructions nor copied the work of contemporaries but rather developed his own style out of what he discovered in others. Success as a composer also meant appearing in public as one, through publication and through performance by professional musicians. Mendelssohn began to accomplish all this in his teenage years.

If only for the sake of forcing a measure of strangeness onto what is familiar, let us for a moment instead regard this effort as an odd choice for a young man embarking on a career as a composer. Seen that way, three experiences he had in the 1820s, all of them staples of his biography, take on fresh relevance—the trip to Paris in 1825, the operatic disappointment of 1827, and the walking tour of Germany later in 1827. By 1825, his father was resigned enough to his son's pursuit of a musical career, and anxious enough that it be a successful one, to take him along on a trip to Paris and

---

[27] Charles Rosen, *The Romantic Generation* (Cambridge, MA, 1995), 569. For a full account of Mendelssohn's compositions in the decade of 1819 to 1829, see Todd, *Mendelssohn,* 47–198.

Felix Mendelssohn Bartholdy at age thirteen. Drawing by Wilhelm Hensel, 1822. By permission of the Bildarchiv Preussischer Kulturbesitz / Art Resource, NY.

there to seek the professional opinion of Luigi Cherubini, then at the height of his influence as director of the Paris Conservatory.[28] The perceived need for Cherubini's opinion reveals the extent to which north Germany felt like a musical backwater, despite visits from such international celebrities as Ignaz Moscheles, who in 1824 has assured the parents that Felix's abilities would "lead to a noble and truly great career."[29] Indeed, esoteric Bach expertise was perhaps the only musical good of which Berlin had an abundance. In the 1820s, no ambitious musicians could have afforded to stay forever in Berlin or measure their achievements only by its standards. Zelter had done so, but Felix had outgrown him by 1825, as both he and Zelter knew. In 1824, at a rehearsal for one of young Mendelssohn's short operas, Zelter had marked the end of his "apprenticeship" with a ceremony, declaring Felix "a journeyman, in the name of Mozart and Haydn, and in the name of the elder Bach."[30] The departure for Paris, then, left behind both the apprenticeship and Zelter's bailiwick.

But Felix found the capital of Europe musically moribund. The celebrated salon musicales seemed devoid of serious purpose; concerts and operas failed to meet his expectations of composers and performers. He did have a successful visit with the "dried up and wizened Cherubini" and received the imprimatur of a smile and a judgment—"this boy is gifted, he will do well."[31] And he impressed a number of other leading musicians of Europe with his performances and his compositions. Either in the course of these encounters or in mulling them over in his letters to sister Fanny back in Berlin, he began to realize he had a rare good in his possession: knowledge of the music of Johann Sebastian Bach.[32] Credit for this insight we should perhaps give to Fanny, who wrote to ask him if he had been introducing people to "our great countryman as scholar and theoretician."[33] In

---

[28] There were no institutions for advanced musical training in north Germany at this time, although Zelter had established a workshop for string players (the Ripienschule) and an institute for the improvement of church and school music (see chapter 4). Mendelssohn established the first true conservatory in Germany—in Leipzig in 1843. France, with its centralized state, institutionalized its music education much earlier; already in 1783 it had the first of a national network of over fifty conservatories. At the time of Mendelssohn's visit to Paris, Cherubini had long been the director of the Conservatoire Nationale de Musique and had helped to found new conservatories in provincial France. Cherubini was an Italian, a composer of grand operas and church music.

[29] Todd, *Mendelssohn*, 135.

[30] Hensel, 175.

[31] Felix to Lea, 6 April 1825, in Richter, *Mendelssohn*, 80–81.

[32] Most of the Paris letters to his family appear in Rudolf Elvers, ed., *Felix Mendelssohn: A Life in Letters*, trans. Craig Tomlinson (New York, 1986); and Eva Weissweiler, ed., *"Die Musik will gar nicht rutschen ohne Dich": Fanny und Felix Mendelssohn Briefwechsel 1821 bis 1846* (Berlin, 1997).

[33] The reference could be to Beethoven, whom she mentioned in her previous sentence, but given the geographical consciousness of the time, for which both Vienna and Bonn were far away,

response, Felix wrote about his efforts to become a "proselytizer" for Beethoven and Bach, the latter seen only as "a wig decked out with learning."[34] Larry Todd regards all this as Felix trying to "brazenly proselytize for German music," but it might just as well have been a pragmatic way of differentiating himself from other musical young men in Paris.[35] Mendelssohn playing both his own works and those of Bach underlined his creativity with evidence of his musical acuity and juxtaposed the old aesthetics with the new. Moreover, it worked. People as celebrated as the virtuoso pianist Friedrich Kalkbrenner were astonished at the beauty of Bach's organ preludes, of which they had no inkling. As Fanny's words at the outset of this book remind us, the desire to bring Bach out into the open underlay the entire project of the *St. Matthew Passion*. The trip to Paris, which Fanny teasingly pronounced a failure of music though a triumph of criticism, demonstrated to Felix the connection between publicizing Bach and establishing his own reputation.[36]

It was followed by two years' worth of compositional brilliance (the Octet for Strings, then the Quintet in A major, the *Midsummer Night's Dream* overture, the String Quartet in A Minor, and a host of piano compositions) and one flop. Mendelssohn's only opera, *The Wedding of Camacho*, was approved for performance by the king's musical superintendent Count Brühl in 1826, had its premier in the Berlin Theater (the Schauspielhaus) on April 29, 1827, received moderate applause (which the composer never heard, having left early, apparently overcome with embarrassed self-loathing), and never again saw the light of stage. The story has as many clichéd morals as people describing it: pride comes before a fall; his reach exceeded his grasp; the public is fickle; money could not buy everything; and so on. At the risk of generating another one, we might consider the opera's failure—for whatever it was, it felt like a failure to Mendelssohn—again in light of the choices open to him as an aspiring composer. Opera

---

Fanny would not have called Beethoven a "*Landsmann*" with its strongly local connotations; nor does it seem plausible that she would have referred to Beethoven as a scholar and theoretician (Fanny to Felix, 11 April 1825, in Weissweiler, *Briefwechsel*, 36). But Bach had lived in the cluster of north German states that included Berlin. Marcia Citron's translation of Fanny's letters inexplicably renders "*unsern grossen Landsmann*" as "our bucolic countryman" and hence takes it as a reference to Beethoven as the composer of the Pastoral Symphony (Marcia J. Citron, ed. and trans., *The Letters of Fanny Hensel to Felix Mendelssohn* [Stuyvesant, NY, 1987], 9). Felix's reply, which refers to Fanny's asking about whether he was teaching people "Beethoven and Sebastian Bach," makes it clear that he at least took her to refer to Bach (Felix to Fanny, 20 April 1825, in Weissweiler, *Briefwechsel*, 40).

[34] Felix to Fanny, 20 April 1825, in Weissweiler, *Briefwechsel*, 40.

[35] Todd, *Musical Education*, 5.

[36] Fanny to Felix, 25 April 1825, in Weissweiler, *Briefwechsel*, 41.

dominated public musical life in the early nineteenth century; it would have been hard to imagine a successful compositional career that did not include it. Apart from Bach, the composers whom Mendelssohn admired the most, namely Mozart and Beethoven, had both composed operas—Mendelssohn had, after all, just been playing parts of *Fidelio* on the piano to Parisian skeptics.[37] According to Eric Werner, he was "throughout his life a theater enthusiast": as a twelve-year-old, he had idolized Carl Maria von Weber and attended not only the premier of *Freischütz* but as many of its rehearsals as he could talk his way into.[38] Before *Camacho*, he had already composed four short comic operas, for which he and his parents had arranged semi-professional performances at their Sunday afternoon musicales. Certainly Abraham Mendelssohn, a great admirer of Gluck, expected an opera from his son. The mid-1820s marked the high point of Abraham's influence on his son's musical career, and the culmination of the young composer's efforts to oblige him came with the two-and-a-half hour *Wedding*.

But apart from the disappointment of the opera's reception (among the same people who would come two years later to hear the *St. Matthew Passion*), the performance failed to meet his own expectations. His friend, the singer Eduard Devrient speculated that "the work represented his musical thought of two years ago," which "he had now outgrown." The "chain of annoyances" associated with its production, thought Devrient, was also "unconsciously the foundation of Felix's repugnance to Berlin."[39] But we need not read so far into the future. The experience led Mendelssohn to postpone—to the disappointment of both Devrient and his father—any further efforts to seek fame through operatic triumph. Nor did instrumental composition alone seem enough. He told Ferdinand Hiller that the reception of his instrumental works often left him with "a feeling of isolation."[40] Much of his composing in 1827 apparently went straight into the desk drawer, so much so that his mother enlisted Felix's friend Karl Klingemann to flush this "closet musician" out into the open.[41] His brilliant *Mid-*

---

[37] He complained that "the people here don't know a note of Fidelio" (Felix to Fanny, 20 April 1825, in Weissweiler, *Briefwechsel*, 40). According to James Johnson, Beethoven's work did not conquer Paris until 1828, when his symphonies (not *Fidelio*) made an "explosive impact" (*Listening in Paris: A Cultural History* [Berkeley, 1995], 257–59).

[38] Werner, *Mendelssohn*, 83; Ferdinand Hiller, *Mendelssohn: Letters and Recollections*, trans. M. E. von Glehn (New York, 1972), 32–33.

[39] Eduard Devrient, *Dramatische und Dramaturgische Schriften*, vol. 10, *Meine Erinnerungen an Felix Mendelssohn Bartholdy und seine Briefe an mich* (Leipzig, 1869), 33–34.

[40] Hiller, *Mendelssohn*, 11.

[41] She worried that his compositions had become like "stillborn children," that they lacked anything "fresh, enjoyable, or lively" and would not become that way without "the light of day." Lea Mendelssohn-Bartholdy to Karl Klingemann, 28 December 1827, in *Felix Mendelssohn-Bartholdys*

summer Night's Dream overture had received its first public performance in February 1827 in Stettin, under the direction of Karl Loewe, but such satisfaction as that afforded paled in comparison to the great hopes invested in the now-submerged *Wedding of Camacho*.

Not knowing what step to take next, the eighteen-year-old set off in the summer of 1827 on a walking tour of middle Germany, accompanied by two friends. One month or so after his return, he assembled "a small and trusty choir" to begin working on the *St. Matthew Passion*.[42] The great project was begun, but the historical record does not tell us why. Devrient's account, which tends, albeit gracefully and amusingly, to overestimate his own contributions to central events in Mendelssohn's life, implies the importance of his own stimulus, along with that of friends he had introduced into the Mendelssohn circle, Julius Schubring and Ernst Friedrich Albert Baur, both students of the theologian Friedrich Schleiermacher.[43] Similarly, Adolf Bernhard Marx, the event's untiring publicist, identified as the catalyst his frequent appearances at the Mendelssohn soirées and his influence over Felix in the years from 1827 to 1829.[44] Both of these perspectives may be true and yet still leave out the importance of what Mendelssohn once again learned on the road.

The walking tour was, significantly, the first extended trip Mendelssohn undertook without the overwhelming presence of his father or his mentor Zelter. On it, he ceased to be the clever, and perhaps indulged, young boy and took on an independent persona.[45] His letters home, which were more voluminous than ever (maternal admonitions are not so easily ignored), made repeated and pleased references to anonymity, invisibility, and strange-

---

Briefwechsel mit Legationsrat Karl Klingemann in London, ed. Karl Klingemann, Jr. (Essen, 1909), 43.

[42] Devrient, *Meine Erinnerungen*, 41.

[43] Ibid., 37. Devrient's emphasis on these new arrivals into the Mendelssohn circle is particularly interesting in light of Michael Marissen's argument that Mendelssohn's choice of "Bach for his conducting debut with the Berlin Singakademie" reflected his Lutheranism, interpreted in light of his Jewish heritage. See Marissen, "Religious Aims in Mendelssohn's 1829 Berlin Singakademie Performances of Bach's St. Matthew Passion," *Musical Quarterly* 77 (1993): 718–26. Jeffrey Sposato disagrees with Marissen's argument that Mendelssohn presented the Berlin public with a philo-semitic *Passion* and points out that this was far from a conducting debut for a young man who had been conducting public performances for several years. He does concur, however, with the notion that the performance was a kind of public declaration of Mendelssohn's Protestant faith. See Sposato, "The Price of Assimilation: The Oratorios of Felix Mendelssohn and the Nineteenth-Century Anti-Semitic Tradition" (Ph.D. diss., Brandeis University, 2000), 73–131.

[44] A. B. Marx, *Erinnerungen aus meinem Leben* (Berlin, 1865), 1:85–87.

[45] Even half a year later, his elation at the experience had not faded. He wrote to his old friend Karl Klingemann, a young Hanoverian diplomat then posted in London, that "this past summer I took a trip—alone! . . . I will always look back on those weeks with emotion, for by God they were wonderful." Felix to Karl Klingemann, 5 February 1828, in Klingemann, *Briefwechsel*, 48.

ness: "If three of the most upstanding families in Berlin," he wrote with cheerful irony from Erbich (a "dump"), "knew that three of their most up-standing sons were roving around the country roads with coachmen, peas-ants, and journeymen, and trading their life stories with them, they would be very distressed."[46] At the same time, the letters emphasized the power of his musicality to establish an identity, if not the same identity he had in Berlin. In a hotel in Baden-Baden, he and his friends gathered a sponta-neous crowd around the piano—literally in the dark, for "the season was al-ready over"—for singing and improvising, as a result of which he received invitations to dine, to visit, and even to compose an opera, all without ever showing his face.[47] The anecdote is farfetched, even dreamlike in its details, but true in its illumination of a state of mind weary of the mixed blessings of *Wunderkind* status. Likewise in Heidelberg, he claimed to have spent two splendid afternoons with the scholar Justus Thibaut without ever properly introducing himself: "I loved music, and the rest didn't matter, for he took me for a student coming unannounced to his office hours."[48]

Of course, Mendelssohn always did get around to introducing himself, with recognition usually following, but his musical undertakings on this trip—and there were several more consequential than jamming in Baden-Baden—came out of a more serious sense of purpose than those in Paris, which still had something of the air of youthful exhibitionism. The stimu-lating September afternoons with Thibaut in Heidelberg, for instance, seem to have been all talk and no playing. Thibaut was a famous jurist at the Uni-versity of Heidelberg and an enthusiastic amateur singer, who had recently created a stir in the educated world with his publication of an aesthetic trea-tise "On the Purity of Music."[49] It consisted of a curious amalgamation of Kantianism, classicism, and romantic philo-Catholicism into a defense of such Renaissance composers as Palestrina and Orlando di Lasso against the alleged sensationalism of modern composers. Mendelssohn recognized that Thibaut, for all his opinions, knew less than he did about music, but he still found the man fascinating. The two argued about who were the greatest composers of the past, and especially about Bach. Thibaut had treated Bach dismissively in his treatise, because he regarded his compositions as too con-voluted and difficult to be truly beautiful. Mendelssohn told him that he simply did not know the "greatest and most important" of Bach's works, in which "everything comes together"—a reference, probably, to the *St.*

---

[46] Hensel, 192.

[47] Ibid., 194–95.

[48] Ibid., 197–98.

[49] Anton Friedrich Justus Thibaut, *Über die Reinheit der Tonkunst* (Heidelberg, 1825). See chap-ter 5 below.

Matthew Passion. When they parted, Thibaut exclaimed, "Farewell, and may our friendship be forever linked to Luis de Vittoria and to Sebastian Bach."[50]

Traveling next to Frankfurt, Mendelssohn visited with Johann Nepomuk Schelble and met up again with his friend (and fellow aging child prodigy) Ferdinand Hiller, who later remembered thinking him "much altered in looks"—"since our last meeting he had grown into a man."[51] An opera singer turned choir director, Schelble was the leader of the Cäcilienverein, a singing association comparable to Zelter's Singakademie but more accustomed to public performances. In 1821, the society began offering regular subscription concerts of choral works, especially those of Handel, Haydn, Mozart, and Beethoven. At the time Mendelssohn visited (late September 1827), the group was in its final rehearsals for a performance of a Handel oratorio: he did not know the work and made considerable effort to pass through Frankfurt again in early October to hear it.[52]

As for Bach, Schelble's sustained interest seems to date to 1826, when the singer Franz Hauser moved to Frankfurt from Berlin, bringing with him his own extensive Bach manuscript collection and his close knowledge of Bach cultivation among his friends the Mendelssohns.[53] Once again we are reminded of how much the knowledge of Bach derived from the intimacies of friendship and musical association rather than from general education, even of musical people. Hauser joined the Cäcilienverein at Schelble's invitation and spurred the group to study Bach's choral compositions. When Felix came to Frankfurt in 1827 (and visited Hauser as well), the group was already looking beyond its Handel concert to the Credo from Bach's Mass in B Minor, which it performed in early 1828—the first time since C. P. E. Bach had directed the Credo in Hamburg in 1784.[54] Schelble may also have had the *St. Matthew Passion* on his mind: Hauser had a copy of it and seems to have been discussing it with his friends.[55] Although we will never know the timing of the group's rehearsals for certain, since the

[50] Geck also believes that Mendelssohn was referring to the *St. Matthew Passion* (Geck, 21). Felix to family, Heidelberg, 20 September 1827, in Hensel, 196–98.

[51] Hiller, *Mendelssohn*, 8–9.

[52] Outlining the complex travel plans that would allow him to take in the performance as well as the wine harvest on the Rhine, he wrote to his father that "it is all too wonderful!" (Hensel, 199–200).

[53] Geck, 75–76. See also Dale A. Jorgenson, *The Life and Legacy of Franz Xaver Hauser: A Forgotten Leader in the Nineteenth-Century Bach Movement* (Carbondale, IL, 1996), 23–27.

[54] Christoph Wolff, "The Kantor, the Kapellmeister and the Musical Scholar: Remarks on the History and Performance of Bach's Mass in B Minor," trans. Mary Whittall, liner notes to J. S. Bach, Mass in B Minor, compact disc (Hamburg, 1985), 4.

[55] Geck, 76–77.

archives of the Cäcilienverein were destroyed in the Second World War, Felix wrote to a friend in Stockholm some months later that "in Frankfurt am Main, they have performed [Bach's] Credo and they are planning to perform the Passion."[56]

The combination of visits with Schelble, Hauser, and Thibaut—rich as they were in rehearsals, revivals, vibrant choral performance, and talk of past music—must have given Mendelssohn possibilities to ponder. Soon after, he wrote to his father, who had been pressing him to find a new libretto and move forward on the all-important opera front. Felix temporized: "The whole trip has convinced me all over again that people expect something special from me, and much more than was achieved in *The Wedding of Camacho*. I also know that I do not have to disappoint these expectations; but I doubt very much that everything depends on having to present myself today or tomorrow in such a manner. . . . I have blazed a path for myself in instrumental music (and those are your own words, dear Father), but in other areas I have yet to."[57] Although the letter discusses only his composing, the phrase "expect something special from me" resonates as much with his experiences in Heidelberg and Frankfurt as with his past and future in Berlin. In Heidelberg he had presented himself chiefly as Sebastian Bach's champion to Thibaut, a man celebrated not for his composing but for his historical erudition. In Frankfurt he had witnessed how a gifted conductor could carry the public along with him in performances of forgotten masterpieces. Feeling no urgency to write another opera (as his letter to his father reveals), Felix could well have thought it time to delve deeper into the performative, as well as ethical-educational, possibilities of Bach. Taken together, the trip to Paris, the opera premiere, and the tour of western Germany all suggested the plausibility, the timeliness, and the dramatic potential of an experiment in historical performance.

REHEARSING

The project to bring the *St. Matthew Passion* out of silence into sound began in earnest shortly after his return to Berlin in the fall of 1827. As Devrient reports, Felix began to gather a group of friends at the Mendelssohn house on Saturdays "for the practice of rarely heard works," soon exclusively the *St. Matthew Passion*. The group was small and drawn mainly from Singakademie acquaintances. It included a handful of instrumentalists as well, chief among them Eduard Rietz, a young violinist (and tenor) who

---

[56] Reprinted in Grossmann-Vendrey, *Vergangenheit*, 29.

[57] Felix Mendelssohn to Abraham Mendelssohn, 29 September 1827, in Elvers, *Life in Letters*, 48–49.

had become Felix's violin instructor in 1820 and for whom Felix wrote a number of compositions in the 1820s. Rietz was already ill with the tuberculosis that would kill him in 1831, and was, according to Devrient, "Felix's constant especial confidant, initiated in all his musical doings."[58]

It was Devrient, however, who formed the center of this group. His own entrée into the Mendelssohn circle had come through the Singakademie, which he joined in 1818 when he was seventeen. Zelter quickly recognized the beauty of his baritone voice and already in 1819, the year Fanny and Felix Mendelssohn joined, made Devrient a soloist in the traditional Good Friday performance of Carl Heinrich Graun's beloved oratorio, *The Death of Jesus* (*Tod Jesu*).[59] In 1820 Devrient joined the company of principal singers at Berlin's Royal Opera. Although he sang a number of significant roles in his first years there, his opera career took off after he returned to Berlin from a study tour in 1822–23, in which he sang and studied Italian opera in Vienna and oratorios with Schelble in Frankfurt. His lifelong friendship with Felix Mendelssohn also dates to this return. Devrient was the most impressive voice and the most significant dramatic talent among Mendelssohn's circle of friends; moreover, by 1827, he had sung more than thirty roles on the Berlin stage. This experience was more crucial to the success of the *St. Matthew Passion* revival than scholars caught in the Mendelssohn-or-Zelter dilemma have acknowledged.[60]

The Mendelssohn house rehearsals continued from late 1827 to late 1828 and have left fragmentary traces in the historical record. The intensity of the singers' engagement with the *Passion* music probably varied. A note from Mendelssohn to Devrient in January 1828 took the tone of light teasing so characteristic of his correspondence—"Surely you haven't forgotten, dear Herr Devrient, that we were going to work up some *Bach* on Saturday."[61] Other letters from the time indicate the absence of a number of the circle's

---

[58] Mendelssohn dedicated the Octet for Strings of 1825 to Rietz. Devrient, *Meine Erinnerungen*, 37–38.

[59] Devrient was a native of Berlin and a nephew of one of the most celebrated dramatic actors of the day, Ludwig Devrient. He married Therese Schlesinger, daughter of the prominent Berlin publisher Adolf Martin Schlesinger. See Ledebur, *Tonkünstler Lexikon*, 110–11. The notorious *Lexikon der Juden in der Musik*, assembled in the 1930s, asserted that the Devrient family were Jews trying to disguise their identity behind a false French exterior (vol. 2). As proof of this, the author of the entry, the anti-Semitic literary historian Adolf Bartels, said of Eduard's marriage to Therese, the "Judin Schlessinger," "by his marriage to a Jew, one can practically assume his own Jewish blood."

[60] Devrient is partially to blame for being overlooked, because he presses his own claim for being at the center of the performance so strongly that critical historians have automatically discounted his role.

[61] Elvers, *Life in Letters*, 51–52.

members throughout the first half of 1828.[62] All of this suggests a provisional quality to the gatherings, although not aimless: Devrient later described a systematic working-through of the entire *Passion*, "piece by piece." Many in this circle already knew excerpts, since Zelter had very occasionally allowed Singakademie members to practice a chorale or chorus otherwise locked up in his cabinet of unsung treasures. But such exposure made little impression. Devrient claimed that "the miscellaneous performance of single numbers at Zelter's Friday rehearsals did not have any effect." By contrast, in the Saturday rehearsals "a new world opened to us." The memoirs of his wife, Therese Schlesinger Devrient, along with Fanny Mendelssohn one of the few women in this early group, described the initial difficulties the singers had in reading the music—"nevertheless we were completely shaken by it and transported into a new musical world."[63]

The decision to attempt a complete public performance of the work with a full complement of singers, instrumentalists, and soloists, as well as an audience to hear it all, emerged sometime in the course of 1828. Devrient's account has become definitive by default, and in it, his own force was the moving one. "I longed more and more ardently to sing the part of Christ in public," he wrote, ever the performer. Others agreed, but the general feeling in the singing circle was one of "dismay" at the "insurmountable difficulties"—"not only in the work itself, with its double orchestra and double chorus" but also with the antiquated attitudes of the Singakademie and its director. In his narrative, written when he was seventy, Devrient remembers the project as something akin to youthful folly: "it seemed a rash undertaking." Pitted against these young enthusiasts—the boy genius, the up-and-coming star of stage and opera, the tragically ill violinist, the singing theologians—were the forces of a calcified establishment and an ignorant public, both too set in their ways to indulge impulse. "Even the parents of Felix" held back, presumably out of fear of another public embarrassment: "Marx [the journalist] doubted and the old ladies of the Singakademie shook their heads."[64]

---

[62] Felix complained to Karl Klingemann, listing all the absences in early 1828—"our circle bears a wretched aspect these days" (Felix to Karl Klingemann, 5 February 1828, in Klingemann, *Briefwechsel*, 48).

[63] Devrient, *Meine Erinnerungen*, 41–42; Therese Devrient, *Jugenderinnerungen* (Stuttgart, 1905), 303. She dates the beginning of these rehearsals to an "October evening" in 1828, but the letter from Felix to Devrient of January 1828 suggests that she was off by a year. Her description indicates that this group of twelve had not met before, so the *St. Matthew Passion* seems to have been its raison d'être.

[64] Devrient, *Meine Erinnerungen*, 49. The eminent Friedrich Blume accepts the implicit explanation here for the performance, that a "young generation entered upon the scene," displaying a

Such a story line provided the perfect setup for the eventual triumph—after all, with no obstacles to overcome, there would be no glory. The climax of Devrient's account comes not with the performance but earlier, with a visit to the lion's den itself, Zelter's studio, where the two young men went to seek permission to use Singakademie singers and space for the project. Once again, Devrient must provide the impetus. Overcome with emotion after a particularly moving rehearsal in the singing circle, he spent a sleepless night plotting a strategy for Bach's conquest of Berlin. When the sun rose, he went immediately to the Mendelssohn house, where Felix lay in a "deathlike sleep." Brother Paul undertook to awake him, and after much shaking, calling out, and lifting up, Felix roused enough to murmur (in reference to his earlier offer to perform the *Passion* on a penny whistle), "Oh leave off, I've always said so, it's all just tootling." Nonsensical or not, the remark revealed that Felix too was dreaming of Bach, and Devrient now persuaded him that the deed must be done and he, Felix, must be its doer. Zelter, argued Devrient, "owed him [Devrient] for nearly ten years of contributions to his concerts," and today he was calling in his chips, in the form of a working chorus and its performance hall. With a shrinking Felix in tow, Devrient "set out at once for Zelter's room"—on the ground floor of the Singakademie's new building, located just off Unter den Linden, in other words, in the heart of official Berlin. "We found the old giant in a thick cloud of smoke with a long pipe in his mouth," sitting at his harpsichord and wearing his worn woolen stockings and slippers, remembered the seventy-year-old Devrient, with a lifetime of stage directing and scene setting under his belt. Devrient delivered his speech, lacing it with references to Zelter's excellent teaching. Zelter declared the plan impossible. When Felix tried to leave, Devrient grabbed him and delivered another speech with more flattery. Zelter accused them of being a couple of "snotty-nosed brats." Devrient laughed, a mortified Felix again tried to leave, but Devrient again grabbed him and flattered Zelter some more. Finally, of course, Zelter gave in, warning them with cheerful misogyny that the "old biddies" on the Singakademie board would likely prove difficult and the choir members would cause them "endless misery," probably not even showing up for the second rehearsal.[65]

According to Devrient, the confrontation—half farce, half morality play—took place in January 1829. That date is almost certainly wrong, for

"spontaneous enthusiasm, an unbounded fervor for Bach's music," in the face of an older generation's grumbling and suspicion (Blume, "Bach in the Romantic Era," 298). As to Marx's doubts, Devrient was quite accurate—see chapter 3 below.

[65] Devrient, *Meine Erinnerungen*, 49–58.

Eduard Devrient. Drawing by Wilhelm Hensel, 1831. By permission of the Bildarchiv Preussischer Kulturbesitz / Art Resource, NY; Kupferstichkabinett, Staatliche Museen zu Berlin, Germany.

already on December 13, 1828, Mendelssohn and Devrient together send a letter of petition to the governing board of the Singakademie, requesting the use of its hall and the participation of its members in the undertaking—something they would not have done prior to consulting Zelter.[66] But other aspects of the narrative are probably right. For instance, Zelter's initial re-

---

[66] Geck, 31.

serve, not to say scorn and incredulity, about the project conforms to his long-standing reluctance to do much of anything in public. And recently, his public performances had not succeeded. A botched effort at Handel's *Judas Maccabeus* had been the latest disaster. Even before the actual perform-ance, Lea Mendelssohn had predicted the worst: she wrote to Klingemann in London that "the Akademie had labored already the whole winter" on *Judas* without coming any closer to performance. "It is heartbreaking," she wrote, "how such vigorous, extensive resources in our city turn mountains into mice." She thought Zelter had become "enfeebled in body and spirit" and was in any case not much of a conductor.[67] Indeed, the performance turned out badly. The choir was ill rehearsed, and Zelter had not bothered to check dates—it turned out to conflict with a Royal Opera event. Zelter's main soloists, Eduard Devrient and Heinrich Stümer (who would sing the role of the Evangelist in the 1829 *Passion*), had to put their professional du-ties over their volunteer ones and so decamped to the opera, leaving *Judas Maccabeus* without Judas Maccabeus (or Simon).[68]

As for the alleged reluctance of Felix Mendelssohn himself to go public with the *Passion*, we can neither confirm nor deny it from sources outside Devrient's account. Devrient depicted this reluctance in terms of youthful modesty and even timidity, particularly when facing the disapproval of a former mentor. His narrative relied heavily on Felix's inability even to imagine such a thing as a public performance—as he recalls it, Devrient must literally, and presumably figuratively also, awaken Felix from deep slumber. Fanny Mendelssohn, writing to a friend a few months after the initial petition, recounted only how the two of them, Felix and Devrient, had decided one evening to undertake the project, then went out the next morning "in newly purchased yellow gloves (on the importance of which they laid much weight)" to speak with the Singakademie board.[69] When one puts together the course of Mendelssohn's career, the lessons of past ex-perience and example, his consciousness of similar projects underway else-where, not to mention his initiation of rehearsals in the first place, enough runs counter to Devrient's version to suggest that, at the least, both young men sought out the encounter with Zelter—supposing it even took place at all. As Mendelssohn had written to his Swedish friend Lindblad in April 1828, seven months before the petition to the Singakademie, "Bach is everywhere in fashion." Not only was Schelble planning to perform the *St. Matthew Passion* in Frankfurt, but Berlin's glamorous Italian maestro, Gas-

[67] Lea Mendelssohn to Karl Klingemann, 28 December 1827, in Klingemann, *Briefwechsel*, 45.
[68] Felix Mendelssohn to Karl Klingemann, 5 February 1828, in Klingemann, *Briefwechsel*, 47.
[69] Fanny to Karl Klingemann, 22 March 1829, in Hensel, 237.

paro Spontini of the Royal Opera—a man not known for his devotion to antiquated contrapuntists—had that very Day of Repentance in 1828 directed a performance of the Credo from Bach's B-minor Mass.[70] Ambitious, exciting, daunting, monumental, even risky—the effort to perform the *St. Matthew Passion* was all of that. But by the end of 1828, it was not unimaginable.

The board of the Singakademie duly granted its permission to Felix Mendelssohn Bartholdy and E. P. Devrient, "royal singer," to hold a public concert in its rooms on March 11, 1829, for the rent of fifty thalers. "Now everything went smoothly," reported Devrient, "obstacles vanish like ghosts when you approach them." More and more singers came to each rehearsal, rather than fewer and fewer, as Zelter had predicted. Copyists worked day and night to provide enough scores for them all. Soon the rehearsals had to move from a small practice room into the drafty main hall, and still the singers kept coming. Several years earlier, Felix's consumptive friend Eduard Rietz had quit his regular position in the royal chapel orchestra in order to found a "Philharmonic Society," an orchestra made up mainly of amateurs recruited from Zelter's Ripienschule (an instrumental ensemble for the practice of older music, established in 1807). Under Rietz's gifted direction, it had reached professional standards of performance, and by 1828, among other engagements, it provided all the instrumental accompaniment to the Singakademie.[71] This Philharmonic, supplemented with professionals from the Royal Orchestra and a few additional instrumentalists, constituted the double orchestra that the score requires. Rietz himself served as the concertmaster of the first orchestra, as well as violin soloist at such emotional moments as the aria "Erbarme Dich." Ferdinand David, another nineteen-year-old and future world-famous violinist, sat in the first chair for the second. The soloists came, without exception, from the Royal Opera and thus were all of them well known to the Berlin public: among them Anna Milder-Hauptmann, celebrated prima donna of the moment, singing the arias for soprano voice, Heinrich Stümer as the Evangelist, Carl Adam Bader as Pilate and Peter, and, of course, Devrient in the role "most essential to the expression of the whole work," that of Jesus.[72]

Mendelssohn conducted the rehearsals often from the piano, playing

---

[70] Mendelssohn also exclaimed, "Aren't you tickled by that absurdity??" (Wie gefällt Dir der Unsinn??), referring to the juxtaposition of Spontini and Bach, not the Credo itself. Mendelssohn to Lindblad, 22 April 1828, in Grossmann-Vendrey, *Vergangenheit*, 29.

[71] Ledebur, *Tonkünstler Lexikon*, 463.

[72] Devrient, *Meine Erinnerungen*, 55–62; Geck, 34–35. In contrast, the modern reception of the work tends to focus on the role of the Evangelist as a more important expression of Bach's musical and theological achievement.

with his left hand and conducting with his right. According to Fanny, Zelter had helped direct the first rehearsal but drew into the background as they progressed.[73] Perhaps to distance himself from Zelter's previous efforts with the work, Felix had decided not to rehearse the many pieces of the *Passion* one at a time, chorus by chorus, chorale by chorale. According to Devrient, he chose instead to work with the singers on entire sections at a time, "with unrelenting strictness until they reached the fullest possible expression of the work" and thereby would receive "a complete impression of its utterly extraordinary nature." Both Devrient and Fanny, one remembering and the other reporting from the scene, described the impact of the music on those rehearsing it. Fanny wrote to a friend of how the members of the Singakademie "marveled, gaped, admired," and of how "within a few weeks of rehearsing, they expressed even greater astonishment that they of all people should have had so little knowledge that such a work even existed."[74] "These were unforgettable times," she wrote: "how from the first rehearsal on, we were all seized by it and devoted ourselves to it with our entire soul; how each rehearsal brought greater love and dedication; how the addition of each element, the soloists, the orchestra, always brought renewed pleasure and astonishment; how magnificently Felix directed it all."[75] Devrient, for his part, remembered people's amazement "not so much at the grandeur of the construction as at the abundance of melodies, the rich expression of emotion, the passion, the singular style of declamation, and the force of the dramatic action." "No one," he observed, "had expected any of this from old Bach."[76]

Meanwhile, as the rehearsals progressed inside the Singakademie building, a general air of expectation gathered outside in Berlin. Singakademie members came from the leading segments of Berlin society—bureaucracy, business, academia, nobility. Opera singers were welcome guests in the city's drawing rooms, and of course the Mendelssohns themselves hosted a constant stream of everyone famous, educated, wealthy, talented, or otherwise interesting. People talked; the news spread. Felix himself was evidently confident enough to invite a few guests of his own. On March 7, only four days before the performance, he sent a note to Johann Friedrich Schneider, asking him for a "personal favor": "You may perhaps know from the papers that I intend to perform the *Passion* by Seb. Bach, a very beautiful and worthy piece of church music from the last century," he wrote, and "the favor I

[73] Fanny Mendelssohn to Karl Klingemann, 22 March 1829, in Hensel, 238.
[74] This is a rather pointed rebuke of Zelter, whom the Mendelssohns believed to have hoarded his knowledge of Bach, even from his own closest associates.
[75] Fanny Mendelssohn to Karl Klingemann, 22 March 1829, in Hensel, 238.
[76] Devrient, *Meine Erinnerungen*, 59–62.

Fanny Mendelssohn Bartholdy. Drawing by Wilhelm Hensel, 1829. By permission of the Bildarchiv Preussischer Kulturbesitz / Art Resource, NY; Kupferstichkabinett, Staatliche Museen zu Berlin, Germany.

request is to ask if it would be possible for you to suffer the inconvenience of undertaking a long trip, thereby granting us the pleasure of your company . . . in order to honor an old master and dignify our musical celebration by your presence."[77] Schneider was court director of music in Dessau, a leading organist who had recently held Bach's own position in Leipzig, the organizer of a series of important music festivals, and the composer of the popular oratorio *The Last Judgment.* More than a polite gesture, the letter reveals the extent to which Mendelssohn regarded this undertaking as both significant to his musical future—significant enough to try to insure the presence of influential men of music—and significant to the musical community in Germany.

But as the letter also indicates, the 1829 performance benefited from a deliberate media campaign on its behalf, perhaps the first ever such campaign. It was conducted, with persistence and a flair for highbrow appeal, by Adolf Bernhard Marx. The son of a Jewish doctor in Halle, he had arrived in Berlin in 1822 with his own great expectations. Initially a student of the law, he moved to Berlin to study music and quickly began to shape a career for himself. In 1824 he founded a new musical journal in the city called the *Berliner Allgemeine Musikalische Zeitung* and used it to develop, among other things, his own school of quasi-Hegelian music criticism.[78] Marx antagonized as many people as he attracted. Among the former were Eduard Devrient, Carl Friedrich Zelter, and Abraham Mendelssohn. Among the latter was Felix Mendelssohn, who took up Marx with something of the adolescent's enthusiasm for parental disapproval. For his part, Devrient blamed Marx for Felix's refusal to compose music to a libretto Devrient had written on the legend of Hans Heiling, king of the earth spirits. Nearly fifty years later, his resentment of Marx had not faded: the normally charitable Devrient denounced Marx's domination of "every conversation," "his adroit flattery," and "his ungainly appearance, short trousers, and clumsy big shoes."[79]

---

[77] Reprinted in Elvers, *Life in Letters,* 53.

[78] See chapter 3.

[79] Devrient, *Meine Erinnerungen,* 38. Descriptions of Marx from people in the Mendelssohn circle have strongly anti-Semitic overtones, which we might plausibly interpret as a defensive reaction against Marx as the embodiment of assimilation's limits—limits that the Mendelssohns knew well yet needed psychically to keep on the margins of consciousness. Beside his own evocation of the stereotype of Jew as base flatterer, Devrient describes Abraham Mendelssohn criticizing "people of that kind, who talk so cleverly and can do nothing, [and who] act perniciously on productive minds"—here the stereotype of the Jews as parasites on the social body, incapable of real creation. In the unbridled reaction of Varnhagen von Ense, a friend and frequent visitor at the Mendelssohn salon, Marx was not only "crawling," "obsequious," "man as bug," but also "unpleasantly pungent and suffocating." For a full account of the notorious "foetor judaicus" or Jewish odor, see Marc Weiner, *Richard Wagner and the Anti-Semitic Imagination* (Lincoln, NE, 1995). On reactions to Marx, see Todd, *Mendelssohn,* 128.

But Marx did not just hold forth; he seems also to have listened, absorbing the musical offerings of the household, especially the *St. Matthew Passion*. He wrote in his memoirs of first hearing parts of it played there in 1823: so moved was he that "day and night I could not separate myself from it." "Here, here," he continued, with Hegelian abandon, "is the full realization of an Ideal of composition." "Naturally," he concluded, "I told everyone about it." Not right away, however. His journal contained no references to the *St. Matthew Passion* until 1827, and then only a handful. In April 1828, while writing in enthusiastic support of a plan to publish Bach's B-minor Mass, Marx switched to verse: "I thought last night / That I saw the moon as I slept / But when I awoke / There unexpectedly came the sun!"[80] Soon, he announced, Berlin would witness the publication of "the greatest work of our greatest master, the greatest and holiest musical work of all peoples, the great *Passion* music of Matthew the Evangelist by Johann Sebastian Bach." Marx exclaimed, "What wondrous times break forth!" When it became clear at the end of that year that the piece would actually be performed before it was published, Marx devoted no fewer than six consecutive issues of the *Berliner Allgemeine Musikalische Zeitung* to proclaiming the coming event.

THE PERFORMANCES OF 1829

Whether because of Marx's efforts or not (and several other Berlin newspapers also urged readers to attend), tickets to the upcoming performance, priced low for the time at twenty silver groschen, quickly sold out.[81] Fanny reported that "over a thousand people" more were turned away ticketless, and every newspaper review noted the high level of public interest and the subsequent demand for more performances. Almost all the performers contributed their services gratis, including the free tickets to which soloists were entitled, and all profits went to a sewing school for indigent girls. The performance took place at 6 p.m. on March 11, 1829, a pleasantly warm Wednesday evening. Again according to Fanny, people stood outside the Singakademie building long beforehand, so that when the doors finally opened, the hall filled up in less than fifteen minutes, including the lobby and the practice space behind the orchestra. Marx estimated that more than

---

[80] "Ich gedachte in der Nacht, / Dass ich den Mond sähe im Schlaf; / Als ich aber erwachte, / Ging unvermuthet die Sonne auf!" *BAMZ* 5 (23 April 1828): 131.

[81] The report on the first performance in the *Spenersche Zeitung* commented approvingly that the low ticket price reflected "the proper conviction that the nobler and greater and truer an artwork is, the more it constitutes a common good for all educated persons" (reprinted by Marx in his *BAMZ* 6, no. 11 [14 March 1824]: 80).

a thousand people came to listen: the new building had been designed to hold an audience of about nine hundred. Add to that about 150 singers, perhaps as many as 30 instrumentalists, 8 soloists, and the conductor himself, and the hall would indeed have been "overflowing."[82]

The list of the people known to have been at that first performance is enough to command one's attention: a large representation from the court including the king and the crown prince, an enthusiastic supporter of the event; intellectuals like Schleiermacher, Hegel, and the world-traveling, world-famous Alexander von Humboldt; literati like Heine and Rahel Varnhagen von Ense; men who would later rise to prominence in Prussia like Joseph Maria von Radowitz and Mendelssohn's friend Johann Gustav Droysen. Contemporaries who wrote about it were impressed by the very phenomenon of the audience. Devrient referred to the "extraordinary sensation" that the concert had excited "in the educated circles of Berlin." Fanny marveled at the "interest it had aroused in every circle and throughout all ranks of society." Zelter's note to Goethe referred, somewhat restrainedly, to the "completely full house"; Rahel von Varnhagen wrote to her husband of having been barely able to find a place among the "people of rank" in the balcony; Johann Wilhelm Loebell wrote to Ludwig Tieck about the "quite extraordinary and unexpected participation" of the public in this "truly remarkable event."[83] So successful was the performance that Mendelssohn repeated it on March 21, on the 144th anniversary of Bach's birth. Fanny reported that opera director Spontini had intrigued against the second performance, but was foiled by the crown prince. In any case, the concert once again sold out: even more people vied for entrance; many members of the original audience came to hear the music a second time.

What these people heard, in the narrowest sense of that question, was a much shortened version of Bach's monumental work, which in its entirety lasts about three-and-a-half hours (of the modern recordings, Otto Klemperer's clocks in at three hours and forty-three minutes; Sir David Willcocks romps through it in just over three hours). With Mendelssohn's cuts, the concert probably lasted just under two hours.[84] Bach's setting of the Passion according to St. Matthew, which he composed in 1727, revised significantly, and conducted only four times, was the second of his efforts at large-scale

---

[82] Fanny Mendelssohn to Karl Klingemann, 22 March 1829, in Hensel, 239.

[83] Devrient, *Meine Erinnerungen*, 67; Geck, 45–47.

[84] In 1992, Christoph Spering and his Chorus Musicus Köln with Das Neue Orchester (also founded by Spering) released a recording of Mendelssohn's 1841 performance of the *St. Matthew Passion* in the Thomaskirche in Leipzig. The 1841 performance included four arias and one chorale cut from the 1829 performance but was otherwise much the same. Spering's recreation is 132 minutes long. The recording is available on the Opus 111 label (OP 20001).

oratorical composition.[85] He had written and performed the *St. John Passion* in Leipzig in 1724 (subsequently revised multiple times); he also wrote three more Passions, none of which has survived. Yet even the question of how to classify such a work has exercised musicologists for some time. When Philipp Spitta, the author of the first definitive biography of Bach, attempted to account for the genealogy of Bach's Passion music, he expressed dissatisfaction with the by-then common definition of it as "a dramatic interpretation of the Gospels with a side glance at the oratorio and the opera." He preferred to classify it as something more complicated, which ought to be regarded "as the culminating effort of Protestant church music." Bach's Passions constituted "a very singular compound" of music and poetry, secular and sacred traditions, drama and contemplation, vocal and instrumental music, the individual and the crowd.[86] Bach himself, Spitta pointed out, carefully avoided calling them oratorios, nor did the term begin to encompass the originality and the comprehensiveness of his creation.

The audience in 1829 did not have such a rich understanding of the Passion tradition; indeed many hardly knew what to expect. Moreover, Mendelssohn presented them with a version that, by cutting ten arias (about a third of them), seven choruses (about half), and only a few of the chorales, emphasized the drama of the Passion story and the congregational tradition of the Lutheran chorale at the expense of the reflective and Italianate solo singing.[87] Still, the overall shape of the work remained one that

[85] He achieved the definitive or final version in 1729, two years after the first. This was the version he carefully recopied in ornamental hand in the 1740s and the one passed on to his son Carl Philipp Emanuel Bach and from there to the early-nineteenth-century admirers. Zelter's manuscript of the score was probably a copy he made not from the autograph score, which did not arrive in Berlin until 1824 (via Bach manuscript collector and Singakademie benefactor Georg Polchau), but from a copy made in the 1740s by J. C. Altnickol, Bach's son-in-law, which came to Kirnberger in Berlin and from thence to the library of Prussian Princess Anna Amalia. Felix's copy is now thought to reflect some kind of access to the autograph score itself and not just Zelter's copy. For a lucid account of these intricacies, see Todd, *Mendelssohn*, 122–24. Mendelssohn believed that he was resurrecting the work on the one-hundredth anniversary of its first performance, and some accounts still repeat this error.

[86] Philipp Spitta, *Johann Sebastian Bach: His Work and Influence on the Music of Germany, 1685–1750*, trans. Clara Bell and J. A. Fuller-Maitland (New York, 1951), 2:477, 497; originally published in 1889.

[87] Todd summarizes the effect of this alteration as one of encouraging Berliners "to discover in Bach's cerebral masterpiece roots of their own spiritual experiences as German Protestants" (Todd, *Mendelssohn: A Life*, 197). Jeffrey Sposato has argued vigorously against Michael Marissen's belief that the cuts reflected an effort to excise the anti-Judaism of the *Passion* narrative. Sposato believes, plausibly, that Mendelssohn sought mainly to make the work more accessible to the public by making it shorter and more dramatic. See Sposato, "Price of Assimilation," 73–131. For further discussion of this issue, see chapter 5.

in its unusual combination of parts was unlike either opera or Handelian oratorio, both of which the audience would have known well. Yet unlike the *St. John Passion*, which relies overwhelmingly on biblical text, the *St. Matthew Passion* had, like an opera, a single librettist, Christian Friedrich Henrici (his pen name was Picander), the postmaster general of Leipzig and sometime poet. Picander drew on a successful Passion libretto written in 1712 by the Hamburg poet Barthold Heinrich Brockes: men as distinguished as Telemann, Mattheson, and Handel had each already composed music for it. Its distinguishing feature, and the key to its great popularity in those early decades of the eighteenth century, was to have turned the gospel story into a poetic narrative and to have inserted additional poems of spiritual reflection and anguish at crucial moments in the story.[88] Picander's libretto, written to Bach's specifications, included three kinds of text, only one of which was his own words: the biblical narrative from Matthew 26–27, Picander's poetical texts, and chorales in strophic form.

Bach created a remarkable balance among all three. The structural background of the work consists not of the Gospel text, as tradition dictated, but of Picander's poems. Bach divided them among soloists and two choruses, one of which represented the lamenting faithful of the New Jerusalem—Brockes's popular Daughters of Zion—and the other the crowd of the old Jerusalem, who witnessed and participated in the actual Passion events. Both halves of the *Passion* begin and end with Picander's texts. In between one finds the gospel story distributed among its actors—Jesus, Peter, Judas, Pilate, and so on—and the Evangelist, or teller of the story, for whom Bach wrote recitative music that in its expressiveness and dramatic coloration went far beyond the perfunctory style of most contemporaneous recitative composition. Finally, he included a number of familiar chorales, some repeated in the course of the work with different words and harmonizations, all placed to enlarge upon the emotional impact of the story and perhaps also to draw the audience into actual or implicit participation in the music.

We have every reason to believe that the force of Bach's creation affected the Berlin audience of 1829 much as it continues to affect listeners today, in its inexorable accumulation of lamentation, anger, anguish, resignation, and faith. Mendelssohn's direction of it, so far as can be told with only contemporary reviews and his annotated score to go on, was a surprisingly true one, neither overlaid with romantic orchestration, as some accounts would have it, nor excessively speedy, as his later conducting was allegedly wont to be. The many markings on his score of the *Passion* (now preserved in the

[88] Spitta, *Bach*, 2:496–97.

Bodleian Library in Oxford) were, in Friedrich Blume's words, "purely technical, bearing on the performance." Mendelssohn, Blume concluded, did not "prettify the dramatic diction of the recitative in any way, nor did he smooth away the surging expressiveness of the arias." In short, he allowed "Bach's mighty language to ring out in its true tones."[89] Mendelssohn did have to make minor adjustments in instrumentation, for unlike today no one in his time played such obsolete instruments as the oboe da caccia and oboe d'amore (a clarinet had to do) or the viola da gamba (a cello served instead). But overall, in Martin Geck's definitive judgment, we are left with the "picture of a performance in the spirit of Bach."[90]

Certainly the listeners of 1829 felt themselves to be in Bach's presence. Of the many and moving accounts of the performance—which subsequent chapters will explore more fully—just a few may suffice. Writing several days after the second performance, Fanny Mendelssohn described how the chorus (of which she was a member) "was possessed by a fire, a pulsating force and at the same time a heartrending tenderness, which I have never before heard in them." The "overflowing hall," she continued "gave the impression of a church: the deepest quiet and the most solemn reverence seized the gathering; one heard only a few involuntary exclamations of deeply stirred feeling; what is said so often without justification may truly be said of this undertaking, that an extraordinary spirit, a universal, transcendent interest, guided it." Devrient too believed that the Singakademie chorus had outdone itself, achieving "perfection" (*das Vollendete*) under Mendelssohn's direction. Of his own performance, he remembered being "carried away by the totality of the performance" and "singing and feeling with my entire soul, such that the shivers of devotion that ran through me in the most moving moments of the work, were surely felt by the absolutely silent listeners as well." Like Fanny, he believed that "the entire assembly of musicians and listeners" were moved by a single spirit of devotion.[91]

Nor was either of them necessarily misreading—or misremembering— the mood of the crowd, out of their own excited sensibilities. Johann Wilhelm Loebell, who with no particular connection to any of the main players and no previous record of admiring Bach's music may be reckoned an average listener, found himself overwhelmed. "I must tell you," he wrote to Tieck, "about what in this moment fills my whole soul, and that is the Passion music of Sebastian Bach." Remembering Tieck's own reflections on

[89] Blume, "Bach in the Romantic Era," 299.
[90] Geck, 41.
[91] Fanny Mendelssohn to Karl Klingemann, 22 March 1829, in Hensel, 239; Devrient, *Meine Erinnerungen*, 66–67.

Shakespeare, he said that "I count the hearing of it to be among those pleasures of which you once spoke in reference to Lear: that it should be granted to humanity to experience such a work of art, that is something great and ennobling." "A new, hitherto unknown world of artistic creation has opened up for me," he exclaimed. "If only you, my great friend, could have experienced it with me!"[92] Perhaps something of this apprehension came through to Goethe, despite his informant Zelter's inept description of the work as "a wonderful sentimental mixture of music and ideas" with melodies that reminded him of Gluck or Mozart. Goethe's reply, as was so often the case in their correspondence, cut through Zelter's jollity to the emotion or experience it masked. "I have been thinking about your report on the successful performance of that great old piece of music," he wrote, and "for me it is as though I could hear in the distance the ocean singing."[93]

Of course the performance had its detractors: some, like Heine, found the music (indeed the whole experience) excessively boring; others, like Hegel (much to Zelter's disgust), found it merely peculiar; yet others expressed the opinion that for good reason it had been stored away and forgotten.[94] Some comic relief came the night of the first performance, and from an unexpected quarter. Therese Devrient wrote in her memoirs of attending a festive dinner that Zelter hosted for a number of the performers and guests. She arrived late—her husband having been detained outside the hall by admirers—and was squeezed in between Felix and an older man unknown to her. The latter proceeded to urge her to drink, tease her, toast her, grab her lacy sleeve, coyly knock against her, and generally make such a nuisance of himself that in exasperation she leaned over to Felix and whispered, "Who is this idiot [*dumme Kerl*] sitting next to me?" He replied, "That idiot sitting next to you is the famous philosopher Hegel."[95]

In early April, Felix Mendelssohn left Berlin to travel to Hamburg and from there to England, where he spent the next eight months conducting, performing, composing, and establishing the warm relationship with the English musical public that endured throughout his life.[96] He left Berlin at

[92] Geck, 46–47.

[93] Geck, 46.

[94] Rahel Varnhagen, for instance, thought the music impressive but said she preferred purely instrumental works—a view not as original as she pretended in the letter. For the letters of Heine, Zelter, and Varnhagen, see Geck, 45–49.

[95] Devrient, *Jugenderinnerungen*, 307–8.

[96] See Wilfrid Blount's biography of Mendelssohn, *On Wings of Song: A Biography of Felix Mendelssohn* (London, 1974).

the height of his first experience of clamorous acclaim. Marx had heralded Mendelssohn's "deed" as a "sign of fulfillment," a "presage of a new and higher period of music," for which he too had worked tirelessly and against all opposition. Other reviews of the performance also singled out Mendelssohn for praise: the Berlin correspondent for the leading musical journal of the day, Leipzig's *Allgemeine musikalische Zeitung*, wrote of Zelter's "brilliant student," whose "sure direction" had led his combined forces in a performance "that left nothing to be desired." Ludwig Rellstab, a Berlin music critic as prolific and as gifted as Marx, wrote of Mendelssohn's "rare talent and zeal," which had produced "so consummate a performance as one has hardly ever experienced."[97] Mendelssohn's own compositions, however extraordinary, had never excited so enthusiastic and even awestruck a response. And although such high excitement soon dissipated, Mendelssohn had unquestionably established his reputation in Berlin and beyond as the premier interpreter of Bach in performance, a reputation he built on in the years to come.

On April 18, Good Friday, Zelter conducted the *St. Matthew Passion* for a third time in Berlin, in place of his traditional Good Friday performance of Graun's *Tod Jesu*, a simple work by comparison but one much loved by the north German public.[98] A flurry of *Passion* performances followed in other north German cities. In late May, Johann Nepomuk Schelble in Frankfurt directed the Cäcilienverein's long-anticipated performance. Although he cut nearly twice as many pieces out of the work as had Mendelssohn, used a smaller chorus and a larger orchestra, and sang the parts of both the Evangelist and Jesus himself, the reaction to his performance seems to have been similar to that in Berlin—amazed appreciation and renewed determination to hear more of the works of "forgotten masters." Schelble, as we have seen, had conceived of the revival independently of Mendelssohn's plans. However, most subsequent Passions in the 1830s took the Berlin performance as their inspiration, along with the linked publication of the full score by the house of Schlesinger in consultation with Felix Mendelssohn in 1831. The Breslau Singakademie under Johann Theodor Mosewius, who had attended Zelter's 1829 performance, sang the work on April 3, 1830. In Stettin, Karl Loewe, the director of the city orchestra that had premiered Mendelssohn's *Midsummer Night's Dream* overture in 1827, reported to his chorus about having heard the work in Berlin: "How great and magnificent it is! Stettin must also have it!" The musicologist Martin

---

[97] Marx, *BAMZ* 6, no. 9 (28 February 1829): 65; other reviews in Geck, 53–55.
[98] On *Tod Jesu* versus the *St. Matthew Passion*, see chapter 5.

Geck believes that the phase of the "true rediscovery" of the ·St. Matthew Passion ended with a performance in Dresden in 1833.[99] Although the work became a regular part of an increasingly historicized repertory in Europe, its performance never again excited the same publicity, the same intellectual ferment, the same sheer amazement as it did in 1829.

[99] Geck, 78–79, 87, 97, 127.

2

Toward a Music Aesthetics

of the Nation

To understand the excitement generated by the 1829 performance of the *St. Matthew Passion* requires more than appreciating Felix Mendelssohn's, or Bach's, achievement. Mendelssohn's readiness to undertake the revival makes sense within his family milieu and his unfolding ambitions as a musician in the public eye. He was a highly imaginative person and, in ways that became apparent in the *Passion* project, a musical leader capable of shaping public opinion. But consideration of these personal qualities raises the intriguing question of his relationship to his larger milieu—to Berlin, to musical life, to the ideas and institutions in which he lived. His readiness to perform the *Passion* points to a broader cultural readiness to hear it, and that in turn raises questions about why and how groups of people value certain things. In this case, cultural readiness for the performance of an antiquated piece of church music involved a positive evaluation of the place of music in collective life, which corresponded to changes in the status of music as a profession. The present chapter takes the long view of these matters, considering developments in the status and meaning of music in the eighteenth century. These developments laid the foundation for a music aesthetics of the nation, by which I mean an effort to define the German nation through the particular qualities of German music and to experience the nation through its performance and appreciation.[1] This music aesthetics of the nation came to full maturity in 1829. The long view of its origins, back in the eighteenth century, allows us to see the circumstances of music making in central Europe slowly transform. The people of 1829 were dependent on this transformation, and subsequent chapters will show how.

To speak in these terms about listening to music and defining a national identity risks sinking into abstraction. Music aesthetics refers to a field of inquiry that the English-speaking world cannot even decide how to spell, let alone appreciate, and thus often regards with suspicion. Yet as Carl Dahlhaus pointed out, aesthetics is "constantly at work." Any attitude toward music, from deploring one's children's taste in it to encouraging them to study it, any "pattern of conduct" in regard to musical activities, reflects "music-aesthetic decisions." These decisions usually refer back, moreover, to eighteenth- and nineteenth-century debates over music, whether consciously or not.[2] Already by the middle of the eighteenth century, German writers were taking the lead in them. German predominance in music aesthetics constitutes, finally, a puzzle, the solution to which tells us much about the historical contexts of music making. Why did Germans reflect so much on beauty and meaning in music, sustaining a longer, more searching, and more widespread discussion of arcane aesthetic issues than obtained in any other European country? Retrospection tempts one to suppose that, surrounded as they were by the likes of Bach, Mozart, Haydn, and Beethoven, German writers were bound to become interested in musical beauty. Music-aesthetic debates must depend on the near presence of musical greatness. But such a supposition distorts the nature of German music-aesthetic writing, which neither in its origins nor in its development took its bearings from actual composers, great or ordinary.

---

[1] Bernhard Giesen uses the phrase "the aestheticization of the national" to express the relationship German romantics believed to exist between their artistic creations and the creation of German national consciousness—the former should mediate the latter, allowing Germans to sense their collective identity. He does not discuss music, but the concept of the aestheticizing of the national works equally well for those involved in late-eighteenth-century musical life. See Bernhard Giesen, *Intellectuals and the Nation: Collective Identity in a German Axial Age*, trans. Nicholas Levis and Amos Weisz (New York, 1998), 97–99.

[2] Carl Dahlhaus, *The Esthetics of Music*, trans. William Austin (New York, 1982), vii. See also Austin's "Translator's Introduction" on the terminology problem (ix–xii).

JOHANN MATTHESON AND THE LITERARY ORIGINS
OF GERMAN MUSIC AESTHETICS

One of the earliest philosophers of music aesthetics in the German-speaking lands was Johann Mattheson of Hamburg, who in 1722 founded *Critica Musica*, the first musical periodical in Europe. Mattheson maintained a separation between his writings on music and his own work as a composer and as musical director in the Hamburg Cathedral, as though to establish an independent existence for musical discussion, apart from the usual venues—courts, churches, theaters—of musical life. Through his writings, Mattheson aspired instead to participate in another milieu, that of literary or print culture.[3] He modeled *Critica Musica* on the scholarly periodicals and moral weeklies of literary culture and gave it a suitably erudite subtitle, boasting of "searching critiques" that would eradicate "vulgar error." Although its subject matter reflected the traditional scholarly interest in music as a branch of practical mathematics, his means for dissemination of such scholarship were new, and the target audience was all educated people, not just experts in "the pure science of harmony." In 1728 he launched a second periodical, called *Der musicalische Patriot* in order to signal its kinship with the *Patriot*, a Hamburg journal for the "German-speaking community."

This use of the term "patriot" gives us a clue to his purpose and to the subsequent evolution of music-aesthetic discourse. In Mattheson's day, the term carried several overlapping connotations, all of which resonated in his writings. First, it meant devotion to one's *Vaterland*, or native land, a unit with an identity as various as the many territories of central Europe but in Mattheson's case designating Hamburg, a free city within the Holy Roman Empire. Second (and especially in free cities like Hamburg), a patriot was someone conscious of citizenship in the empire, which for all its shortcomings did represent Deutschland, or Germany, for most of its inhabitants. Third, the word "patriot" evoked a discourse of "baroque language and cultural patriotism," developed in the seventeenth century by writers seeking to ground national consciousness in speech, history, and custom.[4] To describe oneself as a patriot in this final sense was to appeal to an imaginary community, an "invisible intercourse of spirits and hearts" in Herder's words, the existence of which might be secured through language.

In the early eighteenth century, none of these meanings excluded any

---

[3] For a discussion of print as the "primary source and subject of cultural activity" in literary culture, see Sheehan, *German History*, 153.

[4] On this meaning of "patriot," see the discussion of *"Bürger"* in Reinhardt Koselleck, ed., *Geschichtliche Grundbegriffe*, 8 vols. (Stuttgart, 1992), 1:686.

other, yet neither did they constitute a harmonious convergence within the single idea of the German nation. Instead, the multiplicity of meanings reflected the dispersion of political and cultural life. The only points of commonality among the meanings of "patriot" lay in the idea of devotion to some common good and in an inchoate sense of defensiveness vis-à-vis influences outside the several communities to which the patriot belonged. The historian Reinhart Koselleck has described this defensiveness as a "concrete fear of the cultural infiltration of foreigners and political powerlessness."[5] Literate people knew that German culture existed, but lacking the confident assertion of a deeply rooted existence that Herder would bring to the understanding of nationhood fifty years later, German culture seemed to them a vulnerable, elusive tenuity, too dependent on the fortunes of princes to be secure. The baroque understanding of culture saw it not anthropologically (as a way of life) nor liberally (as the creative work of individuals) but paradigmatically (as the expression of the power and glory of ruler and God).

Mattheson sat down to write about music, then, in a discursive context fraught with significance, and he extended the possibilities of music writing in several directions—a pedagogic one, by providing useful aids to fellow musicians, a learned one, by writing treatises for the scholarly community, and a public, political one, by contributing to debates about the common good and the content of collective life. He was not the first to bring music into such debates, but his contribution was enormous and timely.[6] Although Germans had read printed matter for some three hundred years by his time, the second and third decades of the eighteenth century marked the takeoff point, at which the number of people regularly reading and writing was sufficient to constitute "a sustained, secular reading public."[7] New books and new periodicals published in Germany multiplied dramatically as the century progressed, each feeding off the other. As it coalesced, literary culture provided the German lands with their only national culture. It became the only network of shared concerns crossing barriers that divided one locality from another and the privileged aristocracy from all. The popular cultures of towns and peasantry were bounded by locality and custom. Aristocratic culture, although transcending geographical and political divisions, was not German but cosmopolitan. It adhered to the fashions and

[5] Ibid., 1:305–6. On the patriot as one devoted to a community's well-being, see Mary Lindemann, *Patriots and Paupers: Hamburg, 1712–1830* (New York, 1990), 5.

[6] Gloria Flaherty, *Opera in the Development of German Critical Thought* (Princeton, 1978), 10–65.

[7] Sheehan, *German History*, 144.

languages of the grander courts of other lands, France especially. Literary culture alone expressed the nationality of Germans, a quality becoming more distinct through contemplation of it and works of art intended to express it.

Establishing a national community through print culture thus became the underlying project of participants in literary culture. Historians have understood this project as one of writing literature and developing the expressive capacities of the German language.[8] The participation of music—and especially of people writing about music—in the nationalizing project of literary culture is more mysterious to us, even though the writings of music aestheticians, outside this general context, have interested philosophers and musicologists.[9] But Mattheson's case shows that music writers and musicians did contribute to nationalizing culture. As Gloria Flaherty suggested several decades ago, their discussions of opera in the literary journals shaped modern criticism, anticipated literary romanticism, and helped to develop a "distinctively German version of the classical ideal," more committed to imagination than imitation.[10] Most important from our perspective, their contributions to aesthetic debate made musical life part of nationalizing culture. By the time writers had spent a hundred or more years arguing about the nature of beauty—natural and man-made, ancient and modern, musical, pictorial, and literary, French, Italian, German, and English—the outlines of national differences had become much clearer to them and to their readers. So too had the role of music in expressing those differences.

Mattheson stood near the beginning of the process of articulating nationality, and he lived in Hamburg, the leading city-republic of the eighteenth century, the "point of departure for modern patriotism in Germany."[11] He secured a place for music in nationalizing culture by deciding, simply, that the issues that music, and especially opera, faced in Hamburg were too important for ephemeral pamphlets—a number of which he had

---

[8] English-language overviews are Eric Blackall, *The Emergence of German as Literary Language, 1700–1775* (Cambridge, 1959); Alan Menhennet, *Order and Freedom: Literature and Society in Germany from 1720–1805* (New York, 1973); and Albert Ward, *Book Production, Fiction, and the German Reading Public, 1740–1800* (Oxford, 1974).

[9] Warren Dwight Allen observed more than sixty years ago that "studies of the rise of the spirit of national unity in Germany" had failed to "refer to the part played by music." The situation has hardly changed all these years later. See Allen, *Philosophies of Music History: A Study of General Histories of Music 1600–1960* (1939; repr., New York, 1962), 23. An important exception is Mary Sue Morrow, *German Music Criticism in the Late Eighteenth Century: Aesthetic Issues in Instrumental Music* (New York, 1997).

[10] Flaherty, *Opera in the Development*, 288.

[11] Otto Dann, *Nation und Nationalismus in Deutschland 1770–1990* (Munich, 1993), 39.

already written by the time he launched his first journal.[12] Music deserved the kind of sustained public discussion made possible by the new medium of the periodical. Mattheson knew about the enlightening potential of such periodicals from working for the English Resident in Hamburg as a tutor and secretary. He transmitted English culture, and briefly in 1713–14 he published his own version of the English taste-making weeklies the *Tatler* and *Spectator*. Shortly after that project ended (short-lived periodicals were the rule throughout the eighteenth century), he joined a voluntary association recently founded by city senator and poet Barthold Heinrich Brockes called the Teutschübende Gesellschaft, or the Society for the Promotion of German. It was a new type of social formation, dedicated to general education and the free exchange of opinions. It also expressed the patriotic activism so characteristic of Hamburg's free citizens: Brockes's society aimed to improve the reputation of the German language and extend its expressive capacities.[13]

Music held a prominent place among the society's concerns, especially insofar as it was involved with the German language. A number of members, including Mattheson, were accomplished musicians and composers. Consistent with the society's mission, Brockes turned the gospel story, in Luther's German, into a poetic narrative interspersed with reflective passages. By 1720, more than twenty composers had written music for this work, *Der für die Sünde der Welt Gemarterte und Sterbende Jesus*, making it the most widely heard Passion oratorio in German-speaking lands, and only a few years later it served as the model for the libretto of the *St. Matthew Passion* that Picander wrote for Bach in Leipzig.[14] Meanwhile in Hamburg, Mattheson, Brockes, and their fellow patriots began to define a musical-patriotic position by turning their attention to the sorry state of opera in their city.

The debates over opera, seemingly tangential to the history of the Bach revival, allow one to follow the development of the educated public's atti-

---

[12] Already in 1713, Mattheson had published *Das Neu-eröffnete Orchestre*, according to its title a "universal and fundamental guide" for the educated gentleman to understand "fully the greatness and worth of noble music." In it he included a discussion of "national music" ("if I may use such a term"), which attempted to distinguish among Italian, French, English, and German music. He found the prospects for German musicians very low indeed. See Johann Mattheson, *Das Neu-eröffnete Orchestre* (1713; repr., Hildesheim, 1993), 200–31.

[13] The *Teutschübende Gesellschaft* too was short-lived but had a number of successors. In the 1720s, Brockes founded another society, called the *Patriotische Gesellschaft*, which published the journal *Patriot*, the model for Mattheson's *Musicalische Patriot*. See Christian Petersen, "Die Teutschübende Gesellschaft in Hamburg," *Zeitschrift des Vereins für hamburgische Geschichte* 2 (1847): 533–64.

[14] "Jesus, martyred and dying for the sins of the world." On the Brockes connection, see Christoph Wolff, *Johann Sebastian Bach: The Learned Musician* (New York, 2000), 292, 296.

tude toward music, a fluid mixture of national, social, and aesthetic concerns, from the first rumblings of language patriotism. Opera's domination of music-aesthetic discourse for much of the eighteenth century reflected the degree to which music writers came out of a literary culture in which the focus of patriotic hopes lay in the German language. Their preoccupation with opera also reflected social tension, even competition, between the untitled, middle-class members of literary culture, whose tastes lay in German-language opera, exemplified in the works of Hamburg's Reinhard Keiser, Christoph Graupner, and Mattheson himself, and the nobility, who had long favored Italian opera and Italian musicians in their courts. Patriotic writers were ambivalent about court culture, both admiring the princes for their leadership (by default) of the German nation and despising their preference for all things foreign. In print, this ambivalence translated into enslavement to the culture of the courts, which in turn led writers to try to Germanize court culture rather than reject it altogether. Finally, opera fascinated music writers because of its potential to create the complete aesthetic experience—music, drama, poetry, movement, light, and sound.[15] So the struggle to give German opera a status equal to that of Italian ones brought music within nationalizing cultural circles. At the same time, the fixation on opera meant that music needed language to get any attention at all from German patriots, a tendency only partially blocked by the romantic revaluation of instrumental music at the end of the century.

In any case, opera alone provoked Mattheson's patriotic consciousness. He feared that a native musical form, German baroque opera, was facing extinction: 1738 saw the last performance of a German baroque opera in the Hamburg opera house; in Leipzig, all German-language opera was already gone by 1720, yielding to an entirely Italian repertory. The public, to whose musical enlightenment Mattheson had dedicated himself since the 1720s, had abandoned German art. Mattheson believed it had fallen victim to a delusion, brought on by a cultural infiltration from two directions—from Italy to the south, with its dominating music and carpetbagging musicians (they "make all the money and then return home," wrote Mattheson) and from France to the west.[16] The patriotic sensibility demanded that German musical theater be reformed in a way that would satisfy both popular taste and patriotic feeling. Above all, the German language had to be defended as musical or, in Mattheson's view, as capable of expressing emotion as was Italian. Italy may still have been the "fatherland of music," but, as Jo-

---

[15] Bernd Sponheuer, "Reconstructing Ideal Types of the 'German' in Music," in Applegate and Potter, *Music and German National Identity*, 36–57.

[16] Mattheson, *Das Neu-Eröffnete Orchestre*, 214.

hann Philipp Praetorius wrote, Germans must preserve the native art that expressed the "ingenious character of the German nation."[17]

HERDER AND THE DISCOVERY OF NATIONAL CULTURE

But therein lay the problem. Throughout the first three-quarters of the eighteenth century, the music-aesthetic debates over opera and music puzzled over the unanswerable question of what was, in fact, authentically German in a musical culture shaped by crisscrossing currents of influence from all directions. Back and forth from Mattheson to Gottsched to Scheibe to Marpurg to Nicolai, Lessing, Moses Mendelssohn, and many others, the journals and reading clubs of literary culture debated over whether opera was nonsensical or instructive, world creating or unnatural, soul stirring or intellect impairing, German or foreign, base or elevated. The possibilities did not yet line up on either side of a simple dichotomy, and no writer suggested that music alone was the essential expression of German identity. Such a place of honor remained the preserve of language, hence literature. No mere composer could produce anything so patriotically promising as Lessing's dramas or Klopstock's poetry, which had at least given Germans what Justus Möser called a "literary fatherland."[18]

But in the 1770s the beginnings of a German Enlightenment made it possible to regard music from a new perspective, largely free of court associations. The decisive figure was Johann Gottfried Herder, whose own "self-conquest" of Enlightenment rationalism brought him to understand nations and their differences without reliance on Montesquieu's comparative framework. Herder, as Goethe famously wrote to him, transformed "the rubbish of history into a living plant" by concentrating on the particularity of history, not its uniformity, its constancy, or the existence of principles and ideal types.[19] His philosophy of history, developed over a lifetime of writing and debate, rejected general characterizations of the past in order to grasp the infinite wealth of diverse conditions of the human spirit.

This new conception of the historical world had immediate implications for Germans. German culture had an essence all its own; it was the "great uncultivated garden of the nation," which Germans must grow by means of

---

[17] Johann Philipp Praetorius, introduction to his libretto *Calypso, oder Sieg der Weissheit Ueber die Liebe, in einem Sing-Spiele* (quoted in Flaherty, *Opera in the Development*, 69).

[18] On Möser, see Jonathan Knudsen, *Justus Möser and the German Enlightenment* (Cambridge, 1986). As late as the writings of Triest around 1800, Italy was still called the "fatherland of music."

[19] Ernst Cassirer, *The Philosophy of the Enlightenment*, trans. Fritz C. A. Koelln and James P. Pettegrove (Princeton, 1951), 233, 359, 197–226.

"illumination, enlightenment, sense of community," and the confidence "to be German on one's own well-protected land and soil." "The highest culture of a people," Herder assured his readers, flourished "only in the particular soil of the nation."[20] Herder thus joined Lessing, and soon Goethe as well, in bringing a more ambitious sense of mission to the century-old defense of national culture in Germany. No longer was it enough to converse with an enlightened public or to create for them a national literature. Herder had a wider vision. At its heart was the idea of the people, or *Volk*, who gave a distinctive character to all forms of culture— "unless we have a *Volk*," he wrote, "we lack also a public, a nation, a language and a literature."[21]

Herder's vision had implications for music as well. The surest road to knowledge of the *Volk*, especially in cultures as subject to foreign influence as that of the Germans, came through the study of folk song, which Herder thought had survived largely unaffected by foreign cultural influences. To be sure, he was more interested in the words than the music itself: in Strasbourg, he set Goethe to reading old English and Scottish ballads, not singing them, and when Goethe made expeditions for Herder into rural Alsace in search of remnants of old German folk songs, his transcriptions included only the words.[22] The musical significance of Herder's emphasis on folk song and folk culture lay in its implication that there was more to the promotion of a national music than the production of an opera with a German libretto, and further, that music existed and flourished outside of Italy and the court theaters. His role in sparking the interest of subsequent generations of nationalists in collecting folk songs was a by-product of his message about the infusion of national character into all parts and products of national life, music included. But Herder's view of music's importance went beyond his eclecticism to his intuition that music and language had evolved together as vocal utterances. Thus music lay behind all poetry, as did the melody behind the verse, in an organic relationship of the essence to its particular manifestation. Whatever the shortcomings of this embryonic ethnomusicology, it strengthened Herder's call for Germans to attend to their own genius, in creative disregard of other nations.[23]

A generation of poets and writers would soon come of age and answer this call. But meanwhile, despite a flurry of self-consciously German cultural achievements in the 1770s and early 1780s, the nationalizing project

[20] *Briefe zur Beförderung der Humanität*: all quotations are from Friedrich Meinecke, *Cosmopolitanism and the National State*, trans. Robert B. Kimber (Princeton, 1970), 28–29.

[21] Sheehan, *German History*, 165.

[22] Nicholas Boyle, *Goethe: The Poet and the Age* (New York, 1992), 1:94–100.

[23] Flaherty, *Opera in the Development*, 45, 227, 240, 243, 287.

within literary culture was faltering, and the contribution that music made to it was less certain than ever. One sees the faltering in a flurry of manifestos and joint projects, from Klopstock's highly anticipated but disappointing *German Republic of Learning* in 1773 to Herder's "Idea for the First Patriotic Institute for the Promotion of a General German Spirit" in 1788. Even taken as an integrated whole, which they were not, such writings accentuated the fragmentation of cultural, social, and political life, frustrating those who felt the need for a unity more concrete than the communicative space of language. Literary culture had, in the words of Nicholas Boyle, "something of the sultry stillness in which many flies breed," and Goethe fled it for Italy in 1786, leaving behind a milieu that gave him "neither support nor stimulus." Musical theater in the 1780s filled him with weary disgust. In 1786 he started an opera libretto (as did Herder), hoping to address the German public, but the project came to nothing. Contemporary theatrical companies, he wrote, "brought me almost to despair": "nowhere is there anything worthwhile," he asserted, pitying his "poor little operetta" as like the "child of a negro woman who is to be born in slavery."[24]

Goethe's condemnation only dimly illuminates the contemporary musical scene—one would never know from it, for instance, that he had just seen the 1785 Weimar production of Mozart's *Abduction from the Seraglio*. But music aesthetics really was going nowhere. It was stuck in repetitive debates over the subservience of music to poetry, the relevance of bardic traditions, or the prospect of a German opera. Repetition could be called tradition, but in this case the existence of a century-long debate had not brought independence from literary discourse. Nor by 1780 had music won a secure place among those who championed Germany's cultural integrity. It was still marginal to the ambitious programs of humanistic education (*Bildung*) and professional training for bureaucratic leadership, which were reforming many universities and mobilizing the literary elite in the service of state and education. Indifferent to the quality of contemporary music and unable to value its potential for the nationalizing project, Goethe, for his part, lamented only the wretchedness of words.

GERMAN MUSIC AESTHETICS IN THE ERA OF KANT

Music's status problems only got worse in the 1780s, culminating in 1790 with Kant's publication of his third and final critique, that of judgment. With few exceptions, historians of music aesthetics have treated this dismissive view of music with respect, awed perhaps by its ambiguities, not to

[24] Boyle, *Goethe*, 270, 272, 381.

mention its author. Edward Lippman recognized the inadequacy of Kant's conception of music, but claimed to admire it for forcing a reaction against it, thus bringing "musical aesthetics to fruition."[25] Kant's work did leave open the possibility of misreading it to the benefit of music, like the "fantastically careless and incompetent misreading" of Kant by the French writers who invented the notion of art for art's sake.[26] But for musicians and music writers of the 1790s, existing at the margins of literary culture, the Kantian judgment on music undermined their struggle for citizenship in the "German republic of learning" and impeded recognition of music's importance to cultural nationhood. Had music-aesthetic debate ended with Kant, then J. S. Bach or Mozart or Beethoven might never have acquired, for better or for worse, the nation-bearing status that they did.

The function of Kant's *Critique of Judgment* within music-aesthetic debates, as something more to be refuted than admired, stands in contrast with its overall reputation as the capstone of a grandly synthetic theory of the mind. Ernst Cassirer wrote of the third critique that it "touched the nerve of the entire spiritual and intellectual culture of his time," becoming the essential philosophical text for Goethe and Schiller and the guiding light for "the entire post-Kantian philosophy."[27] More derivative of previous philosophical works than his earlier critiques, the *Critique of Judgment* sought to bring the insights of aesthetic philosophy—chiefly, the subjective nature of beauty, its existence in the eye of the beholder, its seeming lack of universality—into line with Kant's theory of mind. To do so, he had to show how universality entered into the faculty of judgment, which subsumed particulars into a universal ("that particular tree is beautiful") yet lacked an understanding of the universal itself ("beauty"). An aesthetic idea, he wrote, "allows much to be thought without being adequate to a determined thought, i.e., concept, corresponding to it."[28]

The solution for Kant was that judgments had the "possibility" of being not just subjective but universally subjective, that is "valid for everyone." In other words, everyone could make the same judgment about a given object, if these judgments were wholly disinterested. Such disinterest, in turn, derived from the unity, within the mind itself, of imagination and understanding—an argument that makes sense only in light of the first two critiques.

---

[25] Edward Lippman, *A History of Western Musical Aesthetics* (Lincoln, NE, 1992), 133.

[26] John Wilcox, "The Beginnings of *l'art pour l'art*," *Journal of Aesthetics and Art Criticism* 2 (1953): 361. On the misreading of Kant, see Gene H. Bell-Villada, *Art for Art's Sake and Literary Life: How Politics and Markets Helped Shape the Ideology and Culture of Aestheticism 1790–1990* (Lincoln, NE, 1998), 35–56.

[27] Ernst Cassirer, *Kant's Life and Thought*, trans. James Haden (New Haven, 1981), 273.

[28] Cited in Lippman, *History of Western Musical Aesthetics*, 130.

"He who feels pleasure in the mere reflection upon the form of an object without respect to any concept," Kant argued, "justly claims the agreement of all men, because the ground of this pleasure is found in the universal, although subjective, condition of reflective judgments, viz. the purposive harmony of an object (whether a product of nature or of art) with the mutual relations of the cognitive faculties (the imagination and the understanding)."[29] The truly beautiful could thus be distinguished from many things with which it had been confused, like the merely agreeable, the good, or the charming. Kant tried to free aesthetic judgment from all the extraneous ends that art had previously served—religious, pedagogical, hedonistic, nationalizing.[30] Only under conditions of freedom from such ends would judgment achieve universality.

Unfortunately for music, Kant was not at all sure that its listeners could achieve freedom. Music seemed to him to lack form or concept and, potentially even worse, to excite pleasant sensations that posed an obstacle to disinterested judgment. Still, he hedged: "For although it speaks by means of mere sensations without concepts, and so does not, like poetry, leave anything over for reflection, it yet moves the mind in a greater variety of ways and more intensely, although only transitorily." Yet this last phrase proved for Kant more damning of music than its stature as "a universal language of sensations intelligible to every man." In the end, music was "rather enjoyment than cultivation." "The further play of thought that is excited by its means" was just a "mechanical association," and thus "in the judgment of reason," music had "less worth than any other of the fine arts." Returning to its transitory nature, Kant stated that "like all enjoyment, it desires constant change and does not bear frequent repetition without producing weariness."[31]

As we try to chart the path by which music became important to German cultural nationhood, Kant's work presents, then, both a promise and a problem. On the one hand, he did music the favor of concentrating primarily on instrumental music or music without words, thus clearing away, for the moment at least, all the detritus left by nearly a century of futile debate over opera. Debaters had wasted too much of their energy trying to trans-

---

[29] Ibid., 128.

[30] Elizabeth Wilkinson and L. A. Willoughby, introduction to Friedrich Schiller, *On the Aesthetic Education of Man in a Series of Letters* (Oxford, 1967), xxiii.

[31] The charge of transitoriness, and the inevitable boredom caused by trying to combat it through repetition, was answered by Herder in his *Kalligone* in 1801. He defended transience as true to life itself, "an endless longing," and said that repetition of melody created intense enjoyment in the listener (in *Musical Aesthetics: A Historical Reader*, ed. Edward A. Lippman [Stuyvesant, NY, 1988], 2:33–43). All quotations from Kant are in Lippman, *History of Western Musical Aesthetics*, 132–33.

form an art form that, despite Gluck and now Mozart, remained aristocratic, Italianate, and ill suited to contribute to German cultural integration.
But on the other hand, Kant cited a formidable array of new reasons to dismiss music's importance to the national project. Now its problem was its
lack of adequate material for the "play of thought." Thanks to Kant, a loose
distinction between art and entertainment hardened into aesthetic orthodoxy. Kant himself distinguished between the fine arts and the pleasant arts,
between art that evokes disinterested aesthetic judgment (cognition of a
sort) and art that evokes mere enjoyment (sensation only). Music, he
thought, was a fine art but one prone to degenerating into pleasantries; it
was "agreeable" rather than truly "beautiful," and in this way like "fireworks and perfume." Kant thus put himself in the peculiar position of valuing gardens over string quartets, because the former was a "free beauty," un-
fettered by purpose, while the latter were "dependent beauties," contriving
merely to charm.[32]

Music's low status in the Kantian system of artistic ranking could be seen
as bringing to sour fruition the tendency of the creators of national culture,
even music-loving ones, to favor words over tones. Kant himself was not a
propagandist for the German nation, but his unprecedented stature within
the German-speaking and the European-educated elite made his writings
into documents of nation-making significance. Given the existence of people like Kant, Goethe, and now Schiller, even the most Francophile of
monarchs could not deny the richness and profundity of the literary-
cultural fatherland coming into existence among German-speaking people.
But if, as Kant argued, music lacked ideal content, then how could it—or its
practitioners—contribute to this fatherland? Yet immediately in the wake of
Kant, the debate over music aesthetics and the cultural nation entered a new
phase of development, which persisted into Felix Mendelssohn's time. In it,
a reinterpretation of musical meaning brought the riches of instrumental
music to the fore, gave music more than enough ideal content to satisfy the
serious-minded connoisseur, and tethered its newly perceived artistic powers to the national project itself.

All this reached an initial completion by the time of Mendelssohn's birth
in 1809. The reordering had been years in the making and would be many
more years in the maturing. In conventional intellectual histories of aesthetics, the agents of this reordering were the generation of writers and thinkers
known as the romantics, two of whom interest us especially: Wilhelm
Heinrich Wackenroder and Ludwig Tieck, born in the 1770s and producing their first works in the 1790s. Nowhere were these writers' most notor-

---

[32] Lippman, *History of Western Musical Aesthetics*, 129.

iously romantic qualities—their valuation of feeling and expression for its own sake, their pursuit of sublimity and transcendence, their belief in art's capacity to create new realms of experience, their worship of individual genius—more in evidence than in their understanding of music, especially music without words. Herder had provided an intellectual framework for the romantics' departure from rationalism and empiricism and had implied how one might find the ideal content of music, but his own reply to Kantian aesthetics, *Kalligone,* published in 1800, came only after important interventions from the romantics. One of the fullest of these was also among the earliest, Wilhelm Heinrich Wackenroder's *Phantasien über die Kunst für Freunde der Kunst,* which appeared in 1799, published with the accompanying reflections on art by his friend Ludwig Tieck.[33]

True to its purposes, Wackenroder's writing took a form as distant from a Kantian critique as could be conceived. Using a character he had created two years earlier, a musician-monk named Joseph Berglinger, who "poured out his heart" on the subject of art, Wackenroder produced a memorable statement of the superiority of musical language over mere words: "Come, thou musical strains," cried Berglinger, "draw near and rescue me from this painful earthly striving for words." As he mused on everything from naked saints to metallic sounds, Berglinger revealed music to be the only true expression of the "feelings which surge up in our hearts" as gifts from "the Creator," hovering above us "clothed in golden clouds of airy harmonies." In response to long-running debates about music and poetry, Wackenroder claimed that music was in fact a language—the "language of angels." If it still seemed to lack substance for thought, at least in the Kantian sense, then Wackenroder struck a pedagogical note: we not only hear emotion in music, and preserve it through composing and performing, but we also learn to feel, thereby learning to know ourselves and to transcend everyday things.[34]

Wackenroder's prose was easily digestible (unlike Kant's), yet his idealist, humanistic claims for music's importance accorded well with the tenets of Kant and the educated elites. Wackenroder's music aesthetic proved influential because, unlike Kant's, it told the educated elites what one suspects they wanted to hear, that is, that one could enjoy music as a higher pleasure, not a mere low entertainment. Significantly, Wackenroder followed Kant in paying instrumental music the compliment of writing mainly about it. Both

[33] Tieck was still alive in 1829, and although he was not present at the *Passion* performance, he received an ecstatic description of it from his friend Wilhelm Loebell.

[34] The original Berglinger story, called *Herzensergiessungen eines Kunstliebenden Klosterbruders,* or *Outpourings of an Art-Loving Monk,* was published in 1797. The phrases quoted here from the *Phantasien* are from Lippman, *Musical Aesthetics: Reader,* 2:5–32.

men's work came in the midst of revolutionary developments in instrumental music that writers about music could no more ignore than Mattheson could ignore Italian opera. Wackenroder waxed poetic, as always, about "those divine, magnificent symphonic pieces" pouring forth "an entire world, an entire drama of human emotions."[35] Ludwig Tieck also addressed Kant's music aesthetic through a defense of instrumental music, via Schiller's passionate confrontation with Kant in his letters on the aesthetic education of man and Herder's view of music as an "art of humanity." Instrumental music provided, Tieck thought, a free play of artistic expression, purely without purpose and thus fully in accordance with the development of human wholeness and freedom: "these symphonies can represent a colorful, manifold, intricate, and beautifully developed drama such as the poet can never give us."[36]

Tieck and Wackenroder's worshipful attitude toward music informed the next quarter-century or more of music-aesthetic writings. From Schelling to Hoffmann to Schopenhauer, writers acknowledged the transcendent, profoundly important powers of musical sound itself, independent of words, images, or movement. As Bernd Sponheuer has shown, writers met the challenge of Kant's dismissal by dichotomizing musical expression into the sort worthy of dismissal, because forgettable or merely pleasant, and the sort worthy of the most serious attention, expressive of genius, beautiful beyond words, a true "play of thought."[37] In the end, giving music ideal content proved just a matter of words, or more precisely, a matter of deciding when words alone did not suffice, even for a literary culture. For the romantics, music gave immediate expression to the endless longings which their words struggled to describe. The elevating of music provided them with both theme and variation for much writing over the next decades. In Heinrich von Kleist's story of 1810 called "St. Cecilia or the Power of Music," to choose one example among many, music was at the center of a miraculous visitation that both saves and destroys, elevates and transforms, human beings: it brings "a miraculous, heavenly consolation" and raises "souls as if on wings through all the heavens of harmony," as well as causing "horror and dread," making a house tremble and hair stand on end.[38] Ironically, then, music finally achieved full membership in literary culture not

---

[35] Lippman, *Musical Aesthetics: Reader*, 26.

[36] Cited in Lippman, *History of Western Musical Aesthetics*, 206.

[37] Bernd Sponheuer, *Musik als Kunst und Nicht-Kunst: Untersuchungen zur Dichotonomie von "hoher" und "niederer": Musik im musikästhetishcen Denken zwischen Kant und Hanslick* (Kassel, 1987).

[38] Heinrich von Kleist, "St Cecilia or the Power of Music," in *The Marquise of O—and Other Stories*, trans. David Luke and Nigel Reeves (London, 1978), 218, 225.

by setting its words *to* music but by inspiring great outpourings of more words on how music transcended it all.

THE ENTRY OF MUSICIANS INTO NATIONAL CULTURE

Nevertheless, the romantic worshippers of music, even with Herder taken into account, did not single-handedly create a music aesthetics of the nation. The romantics may have elevated music to the status of the sublime, they may have made it an art that suffused creative and critical writing in the German language, and they may have celebrated the ultimate hero of humanity in the person of Beethoven. But they did considerably less to articulate how the appreciation of music fit into the nationalizing project. To find such articulation, we need to return to the concerns of musicians themselves, particularly the ones who aspired, like Mattheson, to participate in national culture through writing. Their efforts fed the outburst of music aesthetics produced in the 1790s by the romantics, whom we could describe as an enthusiastic if self-absorbed audience for the writings, lectures, and general musical advocacy of a generation of musicians unknown to intellectual history and known only partially to musicology. Wackenroder, for instance, had heard the musician and scholar Johann Nikolaus Forkel give lectures at the University of Göttingen. The existence of figures such as Forkel raises the issue of the social status of musicians and their struggle for social mobility and security. While philosophers debated music's value, musicians themselves strove for recognition and pursued an education beyond craftsmanship. In the course of those efforts, they continued the patriotic project of Mattheson and provided the explicitly national framework for the romantics' recognition of musical beauty. Musicians, moreover, in their writings and in their pedagogy, preserved as living practice the works of Johann Sebastian Bach until the general public was ready to hear them.

Thus we can understand neither the nationalism of eighteenth-century musicians nor their aesthetics, let alone the durable intertwining of the two, without the aid of social history. The defense of music that emerged in the eighteenth century consisted of more than paradigm-shifting reevaluations within aesthetics. From the perspective of social relations, this defense was an attempt to respond to, even to control, significant changes in how musicians could earn a living. Many of the people who contributed to this defense, behind the familiar scenes of dueling philosophers, felt overtaken by a crisis in the music profession. One might suppose that people in danger of losing their livelihoods would have more pressing concerns than whether a philosopher in Königsberg considered their music food for thought or love. But, as suggested earlier, such opinions had consequences, probably more so then than at most times in history. The influence of Kant's musical opinions and those of his literary-cultural colleagues derived from the shifting constitution of ruling elites in central Europe and, in turn, the peculiar vulnerability of practicing musicians to this central European version of eighteenth-century revolution. We must consider each in turn.

The question of ruling elites takes us back to literary culture, the only national culture in German Europe and one that paid only fitful attention to musical developments. During the eighteenth century the social core of literary culture—teachers, preachers, state officials and clerks, as well as a self-selected few among the nobility, all of whom had long held a stable place in the old corporate order—began to experience a limited expansion of opportunities for social ascent. New economic opportunities provided a similar, gradual expansion in the horizons of merchants and some trades-men, but such people did not make up the core group of readers and writ-ers who sustained literary culture's growth in the eighteenth century. Rather than economies, the states of the Holy Roman Empire provided the major source of new opportunities for the creators of a national culture. Particularly those states looking to expand their power underwent a historic transformation from personal rule to a bureaucratic system of law and regu-lation. The expansion of state bureaucracies did not have any immediate impact on musicians or musical life; its transformative power worked more directly on religious, administrative, educational, and military institutions. Although the aristocracy was still guaranteed positions of importance and greater ease of promotion, members of nonnoble estates could increasingly rely on their educational, administrative, and commercial achievements to move above their birth rank and acquire influence in public affairs. By the last decades of the eighteenth century, whatever complicated boundaries among the social orders persisted, a combination of aristocratic and edu-cated elites administered the majority of German states.

This gradual alteration in the social composition of ruling elites brought greater prominence to universities, which served as the training ground for nobles and nonnobles who wished to serve the state. Universities too had a stable place in the old order as self-governing corporations and had long provided training in law, theology, and medicine. But newly ambitious states now began to exert greater control over them as a means of monitor-ing the training of their officials. They pressed for educational reforms that would benefit the state itself and made a degree in law a requirement for state service. For men without title, the university was the only route to a change in status and an escape from what the historian Mack Walker has called "the static dull complexities of Germany's predominant hometown and country life."[39] Universities provided a common experience of "mixing and changing," even for the poor students who "arrived at the universities on foot, like vagabonds," and left hardly richer but more capable of participating in a changing public world, even from their poorly paid posts as tutors and rural pastors. A nonservile collective identity emerged in the course of a university education, a self-conception "as individuals, free of social constraints and prejudices," capable of transcending the "limits of provincialism" and gaining an "introduction to cosmopolitan thought patterns and lifestyles"—in short, a collective mentality that shaped the development of German literary culture.[40] The reform of law faculties also brought a slight improvement to faculties of humanities and science. Successive waves of reform created a peculiarly German synthesis of utilitarian training for state service and the free professions, on the one hand, and the neohumanistic education of individual cultivation and self-development (*Bildung*), on the other.[41] This combination provided "the moral core of a new social order"; it shaped the men who became "the chief creators and consumers of a new, national culture."[42]

By the end of the eighteenth century, then, mutual recognition, if not common purpose, marked the relations among the ruling elites of state bureaucracy, the leading writers and philosophers of literary culture, the faculties of the reformed universities, and the dispersed audience of readers linked by print and conversation throughout German Europe. Mutual recognition also sustained a growing market in literary works, which made it possible for writers to earn a living, albeit a precarious one, tentatively freed from the drudgery of tutoring and the servility of patronage. One can overstate the financial comfort of such freedom, but its possibility tantalized musicians as well. "Out into the world with you!" wrote Carl Maria von Weber in 1809, as the opening line of his unfinished novel, *Tonkünstlers Leben*, "for the world is the artist's true sphere": "What good does it do you to live with a petty clique and to earn the gracious applause of a patron. . . . Out! A man's spirit must find itself in the spirits of his fellow creatures."[43]

Weber's exhortation, in Wackenrodian prose, expressed the romantic

[39] Mack Walker, *German Home Towns: Community, State, and General Estate 1648–1871* (Ithaca, NY, 1971), 130.

[40] Ibid., 129; Anthony La Vopa, *Grace, Talent, and Merit: Poor Students, Clerical Careers, and Professional Ideology in Eighteenth-Century Germany* (Cambridge, 1988), 1–2; Charles McClelland, *State, Society, and University in Germany, 1700–1914* (New York, 1980), 3.

[41] Hans H. Gerth, *Bürgerliche Intelligenz um 1800: Zur Soziologie des deutschen Frühliberalismus* (1935; repr., Göttingen, 1976), 34; McClelland, *State, Society, and University*, 34–58.

[42] Sheehan, *German History*, 143.

[43] Weber, *Writings on Music*, 318–19.

revaluation of music as a true art, but between the lines of his hero's strivings we can also read the disintegration of one social identity in favor of another. In the simplest terms, the person of settled station became the free-floating artist; the *Musikant,* or journeyman musician, became the *Tonkünstler,* literally the artist of tones. That this transformation should feature in Weber's story as not just desirable but urgently necessary reflected the unstable state of the social formations that had sustained musical production up through the eighteenth century. The professional musician in the early modern period had, as Henry Raynor put it, "a definite if not exalted place in society and a clearly defined social function."[44] A definite place was not the same as a uniform one, and the social status of professional musicians varied by locality and institution, since for the past century they had experienced something approaching the modern mobility of employment. Church, town, and court constituted the primary sources of employment for musicians, as they had for centuries, and although a court musician might receive a better salary, a town musician had certain privileges, such as the right to play at weddings and funerals within the town walls as a member of an incorporated town guild. A boy would receive early musical training in the Latin schools attached to churches and cathedrals, with the cantor serving as teacher, musical director, and composer on occasion, but the boy would then proceed to a musical apprenticeship within the city musicians' guilds. From there, he could compete for a variety of positions, depending on opportunity and ability. A very few completed the final year at a *Gymnasium* and went on to university study, which enabled them to take up positions of the more scholarly sort, such as cantor or music teacher in a Latin school. But such pursuit of higher education was rare: the miserable salaries of teachers and music directors rarely compensated for the years of income one lost by pursuing higher education.

The lines separating different types of musical career were not impassable, though a man without any university training was unlikely to become a cantor. (Given his lack of university training, Bach's appointment to the most prestigious cantorate in central Europe attested to his extraordinary achievements and talent.)[45] More commonly, a well-trained city musician might leave to serve a prince or pick up extra income by work outside the town walls; a court musician might serve at a different court or even risk a career as independent virtuoso. To be sure, town musicians clung to a guild

---

[44] Henry Raynor, *A Social History of Music, from the Middle Ages to Beethoven* (London, 1972), 9.

[45] Christoph Wolff's biography takes as its major theme his "traversing conventional boundaries" to achieve erudition on his own: see his *Bach: The Learned Musician.*

mentality, bickering constantly with the authorities over the presence of traveling musicians who made their way from court to court, often stopping in the more prosperous cities on the way. All, including Bach, had to police the boundaries between themselves and the "beer fiddlers" and vagabond players, musicians without honor who lived on the margins both of home-town and court. But pursuit of the guild strategy never entirely worked for musicians, in part because opportunities outside the hometown milieu al-ways beckoned and in part because the controlling guilds in communities never accepted them as equals or allowed musicians much chance of eleva-tion into the urban patriciates. Even before the loosening of guild cohesion in the eighteenth century, musicians' guilds had often been the butt of at-tacks from other guilds, a circumstance that in 1653 led to an unusual supra-local effort on the part of German musicians to obtain imperial approval for uniform standards within communities. The Saxon Town Musician Arti-cles, which the emperor himself confirmed, consisted of twenty-five speci-fications of musicians' guild privileges, ranging from a monopoly over local performances to moral instruction of journeymen.[46] And although over one hundred musicians from forty-three localities signed onto them, the ar-ticles did not represent a step toward gradual unification of musical employ-ment across central Europe but only a briefly successful attempt to strengthen the position of musicians in a handful of localities. The outlook for town musicians was never bright. Heinrich Schwab has written of "the artistic stagnation of the town musician" in the course of the eighteenth century, a situation exacerbated by the shrinking ambitions of church music in the same period. By the start of the nineteenth century, most towns were abolishing the statutes that had long since ceased to secure guild monopoly over town musical performances.[47]

Moreover, although guild musicians retained a loosening grip on church music and town entertainment in the eighteenth century, the capacity of the princes to undermine guild strength—amply demonstrated in the princes' residential cities—worked with particular effectiveness against mu-sicians' organizations. Life within the musical institutions of a town still of-fered more security than a court ensemble, which might dissolve if a prince died or suffered financial reversals. The writer and composer Johann Beer noted that the hectic schedule of a court musician meant "there is no dif-ference made between day and night," and "in comparison to this, things

---

[46] Martin Wolschke, *Von der Stadtpfeiferei zu Lehrlingskapelle und Sinfonieorchester* (Regensburg, 1981), 33–36.

[47] Heinrich W. Schwab, "The Social Status of the Town Musician," in *The Social Status of the Professional Musician from the Middle Ages to the 19th Century*, ed. Walter Salmen, trans. Herbert Kauf-man and Barbara Reisner (New York, 1983), 36–37, 51.

are a little calmer in the cities."[48] Still, the growth of a musical marketplace in the course of the eighteenth century compensated somewhat for the decline of traditional musical livelihoods. It provided opportunities to supplement one's income—by playing for the growing numbers of amateur groups (*Collegia Musica*, *Musikkränzlein*, and the like), by performing in the new phenomenon of the public concert, and by participating as middlemen, copyists, publishers, sellers, and of course composers in the expanding commercial realm of music publishing. The instrumentalist Georg Christoph Grossheim of Kassel, who lost his position in the orchestra of Friedrich II when the king died in 1785 and the orchestra was dissolved, began giving music lessons and selling music, all the while looking to return to a regular court position.[49] Organists, who lacked status among town musicians and suffered, especially later in the century, from a fashionable dislike of the organ's sound, often founded local *Collegia Musica* of amateur instrumentalists to supplement their income.[50] And as Erich Reimer has shown, the institutions of court music did much to forward the development of this musical marketplace, overcoming a crisis of court music in the latter decades of the eighteenth century by opening up courtly performances to a limited audience or supporting the development of national theaters.[51] Likewise, the princely courts stood behind the development of the new social groups, which became the consumers in the musical marketplace. The social core of literary culture—educated and culturally ambitious people, often members of the bureaucratic elites—enjoyed music in new settings, in public rooms or private homes. Their activities established the beginnings of an organized public interested in the arts.[52]

These developments also contributed to the decline of guilds and diluted the power of princely patronage, without, on the other hand, destroying either guilds or court musical establishments. Thus musicians were, on the surface of things, enjoying an unprecedented range of economic opportunities: courts and cities both had recovered from the Thirty Years War, and nothing like the experiences of Heinrich Schütz in Dresden—without in-

---

[48] Cited in Richard Petzoldt, "The Economic Conditions of the 18th-Century Musician," in Salmen, *Social Status*, 176–77.

[49] Grossheim wrote an autobiography, itself a sign of his participation in literary culture. See Klaus Hortschansky, "The Musician as Music Dealer in the Second Half of the 18th Century," in Salmen, *Social Status*, 205–6.

[50] Arnfried Edler, "The Social Status of Organists in Lutheran Germany from the 16th through the 18th Century," in Salmen, *Social Status*, 75, 89–90.

[51] Erich Reimer, *Die Hofmusik in Deutschland, 1500–1800: Wandlungen einer Institution* (Wilhelmshaven, 1991), 125–41.

[52] For a recent overview, see Peter Schleuning, *Der Bürger erhebt sich: Geschichte der deutschen Musik im 18. Jahrhundert* (Stuttgart, 2000).

strumentalists, singers, or salary, subject to famine, plague, and marauding soldiers, forced finally to flee to Copenhagen—threatened contemporary musicians.[53] Yet even before the revolutionary armies of France invaded the Rhineland in 1792, initiating twenty-two years of fundamental social and political reorganization in central Europe, musicians had begun to express concerns about their security. These concerns reflected consciousness of the changes underway in the music profession and expressed the anxiety that musicians would not be able to master them. The social historian Klaus Hortschansky has identified a "latent crisis in the musician's life," a lurking fear that music was doomed to become, in the words of the composer J. W. Hässler's father, a "breadless art." Hässler wrote in 1787 that his father "could not be convinced" that distinctions could any longer be made "between beer fiddlers, town musicians [*Musikanten*], and true artists [*Tonkünstler*]."[54] With such status anxieties, the senior Hässler echoed composer Johann Friedrich Reichardt's lamentation, a few years earlier, that the "art" of music was becoming merely "craft," so that "from the prince's *Oberkapellmeister* to the beer fiddler who drags operettas into the peasant pub, everyone has become an artisan producing cheap copies for the going market price."[55]

This latent sense of crisis became a real crisis from the 1790s on. All the institutions that provided a basic livelihood for early modern musicians—princely courts, churches, free cities, and hometowns—had to respond to the revolutionary challenge of French victories in the field, and in many cases, the effort radically diminished their capacity to support musical activities. The rulers of many states shut down their court orchestras and theaters to save money, throwing hundreds of instrumentalists and singers out of work. A precipitous decline in sheer numbers of courts at the start of the nineteenth century added to the redundancies. From 1803, when the Holy Roman Empire began the complex process of its own reorganization, to 1806, when it shut itself down, the number of its sovereign entities declined from several hundreds to about forty. This downsizing hurt native German musicians, already experiencing a crisis of training and professional standards, more than the Italian and French stars at the top of court musical life.[56]

---

[53] Hans Joachim Moser, *Heinrich Schütz: A Short Account of His Life and Works*, trans. and ed. Derek McCulloch (New York, 1967).

[54] Hortschansky, "Musician as Music Dealer," 217.

[55] J. F. Reichardt, "An junge Künstler," *Musikalisches Kunstmagazin* 1 (1782): 5.

[56] Christoph-Hellmut Mahling, "The Origin and Social Status of the Court Orchestral Musician in the 18th and early 19th Century in Germany," in Salmen, *Social Status*, 240. See also Reimer, *Hofmusik*, 125–50.

The reorganization of authority and the condition of financial hardship in times of war and occupation affected musicians in towns as well. Some musical positions in towns had been financed by local aristocracy, some by town councils, some by ecclesiastical sovereigns, each of whom responded differently to French hegemony. Still, it seems clear that the number of available cantorates had declined drastically by the first decade of the nineteenth century, because of both political upheaval and a fifty-year decline in the importance of music within Protestant worship. Surviving cantorates involved few and sometimes no musical duties.[57] Music making in the Catholic churches of Germany, like Catholic intellectual life, was enjoying a revival in the late eighteenth century. The Reich reorganization of 1803–6 reversed that hopeful trend, coming down with its most devastating force on the ecclesiastical principalities, which suffered wholesale loss of land and revenue to middle-sized secular states. Finally, musicians' guilds proved nearly useless in shoring up the positions of town musicians in the maelstrom of those times.[58]

All these threats to traditional musical institutions accelerated the shift of the center of gravity in musical life to the public concert and the publishing house. The early modern complexity of a musician's place, embedded in a dizzying variety of institutions and prerogatives, began slowly to resolve into a simpler status, more and more determined by ambition, aggressiveness, skills, in short, achievement. The historian Mack Walker has coined the term "movers and doers" for those free professionals who were known not by what they had or what they were in a particular setting but by what they did. Performers in independent orchestras, which came into existence because of the new possibilities of public concertizing, had to sustain a certain level of musicianship to flourish; this performance requirement was of course even more stringent in the case of solo players, the famous virtuosi, whose careers of constant moving and striving represented an intensified case of the new musical career, open above all to talent. And many musicians began to move entirely into the commercial realm of publishing and selling music, no longer relying on it as a supplement to uncertain court appointments.

All this took musicians "out into the world," making them more dependent on knowledge, skill, and movement for survival, on being able to take advantage of opportunities whenever they arose and to change when

[57] John Butt, *Music Education and the Art of Performance in the German Baroque* (Cambridge, 1994), 166–92; Hans Engel, *Musik und Gesellschaft: Baustein zu einer Musiksoziologie* (Berlin, 1960); Edler, "Social Status of Organists," 89–93.

[58] On the vulnerability of guilds in the revolutionary era, see Walker, *German Home Towns*, 185–216.

change was all there was. The new man of music came into contact with other movers and doers—state officials, free professionals, clergy, intellectuals, and (to a lesser extent) merchants. These were the members of a new elite marked by expensive secondary schooling and a commitment to refinement, achievement, and self-improvement. These were the "fellow creatures" to whom Carl Maria von Weber longingly referred and on whose approval musicians increasingly relied as the old world changed beyond recognition.[59] Mixing with the commercial bourgeoisie, from this perspective, did not ensure economic security, because the commercial sector held little power in central Europe, whereas the university-educated elites, with their hands on the levers of state, had some. Except in a few cities like Hamburg and Leipzig, the commercial bourgeoisie also lacked a tradition of financial support for arts and learning, and by the end of the eighteenth century it rarely sent its sons on to university training. So even though the commercialization of music was well underway by the late eighteenth century, market forces did not (and never would) support a full range of musical activities. For a musician to rely on the sale of his talents alone meant constant insecurity and meager returns on effort.

It would be a mistake to attribute too much conscious understanding of all these social transformations to individual musicians making more or less independent decisions. Nevertheless we can see the resemblances, or "genetic" links, as Pierre Bourdieu put it, between changes in society and changes in the ways people explain and direct their own lives.[60] Everything—their own mobility and lack of clear status as a group, their association with traditions of Latinate and theological learning, their close acquaintance with the German courts, their familiarity with the activities of leisured people, the limited salability of their product—suggested to forward-looking musicians the desirability of connection to literary culture and especially to the elite in state service. We have already mentioned the mutual recognition among such groups and the literary elite as necessary to the economic viability of a career in writing. In this same context, aesthetic debates over opera libretti or the opinions of Kant had the potential to influence people in decisions as minor as how they spent their money or as major as how a university would be reformed or a state subsidy be directed. Opinions about music had consequences within such a milieu, and the uncertainty of music's aesthetic worth, which under other circumstances

---

[59] McClelland, *State, Society, and University*, 97.

[60] Pierre Bourdieu suggested that genetic resemblances exist between the "objective divisions of the social world" and the cognitive schemata by which people organize their lives—an elegant way of avoiding the chicken-and-egg problem. See Pierre Bourdieu and Loïc J. D. Wacquant, *An Invitation to Reflexive Sociology* (Chicago, 1992), 11–17.

might have been a matter of merely academic concern, began to loom large in the minds of musicians. As long as music seemed only to decorate court culture or accompany moribund liturgical and provincial ceremonials, as long as it seemed a mere craft that one practiced rather than an art of great dignity, its practitioners had little hope of moving fully and successfully "out into the world." Musicians, like writers, relied on a tacit agreement among artists and scholars to aid and support one another in the publication of their works, to sign on to subscription lists for new works, and to spread knowledge of creative work among circles of acquaintances.[61] A Kantian underestimation of music's significance threatened these ties of mutual understanding. It also portended the absence of music scholarship from modernizing universities. As the stakes became higher after 1806, this absence threatened to perpetuate the state's indifference to music as art and all that implied.

BILDUNG AND MUSICAL ENLIGHTENMENT

We can hear the echoes of upheavals in the music profession and changes in the interests of the ruling elites in the strenuous tones with which musician-writers, starting in the late 1770s, expounded on three intertwining themes. The first was that music itself was an art, not a craft, and the concern of all cultivated people. The second was that musicians themselves needed to acquire the kind of professional education and self-cultivation (*Bildung*) that defined the ruling elites. The third was that music held a place of national honor and distinction in the culture of the German people. All three themes had already made an appearance in music journalism earlier in the century. Mattheson, as we have seen, used his publications to associate himself and music with higher learning. His first writing on music, the *Newly Made Orchestra* of 1713, aimed to teach "the *galant* man" to appreciate "the noble art of music" (at the same time railed against the Germans' tendency to admire "everything foreign *because it is foreign*" and dismiss everything German "*because it belongs to us and is familiar*"). *Critica Musica* had scholarly pretensions of the first order, and its successor journal—Johann Adolph Scheibe's *Der Critische Musikus* (1737–40)—urged composers to attend to the "noble and lofty" thoughts of Greek and Roman playwrights.[62] In 1739 Mattheson described opera as "a musical university"; a few years later, he called it "an advanced school of many beautiful sciences," in which "architecture, scenography, painting, mechanics, dancing, acting,

---

[61] Hortschansky, "Musician as Music Dealer," 202.

[62] Mattheson, *Das Neu-Eröffnete Orchestre*, 213; Scheibe quoted in Flaherty, *Opera in the Development*, 116–18.

moral philosophy, history, poetry, and above all music unite."[63] Other writers found a different way to demonstrate music's connection to higher learning. Lorenz Mizler, who had studied in Leipzig with the neoclassical patriot Gottsched and the "learned musician" Bach, worked on proving the mathematical foundations of music, hoping to bring it into university faculties of philosophy. His efforts reflected the same mission as Mattheson's writings—to make the case for music as a serious pursuit. Musical art, as Mizler showed to the satisfaction of his dissertation examiners, "was a part of the education of a philosopher."[64]

Discussions about the importance of musicians themselves acquiring higher learning also had some place in early musical writings. Because a church position required one kind of music, a civic position another, and a court position still another, practicing musicians had to be familiar with a wide-ranging repertoire and acquire mastery of many instruments, if they were to be employable. Bach himself once complained that "German musicians are expected to be capable of performing at once and *ex temporare* all kinds of music, whether it comes from Italy or France, England or Poland."[65] The main purpose of Mattheson's *Vollkommene Capellmeister* was to provide an encyclopedic guide to musical knowledge, less for laymen than for professional musicians. Many used this influential book to aid them in their work and to educate themselves in the first place—a phenomenon that itself presages the entry of musicians into the ranks of modern professionals. Yet important though they were, treatises like Mattheson's could not assuage the fear musicians began to articulate in the late 1770s that they suffered from an educational deficit. Writers in music journals described the deficit not as one of craftsmanship but of artistry, knowledge, aesthetic value, in short *Bildung*. Long-simmering anxieties over whether music was more craft than art found expression in these discussions, as did perennial concerns about the public's inclination to be happy with only the most superficial of musical performances. If the public persisted in admiring only the least of professional musicians' works, preventing them from being true artists, then how could musicians hope to be respected? For musicians at the end of the century, finally, the question of music's national valence seemed as unsettled—and therefore as deserving of strenuous debate—as it had when Italian opera conquered the musical stage at the century's beginning.

To follow the progress of writing about music in the final decades of the

---

[63] The first quotation is from *Der Vollkommenen Capellmeister* (1739), the second from *Die neueste Untersuchung der Singspiele* (1744); see Flaherty, *Opera in the Development*, 84–86.

[64] *New Bach Reader*, 296.

[65] George B. Stauffer, "Changing Issues of Performance Practice," in *The Cambridge Companion to Bach*, ed. John Butt (Cambridge, 1997), 204.

eighteenth century is to feel the professional musicians' sense of "latent crisis."[66] In 1776 Johann Nikolaus Forkel, among the preeminent music scholars of the eighteenth century, founded a periodical called the *Musical-Critical Library*. He intended it as a point of dissemination for the work of music scholars, so often unknown to the reading public. Forkel regretted the gulf between high musical aspiration and low public enjoyment: "never has more been declaimed than now about the great, the sublime, the beautiful," and yet when has there been in music itself "so little of the great, of the sublime, and of the truly beautiful?"[67] His *Library* lasted only a few years. In 1782 the composer and writer Johann Friedrich Reichardt launched a new periodical, more expensively produced (ruinously so, as it turned out) than Forkel's but similarly pitched to the highest "artistic sensibility." He hoped to lead musicians and the reading public through a comprehensive program of musical enlightenment. He began with an unbound address "to young artists," in which he raged against the employment conditions of practicing musical artists, dependent on a multitude of people many of whom were ill intentioned. At the mercy of arbitrary princely power, under the "slavery of note-sellers and fashion-mongers," the musical artists churned out idiotic operettas, unworthy of the name of art, and the world was robbed of the "most noble, indeed most original compositions" that might have been written under better circumstances.[68] For Reichardt, better distribution of the great music that did exist might lead to an improvement in public taste; meanwhile, he pleaded with Germany's princes to establish true schools of art, in which a young artist could receive "instruction in the theoretical and practical aspects of his art" as well as cultivate his heart "through true religion, pleasure in nature, history, and the example of noble teachers" and his head "through knowledge of nature, the ancients, and the world"—the full offerings, in other words, of the humanist education.[69]

Reichardt's journal, like Forkel's, failed, but the discussions continued in a parade of new periodicals. In 1783 Carl Friedrich Cramer founded the *Magazin der Musik* in Hamburg. It lasted for nearly six years, claiming a place in the tradition of Mattheson, Forkel, and Reichardt (our "well-known prophet," as Cramer called him). Cramer too pursued the project of musical enlightenment; he too lamented the gulf between a sophisticated body of writings about music and the public lack of understanding of it; he too believed that the solution lay not in more listening but more reading, by the lay public and musicians themselves, whose educational improvement

---

[66] Hortschansky, "Musician as Music Dealer," 217.
[67] J. N. Forkel, "Vorrede," *Musikalisch-kritische Bibliothek* 1 (1778): vii.
[68] Reichardt, "An junge Künstler," ii.
[69] J. N. Reichardt, "An grossgute Regenten," *Musikalisches Kunstmagazin* 1 (1782): vii.

seemed inseparable one from the other. In 1787 an anonymous pamphleteer lamented the condition of professional musicians who worked as mere "machines," "with their hands and not with their heads," and then urged "public institutions such as the secondary schools and the *Gymnasien*" to "refine the study of music." Poor living, worse studying, and above all the "lack of spiritual development"—these were the factors that produced such a small number of "really musical instrumentalists" and knowledgeable listeners.[70]

In 1795, the music theorist and court concertmaster Heinrich Christoph Koch started yet another music periodical, the *Journal der Tonkunst*, in which he announced his desire to contribute to the "general spread of the correct principles and maxims of the art," especially among young musicians. Aspiring musicians needed to "cultivate their minds," he wrote, and to resist fashion, study music theory, and seek the "essential truths" behind the "accidental beauties" of their art. But Koch also addressed "music lovers and dilettantes," who also inclined to "flower-strewn by-ways and detours" that did not lead to the "highest perfection" of music.[71] A sense of crisis as amorphous as this could not quickly dissipate, and in 1806 the music writer J. F. K. Arnold was still advising musicians on the need for "industry, constant practice," and "aesthetic education" through a "library of books on music" and "critiques of pure artistic taste."[72]

More valuable, in the long run, than music writers' exhortations to learning were their contributions to music scholarship. A number of them during these same decades wrote works aimed at the educated layperson who was interested in music but not well versed in its technical language. Their books were broadly disseminated, perhaps for the first time in the history of music writing. Johann Nikolaus Forkel, with his *General History of Music*, was a leader in creating the foundations of a music scholarship that would serve both musicians and music lovers. More closely identified with university life than any other music writer of his generation, Forkel held positions from university organist to music director and offered private instruction in music theory (in which he was self-taught, thanks once again to Mattheson's *Vollkommene Capellmeister*) on the side. Yet despite his lifelong involvement with Göttingen University, Forkel never held a faculty position there (he was granted an honorary faculty title in 1787) and would not have

---

[70] Pamphlet titled *Philosophische Fragmente über die praktische Musik*, cited in Mahling, "Origin and Social Status," 238–39.

[71] H. C. Koch, "Über die Vernachlässigung der Theorie," *Journal der Tonkunst* 1 (1795): 17–20, 11. See also Nancy Kovaleff Baker and Thomas Christensen, eds., *Aesthetics and the Art of Musical Composition in the German Enlightenment: Selected Writings of Johann Georg Sulzer and Heinrich Christoph Koch* (Cambridge, 1995), esp. 111–36.

[72] Mahling, "Origin and Social Status," 239.

held even the musical-service positions were it not for the years he himself had studied law, philosophy, and mathematics at Göttingen. Music did not have standing in the educational hierarchy, but Forkel, undaunted, spent most of his working life creating the foundational pieces of an entire scholarly system for music, as though he could single-handedly piece together the music curriculum for a nonexistent course of university study. In 1802 Forkel published the first biography of Johann Sebastian Bach, a pathbreaking work for the public understanding of Bach but also a work that allowed Forkel to emphasize the importance of a specific type of person, the learned musician. Bach represented the culmination of musical learning, in Forkel's account, and after him came only decline, unless, he implied, the work of music scholars might stave it off, or at least make it possible for later generations to appreciate the greatness that had once existed.

Despite his marginal position at the university, Forkel lectured as well as wrote, exerting his influence on the educated world of German Europe in all the available ways. Wackenroder, who heard him speak, was almost certainly influenced by Forkel's belief in the seriousness of music and its capacity to express the most profound human emotions and thoughts. Wackenroder's music aesthetic did diverge from Forkel's judgments on beauty in music, but their brief contact illustrates the nature of music writers' participation in literary culture. More bystanders than full participants, pedantic more often than eloquent, they nevertheless provided much of the raw material for the writers who shaped educated society's attitudes toward music.

Moreover, Forkel's voice joined that of a number of other music writers calling for more serious attention to their art, and he influenced a number of aspiring music savants. He was, for instance, the chief intellectual influence on Ernst Ludwig Gerber, who, shortly after Forkel's general history appeared, published a *Historical-Biographical Lexicon of Music Artists*, the first comprehensive dictionary of music biography and the product of years of research, collecting, and correspondence with musicians. Gerber, like so many eighteenth century musicians, straddled the older professional world, in which musicianship was a trade passed from father to son, and the new one, in which educational achievement and talent shaped one's career. His father, Heinrich Nicolaus Gerber, had been a student of J. S. Bach in the 1720s (Gerber's entry about his father in the *Lexicon* provides important information on Bach's instructional methods), then became court organist and instrumentalist at Schwarburg-Sondershausen, a position that Ernst Ludwig eventually held. But with the publication of the *Lexicon* between 1790 and 1792, the younger Gerber made a lasting name for himself among musicians and music lovers, for whom "Gerber's Lexikon" quickly became a single word. For the next fifty years, supplemented by expansions and reissues, it served as the single most widely-read reference work in music, the model for all subsequent efforts of that sort, and the source for the anecdotes that enlivened many a belletristic journal or romantic text.

Gerber himself described the work as "a laborious and wearisome undertaking" requiring only "diligence in reading" (*Fleiss zum Lesen*) and unsuited to the pens of "great men in the great world"—like, for instance, the elegant, charming, and intimidating Friedrich Wilhelm Marpurg, whom Charles Burney had called "the first German theorist who could be read by persons of taste." Gerber painted himself, by contrast, as the tireless reaper of what more accomplished men had sown, including the authors of so many short-lived music periodicals. His audience was the "contemporary enlightened musical public" or, alternatively, "music lovers, budding young music artists, and those for whom the great world is distant, who live in provincial cities, working as cantors and organists, and also for members of music associations." The list was an encompassing one, as was the mission. Despite his workhorse modesty, he sought nothing less than to provide all such people with complete musical knowledge, especially of the past extraordinary sixty years of musical work, both in Germany and outside of it. "In short," he wrote, in accord with Forkel's understanding of music history, the art of music "has achieved its highest peak." And yet, again like Forkel, he warned that music might easily fall from these heights, as it grew "ever more distant from its fundamental principles" and succumbed to the "whims of music lovers and fashion." "Who would believe," he exclaimed, that "throughout this entire remarkable era, in which the true and actual classical masters of now and for eternity have worked," no book made known the lives of the great musicians. No other art, not painting, not architecture, not poetry, suffered such neglect, which in turn made music lovers "indifferent to its history" and crude in their musical pleasures.[73]

Gerber's impassioned plea, remarkable in such a sober undertaking as a biographical dictionary, reflected the certainty that music, like the other arts, had a historical development but, unlike them, had already reached its climax and now stood poised to descend back into mediocrity. Gerber's historical consciousness, so similar to that of Forkel, Koch, and Reichardt, consisted of a peculiar mixture of optimism and anxiety. He believed in the perfectibility of human musical creation and was confident in music's capacity for greatness, yet he was concerned that human society itself seemed unable to sustain or even to recognize musical genius, and he nursed a worry about music's future that bordered on despair. On the one hand, he

---

[73] Ernst Ludwig Gerber, *Historisch-Biographisches Lexikon der Tonkünstler*, ed. Othmar Wessely (Graz, 1977), v, x, iii; originally published in 1790–92.

shared with his contemporaries in literary culture the recognition, as Wilhelm von Humboldt put it, that "the eighteenth century occupies the most favorable place for the examination and appreciation of its own character in the history of all time."[74] From this recognition came Forkel's wish to undertake such massive projects as his general history of music or even more ambitiously his multivolume anthology of musical works.[75] But on the other hand, the strangely pessimistic note in Forkel and Gerber's writings expressed persistent anxieties, shared by the editor of one failed musical periodical after another, that music could neither sustain its place among the arts nor win full appreciation from an audience of educated people. This pessimism can itself be seen as the product of a new understanding of historical change, one that feared decline as much as it hoped for progress.

MUSICAL CLASSICS AND THE GERMAN NATION

One further aspect of this music-historical scholarship deserves attention, and that is its recurrent references to the "classical masters of art" in the recent past—Bach first among them, but also (in Gerber's list) "Benda, Gluck, Graun, Handel, Hasse, Haydn, Hiller, Kirnberger, Marpurg, and so on," along with a few Italian composers who had also contributed to the last sixty years of musical greatness.[76] The use of this term "classical" conveys a number of meanings. It distinguished, first of all, between true artists and mere entertainers or handymen of music; thus it asserted the seriousness of the art. But there was more to it than that. Gerber's reference to classical masters was followed by a list that gave precedence to German-speaking composers and only then, with gentle irony, reminded readers not to forget composers from "foreign parts"—those same ones who had in fact garnered the lion's share of public attention in German Europe for the past century. Gerber's list amounted, then, to an understated but thoroughgoing reorientation of musical valuation. It disassociated music from its "fatherland" of Italy; it lionized largely unperformed composers like Johann Sebastian Bach, who was indeed forgotten or neglected by the "enlightened musical public" to which Gerber addressed his lexicon; it gave equal weight to composers of operatic and instrumental music. Gerber's list represented a much bolder, if still implicit, claim for music's importance to German cul-

---

[74] Cited in Reinhart Koselleck, *Futures Past: On the Semantics of Historical Time*, trans. Keith Tribe (Cambridge, MA, 1985), 251.

[75] Less ambitious projects, like Kalkbrenner's *Short History of Music, for the Pleasure of Music-Lovers*, which was widely read by the musically interested public, reflected this same confidence in being able to achieve a historical perspective on music.

[76] Gerber, *Historisch-Biographisches Lexikon*, iv.

ture than Mattheson's defenses of German libretti. Whatever the future of music in Germany would bring, Gerber suggested, the recent past held treasures which lovers of music had hardly begun to appreciate.

Gerber's list brings us back, then, to the question of where music fit in to German culture. Fifteen years earlier, the Englishman Charles Burney had asserted in the *Present State of Music in Germany, the Netherlands and the United Provinces* that, although "a musical spirit" was "universally diffused throughout the [German] empire," the Germans for the most part lacked a "national music."[77] Burney's work was translated into German in 1778 and reached a broad readership, in part because educated Germans liked to read what other people, particularly those from cultures they admired, had to say about them. Nor were Burney's views on the deficiencies of German musical culture unprecedented. He repeated opinions expressed decades earlier by Scheibe and Gottsched and by Friedrich II in Burney's own time. The greatest music and musicians were Italian; German musicians and composers by contrast had a style marked by "patience and profundity" (so far so good), but also "prolixity and pedantry." But Gerber would have none of this. His *Lexicon* made nonsense of Burney by asserting not only a counter-aesthetics of seriousness in music but also a counterhistory of "classical masters" in an independent, fully developed German tradition. For Gerber, the problem was not the lack of a national music but the absence of a public sufficiently educated in music theory and music history to appreciate the national music they already had.

In describing the distinctiveness of German music, moreover, Gerber reflected tendencies that had emerged over the past several decades of music writing. The musicologists Arno Forchert and Bernd Sponheuer have identified two especially persistent tendencies. The first pattern, "cosmopolitan-universalist," credited German musicians with absorbing the best of Italian and French culture and creating something mixed. The second pattern, which Sponheuer calls "exclusive," identified traits specific to German music and held them up in diametric opposition to foreign music—thoroughness (versus thoughtlessness), profundity (versus superficiality), harmony (versus melody), and effort (versus mere showmanship or ease).[78] These ways of writing about Germanness emerged out of Enlightenment Europe's comparative interest in the characters of national peoples, but by the end of the century, in Gerber's and Forkel's generation, comparison had

[77] Charles Burney, *The Present State of Music in Germany, the Netherlands, and United Provinces*, 2 vols. (London, 1775), 2:70, 340.

[78] Sponheuer, "Reconstructing Ideal Types"; and Arno Forchert, "Von Bach zu Mendelssohn: Vortrag bei den Bach-Tagen Berlin 1979," in *Bachtage Berlin: Vorträge 1970 bis 1981* (Neuhausen-Stuttgart, 1985), 211–23.

begun to yield the conclusion that German music was, in fact, better. Either the German mixture was better than its constituent parts or the traits of Germans were better than the traits of foreigners. Gerber's list, unprepossessing as it appears at first reading, reflected that development, and his book backed it up with biographies recounting native German accomplishment.

Finally, to call this list of German composers "classical masters" was also to invoke decades of literary-cultural debate over the capacity of the German language to produce a "classical" literature. This debate culminated in Goethe's 1795 essay, "Literary Sans-culottism," in which he defended German prose as not yet capable of classical grandeur but full of promise: true classics, thought Goethe, could not be conjured out of thin air but rather developed out of the efforts, good and bad, of one's predecessors and contemporaries.[79] Gerber's use of the term implied that music already had its classics, and Forkel made the case explicit in his 1802 biography of Bach. Forkel placed Bach at the center of an educational project he compared to training in Greek and Roman classics at the *Gymnasium* and university, in other words, the central educational experience of Germany's ruling elites. Bach himself, in Forkel's comparison, was the musical counterpart to the Greek and Roman authors; he "was the first classic that ever was, or perhaps ever will be," at least in terms of the higher musical education of a cultivated person.

Accustomed as we are to referring to such music as "serious" or "classical," the terminology does not seem as striking to us as it should. In their time, these music writers' use of the term "classic" involved an ingenious transposition of classical status from the ancient world to the contemporary one, from the Mediterranean to a familiar German-speaking Europe, from the bastion of neoclassicism in Paris to the cultural backwaters of Hamburg, Berlin, and Leipzig. Forkel's homemade classicism exploited the German educated elite's susceptibility to invocations of Greco-Roman culture and in the same breath confronted the problem of music's shaky status in the neohumanist worldview. Forkel described the preservation of Bach's works as the creation of "an everlasting monument to the artist." The word "monument" (*Denkmal*) evoked antiquities and worthy pieces of architecture and sculpture from the German past; it was redolent with the efforts of Goethe, Herder, and others to find the history of German culture in its enduring creations made of stone. Forkel's use of the same term to refer to music further attests to his determination to place the art he honored in the pantheon of imperishable cultural goods. Against Kant's charge that music moved the

---

[79] From "Literarischer Sanscullottism," cited in T. J. Reed, *The Classical Center: Goethe and Weimar 1775–1832* (London, 1980), 17–18.

mind "only transitorily," Forkel asserted music's endurance, its timelessness, and its "dedication to memory."[80]

But most important, Forkel placed music among the enduring monuments of culture by playing the patriotic card—and playing it more artfully and explicitly than any music writer so far, including Mattheson. The very title page of the biography dedicated it to "patriotic admirers of true musical art." The foreword claimed that "this undertaking" concerned not just art but also "the honor of the German name." Bach's works were "an invaluable national patrimony, with which no other nation has anything to be compared." Whoever undertook to save them from oblivion "performed a service to the fatherland." And even more strongly, whoever cared about the German fatherland had a duty to "support such a patriotic undertaking and, so far as possible, to hasten its further acceptance." Forkel hoped, he wrote, to "remind our public of this duty and to awaken in the heart of every German man this exalted enthusiasm." It would not be enough, he insisted, to be read only by the small circle of those learned in this art: "allow me to repeat myself once again; this is not a concern of art alone, this is a *national concern*."[81]

The strenuousness with which Forkel made his case did not come out of nowhere, nor did it reflect, as has often been suggested, a sudden popular enthusiasm for nationalism, brought on presumably by the presence of the French on German soil.[82] Forkel's Bach biography came at the end of a long century of debate about the place of music in hierarchies of aesthetic value and about who the Germans were and what constituted their national culture. It came also after a century of transformations in the livelihoods of professional musicians, whose worlds of employment and career success looked even more precarious in 1800 than they had thirty or fifty or seventy years earlier. It came, finally, as the capstone of a lively tradition of writing about music, in which Forkel served as an important link between the small numbers of people highly educated in musical things and the larger world

[80] Several decades and large collecting projects later, the Grimm brothers came up with four primary definitions of a monument, which reveal the extent to which music still remained marginal to historicist thinking. A *Denkmal* was defined as (1) buildings, columns, statues, paintings, and tombstones intended to memorialize a person or event; (2) a thing dedicated to memory; (3) preserved works of antiquity; (4) buildings or sculpture from the past (Jacob Grimm and Wilhelm Grimm, *Deutsches Wörterbuch*, 10 vols. [Leipzig, 1854]). See also the discussion in Susan Crane, *Collecting and Historical Consciousness in Early Nineteenth-Century Germany* (Ithaca, NY, 2000), 44–59.

[81] J. N. Forkel, *Über Johann Sebastian Bachs Leben, Kunst und Kunstwerke*, ed. Claudia Maria Knispel (1802; repr., Berlin, 2000), 21–22.

[82] See, for instance, *New Bach Reader*, 418, which evokes a metaphoric "tide of nationalism." On the inaccuracy of such characterizations, see Celia Applegate, "How German Is It? Nationalism and the Idea of Serious Music in the Early Nineteenth Century," *19th-Century Music* 21, no. 3 (spring 1998): 274–96.

of educated people in general. Musicians needed the interest and support of that larger world. They sought to secure it by playing beautiful music and—less obviously to posterity—by invoking notions of music's classical status and patriotic importance. Nationalism, if we wish to call it that, entered into this constellation of social and cultural changes as a strengthening and linking agent, a means to connect the problems and possibilities of musical life to social life as a whole and to larger problems of cultural meaning—a means, in short, of becoming important to the people who seemed to be shaping the world of German Europe as it changed. Inclusion in educated society promised some measure of security to professional musicians and some guarantee of progress in the face of what a number of spokesmen for music considered an impending threat of triviality, superfluity, and decline.

In 1798, shortly before the publication of Forkel's ringing call to action disguised as biography, a young writer named Friedrich Rochlitz began a journal in Leipzig called the *Allgemeine Musikalische Zeitung* (*General Musical Newspaper*). Breaking with tradition in music journalism, the journal endured for more than fifty years, succumbing only to the musical battles that preceded the revolutions of 1848. Rochlitz recruited a large and talented group of writers and secured a loyal and well-placed audience of readers. As a result, his journal became the most influential voice in musical matters and the means by which, for the first time, a unified musical culture could coalesce in central Europe. Rochlitz, as much as Gerber, reaped what others had sown, pressing forward the long-standing desire of music writers and musicians to be taken seriously as part of the nationalizing project. The following chapter will consider the work of music journalists, starting with Rochlitz and ending with Adolf Bernhard Marx, in creating the musical public that would attend Mendelssohn's work of revival.

3

Music Journalism and the
Formation of Judgment

The decade of the 1790s was hard on the German-language musical press. In the late summer of 1792, the expectation that a Prusso-Austrian advance on Paris would restore order evaporated over the battlefield of Valmy, and by mid-October no German soldier remained on French soil. By late October, most of the German-speaking territories west of the Rhine were in the hands of French revolutionary armies; by early 1793, a kingless France went to war against the kings and princes of Europe, pushing into the Rhineland, conquering the Low Countries, and moving into the northwest German lands. Only twenty years later did its soldiers withdraw completely from German Europe. In Speyer, one of the cities on the Rhine captured earliest and held longest by the French, H. P. C. Bossler, editor and chief writer of the *Musikalische Realzeitung*, fled across the Rhine to Darmstadt, suspending publication of his newspaper until "better times" arrived. After founding it in 1788, Bossler had beaten the odds against the survival of a music periodical beyond its first year: by 1792, it enjoyed a healthy distribution network and the services of reliable writers.[1] French armies, with their heavy demands on local economies, ended all that. Before the decade was over, they contributed to the financial failure of many other music journals: three periodicals launched by J. F. Reichardt (a weekly, a monthly, and a yearly), Spazier's *Berlinische musikalische Zeitung*, Koch's *Journal der Tonkunst*, the *Augsburger musikalischer Merkur*, and dozens more. One music writer despaired that "among all the thousands who love and revere music," there were "too few educated minds" to support a journal about its "scholarly side."[2]

MUSIC JOURNALISM IN A NATION OF READERS

In these years when the relationship between music and the nation of readers was fragile, serious-minded musicians often expressed anxiety about the survival of their art. But the travails of music journalism were not out of scale with the general condition of periodical literature in this era of confrontation and defeat. Despite a contemporary consciousness of crisis, they were not all that different from the frequent founding and failing of music journals in the previous decades. The French were the least of the challenges faced by anyone who wished to shape a German musical public larger or more lasting than the audience for an evening's performance. The music press (and the press altogether) in eighteenth-century Germany had developed in fits and starts. Periodicals for the literate classes began, as the previous chapter indicated, in the first third of the century, but their print runs rarely exceeded four hundred copies. Efficient distribution was impossible, given the multiplicity of state boundaries and the difficult conditions of travel. That a German public emerged at all under such circumstances attested to the determination of its members to establish durable institutions—not just the press but clubs, universities, theaters, even orphanages. By 1770 only about 15 percent of the German-speaking population was literate, and although that figure rose rapidly over the next hundred years, the regular purchase and reading of periodicals remained an activity confined to a small segment of the populations of towns and cities.

But a German public did emerge by the end of the eighteenth century. Its defining characteristics were a commitment to earnest discussion and a patriotism expansive beyond the limits of city and princely states. The nature of national identity, as it coalesced in eighteenth-century German Eu-

---

[1] Bossler renamed the periodical in 1790, in association with the short-lived "German Philharmonic Society." See the *Musikalische Korrespondenz der Teutschen Filharmonischen Gesellschaft* (1792), appended to *Musikalische Realzeitung* 5, no. 16 (1792), its final issue.

[2] From the *Erfurtische gelehrte Zeitungen*, in Morrow, *German Music Criticism*, 19.

rope, reflected the form and the content of public life, characterized by a heavy reliance on the printed word and by contradictory tones of enlightened openness to the world and defensive fear of foreign cultural and political domination. Before a nation existed in the form of a political state, the idea of the nation formed the core of the German national movement. As Hagen Schulze has said, the German nation could be found "solely in the heads of its educated members."[3] These mainly middle-class men of central Europe nurtured the idea of the nation—to be literal, they wrote it. The idea expanded, taking on ever more plausibility as they accumulated writings spread across a widening range of fields of knowledge. The expansion of reading, tightly linked to the national movement, in turn stabilized the German-language press, creating a motivated market for its consumption.

All this—the history of the German-language press and the German national movement—speaks to the phenomenon of music periodicals in ways that call for further exploration. The existence of music journalism was essential to the success and long-term impact of the 1829 *St. Matthew Passion*. In the short term, Adolf Bernhard Marx's passionate exhortations to worship at the holy temple of Bach's music created the religio-patriotic aura that surrounded the performance, as well as helped sell out the tickets far in advance of the day itself. To be sure, word of mouth sold tickets too, but the words in people's mouths came from what they read over a lifetime as well as what they heard. Susceptibility to the Bach *Passion* reflected, then, the longer-term workings of music journalism. Writing shaped a German musical public that endured beyond any given performance. It sought to extend the effect of music on the mind by informing readers about composers and works, keeping them abreast of new developments, preparing them for performances, and interpreting those performances when they were over. Music journalists wanted to influence how people judged music, and they did so in ways that tied musical judgments to German culture as a whole.

Music journalism thus constituted the medium in which music participated most fully in Germany's emergent national culture. But we can put this more strongly. Writing about music tried to give substance—musical substance—to the national culture of Germans. To thank for this, perhaps, we have Johann Mattheson's imaginative adoption of the English model of moral weeklies. Right from the start and for a long time without much success, writers on musical subjects were making an implicit claim to contribute to general knowledge. The influential sociologist of nation making, Ernest Gellner, suggested that some degree of cultural homogeneity was a necessary precondition for the establishment of national consciousness;

[3] Schulze, *Course of German Nationalism*, 47.

"sustained frequent and precise communication between strangers" was required, along with institutions to "generate and perpetuate a homogeneous culture."[4] Music journals were part of this process every step of the way, not a late and specialized product of a homogeneous culture—Gellner's model of normal development—but an early and generalizing contributor to it.

Yet their work was, as we have already seen, participation of a peculiarly tagalong variety. On the one hand, sustained discussions of music in any but the music journals themselves were rare. Exceptions did exist. Christian Schubart's *Deutsche Chronik*, which appeared for brief runs in the mid-1770s and again in the late 1780s, included lively reports on musical events; and important literary figures of the later eighteenth century—as famous as Herder and as forgotten as Heinse—crossed over to publish essays in music journals. But for the most part, writing about music was no way to secure recognition from a dispersed set of readers. Writers had enough to worry about in the precarious conditions of literary endeavor in the eighteenth century without championing a music aesthetics that remained for much of the century in the twilight zone of literary culture.

But to look at the situation in terms of what it had rather than what it lacked, music writers had established their own journals far in advance of other fields of artistic knowledge. Although subject to constant closures and characterized by tiny readerships, these journals together generated a nearly continuous succession of musical reading matter, broken only from 1728 to 1736 and again from 1770 to 1778.[5] If we consider these miscellaneous titles as a whole, we see that musical knowledge had accumulated impressively by the end of the century, a phenomenon literalized in such works as Gerber's *Lexicon* or Forkel's *General History of Music*. So too had a consensus emerged on the comparative worth of kinds of music, or to put it otherwise, on a consequential distinction between serious and frivolous music.

The participation of music writing in the nationalizing project of literary culture in the eighteenth century provides us with one more preliminary perspective important to understanding nineteenth-century developments, and that is a geographical one. One of the neglected themes of central European musical life between 1800 and 1900 is its relationship to the reconfigurations of political boundaries during those one hundred years, and in particular to the gradual extrusion of German Austria from the eventual nation-state of Germany. There had, to be sure, always been subtle differences in the musical activities of the Holy Roman Empire, reflecting the

---

[4] Ernest Gellner, *Nations and Nationalism* (Ithaca, NY, 1983).

[5] See the list of German music periodicals in the *New Grove Dictionary of Music and Musicians*.

patchwork of religious affiliations and varied distributions of wealth. But with the advent of print culture and the reading revolution, differences between the Protestant north and the Catholic south took on a new dimension. (The lands in between, which the nineteenth-century ethnographer Wilhelm Heinrich Riehl called the "individualized country" of the central German plateau, more closely resembled the north). Music periodicals tell the story of a striking divergence between south and north in German-speaking Europe. The great majority of early efforts to sustain music journals took place in Hamburg, Leipzig, and Berlin. Until a Viennese imitation of Leipzig's *Allgemeine Musikalische Zeitung* made a tentative start in 1813, the musically interested reading public in the most important city of central Europe had to subsist on a thin gruel of entertainment sheets with the latest opera gossip, supplemented only by whichever north German journals made it past the censors and along the wretched roads. Vienna may have been the place to which aspiring musicians went to play and to write music, but it was in the cities of northern Germany where people wrote *about* it.

Nor was this simply a matter of Adam Smith's invisible hand creating efficient divisions of cultural labor. The state of music journalism reflected persistent and consequential cultural differences. Ironically, given the centrality of the German language to the nationalizing work of literary culture, the growth of the German-language press exacerbated, or perhaps simply exaggerated, the cultural conflict between Catholicism and Protestantism in German Europe. Albert Ward, in his study of the reading public in these years of the German Enlightenment, argued that Austria and southern Germany, "once the leaders of cultural life," lagged behind northern and central Germany in the eighteenth-century "march of culture," playing only "a small and unimportant part in the great intellectual and literary developments." To be a Protestant was to be "intellectually progressive"; to be a Catholic, he suggested, was to be hampered by censorship, harangued by the lower Catholic clergy, distanced from new libraries and reformist universities, cut off from the growing trade in books. As Riehl put it some hundred years later, with his trademark combination of irony and admiration, "these remarkable people" in the lower ranks of Catholic clergy allowed "the Bavarian people to move directly from the seventeenth into the nineteenth century, without taking notice of anything from the eighteenth."[6]

Riehl may have been indulging in some wishful thinking, but it remains the case that the eighteenth-century legacy of serious music writing belonged initially, if not enduringly, to the Protestant north. The implications of this for the insertion of music into the project of German culture are not

---

[6] Ward, *Book Production*, 116.

at all clear. One might be tempted to draw lines of historical development from the nationally inflected music writings of the early nineteenth century to Bismarck's Reich of 1871, which like music criticism was predominantly Protestant, centered in north Germany, and ambivalent about Catholic Austria. To do so would be to follow in the footsteps of earlier generations of political historians, for whom all the expressions of nationalism in the first decades of the century prepared the way for a Prussian-led unification. But even the history of the national movement in politics looks to us today more complicated than that, and the history of German national culture, let alone music's involvement in it, poses further problems of aggregation. Nationalist politics and national culture certainly overlapped and intersected in the lives of nation-conscious Germans. But however much a sense and an experience of common culture sustained the movement toward political unification, the history of a common German culture sometimes diverges from that of political nation building.[7] Music journalism, far from contributing to the creation of a cultural milieu exclusive of Austria, went in the opposite direction, forming and sustaining ties among all the centers of musical Germany, south to north, east to west. Given the great weight of musical creativity in Vienna, how could it have been otherwise? And although the current state of our knowledge makes generalizations difficult, these ties survived the political realignments of the latter part of the century. The first journal in central Europe dedicated to academic music scholarship was a joint German-Austrian venture, the *Vierteljahresschrift für Musikwissenschaft*, edited by Friedrich Chrysander (in Vienna), Philipp Spitta (in Berlin), and Guido Adler (in Prague, then Vienna) from 1885 to 1894.

To return to the century's start, the concentration of music writing in north Germany did nevertheless create a distinctive musical culture there, oriented toward academic learning, personal cultivation, and the promotion of what was understood to be Germany's own musical heritage. But it was more inclusive and extensive than exclusive and narrowing, fixed on education and enlightenment, and oriented toward the tiny number of people who had the leisure and resources to enjoy culture and who saw themselves as the representatives of a broad, if submerged, cultural unity. Music journalism in north Germany tried to make clear to a general public what was at stake in the appreciation of music, and that turned out to be nothing less than the future well-being of the German people, Austrians included. Without this kind of coaching in why music mattered, the public's ecstatic

---

[7] Brian Vick productively re-entangles political and cultural nationalism in his book *Defining Germany: The 1848 Frankfurt Parliamentarians and National Identity* (Cambridge, 2002) through his concept of a "culture of nationhood."

reception of the *St. Matthew Passion* in 1829 is scarcely imaginable. To examine the long preparation for 1829 in the pages of the musical press, we must turn to Friedrich Rochlitz and his discovery of the formula for a successful music periodical.

FRIEDRICH ROCHLITZ AND THE CREATION OF A NATIONAL MUSIC JOURNAL

In 1798, Rochlitz was a typical representative of German literary culture. The son of a tailor in Leipzig, he had won a choral scholarship to the famous St. Thomas School (Thomasschule), where he received a disciplined and thorough musical education. In Rochlitz's time, the cantor was Johann Friedrich Doles, who had followed on Gottlob Harrer and was J. S. Bach's real successor, teaching his own students through Bach's chorales, motets, and keyboard works and laying, in Christoph Wolff's words, "the cornerstone of what can be called a Leipzig Bach tradition." Rochlitz did not care for this version of a classical education. Although he dutifully learned counterpoint and composed cantatas, he claimed that his first real understanding of "the inner, secret essence of music" came from a brief glimpse of a living genius, Wolfgang Amadeus Mozart. In 1789 Mozart had traveled from Vienna to Leipzig, and at Doles's invitation visited the Thomasschule, where—in one of those moments that countless retellings transformed into an essential link in the great chain of German musical genius—he listened for the first time to Bach's double chorus motet *Singet dem Herrn ein neues Lied* and was startled into an astonished and joyful exclamation, as "his whole soul seemed to be in his ears."[8]

Epiphanies abounded that spring. Rochlitz had his own when he listened to Mozart play the organ and piano and thereafter immersed himself in the new world of Mozart's and Haydn's compositions. At this point in his life, he had already put aside his study of music in favor of a university degree in theology and philology, but now these compositions aroused in him such "ideas and feelings" that he "sank into dark brooding, melancholy, and constant yearning that gnawed away at my body and soul."[9] Still, Rochlitz felt that he had to renounce such yearnings, and he sold his piano and all his

---

[8] Wolff, *Bach: The Learned Musician*, 463; Ernst Ludwig Gerber, *Neues Historisch-Biographisches Lexikon der Tonkünstler*, repr., ed. Othmar Wessely (1812–14: Graz, 1966): s.v. "Rochlitz." The source for Gerber's Mozart anecdotes was in fact Rochlitz, who published a series of them in the first year of the *Allgemeine Musikalische Zeitung* (hereafter *AMZ*): "Verbürgte Anekdoten aus Wolfgang Gottlieb Mozarts Leben, ein Beytrag zur richtigern Kenntnis dieses Mannes, als Mensch und Künstler," *AMZ* 1, no. 8 (21 November 1798): 117.

[9] Gerber, *Neues Historisch-Biographisches Lexikon*: s.v. "Rochlitz."

musical scores in order to devote himself to nonmusical studies. The story, which he told to the diligent Gerber some twenty years later for inclusion in a new edition of the *Lexicon*, neatly encapsulated the curious place that music held in educated society. The romantic aesthetic of music that shaped Rochlitz's account of his own response to Mozart endowed music with incalculable worth in his eyes but placed it in a realm far beyond the reach of the son of a city craftsman struggling to raise himself above his father's station. Risky and grueling though it was for a poor young man to acquire the education that would make social advancement possible, a musical career was riskier still—especially since Rochlitz convinced himself, again in romantic mode, that nothing less than possession of musical genius would justify such a choice. Chronically short of funds, he completed two years of theological study, quit to take a position as a private tutor in the house of an industrialist, then returned to Leipzig to study theology again. But as he came to realize that without private fortune he would never snag the prominent position among clergy or faculty that he wanted, he renounced those goals as well and embraced the more poetic poverty of a writer. If one is going to starve, it's better to do so (he may have thought) while translating Sophocles in Leipzig than delivering dull sermons to uncultivated villagers.

Astonishingly, Rochlitz succeeded. Starting out with the publication of a learned treatise on the application of Kantian aesthetics to the construction of church buildings, he became a frequent contributor to a number of literary periodicals, writing enough to achieve a financial independence that he held on to for the rest of his life. (It did not hurt that in 1810, at the age of forty and after an earlier engagement that broke off when both mothers announced plans to move into the new couple's home, he married a wealthy and, happily, motherless widow named Henriette Hansen.) His writing brought him to the attention of Goethe, who sponsored several productions of his plays in Weimar, including a much-admired translation of Sophocles' *Antigone* in 1809. Goethe's patronage and friendship also brought Rochlitz the honorary title of "Saxon Ducal Councilor"—not income bearing but a fine proof of success for the son of Leipzig tailor. Rochlitz further cultivated ties with Schiller, Herder, and the whole gamut of his literary contemporaries, whom—if the dedication of his subsequent books is any indication—he perceived as the audience for his music writings as well.

The success of his plays and translations aside, Rochlitz's most effective claim to attention in his own times and ours came from his services to music writing and journalism.[10] In the summer of 1798, not long after his

---

[10] Yet no consensus exists that his, or anyone else's, writing on music constituted an important contribution to German literary culture. The *Oxford Companion to German Literature*, for example,

decision to earn a living by his pen, Rochlitz met Gottfried Christoph Härtel, a thirty-five-year-old entrepreneur who had recently bought into the
Leipzig music-publishing house of Breitkopf, which had fallen upon hard
times. The French had significantly disrupted the publishing trade; moreover, Johann Breitkopf's once-brilliant business strategy, to outmaneuver
musical engravers by producing large numbers of type-set copies and many
tiny runs of hand-copied editions, was no longer keeping pace with the
spread of music engraving. Härtel took over the firm, renamed it Breitkopf
& Härtel, and then began to look for new initiatives to put it in the black.
Well-educated in the law and classical languages, Härtel came up with two
schemes for his business: first, to publish the complete works of Mozart and
Haydn, and second, far less likely to succeed, to start a new music periodical. He had heard of Rochlitz, the writer with the excellent musical education, and offered him the editorship. Together the men worked out a business plan and in the fall of 1798 sent the first issue out into the literate
world.

Perhaps even more astonishingly than Rochlitz's writing career, this too
succeeded. The *Allgemeine Musikalische Zeitung*, begun in such unpropitious
times, endured for twenty consecutive years under Rochlitz's editorship and
another thirty under various others. By the end it was just hanging on in
order to make a dignified departure in its fiftieth year of publication, but
throughout its early decades, it enjoyed an unprecedented prominence
among periodicals in general, becoming both the journal of record for musical happenings and the journal of authority for musical opinion. How this
success, against the backdrop of so many failures, was achieved involved a
number of factors, starting perhaps with the title itself. A small masterpiece
of marketing, it suggested a subtly different periodical than the one to
which it actually belonged. The use of the word *Zeitung*, "newspaper," for
instance, implied daily (not the actual weekly) editions and an extensive
readership. The effect of the word *allgemein*, "general," was similar. Evoking
a series of periodicals essential to the collective existence of German educated society, from Friedrich Nicolai's *Allgemeine Deutsche Bibliothek* to
Cotta's recently established *Allgemeine Deutsche Zeitung*, this simple little
word contained within itself the philosophical outlook of the German Enlightenment and claimed a readership as broad as the entire enlightened
public. Moreover, Härtel and Rochlitz created a paradox and denied its
force in their linking together "general" with "musical." Such a linkage had

includes Rochlitz only because Goethe liked him and because he "was regarded as one of the better purveyors of light novels" (Henry Garland and Mary Garland, *The Oxford Companion to German
Literature*, 2nd ed. [New York, 1986], 758).

not been tried before by music journals and was surreptitiously bold, a claim, for those who could perceive it, that music itself constituted a general interest for educated people everywhere. Just as Cotta's title had elided the implications of his paper's local placement in Stuttgart, so too did this one elide the specialized nature of musical undertakings. And however imperfectly the journal fulfilled the promises of its title, the potential magic of those words to attract the widest possible readership inspired imitations for the next three decades: by 1827 Berlin, Frankfurt, Vienna, Munich, and Zurich had all had some version or other of an *"allgemeine musikalische Zeitung."*

And the claim to a broad readership did not end with the title. In search of a unified public, Rochlitz saw himself as "mediator" between artists and the public, with his "first duty to clear away misunderstandings, to overcome mutual suspicions, to alleviate the difficulties both have with each other, to bring them closer together, and if possible to unite them."[11] From the outset, he exploited the ambiguity inherent in such eighteenth-century terms as "music lover" (*Musikliebhaber*), "friends of music" (*Musikfreunde*), and "musical experts" (*Musikkenner*) to suggest an inclusive, expandable set of people. Despite conventional associations with each of these terms, they were voluntaristic, not ascriptive categories; like voluntary associations themselves, they served as capacious tents under which people could choose to gather without special degrees, ranks, or titles. Rochlitz emphasized their open-endedness in a way that highlighted the generalist aspirations of enlightenment over its tendency to grant special privilege to those who already had expertise. For a "general musical newspaper" edited by a literary figure with his eye on literary, not just musical, culture, such an emphasis was important. It distanced the *Allgemeine Musikalische Zeitung* from the existing tradition of musical expertise, from Mattheson to Mizler to Marpurg, in favor of the larger and more influential readers of literary journals.

Take, for instance, the terms "expert" and "music lover," *Kenner* and *Liebhaber*. They went hand-in-hand in the eighteenth century, as in the frequent advertisement of concerts *"für Kenner und Liebhaber,"* but as the philosopher Johann Georg Sulzer had shown, they were not the same. In his widely read *General Theory of the Fine Arts*, written in the 1770s, the key element in distinguishing them was judgment. A *Kenner* could judge not only the "mechanical" aspects of a work of art but also "that which lies outside the art" and could discuss rationally matters of taste, ideas, structure, originality. A *Liebhaber*, by contrast, knew only what he liked: he judged a work

---

[11] Friedrich Rochlitz, letter to publishers, 1838, in Martha Bruckner-Bigenwald, *Die Anfänge der Leipziger Allgemeinen Musikalischen Zeitung* (Hilversum, 1965), 24.

"entirely in terms of the unconsidered impressions it made on him, praising what pleases him and finding fault with what does not, without offering any further grounds."[12]

Without rejecting this distinction, Rochlitz suggested that his journal would help the *Liebhaber* become more like the *Kenner*. In his 1798 "Thoughts on the Opera," Rochlitz criticized the neglect of music in aesthetic works that sought to improve the public's capacity to judge fine art. Why was it, he wrote in an echo of Gerber's introduction to his *Lexicon*, that this art, "the products of which have achieved in our times the greatest perfection," should be almost completely ignored in this decade "rich in critiques, theories, and analyses" of every other art? Rochlitz, the published admirer of Kant's aesthetics, singled him out for rebuke: "even the greatest critic of our times, Kant, treats music so casually" that "one would think there existed nothing but dinner and dance music." One could not expect his followers, continued Rochlitz ("and who among us is not a follower of Kant?"), to do any better by music. Still, Rochlitz believed that the "coldness" toward music among so many educated people masked a capacity to be moved by it. And this basic emotional response to music could turn into "a much higher and nobler pleasure" if one made "reasoned judgments by oneself rather than blindly giving oneself over to mere impressions"—if, in other words, the differences between *Liebhaber* and *Kenner* could dissolve.[13]

Half a year later, his widely quoted article on "The Differences in Judgments of Musical Works" made more explicit the qualities needed in a musical public. Invoking the authority of such well-known authors as Lawrence Sterne and the German romantic Jean Paul Richter, Rochlitz suggested that the art-consuming public fell into four classes. His first three followed conventional Enlightenment distinctions among philistines, experts, and art lovers. The first and least redeemable group, the "wretched" class of the "mightiest" and "highest ranking," saw musical performances solely as occasions to display themselves. The second were "so-called art experts," who listened only "with their intellect," like "scholars whose lives are spent trying to prolong the perfection of their performance on the school exams of their youth." Third were those who listened "only with their ears," a category of sensualists with an instinctive understanding of music's fundamental humanity. And the fourth group, with which Rochlitz abandoned Sulzer for Schiller as his aesthetic guide, consisted of those who listened and heard with "their whole soul." They understood music as they

---

[12] For an English translation and an introduction to Sulzer's aesthetic theory, see Baker and Christensen, *Aesthetics and the Art*, 3–110.

[13] Friedrich Rochlitz, "Gedanken über die Oper," *AMZ* 1, no. 1 (3 October 1798): 1.

understood all art, as "a means toward the perfection and the ennobling" of the human race. For these precious few, knowledge and art came together to "lead on to the temple of perfection and freedom."[14]

Rochlitz wanted more people to share this last, Schillerian vision.[15] So he published essays on musical subjects written so that "every thinking musician and music lover might understand, enjoy, and find them interesting"; he introduced readers to new theoretical writings and reviewed new musical compositions; and he reported on matters of "general interest from the musical world," including all the cities of Germany and Europe.[16] Still, ambitious plans and hopeful opening statements had never before saved a music journal from quick oblivion. What made Rochlitz's journal different went beyond this talk of a unified public to the practicalities of business and management.

In the first place, no other music journal had had the consistent support of a savvy entrepreneur like Härtel. As the eighteenth century turned into the nineteenth, he expanded the publishing house and established a printing works and a piano factory. The latter never became more than a regional undertaking, but it allowed Härtel to diversify his business interests in the fledgling music industry. The new journal benefited from the distribution networks of an established book dealer, which helped in managing the delays and expenses that characterized trade across Germany's many state borders. The journal's placement in Leipzig, which Rochlitz admitted was far from the major centers of music making in Europe, also brought direct connections to an expanding and Leipzig-centered book trade. After initially high investments to get the newspaper established, Härtel saw costs sink to the point where the paper actually made a modest profit, even with slowly decreasing sales over its lifetime.[17]

The viability of the paper as a business venture fed its success as a literary undertaking. Rochlitz was able to pay his contributors more than other music journals did; in fact, the burden of paying for contributions was often the proximate cause of many a music journal's demise. A healthy fee structure, combined with his own talents as an impresario of writers, helped him to create what was the largest, most geographically far-flung, and most gifted group of musical writers ever assembled. By the time he resigned from the journal in 1819, he had managed over a hundred correspondents

[14] Friedrich Rochlitz, "Die Verschiedenheit der Urtheile über Werke der Tonkunst," *AMZ* 1, no. 32 (9 May 1799): 497–505.

[15] Rochlitz, "Gedanken," 4.

[16] Friedrich Rochlitz, "Nochmalige Uebersicht des Inhalts dieser Zeitung, aus dem ausführlichern Plan gezogen," *AMZ*, Intelligenz-Blatt 1 (October 1798); Bruckner-Bigenwald, *Anfänge*, 60.

[17] Bruckner-Bigenwald, *Anfänge*, 29–33.

and writers in more than fifty cities. His list ranged from the enduringly famous like E. T. A Hoffmann to the vaguely remembered like J. N. Forkel to the unjustly obscure and the utterly forgotten. But then, achieving fame through their musical reportage was beside the point for most of Rochlitz's correspondents, who might be traveling virtuosos recruited to write accounts of their own performances, or organ technicians describing new installations, or just professional musicians reporting on the outcome of a local singing competition or the program of a regional music festival. All told, this network brought in news from an astonishing 224 German communities, most of which were in the geographical area of middle Germany, including Saxony, Lower Saxony, Thuringia, and Brandenburg Prussia.[18] In German-speaking Austria, he received regular reports from Vienna and Salzburg; in German-speaking Switzerland, from Basel and Zurich. Occasional news also came in from Amsterdam, Paris, Warsaw, Moscow, St. Petersburg, Stockholm, Copenhagen, Milan, Genoa, Rome, Lisbon, Livorno, London, and Leeds.

Given that most of the information provided by these correspondents was ephemeral, and intended as such, the import of Rochlitz's painstakingly assembled network remains obscure. One could analyze its reports for trends in concert life or tendencies in musical taste, but the more striking implications of Rochlitz's network have to do with time and place and the particular construal of both that characterized the national imagination at its inception. Benedict Anderson, the theorist of modern nationhood, argued that "the hallmark of modern nations" was a "remarkable confidence of community in anonymity." By this he meant the belief shared among people unknown to one another that they held something significant in common, that is, an identity. This confident sense of commonality derived, he thought, primarily from the "convergence of capitalism and print technology on the fatal diversity of human language."[19] Anderson suggested that both newspaper and novel created a fictive reality for their readers characterized by simultaneity of various experiences across a delimited space. The nation operated cognitively in the same way; the fictive reality inhabited by readers, especially in the case of newspapers, was the nation itself, the "imagined community."

From such a perspective, the main contribution of Rochlitz's network to the history of Germany becomes its participation in the making and sus-

---

[18] For an analysis of this "correspondence network," see Reinhold Schmitt-Thomas, *Die Entwicklung der deutschen Konzertkritik im Spiegel der Leipziger Allgemeinen Musikalischen Zeitung (1798–1848)* (Frankfurt am Main, 1969), 127–32.

[19] Benedict Anderson, *Imagined Communities: Reflections on the Origin and Spread of Nationalism* (London, 1991), 36, 44.

taining of a German community, imagined in the case of the *AMZ* as music loving and musically gifted. One could argue contrariwise that such a category is too limited, given the wide scope of the magazine's geographical coverage, or too broad, given the distinctive and localized character of musical life in each of the many places from which Rochlitz's correspondents reported. But several factors speak for the mid-level designation of Germany, between the local and the international. First is Anderson's point about the accident of language. German patriots had been pointing to the significance of the German language throughout the eighteenth century, and many publications had been dedicated to its improvement. The *AMZ* was a music journal in German, and as we have already indicated, the most literary of music journals, seeking the approval of Möser's "literary fatherland." For Rochlitz himself and for his most literary of recruits, E. T. A. Hoffmann, the writing of an article on music posed problems of language itself. If Hoffmann's main purpose in writing about music was to secure its rightful position as the "most romantic" of arts, his greatest challenge was not a musical one at all but a literary one, a problem of writing. His choice of an elliptical, often fragmentary, and sometimes fantastical approach to this problem reflected his stretching of the linguistic resources of musically descriptive German beyond the scientific-technical and aesthetic–philosophical discourses of the eighteenth century into some intuited fusion of music and word. His writing aimed not just to describe Beethoven's Fifth Symphony, not just to identify the romantic sensibility that resonated in its tones, but to instill in the reader some of that "nameless, haunted yearning" felt by "every sensitive listener."[20] Hoffmann stood apart from most of Rochlitz's writers in the reach of his imagination and the intensity of his ambitions for music writing. Lesser writers were nevertheless linked to him in their efforts to address an audience as demanding of literary excellence as it was of musical news. Rochlitz invoked this audience in his defense of the newspaper's placement in Leipzig, admittedly a minor musical center but the "center point, gathering place and trading center" of "everything literary in Germany."[21] Even a writer so ostensibly unstylish as Zelter, who produced a series of reports for Rochlitz on the Berlin musical scene, knew how to deploy that tone of Berliner plain speech that so endeared him to Goethe.

But we need not rely on the national subtext of the journal's attention to

---

[20] The reader wishing for a fuller understanding of Hoffmann's work should consult *E. T. A. Hoffmann's Musical Writings: Kreisleriana, The Poet and the Composer, Music Criticism*, ed. David Charlton, trans. Martyn Clarke (Cambridge, 1989); hereafter Charlton. See his famous review of Beethoven's Fifth Symphony, 236–51.

[21] Rochlitz, "Uebersicht."

the German language in order to see a community of music-loving Germans as the product of Rochlitz's efforts. He and his correspondents continually spoke of Germany with a sense of commonality that went beyond language. The emphasis on actual geographical places in the weekly section on musical news had the effect of creating, over the course of decades of reporting, a map of musically active Germany. This map remained vague in its geographical reach, without definite borders and therefore without clear political implications. But one should not expect clear borders to this imagined community. The map of cultural Germany had always lacked them, and its sense of commonality did not require explicit discussion of political reform. When Rochlitz wrote that he would include "information on the reigning taste in this or that major location not only in Germany but also in other countries," he deployed a simple distinction between here and there, our places and theirs, which would have been obvious to his readers. He clarified only to the extent of judging remoteness in terms of distance from Leipzig, which was the intellectual center of his Germany. This attitude communicated itself to some of his correspondents: one from Stettin referred to the "dearth of imagination" in the "northern regions of Germany"; another lamented the "defective state" of music in "east German" schools. Still, Rochlitz's Leipzig-centered vantage point belied the polycentric impression of Germany that emerged from the reports, from the "hotbed" of musical activity in Hamburg to the French-plundered music libraries of Württemberg to the "hordes of virtuosi" in Vienna. Even reports from remote outposts emphasized their commitment to musical life, in effect affirming the community of musicians and music lovers throughout this Germany. The repeated use of the term *Deutschland* as a place with, for instance, too few music schools or too many Italian operas on its stages or too little understanding of its own music history suggested that it was indeed a meaningful collectivity, a musico-cultural reality if not a political one.[22]

And as a musico-cultural reality, this Germany had a number of problems. It would be an exaggeration to say that these problems defined Germany, but several of them went some distance toward clarifying the substance of national difference. First, and familiar to the point of cliché, was the problem of Italian music. Evoking Mattheson's lamentations of 1713 (in *The Newly-Made Orchestra*) on German musical stagnation, the journal updated the old image of native musical culture bombarded by bravura arias

---

[22] *AMZ*, Intelligenz-Blatt 1 (October 1798); *AMZ* 1, no. 18 (30 January 1798): 285; no. 3 (17 October 1798): 46; no. 14 (2 January 1799): 224; no. 30 (24 April 1799): 465; *AMZ* 2, no. 3 (16 October 1799): 49; *AMZ* 1, no. 11 (12 December 1798): 166; no. 14 (2 January 1799): 216; no. 40 (3 July 1799): 627.

and other incursions of foreignness. Discussions of Italian music did not express hostility to it or nativist bigotry. On the contrary, one writer admired the "advanced culture of music" in Italy, which he attributed to excellent conservatories; several made neutral references to the predominance of Italian opera composers, in one case, to be sure, as a means of highlighting Mozart's remarkable achievements as a German composer of opera.[23] The general consensus was that the Italians, as a consequence of speaking the "loveliest-sounding, most supple language on our half of the globe," had perfected the art of sweetly melodic song.[24] Germany's Italian problem emerged in the pages of the *AMZ* as one of musical ignorance on the part of German audiences infatuated with off-the-rack Italian or Italianate music. Such music pleased without effort and thus had a meager impact on the emotional and intellectual development of its listeners. One could think of this as musical nationalism, but the remedies the journal proposed consisted of educational, not exclusionary, impulses. Germans must learn better judgment, and as their judgment improved so too would their appreciation for less immediately pleasing pieces of music, most especially German ones. Rochlitz drew attention especially to the works of contemporary Germans, "who with a calm spirit, a rich understanding, a pure taste, and their own distinctive style" sought to "unite the best of the old and the new music of Italy, France, and Germany."[25] The meaning of difference, then, in the case of the Italian problem was a kind of cultural backwardness on the part of Germans which made them receptive not only to the best of foreign cultural offerings but even more to the worst.

Consequential in a different way was the French problem, which by 1799 was more political than aesthetic. While Rochlitz and Härtel planned their new periodical, representatives of the disintegrating Holy Roman Empire met with the French in the western German city of Rastatt to negotiate a series of annexations and compensations that showed how powerless the old empire had become. Diverse, complicated, and irregular, the Holy Roman Empire had still been for most Germans the most obvious political expression of "Germany." Its demise meant that Germany was "no longer a state," as Hegel put it in the first political essay of his career, and that its members were now caught in a condition approaching insanity, "the perfected isolation of the individual from his kind."[26] Germans now had to wonder whether cultural commonality was enough. The Rastatt Congress began a

---

[23] *AMZ* 1, no. 11 (12 December 1798): 166; no. 3 (17 October 1798): 38.

[24] "Kritische Bemerkungen über Verschiedene Theile der Tonkunst: Über die italiänisch-französische Musik," *AMZ* 2, no. 14 (1 January 1800): 241.

[25] *AMZ* 1, no. 3 (17 October 1798): 38.

[26] Cited in Sheehan, *German History*, 242.

process, hardened into Prussian policy with the Treaty of Tilsit in 1807, of articulating a conception of nationhood more capable of mobilizing people to action than cultural participation had been.[27] Political nationalism began to circulate in German public life from the 1790s on. Often at odds with the state interests of the German princes, its propagandists attempted to fill a largely French form of popular nationalism with an aggressively anti-French content.[28]

The reverberations of such thinking echoed in the cultural activism of Rochlitz's *AMZ*. Although the journal neither took a nationalistic stance nor ventured into open political journalism, the French Revolution was a palpable presence in its pages. Rochlitz and several of his writers were fascinated by the developments in France, appalled by their consequences in central Europe, and eager to sort out their implications for musical Germany. Rochlitz, however courtly a gentleman he may have appeared to his contemporaries, had no love for aristocratic culture as such, which he thought contributed to musical frivolity.[29] He recognized the importance of the aristocracy's traditional patronage of music, but at the same time he made the stupidity of aristocratic taste the source of humor in his many anecdotes of musical life. Nor could Rochlitz easily forgive a set of people whom he blamed for the miseries of Mozart, the man he considered the greatest musical genius ever. Consequently, he kept a close eye on the role that music would play in this new republican society of France. An article by Johann Friedrich Christmann, a musical pastor in French-dominated Württemberg and one of Rochlitz's earliest collaborators, examined the close connection between song and state in revolutionary France, quoting Mirabeau's "Discourse on a National Education" at some length. Christmann admired Mirabeau's emphasis on the vital role that the arts made to the common good and claimed that the French use of "national singing" as a "medium of national education" accorded well with the "German feeling for humanity" and the journal's own efforts at moral improvement through musical education.[30] Rochlitz did report on the destructive impact of the revolution, but he thought it possible that it had improved the state of

[27] On Stein's use of writers to mobilize national spirit, see Otto W. Johnston, *The Myth of a Nation—Literature and Politics in Prussia under Napoleon* (Columbia, SC, 1989).

[28] Michael Jeismann, *Das Vaterland der Feinde: Studien zum nationalen Feindbegriff und Selbstverständnis in Deutschland und Frankreich 1792–1918* (Stuttgart, 1992), 27–158.

[29] One contemporary writer thought that "his whole outward appearance gave the impression of belonging to an earlier age"; quoted in Hans Ehinger, *Friedrich Rochlitz als Musikschriftsteller* (Leipzig, 1929), 7.

[30] J. F. Christmann, "Einige Ideen über den Geist der französischen Nationallieder," *AMZ* 1, no. 15 (9 January 1799), 228–31; no. 16 (16 January 1799): 249.

music among Frenchmen, turning them toward a more serious appreciation of it.[31]

Rochlitz went so far as to claim that the revolution had "germanized" the French, at least from a musical perspective. The notion was both fanciful and unprecedented: the word "germanization" had been virtually absent from the vocabulary of music journalism. Its first use in the *AMZ* came right after a playful piece by Gerber, "Something Political in the Realm of Harmony," which suggested that Gluck's operas in Paris had stirred up revolutionary sentiments among people used to sleeping through Lully and Rameau.[32] But germanization was more than the conceit of one author. It was the subtext of many reports from non-German countries, which often seemed designed to draw attention to Germans abroad. In 1799 a report from England contrasted its lack of native musical genius to its preference for German music and musicians, whom the English seemed to honor more than did the Germans themselves. Likewise, a Haydn symphony was touted in the *AMZ* as "a favorite in Petersburg as in Naples, in Moscow as in Madrid, in Paris and London as in Lisbon or Stockholm, throughout all of Germany as in Philadelphia."[33] Such imaginings of a wide world echoing with the music of German composers point to an increasingly positive conception of musical nationhood, marked neither by rejection of foreign things nor by fear of outside domination but rather by the assertion of distinctive character, of canon and native genius, in short, of all the markers of a nationalizing culture. National existence, to which musical life attested, was both the program of the journal and its unspoken assumption. The presence of the nation, similarly to that of the French Revolution, often lay between the lines of the journal.

Such implicit affirmation characterized Rochlitz's presentation of the German musical past. This aspect of the *AMZ*'s content provides further evidence of the way in which he turned a so-called newspaper devoted to happenings in musical Germany into a journal with far-ranging educational ambitions. Historical education took a variety of forms. Each time Breitkopf & Härtel produced the bound volume of a year's issues, they presented

---

[31] "Etwas über den Werth der Musik überhaupt und die Mittel, ihn zu erhöhen," *AMZ* 2, no. 49 (3 September 1800): 833.

[32] Gluck's Germanness was ambiguous. His name and native language may have been German, and he was born in a German enclave in Bohemia. But his musical career was cosmopolitan, taking him from Bohemia to Italy to central Germany to Vienna and most triumphantly to Paris. Nevertheless, the notion of Germanness that informed turn-of-the-century music journalism embraced him as a native son, as it did Handel.

[33] "Ueber den Zustand der Musik in England," *AMZ* 2, no. 1 (2 October 1799); on Haydn, *AMZ* 11, no. 8 (20 November 1808): 150.

it with a frontispiece engraving of a musician, starting with J. S. Bach himself, and including in the two decades of Rochlitz's editorship Bach's son Carl Philipp Emanuel, Handel, Haydn, Gluck, and Beethoven, among others.[34] The full list of twenty men included an Italian, a Frenchman, and an expatriate Italian in France (Cherubini) but was otherwise a German construction, characterized by a broadly inclusive understanding of musical work.[35] From the acoustical scientist Chladni to the *Lied* composer Schulz, these men belonged together by virtue of their Germanness and, in close dependence on that notion, their contributions to a distinctively German musical excellence. The frontispiece musicians suggested its defining characteristics: seriousness, excellence in scientific research and scholarship, harmonic and formal complexity, and a closely mutual interaction of word and tone.

They were also men of the recent past or actual contemporaries. By the standards of turn-of-the-century music historiography, preoccupied with the classical or the sacred origins of music, these men were scarcely historical at all. Forkel's own history of music, completed in 1801, ended somewhere in the sixteenth century—"right at the point where history, for us, can begin," as Zelter wrote to Goethe. Christian Kalkbrenner's popular history for "music lovers" included two final pages on the Reformation and music, after somehow managing to devote one 120 pages to ancient music without having the slightest idea of what it sounded like.[36] This long-range view of the musical past was typical. Rochlitz was well aware of it and clearly, like Zelter, unimpressed.

Rochlitz had something else definite in mind, something more like what we would call contemporary history. In his "reflections on the most recent history of music," he suggested that authors neglected the most recent past because it was easier to write about ancient Greek music one has never heard than the "culture of music among contemporary Germans and about the training of the nation in this art." Yet that is precisely what we ought to be writing about, argued Rochlitz, or we will never understand "from whence we came and to where we are going" and consequently will never

---

[34] Many people received the journal as an annual compendium of issues. Goethe, for instance, wrote to Härtel ordering the first three compendia and promising to find an opportunity "to say something publicly to the benefit of the journal, which has earned the applause of all friends of art." In Oskar von Hase, *Breitkopf & Härtel: Gedenkschrift und Arbeitsbericht*, 5th ed. (Wiesbaden, 1968), 1:150.

[35] In order, the men were J. S. Bach, J. A. P. Schulz, C. P. E. Bach, G. F. Handel, C. Gluck, J. A. Hiller, J. Haydn, Mozart, J. P. Kirnberger, E. F. F. Chladni, C. F. Fasch, Rameau, J. A. Hasse, Forkel, Cherubini, J. F. Reichardt, Palestrina, Abbé Vogler, Beethoven, P. v. Winter.

[36] Zelter quoted in Allen, *Philosophies of Music History*, 84; Christian Kalkbrenner, *Kurzer Abriss der Geschichte der Tonkunst, zum Vergnuegen der Liebhaber der Musik* (Berlin, 1792).

progress. Rochlitz's "dream" was that one day Germans would have just "such a history of music and the shaping of a nation." This history would not be the "conventional sort about accomplished individuals" but would concern itself, again, with the "development of the nation overall," especially as the arts contributed to it.[37]

Rochlitz's call for as full as possible a description of this nation reflects how art mediated the experience of nationhood for him and, just as telling, how incoherent art seemed to him outside of a national construct. The German nation was real for Rochlitz, shaped by art and perhaps especially by music. The vagueness of such phrases as "shaping of a nation" reflected the abstract nature of this nation. But at the same time, Rochlitz and his contemporaries had confidence that becoming national—germanization, perhaps—was a process of progressive enlightenment, a "slowly sharpening vision" in Friedrich Meinecke's phrase, turned both inward on the self and outward on the world. Germanness represented for them "a great extension of the individual personality and its sphere of life," and the cultural nation "a jointly experienced cultural heritage," one that in Rochlitz's case included music. This gradually nationalizing perception of the world had affinities with the neohumanist project of self-discovery or *Bildung* in general. Becoming "national" was an expansive effort of education, a search for knowledge about self and surroundings, and Rochlitz wished to make his journal part of it. Men like Wilhelm von Humboldt, whom Rochlitz had met, believed that the more society became educated, the more national it would become: a "finer cultivation of language, philosophy, and art" would lead to more "national differentiation," which would inspire higher efforts at understanding, hence more education. "Whoever occupies himself with philosophy and art belongs to his fatherland more intimately than others," wrote Humboldt to Goethe from Paris, and Rochlitz would not have disagreed.[38] But whereas Humboldt thought such intimacy the direct result of language in its constant interaction with "emotion and reflection," Rochlitz's whole effort was to draw music into the magic circle of distinctive national creations.

Meanwhile, he could forward the process of greater self-knowledge by publishing such articles as would bring specificity to abstraction, making people's understanding of the musical past and the German nation less "imperfect."[39] His most important colleague in this effort was a pastor from Stettin named Johann Karl Friedrich Triest, about whom almost nothing is

[37] Friedrich Rochlitz, "Vorschläge zu Betrachtungen über die neueste Geschichte der Musik," *AMZ* 1, no. 40 (3 July 1799): 625–27.
[38] Meinecke, *Cosmopolitanism and the National State*, 10–15, 42.
[39] Rochlitz, "Vorschläge," 627.

known other than his authorship of an eleven-part essay on the development of the art of music in Germany in the eighteenth century, which appeared in 1801.[40] Triest began with the same question to which Charles Burney had applied himself some thirty years earlier: Do the Germans have a distinctive music? to which he added, And have they always had it? His essay argued that yes, a distinctive German music did exist, but no, it had not always existed but was the product of the past century of musical greatness.

Triest divided the eighteenth century into three periods, the first lasting fifty years, the second thirty, and the final twenty, in a telescoping development that culminated in Haydn and Mozart. This system, based on a twin dynamic of musical improvement and a fine-tuning of the distinctively German, demanded that Triest place not just Haydn and Mozart but also C. P. E. Bach, Carl Heinrich Graun, and Johann Adolf Hasse above Johann Sebastian Bach, the acknowledged master of the first period. And though Triest was probably influenced by the recent adoring reception of Haydn in London, he also suffered from German literary culture's inability to imagine something distinctively German without language being involved. As far as Triest (and Rochlitz and Forkel) was concerned, J. S. Bach had distinguished himself through his "profound" understanding of harmony but had neglected melody and rhythm, those elements most closely linked to language and hence most expressive of human emotion. His successors, though, had incorporated "Italy's expressive charm, France's energy," and "Germany's profundity" into a new style, still distinctively German but at a higher level—"for the German genius, like the busy bees, extracts the pollen of foreign art and carries it back to the homeland to work upon with its own distinctive powers." The result: "in its instrumental music, Germany has advanced beyond all other lands of the earth."[41]

Several years later, another of Rochlitz's writers, reviewing a Handel chaconne that had only recently come to light, quipped that "in the musical world today we are witnessing the resurrection of the dead, but luckily it extends only to the righteous." For this anonymous writer, as for Rochlitz himself, the "righteous" included a Jomelli or two alongside the German Bachs, Haydns, and Handel. Cultivating a German distinctiveness

---

[40] Triest was recognized by musical contemporaries not only for his knowledge of music history but for his devotion to the promotion of musical amateurism, through the Stettin Singinstitut. See Johann Friedrich Reichardt's remarks in the *Berlinische Musikalische Zeitung* (hereafter *BMZ*) 1, no. 37 (1805): 148.

[41] Triest, "Bemerkungen über die Ausbildung der Tonkunst in Deutschland im achtzehnten Jahrhundert," *AMZ* 3 (1800/1801): 224–35, 241–49, 276, 437–45. See also Erich Reimer, "National-albewusstsein und Musikgeschichtsschreibung in Deutschland 1800–1850," *Die Musikforschung* 46 (1993): 17–24.

in music did not mean asserting superiority over all others, though in some cases the journal did not hesitate to do so. It meant, rather, the pursuit of a consensus about the present and past from which the nation was constituted. It meant striving to achieve that "unity of taste and judgment" that historian Hagen Schulze sees as the hallmark of eighteenth-century literary nationalism. It meant overcoming centuries of musical narrowness in order to achieve universal acclaim for German music and centuries of musical fragmentation in order to achieve common recognition of what was excellent about it.

Rochlitz's journal, in the twenty years of his editorship, worked toward progress on all these fronts, and to a large extent succeeded, certainly among Germans themselves. Of course, not all the journal's readers held opinions identical to it, but at least Rochlitz laid out for them the evidence of German-wide musical activity, of international recognition of German musicians, and of a continuous line of German musical creativity leading back through the previous centuries. He argued that the ability to make fine musical judgments lay within the grasp of any reader who wished to apply him or herself to the discipline of it, and he implied that such discernment, once acquired, would reveal the greatness of native musical genius. It is perhaps one marker of his success that by 1821 his one-time protégé E. T. A. Hoffmann could write of gentlemen and ladies with musical aspiration but "little talent" who nevertheless could "speak and pass judgment about the works of great composers."[42]

FEUILLETONS AND MUSICAL FASHION

Those whom Hoffmann mocked were participating in a great cultural transformation when they flaunted their insubstantial musical judgments. Their demonstrations of musical prowess—"performing a solo at the choral society" or playing "badly but charmingly on the piano" in Hoffmann's version—provide evidence of what Wolfgang Kaschuba has called the "bourgeois awakening" of the period between the revolutions of 1789 and 1848. In the course of it, a "new economic, social, and cultural profile" emerged among people recasting the society of their parents and grandparents. The term *Bürgerlichkeit* encompasses this "historically developing cultural praxis."[43] Novelists and historians have long recognized musical activity as a characteristic piece of nineteenth-century bourgeois lives, and a later chap-

---

[42] E. T. A. Hoffmann, "Further Observations on Spontini's Opera *Olimpia*," in Charlton, 442.

[43] Wolfgang Kaschuba, "German Bürgerlichkeit after 1800: Culture as Symbolic Practice," in *Bourgeois Society in Nineteenth-Century Europe*, ed. Jürgen Kocka and Allan Mitchell (Providence, RI, 1993), 392–93.

ter will consider amateur musicianship's role in the 1829 *St. Matthew Passion*. But drawing-room demonstrations of musical ability extended beyond playing and singing to discussion about musical matters in general, and here the role of periodicals was of central importance.

Writing of all kinds, from letters to memoirs to proliferating genres of periodical literature was not only the expression of an emergent national consciousness among Germans but also an essential tool in the making of a modern bourgeois person, a means of expressing cultural values and experimenting with new identities and cultural practices. The formation of judgment, which counts among the most definitive of bourgeois practices, matured through the medium of writing, whether one is talking about aesthetic or political matters.[44] In the case of the *AMZ*, the teaching of judgment—how to make distinctions among musical compositions, what kind of language was appropriate to use—could form a substantial part of a periodical's raison d'être. Reading periodical literature and expressing opinions culled from it became as revealing a marker of bourgeois identity as dress, career, manners, or accomplishments. Moreover, bourgeois identity drew much of its coherence from its creation of national culture, for as one contemporary explained it, reading what everyone else read gave one "the feeling of being in the best society, that society which represented German culture in Europe and beyond."[45]

The *AMZ* was one among many such periodicals during the period of the bourgeois awakening and, as the historian Ulrich Tadday speculates, the first choice only of the most sophisticated musicians, not of readers in general. Many lesser journals also helped to create a musical public, in particular the entertainment sheets or feuilletons, which conveyed information about musical happenings just sufficient to allow one to hold one's own in polite conversation. Such journals as Leipzig's *Zeitung für die elegante Welt* (Newspaper for Elegant Society) and Berlin's *Der Freimüthige oder Scherz und Ernst* (The Free-Spirited Man, or Jest and Gravity) focused on news of operas and traveling virtuosi, almost to the exclusion of all else, and cultivated a tone of breezy joviality that mocked the educational seriousness of Rochlitz's writers. In their heydays during the first decades of the nineteenth century, these sheets boasted circulations roughly double that of the

---

[44] See Jürgen Habermas, *Structural Transformation of the Public Sphere: An Inquiry into a Category of Bourgeois Society*, trans. Thomas Burger and Frederick Lawrence (Cambridge, MA, 1989), which posited rational communication, defined largely as the exercise of critical judgment, as the constituent feature of a new public life. See also Howard Caygill, *Art of Judgement* (Cambridge, MA, 1989), esp. 11–38.

[45] Heinrich Laube on the *Augsburger Allgemeine Zeitung*, cited in Kaschuba, "Bürgerlichkeit," 392.

AMZ and distilled the complexities of high artistic culture into simplicities that could be communicated and commercialized.[46] The effect of this process of reduction was, in Tadday's view, to reinforce a sense of community among the new bourgeoisie and open up the possibility of acquiring a bourgeois identity to whomever chose to buy these modestly priced papers. They created a "socially privileged discursive community that was nevertheless without rigidly exclusive social lines." By making cultivation into something that could be acquired almost like a fashionable piece of clothing (*Bildung* without suffering), the entertainment sheets disseminated common knowledge and norms—and made life a little easier for the tone deaf.[47]

Still, the renunciation of critical judgment in favor of entertainment and information came at a price, and that price was provincialism. Tadday is certainly right in asserting that under Rochlitz's editorship, the *AMZ* was not, in fact, "general" at all, but complex in its musical analyses and comprehensible only to those with or willing to acquire a musical education. A concert review in a feuilleton, with its chatty accounts of who came and who played and whether they were brilliant or disgraceful and how much the audience applauded and the performers earned, was a far cry from the careful assessments that filled the pages of the *AMZ*. But what the simple reviews gained in accessibility, they lost in consequence. Why, after all, should anyone not living in Berlin or Leipzig or Tübingen care to read about whether or not the local opera society was heading into bankruptcy or a popular soprano inclined to screech on the high notes? In a society as geographically fragmented, as separated by political borders and road conditions as was German Europe, rising above locality required more than fashion; in the view of men like Rochlitz, it required intellectual aspiration. Nationalists in the eighteenth century had felt that way, and the new century had not yet proven their vision wrong or inadequate. Not surprisingly, the feuilletons reached only the limited area in which—and for which—they were produced. In contrast, Rochlitz's *AMZ* may have been read by fewer people, but it was read in more places across the German-speaking world.

Still, one might argue that in their very conformity, the feuilletons created a sort of lowest cultural denominator, capable of creating ties among places by the sheer banality of their common concerns. Repetitive in the performances covered, as traveling musicians moved from one major town to another or opera directors in one place imitated a successful production

---

[46] Ulrich Tadday, *Die Anfänge des Musikfeuilletons: Der kommunikative Gebrauchswert musikalischer Bildung in Deutschland um 1800* (Stuttgart, 1993), 65–67, 155.

[47] Ibid., 13–14.

from elsewhere, the feuilletons might indeed, as Tadday supposes, have contributed to the canonization of certain musical works whose popularity hinted at a common culture.[48] But if there was such a culture, it was not particularly German. The feuilletons' perspective was that of provincials looking out on the wide world and doting on what came their way. Except for coverage of oratorio performances, which seemed to point to the national-cultural work of oratorio societies later in the century, the feuilletons described a musical world filled almost exclusively with the sound of Italian opera and its imitators.

ADOLF BERNHARD MARX AND MUSIC JOURNALISM IN BERLIN

Still, the connection between sophisticated musical judgment and national consciousness remained mainly between the lines in the *AMZ*, implicit in the totality of Rochlitz's efforts to write about music in the context of German philosophy, science, and literature and to report on the musical scene in all of German Europe. This connection became explicit, however, in the work of Rochlitz's most important imitator in Berlin, the man who became the self-appointed herald of the 1829 *St. Matthew Passion*, Adolf Bernhard Marx. For Marx, as for many a patriot before him, Germans betrayed their provinciality, not their sophistication, when they admired the cultural products of other nations. The feuilletons, catering to fashion rather than seeking to shape it, only strengthened a provinciality masquerading as worldliness. It followed that if musical judgment among the general public improved, an appreciation for the greatness of a newly recognized German musical tradition would emerge, and along with it would come the strengthening of national feeling. This mixture of highbrow cultural aspirations with outspokenly national preferences became, then, the hallmark of Marx's *Berliner Allgemeine Musikalische Zeitung*, which had its brief moment in the forefront of music journalism in Berlin during the half-decade ending in the *Passion* revival.

Marx's foray into music criticism did not mark the first time a serious music journal with high intellectual aspirations had tried to shape the notoriously uneven taste of the Prussian capital. The eighteenth century had seen the coming and going of dozens of music periodicals, many of them based in Berlin. During the 1770s and 1780s, music journalism in the Prussian capital had flourished; even the 1790s demonstrated the centrality of

[48] Ibid., 144.

Berlin to a type of serious music criticism modeled on its literary counterpart. Its leading representative was a composer and musician, perhaps the most distinguished composer in all of north Germany at the end of the century, Johann Friedrich Reichardt. Born in 1752, two years after the death of Johann Sebastian Bach, Reichardt was only twenty-three when he rose to the exalted post of royal Prussian kapellmeister, or conductor of the royal household's orchestra and director of court music. Reichardt achieved this post in the waning years of the Frederican court. Friedrich II, famous for his patronage and performance of music, had paid little attention to musical matters since 1763 and did not personally appoint Reichardt, as he had the kapellmeisters of the past. Reichardt held on to his post until 1794, when he was dismissed by Friedrich Wilhelm II for his republican political views. His support of the French Revolution, even in its most radical phases, also estranged him for a time from Goethe, whose poetry Reichardt set to music and with whom he had collaborated in a number of *Singspiele*.

But alongside his active career as composer and performer, Reichardt also wrote prolifically about music, beginning in the 1770s with a short pamphlet of technical advice to the "underappreciated" orchestral violinist, and soon joined the ranks of what Mary Sue Morrow has dubbed the "review collective" of north German writers on instrumental music.[49] Reichardt's ambitions led him already in 1782 to start his own journal, the glitzy *Musikalisches Kunstmagazin*, which failed within a year, engulfed in unrecovered production costs and criticism of its founder's "transparent egotism."[50] Reichardt founded at least five more periodicals, all short-lived, and wrote a biography of Joseph Haydn, several collections of short essays for "musicians and friends of music," and a series of musical travelogues about German cities, Paris, and Vienna. In 1805, shortly after returning from Paris, where he found little to admire in French singing, he joined with the publishers Heinrich Frölich of Berlin and Rudolph Werkmeister of Oranienburg to produce what would be his last attempt at a music periodical, the *Berlinische Musikalische Zeitung*. Like Rochlitz, Reichardt believed that great art required great criticism for its sustenance and that Germany could boast of excellence in both.[51] Yet his renewed effort to provide

---

[49] Johann Friedrich Reichardt, *Ueber die Pflichten des Ripien-Violinisten* (Berlin, 1776); Morrow, *German Music Criticism*, 18.

[50] This critic of Reichardt rebuked him for creating a journal "too fancy in its outward form," but he admired his writing so much that he devoted much of his own journal to summarizing the substance of Reichardt's. See Carl Friedrich Cramer, *Magazin der Musik* 1, no. 1 (1783): 29–56 (repr., New York, 1971).

[51] J. F. Reichardt, *Beleuchtung der vertrauten Briefe über Frankreich* (Berlin, 1804), 32.

Berliners with a "precise and highly sophisticated criticism," free of both "pedantry" and "frivolous nonchalance," also ceased publication after only a handful of issues.[52]

The concern for cultural awakening and self-recognition among Germans became militant in the journalism of Marx a decade and a half later. One need not seek far for an explanation. The time between the last issue of Reichardt's *Berlinische Musikalische Zeitung* in July 1806 and the first issue of Marx's *Berliner Allgemeine Musikalische Zeitung* in January 1824 amounted to the first sustained episode in the development of political nationalism in central Europe, the first period in which nationally minded people could be found in significant numbers outside of literary culture. For people of the eighteenth century, who experienced the German nation in literature, art, and music, the wars with France raised questions about both their theories and their practices. The decisive confrontation came in October 1806 on the battlefields of Jena and Auerstadt. Prussia's defeat imbued commonplace words like "Fatherland," "Volk," and "Nation" with a political charge. Even if one does not dwell on Fichte's "Addresses to the German Nation" (Zelter, for one, resisted yielding his Singakademie practice space to Fichte in that cold winter of 1807–8, national crisis or no), the aggressive, even sacralized nature of German nationalist discourse in those years was strikingly evident. The popularity of such rhetoric among urban populations was considerable, especially as the French occupation turned into an extended recruitment and provisioning expedition for the Grande Armée. Small but determined societies began to disseminate nationalist propaganda, which they hoped would combat both indifference and particularist loyalties. Finally in 1813, the formation of Prussian volunteer units to fight against the French provided an opportunity for patriotic men to put ideas into action, and members of the educated middle classes along with artisans and apprentices flocked to what they believed to be the national cause.

By the time the central European princes had reasserted the principle of monarchy in 1815 and circumscribed the public sphere in 1819, no one who frequented the educated circles of Prussian life could fail to have encountered this heightened rhetoric of Fatherland. As Matthew Levinger has shown, even King Friedrich Wilhelm III, along with a significant segment of the Prussian nobility, adopted the discourse of "enlightened nationalism" briefly, before once again rejecting it in the years after 1815.[53] The subsequent development of German nationalism takes one through many de-

---

[52] J. F. Reichardt. "Etwas zur Einleitung," *BMZ* 1, no. 1 (1805): 3–4.

[53] Matthew Levinger, *Enlightened Nationalism: The Transformation of Prussian Political Culture, 1806–1848* (New York, 2000), 93–96, 158–59.

tours, disappointments, and transformations in political purpose to the foundation of a German state more than half a century later. But a concern for the high cultural achievements of the German nation, overburdened with states as it was, never disappeared. Even the most ardent of activists during the struggle against the French still conceived of the wished-for nation in terms of a kind of cultural wholeness gathered beneath the "high center" of kingship. Ernst Moritz Arndt's poem of quest for the borders of a Fatherland not yet quite real, "What Is the German's Fatherland?" relied for direction on the old markers of cultural unity, language and song: "As far as the German tongue rings / And to God in Heaven Lieder sings / That's where it should be! / That, bold German pertains to thee!" And while the opportunities for political activism diminished, decisively with the Karlsbad Decrees of 1819, the promotion of cultural unity and national fulfillment through the consumption of culture and the contemplation of history remained, and not simply as cover for forbidden political gatherings. The 1820s thus became a decade of history writing, of aesthetic and philosophical exploration, of religious awakening and poetic experimentation, of collecting and displaying, traveling and comparing, all still imbued with the spirit of Arndt's search for the German Fatherland.[54]

Marx's Berlin journalism falls within the nation-making project of German cultural exploration. Like his younger contemporary and namesake Karl, who was enjoying a bourgeois childhood in distant Trier at the time of Adolf Bernhard's introduction into Berlin society, Marx found his first intellectual mentor in the towering figure of G. W. F. Hegel, and he fashioned himself into the first important exponent of Hegelianism in music criticism. Such an intellectual gambit had much to recommend itself for a young man (Marx was twenty-one when he arrived in the city in 1821) coming to Berlin to make a name for himself in the 1820s. Hegel was at the height of his social success, the focus of cultlike adoration among the new generation of students at the university and a guest in all the liveliest salons, the Mendelssohns' included. Marx sought entrée into such circles—where better to display his mastery of ideas that few understood but all, as a matter of fashion, admired? Eduard Devrient, as we have seen, found his posturing unbearable: "His intellectual and flowing speech dominated every conversation, his many new and striking ideas, . . . his adroit flattery, so discreetly veiled, made him for a time, very popular with the [Mendelssohn] family," he reported in his memoirs with unconcealed dislike.[55] Still, Marx's music

---

[54] On cultural and political nationalism, see Vick, *Defining Germany*, 16–17.

[55] Devrient, *Meine Erinnerungen*, 38. See chapter 1, footnote 79, for discussion of the anti-Semitic overtones of such descriptions.

Adolf Bernhard Marx. Drawing by Wilhelm Hensel, c. 1829. By permission of the Bildarchiv Preussischer Kulturbesitz / Art Resource, NY, Kupferstichkabinett, Staatliche Museen zu Berlin, Berlin, Germany.

journal represented the first stage in a distinguished career as music theorist, biographer, and popularizer of musical arcana. It became the finest music publication in the city, a mouthpiece of his determined, sometimes intemperate efforts to raise the musico-national consciousness of Berliners.

The Berlin in which Marx arrived had only weak claims to musical distinction, much as did the Leipzig about which Rochlitz could be so apologetic. It had declined musically during the years of warfare and economic depression. In 1817, one of its opera houses had burned to the ground, leaving the city with only one stage of any note, the Royal Opera House, and no concert hall as such, despite a steady growth in numbers of subscription concerts. The 1820s were a decade of expansion of public venues for musical performance, starting with Schinkel's new theater on the Gendarmenmarkt, which opened in 1821, and culminating in the erection of a new building for the Berlin Singakademie in 1827, the place where Mendelssohn performed the *St. Matthew Passion* in 1829. Even so, Berlin had nothing of the musical reputation of Vienna, premiered few works, and owed what reputation it had in musical Europe entirely to the Royal Opera and its well-regarded orchestra.[56] Contemporary observers saw it as a claustrophobic place of "sedate dullness," despite what was in retrospect a quickening pace of social change and an increasingly diverse intellectual and cultural life.[57] The musicologist Arno Forchert suggested that the juxtaposition of "intimacy and fragmentation, of narrowness and breadth, of close-mindedness and worldliness," along with the stifling of political debate by the Karlsbad Decrees, created a context in which art took on "a disproportionately great importance" in conversation and publication. Certainly, the American Henry Dwight felt the "omniscient eye of the government" turning every Prussian into a mealymouthed exponent of "those indefinite opinions which are harmless," and the musician and writer Heinrich Dorn lamented the relative dearth of political newspapers.[58] Dorn noted how "the theater, including concerts or art in general" formed not just the "favorite" but "strictly speaking the only" form of entertainment. A number of entertainment sheets and newspaper supplements catered to the local appetite for theater gossip, flattering or disparaging one opera singer after another, sniffing out conflicts among cultural intendants, and heralding the arrival of virtuosi and prodigious children into the round of city events.

Against the backdrop of so much studied frivolity, Marx's new journal began—and meant to continue—on a sustained note of seriousness. His opening article denounced the ignorance and arrogance with which people made their pronouncements on artistic matters. Instead, Marx promised a new music criticism marked by "thoroughness and substance." Artistic criticism should be more than a "higher form" of advertisement, and the "reading world" deserved a greater challenge to its intellect. True criticism

---

[56] Adam Carse, *The Orchestra from Beethoven to Berlioz* (Cambridge, 1948), 108–16.

[57] See Mary Lee Townsend, *Forbidden Laughter: Popular Humor and the Limits of Repression in Nineteenth-Century Prussia* (Ann Arbor, 1992), esp. 15–34.

[58] Dwight quoted in Levinger, *Enlightened Nationalism*, 191; Dorn in Arno Forchert, "Adolf Bernhard Marx und seine Berliner Allgemeine musikalische Zeitung," in *Studien zur Musikgeschichte Berlins im frühen 19. Jahrhundert*, ed. Carl Dahlhaus (Regensburg, 1980), 382.

should aim to "refine, broaden, and enrich the reader's mind"; true criticism was never "vacuous," "ingenuous," or "pretty-sounding."[59] Nor was it arcane. Too many erudite theoreticians missed, in Marx's metaphor, the whole of St. Peter's Cathedral by gazing too intently at individual columns. Mathematics and physics, despite their valuable contributions to a scientific understanding of musical tones, could not reach music's essence, which lay rather in the "artistic principles embodied and further developed" in each artist and work of art.[60]

We need not read between subsequent lines to find Marx's views, for scarcely an issue appeared over the seven years of the journal's existence (once a week from 1824 through the end of 1830) without some kind of exhortation or fulmination written by Marx himself, often dropped into a review of a new score or a notice on a forthcoming concert. His themes were few and frequently repeated. He believed that Berlin musical life, especially concert life, was in terrible shape—"sunk nearly to the lowest level possible," a junkyard of "one virtuoso after another," possessing only "technical fluency, decked out in fashionable mannerisms." Yet the public was not entirely to blame, argued Marx. The fault lay with those who catered to what they assumed to be the low taste of the public, never offering "artistically rich performances that might challenge listeners to greater attentiveness." The public was at the mercy of bad decisions and low expectations: if only concertgoers could "regularly hear good music, then they would become receptive to it and be awakened to a finer, nobler interest in artistic endeavors." Without help, the public could not improve, and Berliners would remain mired in the fleeting pleasures of "veil-dancing virtuosi," "painted singers," and "charming women seated nearby."[61]

Shoddy performances and cheap thrills only headed the list of Marx's complaints. He objected to the performance of only short works, or senseless excerpts of longer ones; he objected to confining instrumental music to the brief intervals between acts of an opera; he objected to the neglect of the unfamiliar or difficult works of known composers, the neglect of great works of forgotten composers, and the neglect of all the work of young, unknown composers, who with some encouragement might develop musi-

[59] A. B. Marx, "Ueber die Anfoderungen [*sic*] unserer Zeit an musikalische Kritik; in besondrem Bezuge auf diese Zeitung," *BAMZ* 1, no. 1 (7 January 1824): 2–4.

[60] Marx, "Anfoderungen," *BAMZ* 1, no. 3 (21 January 1824): 17–19.

[61] *BAMZ* 1, no. 48 (1 December 1824): 415–16; *BAMZ* 1, no. 41 (13 October 1824): 349. Another full statement of what was wrong with concerts is "Einige Worte über das Konzertwesen, besonders in grossen Städten," *BAMZ* 2, no. 44 (2 November 1925): 349–51; no. 45 (9 November 1825): 357–61.

cal greatness; he objected to gifted performers wasting their talents on trivial pieces and poor performers making a hash of difficult ones.[62] Indeed, Marx's ability to perform variations on his central theme of the need for musical seriousness was itself virtuosic. In one setting after another, he instructed the reader in the ways of his musical universe, divided between profound and superficial music, between music of lasting value and music of ephemeral pleasure.

So familiar is this dichotomy to us today, and so ubiquitous the efforts to deconstruct it, that it takes some effort to appreciate the work that went into its construction.[63] For Marx was not mainly interested in sniping at the Italians, as some have suggested, nor was he a snob, a show-off, a maverick, or a curmudgeon. His calls for free and rational debate on serious issues, his criticism of frivolity (which he explicitly linked to the influence of the aristocracy), and his insistence on the need for leaders to sustain a public life of substance and intellectual challenge for the people amounted to a critique of the Prussian state overall, especially the moribund public sphere of its capital. Moreover, Marx represented the continuation of the long-standing concern among German musicians and musical intellectuals for the status of music among the educated and ruling elite. He simply added a further layer of intellectual justification to those already laid down in previous generations by Mattheson and Marpurg, Rochlitz, Reichardt, and others.

His distinctive contribution was, as indicated earlier, to introduce a measure of Hegelian philosophy into the interpretation of music's significance. He did not draw on Hegel's own thinking about aesthetics, which Robin Wallace believes Marx knew but "chose simply to ignore."[64] Like Rochlitz, the Kantian who sought to overcome Kant's ill-considered dismissal of music, Marx became the Hegelian who used Hegel's ideas (specifically on the historical unfolding of human understanding from the *Phenomenology of Spirit*) to prove Hegel wrong about music's relation to the other arts, wrong about its relation to thought and human emotion, and

---

[62] On several of these issues, see Forchert, "Adolf Bernhard Marx," 381–404. On Marx's championing of Beethoven, his prime example of an underappreciated contemporary composer, see Robin Wallace, *Beethoven's Critics: Aesthetic Dilemmas and Resolutions during the Composer's Lifetime* (New York, 1986), 45–64; and Sanna Pederson, "A. B. Marx, Berlin Concert Life, and German National Identity," *19th Century Music* 18, no. 2 (fall 1994): 87–104. English translations of Marx's Beethoven articles may be found in *The Critical Reception of Beethoven's Compositions*, ed. Wayne M. Senner, Robin Wallace, and William Meredith (Lincoln, NE, 1999), 59–77, 90–95, 111–12.

[63] On the philosophical origins of this dichotomy, see Sponheuer, *Musik als Kunst und Nicht-Kunst.*

[64] Wallace, *Beethoven's Critics*, 51–52.

most of all wrong about the inferior place of instrumental music in the historical scheme of things.[65] Whereas Hegel knew little of instrumental music and seemed to have had no notion of musical progress (it was left to Robert Schumann two decades later to make the great analogy between Napoleon and Beethoven as avatars of World Spirit), Marx believed fervently that music did progress, specifically in its ability to express objective ideas. Against the persistent dismissal of music's higher intellectual appeal, his writings drew attention to the "objective content" of music, to its "richness of ideas" (or lack thereof), to its ability to nourish "our minds and our hearts," to a composer's "grasp of all sides of the human mind" (Handel, in this case), to music's contribution to the "mature culture of the mind."[66] The worst he could say of a piece of music was that it provided a "mindless amusement of the senses" and "destroyed [the public's] capacity for more profound, more introspective listening."[67] The best he could say, as when he challenged the Berlin public to prove its mettle by listening to Beethoven's Ninth Symphony, was that a work was "too great, too rich and too deep to be grasped in its completeness and its full grandeur upon hearing it for the first time."[68]

Marx's sensibility thus embraced the hard work of achieving enlightenment. As his remarks on the Ninth Symphony indicated, to appreciate the most difficult—and most important—music required listeners to improve their own capacity to hear and, in turn, to be fully human. Marx wanted his journal to serve that enlightening function for the Berlin public. In one of his Hegelian disquisitions, Marx tried to prove the necessity of such a musical education by presenting a history of music in its relation to music writing and education. In his scheme, each era was characterized by a distinctive "consciousness," beginning with a religious one that allowed only writing about technical aspects of music and precluded any "engagement in the free play of ideas." An antithetical era of "pleasure in life for its own sake" followed, marked by "bravura singing and virtuosic performances" all for the pleasure of the ruling elite. Composers treated "deep knowledge of the meaning of their art" as "completely dispensable"; music writers busied themselves in theoretical elaborations.

[65] Marx compared the Kantian era of the Leipzig *AMZ* and the "new period" of his journal, which he described in a torrent of Hegelian concepts: "coming into being," "development and further development." "concatenation of emergence and consciousness," and so on. See Marx, "Andeutung des Standpunktes der Zeitung," *BAMZ* 2, no. 52 (28 December 1825): 421.

[66] *BAMZ* 2, no. 52 (28 December 1825): 421; no. 45 (9 November 1825): 358; no. 51 (21 December 1925): 407; *BAMZ* 5, no. 1 (2 January 1828): 1.

[67] *BAMZ* 2, no. 52 (28 December 1825): 421; no. 35 (24 August 1825): 281.

[68] *BAMZ* 3, no. 47 (22 November 1826): 384.

Now a new era of musical endeavor was slowly emerging, thought Marx, in accordance with the advent of rights and freedom for people in the political world (a development that Marx, perhaps with one eye on the censor, attributed improbably to Friedrich II). Art turned to the "free and full life" of individuals, and the "interests of all mankind" took precedence over "religious interests" and "court pleasures." Art could at last become the "common wealth of the entire public."[69] But growing popular participation in music, from music making to concertgoing, brought new responsibility. That, not surprisingly, was the responsibility to understand art at a deeper level. Presumably reading his journal would be a first step in the right direction, since it included plenty of intellectually demanding content: learned discussions of singing styles, theories of instrumental music, instructions on what to listen for in a particular piece. But Marx had greater ambitions for this lazy Berlin public than a reading program and even cautioned his readers against an excess of publications on musical controversies.[70] What he really wanted was for people to go to concerts and listen actively, and so he promoted, forcefully and persistently, musical events he thought would be most enlightening.

Scholars have long noted his reviews of the compositions of Beethoven, which contrasted to the lukewarm reception Beethoven received in the 1820s, especially in the Leipzig *AMZ*. Marx explained how Beethoven had moved music to a more advanced stage in its development and campaigned for more frequent, complete performances of Beethoven's works, especially his symphonies.[71] The year 1825 was a happy one for Marx, because Berliners were able to hear Beethoven's *Pastoral* Symphony no fewer than four times. He noted approvingly that the audience for these concerts was not just "elegant society" with its "Parisian hats and Italian feathers" but a "gathering of true friends of music and of those who had the sense to want to become such."[72]

As such language indicates, he understood his advocacy of Beethoven in the context of European nations.[73] In this, he shared a tendency, in com-

---

[69] A. B. Marx, "Wer ist zu der Theilnahme an der Zeitung berufen?" *BAMZ* 4, no. 1 (3 January 1827): 2–3.

[70] *BAMZ* 3, no. 52 (27 December 1826): 423.

[71] Wallace, *Beethoven's Critics*, 45, 50. See also Elisabeth Eleonore Bauer, *Wie Beethoven auf den Sockel Kam: Die Entstehung eines musikalischen Mythos* (Stuttgart, 1992); Pederson, "A. B. Marx," 89–105.

[72] *BAMZ* 2, no. 12 (14 March 1825): 95.

[73] Musicologist Sanna Pederson argues that Marx's advocacy of Beethoven's symphonies reflected a "strategy" to "delimit the symphony by positioning its 'other,' foreign opera, and by establishing this other's undesirable nature." See Pederson, "A. B. Marx," 89; and Applegate, "How German Is It?" 274–96.

mon with most nationally minded Germans, to explain perceived differences among societies in terms of nationality. Also in common with his contemporaries, he believed that a heightened understanding of the role of nationality in human affairs would lead to fuller development of individual and national identity. Marx, like Rochlitz before him, differed from men like Humboldt only in believing that music was crucial to the process of developing oneself and becoming national. For him, *Bildung*, musical judgment, and national consciousness were inseparable. Thus his concern for the state of musical affairs in Berlin and in Europe reflected a broader concern for cultural awakening among Germans. To improve the capacity to judge music was to strengthen an understanding of what it meant to be German in a world of nations, and Marx's program for the educated public included first learning about all nations' music. He approved of a "greater diversity in the repertoire," which he attributed to "rapidly spreading education" and a "closer community with other nations."[74] He urged Berliners to listen to as wide a range of compositions as possible, from all nations, because musical works "have their true foundation in our time and in the spirit of nations worthy of our attention." "If we wish to understand our times and ourselves," he concluded, we must study them all.[75]

Marx believed, moreover, that the educated public understood much less about nationality's influence on music than it did about, for instance, national schools of painting or the differences between French and German tragedy. National differences, he argued, were not just a matter of "incidental traits, styles, or fashions"; nor was "the essence, the heart" of an artwork everywhere the same. The truth was just the opposite, thought Marx. Italians and Germans may both have had the "the gift of artistic creativity," but general knowledge of the world could never advance on the basis of such banal observations. Real knowledge required "the recognition of differences," among the "temperature, the local manners, the mode of life, the state and religious circumstances, and so forth, of ourselves, the Italians, and the French." To deny such was to "lose consciousness of one's own intentions and tendencies."[76] To know others one must also understand oneself.

Yet for Marx, the study of nations usually yielded the same conclusion—that Germany's contributions as a nation were underappreciated, at home and in the world. Marx, like Rochlitz and even Mattheson before him, observed a lack of balance in musical life, an unthinking preference for Italian music, and a corrigible ignorance about German music. "A proper cultural

[74] "Ueber die Musik bei Schauspielaufführungen: ein Vorschlag zu Gunsten der Bühnen-Orch-ester," *BAMZ* 2, no. 42 (19 October 1825): 333.

[75] *BAMZ* 3, no. 52 (27 December 1826): 421.

[76] *BAMZ* 3, no. 45 (8 November 1826): 357–59.

life will begin," he asserted, when as many German operas were produced on the stage as French and Italian ones.[77] Marx clearly thought that German music was simply better, not just neglected. If people would only listen to more of it, then this fact would become clear to them too—so he hoped. Marx's sense of national identity had a harder, less universalist edge to it than that of some of his predecessors. As Sanna Pederson notes, his disdain for Italian music reflected a quasi-Hegelian analysis of how music history had progressed and where it was ultimately heading. "Just as surely as we Germans stand intellectually higher than does Italy with its Rossini," he wrote in 1825, so too would Germans eventually demand "a higher music."[78] And, thought Marx, they would eventually get it.

Marx's references to national differences in his writings consistently associated transient pleasures with the Italian national character and seriousness with the German. "The German," wrote Marx, "is too serious, too much inclined to reflection, to be able to apply himself happily and seriously to something that will lead to no results." The Italians, by contrast, tolerated ridiculous operatic plots for the sake of beautiful melody, and the French, a people "of very meager musical gifts," were "well entertained by cold, witty conversation pieces," valuing music "only as a superficial accompaniment" to such works. How could it be a coincidence, he wrote in another context, that all Italian composers "dispense with harmony" and "subordinate instrumentation to the requirements of the singing melody"? How could it be accident that the Germans should develop the symphony "to the highest state of perfection," while Italy or France contributed "as good as nothing" to it?[79] But the Germans were more than serious and instrumentally gifted. As Bernd Sponheuer has documented, Marx also refined, again through a Hegelian model of synthesis and transcendence, a century-long discourse on Germanness in music, in which the Germans became the culture that included all others, incorporating the best of all national styles into their own.[80] "German art," as he once put it, "is not exclusive but inclusive of Italian art."[81]

The question of national distinctions spoke, in Marx's view, to the future of music itself, especially among the Germans, who were the people best equipped to raise music to higher levels. In the lazy listening habits of

[77] *BAMZ* 2, no. 35 (24 August 1825): 283.
[78] *BAMZ* 2, no. 3 (19 January 1825): 23 (translation my own). Cited also in Pederson, "A. B. Marx," 91.
[79] *BAMZ* 1, no. 12 (15 March 1824): 108; *BAMZ* 2, no. 3 (19 January 1825): 23; *BAMZ* 3, no. 45 (8 November 1826): 358.
[80] Sponheuer, "Reconstructing Ideal Types," 36–58.
[81] *BAMZ* 2, no. 21 (25 May 1925): 168.

Berliners, Marx saw a vicious circle of incomprehension that threatened to stifle progress in musical life. If Germans only listened to Italian operatic music, which Marx considered a dead end in historical development, then they would always regard music as trivial, irrelevant to the serious matters of mankind. And if music was trivial, then no one need bother to listen to anything serious that might change their minds about music and raise them to a finer level of cultivation.

Marx's year of reckoning came in 1827. The April 11 issue of his journal carried on its front page the simple announcement, bordered with black, "Beethoven is dead." The news seemed to inspire Marx to new heights of righteous anger, or anxiety, on behalf of German music. Germans, he wrote a month later, had produced music at "a level far beyond" that of any other nation, yet they barely "recognized the value of their own native musical art." In June he harangued theater directors for allowing "foreign legions" of French composers, "in alliance with the Italians," "to occupy our stages" and shut out German works. "Have the courage," he urged them in October, to "create a German opera where you find none." Calling for a "patriotic fervor to mobilize for our own," he nevertheless insisted that "an equitable recognition of things foreign remains the honor of our people." Foreign music may have been "shabby, bare, superficial, and totally lacking in artistry and culture," but until Germans achieved "a more general progress" in their own cultivation, it achieved little to point that out.[82] As if to prove him right, at least about the uselessness of criticizing other nations' music, he saw the year ending with concert life "sunk so far in the public's estimation" that worthy performers could find no audience. The operas monopolizing the stages pulled the public down "into ever greater insipidness, corruption of the senses, and emptiness of the mind." He concluded gloomily that, despite his own "four years of effort," Berliners were in danger of losing sight altogether of "the majesty and the essence of art."[83]

MARX, BACH, AND THE *ST. MATTHEW PASSION*

The force that eventually drew Marx out of his pit of despair was not some hoped-for music of the future but old forgotten Bach, and in particular Bach's *St. Matthew Passion*. His paeans to Bach's genius were slow in coming. Before 1828, the elder Bach—indeed all the Bachs—had been a marginal presence in the journal, despite Marx's ties to the circles of Bach cultivation in Berlin. The reasons for his comparative neglect of Bach lay in

[82] *BAMZ* 4, no. 22 (30 May 1827): 173; no. 26 (27 June 1827): 201; no. 41 (10 October 1827): 328.; no. 26 (27 June 1827): 201.

[83] *BAMZ* 4, no. 52 (26 December 1827): 423–24.

his twin preoccupations with reviewing contemporary music and improving concert and theater life, neither of which projects brought Bach to the fore. Marx was not much interested in older music, except as a stick with which to beat up on Berlin's music directors for their shallow present-mindedness. References to it were few and far between. In 1825, he did suggest that one way to improve concert life would be to forage in the "treasure chamber" of old music. "Our own great countryman Handel," the "profundity and truth" of whose music had "hardly an equal," deserved attention, he thought, as did the "instrumental compositions, symphonies, concertos, etc. of the musical giant Sebastian Bach," whose "eternally youthful works have been lost to us through the fickle ways of public opinion."[84] A year later, he regretted in passing the paucity of available works of the "eternal J. S. Bach." Although he wrote more than once that contemporary music lovers ought to know more about older composers, his attitude toward actual performances of older music was distinctly lukewarm.[85] Even when he recommended it, he advised dispensing such music in small doses, lest the untrained ears of the public find it dull and refuse ever to listen to it again. A poor performance of an older work struck him as worse than none at all: in 1827, for instance, he took Zelter and the celebrated soprano Anna Milder-Hauptmann (who would later sing in Mendelssohn's revival) to task for an ill-conceived and ill-performed revival of Handel's *Joshua*.[86]

But in the course of the terrible year of 1827, Marx's interest in Bach intensified. He began to characterize him as not just great but "the greatest" and focus his growing concern for the neglected past fully on Bach. This change in tone may indicate that Marx had just learned of the existence of the *St. Matthew Passion*. He referred to it for the first time in the pages of the journal in January 1827, placing it alongside Beethoven's Ninth Symphony and Handel's *Messiah*, both oft-acknowledged treasures in his pantheon, as "our art works of the greatest genius."[87] According to his memoirs, written many years later, he had heard portions of the *Passion* at the

---

[84] A. B. Marx, "Einige Worte über das Konzertwesen," *BAMZ* 2, no. 45 (9 November 1825): 360–61.

[85] Marx's notice on the publication of Michael Haydn's *Missa solemnis*, *BAMZ* 3, no. 15 (12 April 1826): 113; see also, for example, Marx's review of *Klassische Werke älterer und neuerer Kirchenmusik*, *BAMZ* 3, no. 51 (20 December 1826): 409; and Marx, "Wer ist zu der Theilnahme an der Zeitung berufen," *BAMZ* 4, no. 2 (10 January 1827): 11.

[86] A. B. Marx, "Konzert von Madame Milder-Hauptmann," *BAMZ* 4, no. 2 (10 January 1827): 18.

[87] The context was a discussion of how much intellectual effort it took to be a great composer, with Marx arguing that works of genius invariably reflected "study, reflection, and the participation of all the capacities of mind." Marx, "Wer ist zu der Theilnahme?" 14.

Mendelssohns' house already in 1823 and had proceeded to "tell everyone about it." But nothing else in Marx's extensive written legacy confirms such timing, and several other pieces of evidence contradict it. For instance, as he prepared Berliners for the performance in 1829, he "freely" admitted that "five years ago [i.e., 1824]," he had "no notion of the existence of Bach's Passion music."[88] Between 1824 and 1827, his references to Bach in the journal also made no mention of its existence. In any case, in late January 1827, Marx did have Bach's "great double-chorus Passion" very much on his mind as he reviewed the recent publication of Handel's *Joshua*. Indeed, he abandoned Handel to lament Bach's obscurity, a composer "still unrecognized" despite the admiration of his contemporaries, despite "biographical sketches and carefully preserved manuscripts," despite "the legacy of his sons and students," despite our "endless reiteration" of his status "as the greatest composer ever." Recognition, intoned the prophet Marx, would have to wait upon "the appearance of his greatest work," but that would itself have to wait upon "such a time as people are capable of perceiving its essential idea, not simply its outward appearance."[89]

In 1827 Marx himself thought such a time lay far distant. His next reference to Bach, in May 1827, again suggested that "the time [had] not yet come" when the public could appreciate music of the past or "see its relevance to ourselves." People would have to "be awakened to full consciousness, know themselves fully" before something so distant from their own experience could make sense.[90] He favored more publication of scores and devoted an entire front page to announcing H. G. Nägeli's plans to publish an edition of Bach's B-minor Mass, "this precious patent of the nobility of the German spirit and German music, unattained by any other nation."[91] Throughout 1828, publishing plans for Bach's music remained at the top of his agenda: nothing was "more important" than "the task of broadening [its] availability."[92] The publication of Bach's English Suites, reflecting the "ever more public inclination of music lovers to Sebastian Bach," struck Marx as "one of the most remarkable and profound developments in the cultural history" of music, the "sun of a new day in the fog of our times."[93]

Meanwhile, he was working with his own publisher Schlesinger to guide the full score of the *St. Matthew Passion* to publication. In April he formally

---

[88] A. B. Marx, "Erster Bericht," *BAMZ* 6, no. 10 (7 March 1829): 74.

[89] *BAMZ* 4, no. 4 (24 January 1827): 28.

[90] A. B. Marx, review of *Kirchengesänge der berühmtesten ältern italienischen Meister*, *BAMZ* 4, no. 22 (30 May 1827): 170–71.

[91] A. B. Marx, "Wichtige Nachricht," *BAMZ* 4, no. 51 (19 December 1827): 409.

[92] A. B. Marx, review of *Klassische Werke*, 89.

[93] *BAMZ* 5, no. 13 (26 March 1828): 97; *BAMZ* 4, no. 52 (26 December 1827): 424.

announced the plans for "the greatest work of our greatest master, the greatest and holiest musical work of all peoples, the great Passion music of Matthew the Evangelist by Johann Sebastian Bach." Overwhelmed by the significance of the moment, he broke into verse: "I thought last night / That I saw the moon as I slept / But when I awoke / There unexpectedly came the sun!"[94] So unbounded was Marx's enthusiasm for this project that he began to write as though the publication of Bach's *Passion* would fix everything wrong with the contemporary musical world, scattering the corrupters of art and invigorating the forces of good. "What wondrous times break forth!" he exclaimed, beyond what "the boldest prediction" foretold. Moving on to the chief significance of the event, he declared it "the total vindication of everything this journal has advocated." We have never followed fashion or courted popular opinion, he pointed out, seeking only to prepare the public "for a new and higher period of musical art." Now the time of "fulfillment" had arrived, when Germany would not longer be "deprived of its greatest treasure" by its ignorant pursuit of the "lower sensuality of the Italians" and the "soulless play of the French." Thanks to Marx's journal alone, he implied, the way had been prepared for the public to receive "this greatest work of German music."[95]

Rhetorically excessive though such claims were (and strangely decoupled from any discussion of performance), Marx was right in asserting that the rediscovery of Bach and the *St. Matthew Passion* fit comfortably within the project he had set himself in establishing the *Berliner Allgemeine Musikalische Zeitung*. Marx's conception of the essential character of German music, though modeled initially on Beethoven and the symphony, could accommodate Bach and his *Passion*, largely through the category of seriousness, of intellectual, spiritual profundity. In the months to come, these became the oft-repeated themes of his analysis of Bach. But the advocacy of Bach also allowed Marx to demonstrate the links among national identity, self-knowledge, and musical judgment. Knowing Bach, one would come to know oneself as a German, because knowing Bach entailed understanding not only the Christian, Protestant heritage of Germany, not only the intellectual, inward turn in German character, but also the musical complexity that was as much a part of being German as was the German language itself.

To be sure, a tension existed between Marx's powerful future orientation and this sudden turn to the past. He seemed aware of it and set about explaining why, especially in light of his own theories of historical progress,

---

[94] "Ich gedachte in der Nacht, / Dass ich den Mond sähe im Schlaf; / Als ich aber erwachte, / Ging unvermuthet die Sonne auf!" *BAMZ* 5, no. 17 (23 April 1828): 131.

[95] A. B. Marx, "Hoechst wichtige und glückliche Nachricht," *BAMZ* 5, no. 17 (23 April 1828): 131–32.

studying Bach was so necessary a part of the present. The anomaly, it seems, lay not with composers themselves, who had not forgotten Bach: Mozart and Beethoven had studied and admired him. Hence the symphonies of Beethoven, which Marx had long depicted as the apogee of musical development, had already taken Bach into account. The music-loving public was another matter. Its long neglect of Bach had, in Marx's new perspective, almost certainly contributed to the current depraved state of musical taste and the alienation from German character that such taste reflected. To recover Bach was to recover oneself and to restore musical life to its properly progressive course of development.

But performance was still another matter, and here Marx was overtaken by developments that he did not instigate, most likely to his regret. We have only Devrient's memory that Marx doubted the viability of any plan to perform the *St. Matthew Passion*—and the implications of Marx's writings in 1828, which in one prominent case drew attention to the dangers of introducing a difficult and unfamiliar work to an unprepared public. In April 1828 Gasparo Spontini, the Italian-born French citizen brought to Berlin by Friedrich Wilhelm III as the director of court opera, conducted a concert in the Royal Opera House to mark *Busstag*, the Day of Repentance. For Spontini to be conducting a concert was notable in itself. He rarely ventured beyond opera, indeed rarely beyond his own operas. That this concert should have consisted entirely of German church and instrumental works, including the first public performance in Berlin of the Credo of Bach's B-minor Mass, along with works of Haydn, Handel, and Beethoven, was richly ironic. Spontini, who had been in Berlin since 1819, had never learned German and never expressed interest in bringing German music to the Berlin public. Nor would such an exercise in national education have made any sense to him. Marx, in his frequent calls for just such concerts as this one, had probably expected that a figure like Zelter would bring them forth, never Spontini. And although he had maintained good relations with the powerful director, defending Spontini even while publishing Ludwig Rellstab's devastatingly negative critiques, Marx could not on this occasion act the courtier. No matter how "worthy of respect and thanks" the idea of this concert may have been and no matter how "well-meaning" Spontini himself was, the execution of it represented a disaster, for the Berlin public and for German music. The problem was not just that Spontini, in the fashion of the day, had presented mere bits and pieces of great works, but that his execution of them missed their point entirely. He seated the orchestra "in the Parisian fashion" such that the brass section overwhelmed everything else, he had no sense of rhythm, he exaggerated tempi (taking everything either too slow or too fast), and he demonstrated a total inability to conduct anything fugal. Moreover, he made alterations to Bach's harmonization and orchestration that changed the piece practically beyond recognition. "Had the public had previous knowledge of this masterwork," wrote Marx, then someone might have corrected his errors.[96] But ignorance had bred error, and the error of this poor performance now threatened to leave intact Bach's reputation as a tedious harmonist with no sense of either melody or drama.

Meanwhile, Mendelssohn had been rehearsing the *St. Matthew Passion* among friends probably since the fall of 1827. By the end of 1828, he and Devrient had obtained both Zelter's and the board of the Singakademie's permission to perform the *Passion* in public in March 1829, rehearsals with the entire Singakademie had begun, and the initiative in the greater project of Bach revival had slipped out of Marx's hands. Neither Schlesinger in Berlin nor Nägeli in Switzerland had yet managed to publish the *St. Matthew Passion* or the B-minor Mass, these "greatest works of Bach," despite Marx urging them publicly to hurry up.[97] On February 21, 1829, Marx conceded the inevitability of the performance and appointed himself its publicist. His journal announced, in another of his full-page displays, the imminence of "an important and happy event for the musical world and for Berlin": "In the first days of March, under the direction of Mr. Felix Mendelsohn [*sic*] Bartholdy, the Passion music, following the Gospel of Matthew, by Johann Sebastian Bach, will be performed. The greatest and holiest work of the greatest composer will come to life after nearly a century of obscurity, in a high festival of religion and of art."[98] To prepare the public, he devoted almost the entirety of the next two issues to extensive analysis of the work, followed in subsequent issues with lengthy reviews of the performances. The *St. Matthew Passion* did not leave Marx's front page for six weeks running in 1829, an extravagant feast of attention never before granted any other composer or piece of music in any music journal. After the initial performances in Berlin, Marx published reviews of performances elsewhere in Germany. This "press campaign" was, in Martin Geck's estimation, something new in the history of music, the first time "the ground was systematically prepared for a particular musical work"—and, one might add, the first time so sustained an effort was made to instruct people's reactions to it after the performance was over.[99] With or without the published score, Marx intended that no readers of his journal have any doubt that they

[96] A. B. Marx, "Spontinis grosses Konzert im Opernhause," *BAMZ* 5, no. 19 (7 May 1828): 152–53.

[97] A. B. Marx, reviewing recently published Bach cantatas, *BAMZ* 5, no. 31 (30 July 1828): 243.

[98] A. B. Marx, "Bekanntmachung," *BAMZ* 6, no. 8 (21 February 1829): 57.

[99] Geck, 25.

had heard in the *St. Matthew Passion* the "full realization of the Ideal of composition."[100]

This remark, made many years later, sheds light on the goals of Marx's writing on the *Passion* in those weeks of March and April 1829. Although (as a later chapter will discuss) his main purpose was to show how Bach's music realized the message of Christianity, he also sought to explain the meaning of Bach's resurrection in Marx's time. This allowed Marx to recapitulate themes which had always preoccupied him, chief among them his own role in championing the improvement of Berlin and German musical life. Not shy about appropriating Mendelssohn, he saw "in this act of a young artist" the sign that "our prediction of a new and more thoughtful period of music" had arrived. His journal, he wrote, had always articulated a progressive vision of musical life despite the "enervation and hopelessness of most of our contemporaries" and the "misunderstanding and opposition of so many of our fellow artists": "Every word I have written on music, every resistance I have offered to the errors and delusions of our times, finds meaning and vindication only in the expectation and prediction of a time when the trumpery of today's fashionable shallowness and vanity will be cast off and thrown away."[101]

That Bach should be the instrument of this awakening struck Marx as fate or perhaps the cunning of history that brought this music to the public precisely at "the moment, in which Bach's song of the sacrifice of Jesus must be heard again."[102] Even Forkel, the former emissary of Bach and herald of his patriotic significance for Germans, had missed the significance of the *Passion* music. Bach's "importance to German self-understanding" stood now revealed in all its fullness and profundity.[103] Marx believed, moreover, that the Berlin public had finally gotten the point. They had flocked to the performance, not once but three times, each time filling the hall to overflowing. Unlike his usual suspicion of popular events, Marx put the best possible interpretation on the objective fact of public interest in the *Passion*. The music had "made a deep impression on the sensibilities of all its listeners," he wrote. It had affected a broad swath of the Berlin public and drawn them away from all other "attractive and remarkable events" that the city offered. Even better, people had listened to the *Passion* several times over, thus following one of his own dictums for increasing musical understanding. He still urged people to study the score when it was finally published, but

---

[100] Marx, *Erinnerungen aus meinem Leben*, 86.

[101] A. B. Marx, "Bekanntmachung," *BAMZ* 6, no. 9 (28 February 1829): 65.

[102] Ibid., 66.

[103] A. B. Marx, "Zweiter Bericht über die Passionsmusik," *BAMZ* 6, no. 11 (14 March 1829): 80–81.

meanwhile, he expressed himself satisfied with public reception of the work.[104]

Finally, the Berlin reception of the *St. Matthew Passion* expressed for Marx a growing consciousness of German identity itself, because not only had no other nation produced a Bach but no other nation was capable of appreciating him. With what one can imagine was the satisfaction of prejudices confirmed, he quoted what the French press had to say about the Berlin musical scene. According to the view from Paris, "nothing of interest" was going on there in March 1829 except for "a couple repetitions of old works, with mixed success, in short the very picture of stagnation." From the perspective of the *BAMZ*, of course, the case was just the opposite. Such revivals represented "a spiritual armament" in which "the German character" revealed itself "at its best" and in contrast to "French coldness and paralysis."[105] An anonymous contributor was even more explicit on the national significance of an immersion in Bach's work: "Finally the German recognizes the outstanding value of his fatherland and is filled with noble pride." In short, there was "no land in the world today in which true learning and art are more valued and more cultivated than in Germany."[106]

Marx's media campaign represented, then, both a new use for the music periodical and the culmination of a journalistic tradition going back more than a century. His promotion of the *St. Matthew Passion* embodied a long-standing concern for the valuation of music among the educated public. It expressed the conviction, common to so many music periodicals over the years, that the distinctively German contribution to music was lost in a flood of foreign music, and it represented the hope that greater learning could correct the public's "errors and delusions." Music journalism continued to reflect such attitudes in the years to come, although Marx himself left the business at the end of 1830 for a position at the University of Berlin. In taking his leave, he urged his readers to "stay true to the task" of striving toward "pure thinking and pure judgment of music." "The progress of art and of a people" were inseparable, he once again reminded his readers, and both required the most stringent truth-telling, the highest standards, and the greatest possible freedom of opinion.[107]

Still, neither Marx nor Rochlitz thought that reading about music or even listening to a great deal of it would result in the understanding both

---

[104] A. B. Marx, "Dritter Bericht," *BAMZ* 6, no. 12 (21 March 1829): 89, 91.

[105] A. B. Marx, "Blick ins Ausland," *BAMZ* 6, no. 11 (14 March 1829): 86; Marx, "Vierter Bericht über die Pasionsmusik," *BAMZ* 6, no. 13 (28 March 1829): 100.

[106] B., "Grosse Passion von Johann Sebastian Bach," *BAMZ* 6, no. 12 (21 March 1829): 93.

[107] A. B. Marx, Marx, "Abschied des Redakteurs," *BAMZ* 7, no. 52 (24 December 1830): 414–16.

considered so crucial to the development of the German nation. Both advocated the amateur practice of music, through school and private instruction, as well as voluntary associations. Marx frequently reviewed manuals of musical instruction or printed articles by musical pedagogues. The 1829 performance of the *St. Matthew Passion* represented, among other things, the triumph of Zelter's chorus of amateur singers. After six years of carping about the infrequency of their public appearances and the halfheartedness of their delivery, Marx had nothing but praise for these "outstanding dilettantes" after the first performance, wondering at their "sense of artistry and religiosity." As for Zelter himself, the man who had for almost thirty years stood at the intersection of professional and amateur music making in Berlin, Marx finally conceded his worth. The third performance, conducted by Zelter on Good Friday, seemed to Marx the best one yet, enhanced by the solemnity of the day itself.[108] Perhaps Marx was looking ahead to quitting the journal and thought to enlist Zelter's help in obtaining a position at the university, or perhaps the Singakademie and Zelter really had achieved their finest hour. What one cannot doubt is the centrality of amateurism to the distinctive way that musical culture developed in Germany, and to that we now turn.

[108] A. B. Marx, Marx, "Fünfter Bericht über die Passionsmusik," *BAMZ* 6, no. 16 (18 April 1829): 121.

Musical Amateurism and the Exercise of Taste

Amateurism flourishes when people take art seriously, and the early nineteenth century in Germany was such a time, particularly for music lovers. The more important the existence of serious music became to the educated elites, the more widespread became their desire to make music themselves, and the more journals, manuals, teachers, and organizations flourished to feed this desire. The 1829 performance of the *St. Matthew Passion* could not have succeeded without such "second-hand artists" as audience and performers.[1] Yet the amateur practice of music, so expressive of music's origins as a communal activity, usually retreats into the shadows cast by concerts, composers, and professional orchestras. Amateur musicianship discourages analysis by its ordinariness; even social historians mention it only in passing.

---

[1] Helmut Koopmann, "Dilettantismus: Bemerkungen zu einem Phänomen der Goethezeit," in *Studien zur Goethezeit: Festschrift für Lieselotte Blumenthal*, ed. Helmut Holtzhauer and Bernhard Zeller (Weimar, 1968), 178. For an overview of Bach cultivation in nineteenth-century amateur groups, see Susanne Oschmann, "Die Bach-Pflege der Singakademien," in Michael Heinemann and Hans-Joachim Hinrichsen, eds., *Bach und die Nachwelt*, vol. 1, *1750–1850* (Laaber, 1997), 305–47.

The music writers of the early nineteenth century were not so reticent. *Liebhaber* and *Dilettanten*, who seemed both to misunderstand art and yet were needed to support it, were the object of much attention and anxiety. Amateurism expressed a modern tension between the creators of art and its consumers, and it reflected expectations about the differing roles of men and women in society. But it also hinted at an older class relationship: the professional artist was a servant, whereas the amateur artist was an aristocrat, a leisured practitioner of something that the lower orders (with a whiff of moral inferiority) did only for money.

A reconstruction of the amateur musical scene in the early nineteenth century in Berlin and Germany thus illuminates the changing values of this society. Those who practiced music as amateurs were less troubled by questions of artistic autonomy or class or gender than were their commentators. But for both amateurs and their observers, music making demonstrated taste, and as Carl Dahlhaus has observed, taste "served an unambiguously social function," helping a group "to cohere from within and to insulate itself from without."[2] The group whose coherence chiefly concerns us here is the German nation, experienced by its members in the practice of music. Amateurism was a kind of citizenship in the nation, a realm not of necessity but of self-expression and of freedom.

DEFINING AMATEURISM

A dilettante, wrote Goethe in 1797, was "a lover of the arts who not only observes and enjoys them but also wants to take part in their practice." Because the dilettante existed, thought Goethe, in between recognized social roles, dilettantism spoke to his own sense of being all things—poet, scientist, courtier, traveler, civil servant, artist, human being.[3] Yet whatever kinship he felt with those only half engaged in their pursuit of some art or knowledge was tempered by his condemnation, self-directed as well, of "everything arbitrary and partial, everything only subjectively understood, incapable of intensity or consequence, everything thrill-seeking and artificial."[4] The dilettante, suggested Goethe and after him generations of critics, simply followed the "tendencies of the time," whereas the artist "com-

---

[2] Carl Dahlhaus, *Nineteenth-Century Music*, trans. J. Bradford Robinson (Berkeley and Los Angeles, 1989), 246.

[3] Goethe wrote about amateurism in the context of his effort to reinvigorate the Renaissance ideal of the gentleman-artist. See Hans Rudolf Vaget, *Dilettantismus und Meistershaft. Zum Problem des Dilettantismus bei Goethe: Praxis, Theorie, Zeitkritik* (Munich: Winkler Verlag, 1971). See also Helmut Koopmann, "Dilettantismus," and Gerhart Baumann, "Goethe: 'Über den Dilettantismus,'" *Euphorion: Zeitschrift für Literaturgeschichte* 46 (1952), 350.

[4] Quoted in Baumann, "Goethe," 353.

mands the times." The dilettante was an avid follower of rules, and a plagiarist at heart, expecting recognition for just trying. The artist, and here Goethe anticipated the European reception of Beethoven, "makes the rules" or "gives them to himself."[5] But defiance of rules merely to defy them betrayed dilettantism as surely as did slavish respect for them. Difference did not constitute originality, and following rules did not suggest one understood their essence. Goethe believed, finally, that dilettantism showed the greatest presumption "where the art itself has no firm regulating principle, as in poetry, gardening, and theater." Music, the most suitable arena for the dilettante, did reward sheer effort, he thought, and by its containment of expression within clearly regulated structures—his model was J. S. Bach's *Art of the Fugue*—prevented the dilettante from "losing himself along purely subjective false paths."[6]

Goethe was writing about dilettantes just as other writers began to regard music not as the most regulated but the most free, subjective, and expressive of all the arts. At the same time, a "crisis in the teaching of musical craftsmanship" was emerging, expressed in Beethoven's insistence on "the inviolability of the figured bass" even as he violated it or Schubert's single lesson in 1828 with Simon Sechter, the Viennese master of the figured bass, or even Mendelssohn's loyalty to Carl Friedrich Zelter. "The instruction that was meant to make professional composers superior to dilettantes," writes Dahlhaus, "resembled exercises in a dead language," codifiable but irrelevant.[7] Aesthetic transformation and crisis of craft both reflected the "existential unsettling" of the musical profession itself, with guilds dissolving, courts and churches shedding their musicians like excess baggage, and no alternative means of employment widely available.[8]

As professional musicians doubted and scrambled, the amateurs flourished. Yet the professional crisis did not beget amateurism as response; new amateur music groups did not replace their professional counterparts. The expansion of musical amateurism resulted from the convergence of new forms of sociability, new aspirations to cultivation, and new technologies of print and keyboard. It took professional musicians many decades to develop an independent professional culture with conservatories, big-city orchestras, university chairs in musicology, and scholarly journals. Amateurs, in contrast, achieved their simpler goals earlier, through the means of voluntary associations, private instruction, and musical self-help manuals—all of which

---

[5] Ibid., 351.

[6] Ibid., 352–53.

[7] Dahlhaus, *Nineteenth-Century Music*, 26–27, 245–46.

[8] See Georg Sowa, *Anfänge institutioneller Musikerziehung in Deutschland (1800–1843)* (Regensburg, 1973), 17–22; see also the discussion in chapter 2 above.

were easy to maintain and relatively inexpensive. Even some of the institutional foundations for the training of professional musicians—like the Ripienschule in Berlin—were laid to serve dilettantes as much as professionals.

All this speaks to the crucial role that amateurism played in the evolution of Germans as the "people of music." Throughout the nineteenth century, amateur musical associations flourished in the German lands as in no other European country, and they provide us with an important clue to, in Marcel Beaufils's phrase, "how Germany became musical."[9] Amateurism, with its notions of enlightenment and moral improvement through music, animated activities from book writing to institution building, school reform, and of course a lot of singing. Although amateurs, like visitors to museums, are hard to catch in the act of artistic appreciation, we learn much about them in the publications and organizations through which they learned. In Berlin itself, the best-placed guide to amateur musical culture is the man who became its unofficial guardian, Carl Friedrich Zelter.

ZELTER AND THE SINGAKADEMIE OF BERLIN

So central is Zelter to institutional histories of musical life in Germany that it is easy to overlook the extent to which his achievements almost entirely involved the encouragement of amateur participation in music making, and by extension amateur support for those who earned their living by music. Carl Dahlhaus called the institutions he founded "a nearly complete system . . . through which the participation of music in the *Bildungsidee* of the classical-romantic era was institutionalized"—an oblique reference to the amateur focus of Zelter's work, for what was the "idea of *Bildung*" but the battle cry of dilettantes.[10] At the same time, music's capacity to participate in this idea came to the rescue of artists surviving on the dwindling resources of aristocratic patronage and looking to other social classes to support their work.[11] Zelter's life extended across the full range of the changes in musical life in the fifty years leading up to the 1829 *St. Matthew Passion*. His lobbying, teaching, and association building set patterns of interaction between musical amateurs and professionals that lasted for generations and gave a distinctive shape to German national life.

His own pursuit of music, as he recalled it, initially followed the *stürmish* trope of young Werther's flight from practicality to sensibility and from health to febrility and illness. It also illustrates the extent to which a life in

---

[9] Marcel Beaufils, *Comment l'Allemagne est devenue musicienne* (Paris, 1983).
[10] Carl Dahlhaus, foreword to *Studien zur Musikgeschichte Berlins*, 7.
[11] Applegate, "How German Is It?," 274–89.

music conflicted with the "static dull complexities" of the guild towns and cities of central Europe.[12] Zelter was the second son of a successful mason in Berlin who owned his own brickyard on the outskirts of Potsdam. Both sons were trained from childhood to join the trade, a natural path made all the more irresistible by the early death of young Zelter's elder brother.[13] As Zelter told the story, music entered his life at age eight when he received a violin for Christmas, then later instruction in piano and organ.[14] But he also met court musicians during construction breaks: he listened to orchestra rehearsals at Sans Souci while his father repaired palace buildings and met military musicians while working on the cadet academy in Berlin. In 1775, at age seventeen, he nearly died of smallpox and during his convalescence practiced the violin to promote his return to "bodily health." But practice soon became a passion—an unhealthy one, to which his father objected, saying that "one cannot eat bread" from music and "a true craftsman may sink a little but he will never drown."[15]

The next twelve years brought after-hours efforts to learn music while serving the building trade. The latter culminated in Zelter achieving master-mason status in 1783. The former had miscellaneous outcomes. He hung out with Johann Friedrich George, the "rough" but "talented" city musician of Berlin; he played in the Döbbelin'schen Theater orchestra; he composed a cantata for the dedication of a church organ. Another paternal maxim held that "the craftsman is the true *Bürger*," and a number of these musical episodes skirted the edges of *bürgerlich* respectability. During his association with the free-spirited city musician George, who had farm animals ranging free in his city yard, dogs sleeping in his bed, and fireworks going off in his garden, Zelter serenaded women and blew trumpets from city towers.[16] Both were legitimate parts of the job, to be sure, but at the same time indications that this was no employment for an honorable guildsman or an aspirant to the higher dignities of court service.[17] According to

---

[12] Walker, *German Home Towns*, 130.

[13] Ledebur, *Tonkünstler Lexicon Berlins*, 661–62.

[14] Karl Friedrich Zelter, *Selbstdarstellung*, ed. Willi Reich (Zurich, 1955), 16; see also Dietrich Fischer-Dieskau, *Carl Friedrich Zelter und das Berliner Musikleben seiner Zeit* (Berlin, 1997), 9–30.

[15] This is a nonliteral translation of the expression "Handwerk könne wohl sinken, aber niemals ertrinken" (Zelter, *Selbstdarstellung*, 19). On Zelter's illness, see an earlier edition of his autobiographical writings: Karl Friedrich Zelter, *Darstellungen seines Lebens*, ed. Johann-Wolfgang Schottländer (Weimar, 1931), 3–5.

[16] Zelter, *Selbstdarstellung*, 22–25.

[17] The life of the court musician carried its own moral hazards for the "*wahre Bürger*," and Zelter's father did not approve of that either: "craftsmanship alone," he lectured his son, "prevails over everything, especially over high status and lordly dependency" (Zelter, *Selbstdarstellung*, 19).

the chronicler Ledebur, the city-musician period was bad for Zelter's morals, and George himself eventually sent him away.[18]

Even the composition of the church cantata, seemingly pious enough to suit any parent, had too much of the public world of concertizing and publicity. Zelter's father read about the performance of his son's composition in one of the Berlin dailies and was more confused than angry—who was this Zelter, he asked his son, did he know him, had he met him?[19] The hometown citizen was known by who he was: his *Eigentum* referred not to the property he owned but to the qualities, the worthiness, inherent in him and his place. *Eigentum* was earned by steady effort and proper behavior, not striving and pushing. In contrast, young Zelter had thrown himself before the public as an unknown quantity and let the equally anonymous public make its own judgment on his worth. To be a musician at the end of the eighteenth century meant that one had to live in such public space.

After the death of his father in 1787, Zelter entered the circles of movers and doers, like the *Kenner* and *Liebhaber* (both voluntary statuses and therefore amateur ones of a sort) of J. C. F. Rellstab's public concerts. As Zelter's life indicates, the contrasting worlds of static hometown and mobile city existed side by side in central Europe up to the founding of the German Empire in 1871, by which time most traces of hometown constitutions had disappeared. Berlin at the end of the eighteenth century had characteristics of the guild town, the residential city on the prince's payroll, and the modernizing city of free enterprise and public spheres. This hybrid urbanity enabled ambitious men from the guilds, like Zelter, to mix with people of higher education, wealth, and birth. Zelter had attended a *Gymnasium*, the Joachimsthalsche, for a few undistinguished years, and good masons were among the most scientifically adept of the guildsmen. Still, his acquaintance with literature and philosophy was meager, and his expectations of musical employment were confined to court and guild. In 1782, in the manner of apprentice to master, Zelter had laid his compositions before Johann Philipp Kirnberger, the great musical theorist and guardian of the Bach legacy. Kirnberger became the first in a long line of people unimpressed by Zelter the composer. He, like Zelter's father, told him that "a common craftsman is always a respectable person, whereas nothing is more pitiable than a common artist, such as you will become. . . . Stay with your trowel!"[20]

Characteristically seeking to mediate between old ways and new, Zelter

[18] Ibid., 23.
[19] Fischer-Dieskau, *Zelter*, 17.
[20] Ibid., 23.

threw away neither his trowel nor his music. Instead, he sought out another master and found another way into music. Carl Friedrich Christian Fasch, court harpsichordist and composer, had probably first encountered Zelter as a builder around the court. From 1784 to 1789 Zelter took as many lessons from Fasch as he could, while continuing his paying job as a mason in charge of several major projects. Fasch gave Zelter instruction in the rules of harmony as codified in the writings of C. P. E. Bach, Kirnberger, and Marpurg—in other words, the professional training in the craft of composition that this guildsman sought. Zelter absorbed the teachings as binding guides to proper composition and stuck to them ever after, lending his own music the antiquated air that Goethe favored but more forward-looking musicians could not admire. Fasch's work in turning the mason into a composer gave Zelter an eighteenth-century version of credentials but was not, in the end, what eventually made him a leader in Berlin musical life. What mattered more was Fasch's side project, into which he drew Zelter because he increasingly lacked the energy to supervise it himself. It was an amateur singing group, and in this new style of musical organization Zelter found his footing in a musical world neither dependent on court patronage nor ruled by guild statutes.

In its origins, Fasch's singing group reflected a general sense among north German musicians, to which many a music periodical attested, that musical life stood in need of reform and revitalization. Johann Friedrich Reichardt, believing the new audiences would respond to musical experiences that demanded more of them, did not just write about it; in 1783 he also sponsored serious concerts, the so-called *concerts spirituels* on the Parisian model. In the right hands, he considered church music well suited to the task of musical improvement, but unfortunately, he claimed, "not a single choir" could be heard "singing cleanly and well."[21] Other musicians, reform minded like Reichardt, proposed ways to improve the state of choral singing. The most utopian among these reformers was probably J. C. F. Rellstab, who sought to support destitute women by training them for paid work in choirs. Nothing came of any such schemes until Fasch heard a performance, under Reichardt's direction, of a sixteen-part mass by the early baroque composer Orazio Benevoli (1605–72) and was seized by the desire, according to Reichardt's account, to create a capstone for his distinguished career with the composition of his own sixteen-part mass. Fasch, remembered Zelter, wanted "to leave behind a work" in which "knowledgeable"

[21]Johann Friedrich Reichardt, *Briefe, die Musik betreffend*, ed. Grita Herre and Walther Siegmund-Schultze (Leipzig, 1976), 141. See also chapter 5.

Carl Friedrich Zelter. Lithograph after a painting by Carl Begas, c. 1826. By permission of the Bildarchiv Preussischer Kulturbesitz / Art Resource, NY.

people of the distant future would recognize the capabilities of a "German harmonist."[22] Whether with an eye to posterity or an appetite for canonization, Fasch certainly wanted to hear his work in his lifetime. Disappointed with the efforts of school choirs and court singers, he put his own little circle of private music students to work. They began gathering to practice

[22] Karl Friedrich Zelter, *Karl Friedrich Christian Fasch Gedenkschrift* (Berlin, 1801), in *AMZ* 4, no. 2 (1801): 24.

multipart singing probably in 1790 in the summer gazebo of Charlotte Dietrich, stepdaughter of a government official. Presented with the challenge of Fasch's mass, they settled in for the long haul, establishing regular Tuesday evening rehearsals, recruiting a few professional singers, and even stepping out into the public to perform a few simple choral works in 1791.

The story of the origins of the Singakademie, a group that was to be the model for hundreds of other amateur choral groups across German-speaking Europe and North America, shows the disparate forces at work in musical culture at the turn of the eighteenth century. Not only were financially strapped courts opening up performances to a paying audience, but underemployed court musicians were themselves looking for both work and influence in an amorphous new marketplace for music.[23] Fasch and Reichardt both earned a living from the Prussian court, but in neither case was the court musically active enough after 1778 to engage fully their productive energies or (especially in the case of Reichardt) give them the arena for the influence they wanted. So underemployed was Fasch that he had taken to studying medicine, chemistry, and mathematics; he also assembled "an exact register of all European military forces on land and sea," invented a card game called Grand-Patience, and built three-story high houses out of playing cards.[24] Little wonder, then, that he could find the time to teach on the side and direct an amateur singing group. Always ailing, Fasch seems not to have immersed himself in this new musical public to the extent that Reichardt and Zelter did—the former out of necessity (he lost his court position in 1794 because of his radical political views) and the latter out of choice. Still, this variety of motivations and goals, in which necessity, personal ambition, social improvement, and the search for diversion all jostled against each other, typifies engagement in these new public spaces. There seemed to be no point to an amateur singing group in 1791, no compelling cultural meaning behind its existence—even the stories of Fasch's desire to hear his own compositions have a ring of retrospective invention. But precisely this emptiness made it the ideal vessel in which over the years a number of new ideas about why music existed and what role it played in society could gather and cohere.

Zelter joined the group in the summer of 1791, Fasch paying him the compliment of allowing him the professional musicians' waiver of dues. At the time, the group had about twenty-two singers and no name; within two

---

[23] Reimer, *Hofmusik in Deutschland,* 125–41.

[24] Zelter believed that he first won Fasch's admiration by advising him on roofing for the card house. On Fasch's eccentricities, see Zelter, *Selbstdarstellung,* 82–84.

years, its numbers had grown to forty-one. It still had no name and, in Zelter's view, no sense of purpose either. He complained that the rehearsals were more like "singing teas" and that the pieces they attempted were too difficult for such lackadaisical practitioners. He longed "to bring order and seriousness to matters."[25] Through his acquaintance with members of the Royal Academy of Fine Arts, he obtained permission for the group to rehearse in the academy's large but leaky entrance hall, and at the same time pushed Fasch to obtain formal associational status for the group. The move to the academy's foyer gave the group its name, the Singakademie, but more importantly it lent it the dignity of the place itself. "Here we could practice among the arts and sciences," he wrote in 1800, "undisturbed, independent, and free."[26]

There could have been no more eloquent expression of the dignity of amateurism or music's claim to equal status among the works of intellect and creativity. Music had never held even a minor place among the fine arts or the sciences that the two royal academies had been founded to promote. In subsequent years, Zelter made the claim to inclusion even more explicit. But for the time being, his vision of musical improvement extended only to instituting extra rehearsals without tea and cookies and substituting for the ever-weakening Fasch as musical director of the group. Although many early members drifted away in the face of extra demands, the Singakademie gathered plenty to replace them. By the time of Fasch's death in 1800 it numbered around a hundred and included many representatives of the educated elite of the city as well as a smattering of professional musicians. It rarely performed publicly, but its rehearsals became semipublic performances themselves. They attracted visitors from Berlin and other cities, most famously Beethoven during his tour of northern Germany in 1795–96. Its musical emphasis remained sacred choral music, so important in the eyes of reformers to music's mission of moral improvement. In its first three years, the group mainly rehearsed works of Fasch himself, perhaps still hoping to master that sixteen-part mass. Then in January 1794 Fasch introduced J. S. Bach's double-chorus motet *Komm, Jesu, Komm* into rehearsals, thus sending the Singakademie off on its thirty-five-year journey to the *St. Matthew Passion*. The first decade also saw it revive interest in Handel among Berliners. A first Handel revival had begun auspiciously in 1786 with Johann Adam Hiller's large-scale performance of *Messiah* modeled on the London extravaganza of 1784, but had dwindled to nothing, that is, until Fasch

[25] Ibid., 64–65.

[26] This is Zelter's 1800 entry into the daybook of the Singakademie, outlining its first decade of existence, reprinted in Zelter, *Selbstdarstellung*, 66–68. The academy's building on Unter den Linden housed both the Academy of Fine Arts and the Academy of Learning.

began regular rehearsals of choruses from *Messiah*, *Judas Maccabeus*, and other oratorios.[27]

By 1800 the meaning of the group could be deduced from the name it-self, or so Zelter felt confident enough to claim in his obituary of Fasch: it was a real academy, Zelter wrote, "a kind of artistic corps for the cultivation of holy music," and "every serious-minded friend of art" will find in join-ing it "as much satisfaction through serious art as is possible."[28] Steeped in the language of enlightenment, the Fasch obituary expressed Zelter's devel-oping sense of music's capacity to enable the moral improvement of all who engaged seriously in it. He depicted a community in which class differences ceased to exist and the pursuit of art, separated from commerce and profit, established a place for self-fulfillment and service. "Virtue dwelt" there, he wrote, for "every outsider and every member": "attentiveness without visi-ble exertion, beauty without privilege, multiplicity of all estates, ages, and trades, without affectation; delight in a fine art without weariness; the young and the old, the aristocrat and the burgher; the joy and the discipline; the father and the daughter, the mother with her son, and every possible mixing of the sexes and the estates." The Singakademie, he concluded, was "like a flower garden in the spring," delighting "the most refined sensibility of the educated and cultivated person."[29]

WOMEN IN THE RISE OF MUSICAL AMATEURISM

The presence of women's voices among the singers has often invited cel-ebratory reflections on the march of musical progress. On the occasion of the two-hundredth anniversary of the Singakademie's founding, its official historian Gottfried Eberle wrote that the first performance "must have caused a small sensation," because "for the first time in the history of Berlin, indeed in Germany altogether, women and men sang sacred music together in a choir." "A new 'sound' . . . was heard," he continued, and "it must have been fascinating."[30] Strictly speaking, Eberle is right: women and men in Protestant Europe had not sung together in church as choir mem-bers (though they had sung together as worshippers); Bach's cantatas, motets, and Passion music had employed the voices of the all-male student choirs of the Thomasschule. Yet professional women had sung together

[27] When Beethoven visited a rehearsal, the group was practicing a chorus from Handel's *Judas Maccabeus*, which Beethoven had already heard in Vienna.

[28] Obituary reprinted in Zelter, *Selbstdarstellung*, 71.

[29] The reference to gardens evokes both Kant's notoriously greater respect for the aesthetics of gardening than music and Goethe's interest in gardening as art. Ibid., 71–72.

[30] Eberle, *Sing-Akademie*, 27.

with professional men, both as soloists and in the mixed choruses of opera companies.[31] Most recently, Hiller's performance of Handel's *Messiah* had used a mixed chorus drawn mainly from the royal opera company and local school choirs, with other available professional female and male singers and a few exceptionally well prepared amateurs included as well.

Indeed, women had been professionally involved in music making since the latter half of the sixteenth century, when they had achieved recognition in the north Italian courts as professional performers in a new style of madrigal singing. Within a generation, opera had emerged as a further experiment in sung drama, also requiring professional women singers, whose art was the object of intense scrutiny and admiration. Women composers followed in the wake of women's performance successes. The Italian vogue for women musicians moved to France, and professional women singers soon became an essential part of French court ballet and opera—at some point in their career most also became the mistresses of princes, dukes, or counts, a phenomenon that influenced attitudes toward women musicians even a century later. The first public concerts in Paris, a model for central Europe, brought new opportunities for women singers, instrumentalists, and composers. German courts, imitating the French and Italians, employed female singers (usually Italian ones), and a number of German women became active as composers. In the eighteenth century as in the sixteenth, most women musicians were the daughters and wives of court and other professional musicians and thus could receive the necessary training for a musical career at home.

What was new about the sound of the Singakademie in 1791, then, was not the sound of men's and women's voices combined but two things, neither having much to do with actual voices. First, the 1791 performance took place in a church (the Marienkirche), a circumstance that signals changes in religious practice as well as the dearth of public venues for choral concerts. Second, the Singakademie included amateur women, not professional ones. In this regard, it reflected new expectations of what women, especially middle-class ones, should do, and in its own way contributed to the contradictory notions of what music meant when performed by women.

The last decades of the eighteenth and the first decades of the nineteenth centuries represented an awkward turning point for musical women, both professional and amateur. A number of trends—intellectual, economic, and political—combined to frustrate any expansion of opportunities for women

---

[31] Barbara Garvey Jackson, "Musical Women of the Seventeenth and Eighteenth Centuries," in *Women and Music: A History*, ed. Karin Pendle (Bloomington, IN, 1991), 55, 57–58.

musicians comparable to those for men. The era of revolution and warfare reduced many court ensembles, with devastating consequences for female musicians. Women found fewer chances than men to earn a living in the growing musical marketplace. Few women taught private music lessons, despite the demand for tutoring in the home. Virtually no women wrote for musical journals, paid female instrumentalists were practically unheard of, and women composers became equally rare. The only female musicians who did not disappear were opera singers, the most famous of whom were feted across Europe, and a handful of female keyboard players. The general rule, that professional women musicians came from families of professional musicians, continued to hold true, long after men no longer depended on the circumstances of birth for their choice of profession. The more institutionalized musical training became, and the more removed from the intersecting efforts of guild and family, the more women were shut out from even the basic training necessary to compose or play instruments (as compared to sing and play a little piano), led alone conduct and direct.

The decline of the professional female musician had an ironic counterpart in the growth of amateur musicianship among women as well as men, a trend that the Singakademie helped to initiate. The rise of amateurism among both sexes speaks to the changing nature of the household as it evolved from an economic unit to an "emotional and reproductive" one.[32] On the one hand, the men of the new bureaucratic elites, whose work neither took place in the household nor relied on its members' labor, used the private home as a site for the pursuit of cultivation. This was especially the case for those men and women who hosted salons. By setting aside a room for the expression of their cultural aspirations, householders expressed the new importance of being cultivated, just as did the establishment of more public venues for reading, discussion, artistic appreciation, and eventually music.

However, the pursuit of music within the household carried a different set of implications for wives and daughters in these new urban social groups. A curious aspect of the rise of amateurism in this period is the divergent cultural implications of the same music, performed under the same circumstances, for men and for women. The ideology of domesticity began to engulf the female practice of music, appropriating it to the work of courtship, child rearing, and the general maintenance of a strictly domestic harmony. Although the ubiquity of pianos in middle-class parlors is a phenomenon of the latter half of the nineteenth century, already by the close of the eighteenth century girls of a marriageable age staged performances of

[32] Sheehan, *German History*, 538.

keyboard works or songs at home as an accepted part of sociability. Mothers were expected to sing to their children and teach them a little music. At the same time, the long-standing association of a woman's public music making with sexual availability lingered on—one need only look at the efforts of women like Clara Schumann to prove their respectability or at Fanny Mendelssohn's almost complete avoidance of public music, under orders from her father and her brother, to understand the toll such attitudes took.[33] To take music too seriously or practice it too assiduously invited the kind of remark made in 1789 by Johannes Campe, that among females even "the most virtuosic performer, the greatest singer, or the most learned and adept artist will be a bad wife, a bad housekeeper and a bad mother."[34]

The most acceptable way, then, for most women to go public as musicians was to wear the protective cloak of amateurism, with its connotations of private life and domesticity. The first organization to make this respectable publicity possible, crossing the invisible line dividing domestic and public music making, was the Singakademie. The line was no Rubicon. The decision to perform publicly left no traces in the historical record, no indication that anything extraordinary was happening. Yet hints of ambivalence linger in what we do know. For example, the group performed only rarely and gave what proceeds it earned in performance to charities. Zelter frequently compared the group to a family, with mothers and sons, fathers and daughters.[35] The focus of the group on religious music represented still another indication of its concern for respectability, even though women had not originally sung the higher parts in complex church music and certainly not in public. And when the press took rare notice of accomplished women, their piety earned as much attention as their musicianship. Louise Reichardt, daughter of Johann Friedrich Reichardt and a prolific composer of lieder, was among the earliest members of the Singakademie and went on to Hamburg to found a *Gesangverein* in 1819, modeled on Fasch's Berlin group. Described as nunlike in her good works and pious devotion to "clas-

---

[33] On Schumann, see especially Nancy B. Reich, *Clara Schumann: The Artist and the Woman* (Ithaca, NY, 1985). On Fanny Mendelssohn Hensel, see Hensel, 141–56; Citron, *Letters of Fanny Hensel,* esp. xxxi–xliv; and Marian Wilson Kimber, "The 'Suppression' of Fanny Mendelssohn: Rethinking Feminist Biography," *19th-Century Music* 26, no. 2 (summer 2002): 113–29. Even in 1863, when the violinist Joseph Joachim wrote to Brahms about his engagement to the contralto Amalie Schneeweiss, he warned Brahms "not to run away with the usual notions which are unfortunately connected with the life in our operatic circles, [for] her mind and appearance have remained simple and refined" (Jan Swafford, *Johannes Brahms: A Biography* [New York, 1997], 171).

[34] Quoted by Nancy B. Reich, "Women as Musicians: A Question of Class," in *Musicology and Difference: Gender and Sexuality in Music Scholarship,* ed. Ruth Solie (Berkeley, 1993), 133.

[35] Besides the Fasch tribute cited above, see Zelter's speech to the membership in 1803, quoted in Eberle, *Sing-Akademie,* 45.

sical church music," Reichardt's great achievements as a musician seemed less important than her exemplary character.[36]

Participation in amateur singing groups was not the only way that women were able to shape musical life, though it was certainly the most accessible. The case of Nina d'Aubigny von Engelbrunner (1770–1848), occasional writer in music periodicals, illustrates the roundabout means by which women made use of their musical talent. D'Aubigny was the daughter of a high-ranking civil servant in the court of the elector of Trier and prince archbishop of Augsburg, Clemens Wenzeslaus, and received a humanistic education as well as musical training from court kapellmeister Pompeo Sales. Under his tutelage, d'Aubigny and her sister achieved an early, ephemeral fame as exceptionally talented "dilettantes," performing at court and in semipublic concerts.[37] She was subsequently influenced by Johann Adam Hiller, a composer and musical reformer, who in the 1770s founded a short-lived coeducational singing school in Leipzig to redress the sorry state of choir performance.[38] Rochlitz, a student of Hiller, lamented the obscurity of a man who had "prepared the way for an epoch," and indeed Hiller had forward-looking notions especially about women singing in public.[39] He believed that men and women, amateur or professional, should sing together in public concerts and put his ideas into practice in his celebrated performance of Handel's *Messiah* in 1786.[40] From Sales and Hiller, d'Aubigny developed firm ideas about how singing should be taught, and in 1803 she published them in the form of instructional letters to a young girl.

Unlike Hiller's earlier writings, however, d'Aubigny presented her work simply as "advice" concerning "song as the encouragement of domestic happiness and convivial pleasures." She wrote for those "who would like to develop this art in themselves" and "for mothers and schoolteachers" who had similar goals for their children. Yet d'Aubigny had much less to say about domestic harmony than about the importance of women receiving

---

[36] *AMZ* 29 (12 December 1827): 167.

[37] Limited details of d'Aubigny's early life can be found in Gerber's *Neues Historisch-Biographisches*. See also Wilfried Gruhn, *Geschichte der Musikerziehung: Eine Kultur- und Sozialgeschichte vom Gesangunterricht der Aufklärungspädagogik zu ästhetisch-kultureller Bildung* (Hofheim, 1993), 101–3; Eva Rieger, ed., *Frau und Musik* (Kassel, 1990), 43–47.

[38] See Johann Adam Hiller, *Anweisung zur Singekunst in der deutschen und italienischen Sprache* (Leipzig, 1773); Hiller, *Musikalisches Handbuch für die Liebhaber des Gesanges und Claviers* (Leipzig, 1773); Hiller, *Anweisung zum musikalisch-richtigen Gesange* (Leipzig, 1774); also Gruhn, *Geschichte der Musikerziehung*, 84; Eberle, *Sing-Akademie*, 17.

[39] Rochlitz quoted in Karl Peiser, *Johann Adam Hiller: Ein Beitrag zur Musikgeschichte des 18. Jahrhunderts* (Leipzig, 1894), 3.

[40] Ibid., 60–66.

serious musical training. She believed, for instance, that proper singing technique would protect young women against consumption and cited the lower rates of the illness in Italy as evidence: "in the shadow of many a [German] church steeple lie the victims of musical ignorance." Contemporary assumptions about women's innate frivolity angered her even more. Vanity, she declared, was not "the special marriage portion of the female sex." Men were as vain as women, and it was men who actively encouraged vanity in women by discouraging genuine musical accomplishment and rewarding "mere prettiness and minimal musical achievement with excessive and insincere flattery." "In the behavior of men in regard to us," she concluded, lay "a powerful obstacle to our true fulfillment."[41]

As such statements indicated, d'Aubigny's recommendations for better musical instruction for women formed part of her larger vision of women's equal capacity for *Bildung* or self-development. Unlike "so many other lands" where they were treated as "slaves" or "fashionable dolls with empty heads," women in "our German Fatherland," thought d'Aubigny, had a chance at "rational development," as their "intellectual and moral powers" unfolded under the "influence of the Muses." "Lively powers of judgment" and "a developed understanding" were the "real treasures decorating the young woman's room," and she intended her book to contribute to both through systematic instruction in the art of singing.[42]

If, by the end of the book, one felt prepared to face a recital hall and perform the works of "Pergolesi, Graun, Haydn, and Mozart" but remained hopelessly ill informed about proper lullaby technique, all the better. The book went through several editions and won its author some small renown in her lifetime.[43] Perhaps Zelter knew of d'Aubigny or her book: he read Rochlitz's journal, to which she contributed several short articles, and in which a favorable review of the book appeared, and he took a lively interest in contemporary trends in musical instruction.[44] Certainly Zelter strove, like her, to raise the musical awareness of those with sufficient means to undertake the great project of self-development. His approach to the women and men of the Singakademie reflected the same understanding of music's

---

[41] Nina d'Aubigny von Engelbrunner, *Briefe an Natalie über den Gesang als Beförderung der häuslichen Glückseligkeit und des geselligen Vernügens: Ein Handbuch für Freunde des Gesanges, die sich selbst, oder für Mütter und Erzieherinnen, die ihre Zöglinge für diese Kunst bilden wollen* (Leipzig, 1803), 113–14, 34–37.

[42] Ibid., 1–2, 34–37.

[43] Rieger, *Frau und Musik*, 226.

[44] "For the purposes and the public for which this book is directed, nothing so suitable is available, neither in German, nor in French, nor in Italian musical literature"; anonymous reviewer, *AMZ* 5, no. 51 (14 September 1803).

cultural and moral significance and the same valuation of the capacity of amateurs to practice music for higher ends than mere amusement.

ZELTER AND THE PRUSSIAN STATE

As the reputation of the Singakademie began to grow, in part through its performances at the funerals of Hohenzollerns, membership expanded to nearly two hundred, and Zelter's conception of what the group signified grew with it.[45] Under the influence of his second wife, the professional singer Juliane Pappritz, he turned his Monday rehearsals into a singing school, where he worked on producing a consistent sound from his motley collection of professionals and amateurs. The Berlin correspondent of the *AMZ* was impressed: "It is truly intriguing to hear a chorus of over 100 people perform the most difficult four-part songs with a purity and precision nearly impossible to believe."[46] Three mornings a week Zelter also provided individual instruction in notation, harmony, and voice production. He began to require auditions of prospective members and to deliver regular, often admonitory speeches to the group on the need for greater discipline in the ranks. In 1803 he declared that of his 200 members no more than 110 "did their duty" or saw themselves as something other than "blanks in a lottery, from which nothing is to be won." Ninety members of the Singakademie, he spelled out, were "fully useless, inert, and unprofitable for the whole." "Will it remain like this?" he asked, "can someone really wish to remain a member of a free and happy association," contributing nothing to its success?[47]

More than poor attendance and unpaid dues were on Zelter's mind when he delivered such speeches. Most amounted to disquisitions on the seriousness of the group's contribution to society and Germany's musical future. Zelter had come to believe, like Rochlitz and Reichardt, that the state of music in central Europe constituted a matter of national concern. Singakademie members had to rise to the challenge, pushing beyond the more limited Faschian agenda of respectable music making in someone's living room. For Zelter, serious music drew people and art more closely together, creating an ethical community of the whole. As he said in another

---

[45] In the 1790s alone, the Singakademie performed at the funerals of Prince Ludwig, the widow of Friedrich II, and Friedrich Wilhelm II, as well as at a few birthday celebrations. See Eberle, *Sing-Akademie*, 35.

[46] *AMZ* 3, no. 33 (14 May 1800): 587.

[47] In Eberle, *Sing-Akademie*, 45.

speech to the membership, art was not "a secondary matter in human existence" but a national mission: "The level of the culture of a nation may be found in its cultivation of the fine arts." The practice of art led, on the inside, to "self-recognition" and, on the outside, to a single unified impression of the whole.[48] This view placed Zelter among those whom Carl Dahlhaus saw as advocating a "strong concept of art," by which music could "stand on a par with literature and the visual arts."[49] To hold such views in 1800 was to align oneself with poets and philosophers, rather than with courtiers and guildsmen.

Why a man whose knowledge of music had once been confined to visiting a few opera rehearsals and working for a town musician should have come to stand so firmly on the side of a serious, German concept of art, against frivolous and foreign art, constitutes something of a mystery, but poets and philosophers were close at hand for Zelter and already by 1799 he had contact with the best among them. One year before Fasch's death, he received a letter from the man already regarded as the living exemplar of German cultural greatness, whose authority was unique in the German-speaking lands. Goethe's interest in Zelter sprang initially from his pleasure in the musical settings Zelter had composed in 1796 to a few of his poems.[50] Yet Goethe's willingness to pursue an acquaintance derived less from Zelter's music or admiration than from the piquancy of his dual career as mason and musician, which appealed to the collector in Goethe.[51] Goethe wrote directly to Zelter only after his interest had been aroused a second time by August Wilhelm Schlegel, who wrote to Goethe in 1798 comparing Zelter's masonry to Orpheus's ability to raise structures with his music. Schlegel's letter cast Zelter in the role he would play throughout his correspondence with Goethe, that of a plainspoken man of practicalities, as ready to discuss Teltower turnips as musical meters, yet still with the tender sensibilities of an artist. As Goethe wrote to Charlotte von Stein in 1805, "one begins to have faith in human beings again when one sees such a man, liv-

---

[48] Ibid., 44.

[49] Dahlhaus, *Nineteenth-Century Music*, 8–11.

[50] Zelter made the first direct contact by writing to thank Goethe effusively—"Your works are the gods of my house," and so on—for approving of the Zelter settings sent to Goethe by the publisher Unger. See Zelter to Goethe, 11 August 1799, in Zelter, *Selbstdarstellung*, 61. Zelter was already on comfortable, if formal terms with Schiller.

[51] Goethe said as much to A. W. Schlegel: "If ever I have been curious to make the acquaintance of an individual, it is with this Herr Zelter. This union of two arts is so important, and I wish to know much about both and their mutual connection" (letter in Cornelia Schröder, *Carl Friedrich Zelter und die Akademie: Dokumente und Briefe zur Entstehung der Musik-Sektion in der Preussischen Akademie der Künste* [Berlin, 1959], 46; hereafter Schröder).

ing so vigorously and honestly" and salvaging for this sorry world an "excellence in ordinary things."[52]

The Weimar connection, as it played itself out over the following thirty-three years, was of inestimable value to Zelter and the institutions closely associated with him. Scholars who have looked at this friendship have mostly bypassed this aspect, wondering instead at what Goethe saw in the man ("at times uncouth and unintelligible," wrote the English translator of the correspondence) when there were so many more literary musicians around, or waxing sentimental about the affection between two such dissimilar German men. Despite its eventual intimacy (after the suicide of Zelter's stepson), the relationship also had a purposeful quality to it. Zelter was Goethe's connection to Berlin, where he rarely visited yet with which he wished to stay current, and to music, to which he felt he needed a trustworthy guide.[53] And Goethe was Zelter's entrée into European culture, in the wide, cosmopolitan, nationalizing sense that characterized the "classical center" at Weimar. Zelter learned much from both Goethe and Schiller. Perhaps through them he joined Friedrich Rochlitz's stable of musical correspondents, contributing occasional reports on musical events in Berlin already in 1800.[54] Quick learner and practical guildsman that he was, Zelter applied their ideas about art and music to the Singakademie and his circle of amateur musicians.

The approval of these men may have emboldened Zelter, one year after his first long visit to Weimar, to write directly to the Prussian state seeking official recognition for his musical activities. In 1803 Karl August von Hardenberg, a trustee of the Prussian Academy of Fine Arts and part of the reform-minded clique in the Prussian bureaucracy, had asked academy members for suggestions on how it could "have a sure and measurable impact on the spirit of the age and the productivity of this epoch," as well as "awaken the artistic energies of the country." Zelter, a member neither of the academy nor of the bureaucratic elite, sent Hardenberg a response.[55] His suggestions were bold in their simplicity and earnest in their optimism: include music in the academy, he urged; make the promotion of serious mu-

---

[52] In Walther Victor, *Carl Friedrich Zelter und seine Freundschaft mit Goethe* (Berlin, 1970), 25. Unmoved, the English translator of the Zelter-Goethe correspondence, A. D. Coleridge, wrote that in the case of Zelter, Goethe showed himself capable "of a real affection for at least one of his blindest worshippers" (*Grove's Dictionary of Music and Musicians*, 1910 ed., s.v. "Zelter").

[53] Robert Spaethling, *Music and Mozart in the Life of Goethe* (Columbia, SC, 1987), 21–23.

[54] See, for instance, Zelter's report in the *AMZ* 3, no. 33 (14 May 1800): 585.

[55] In the conclusion of the memorandum, he apologized if his ideas seemed to "forward" (*dreist*); memorandum in Schröder, 79.

sical practices among the people one of its basic goals; improve music in churches and schools and you will improve people.

Zelter's memorandum, informed by his earlier musical experiences as an outsider and amateur, described Germany as a land in musical crisis. The cultivation of music had fallen to a low level, and church music, particularly singing, had nearly ceased to exist. Although he hoped that the state would improve professional training and employment, his main concern was for the population as a whole, who had, he implied, suffered in the recent past under rulers with a preference for operatic spectacle over serious music. Yet music alone, he wrote to Hardenberg, had long "exerted its beneficent influence on the formation of the German nation and the peaceful condition of its people." No other art had so distinguished the Germans among the nations of Europe or expressed so clearly the essence of Germanness. Its deterioration "threatened the German nation in its most essential characteristics of constancy and seriousness."[56]

His proposal, which both Goethe and Schiller amended, articulated Zelter's vision of the Singakademie as an institution of national significance. The Singakademie's importance derived for him both from its essential Germanness and its potential to strengthen German culture in ever-widening circles. A group that "could only have grown out of Berlin's soil," it embodied a "genuine Brandenburger Germanness." It was "bound together by love and faithful effort, knowledge and noble morality," and bore witness "to the German genius" itself. Zelter therefore urged Hardenberg to secure music's beneficent influence, first by appointing a "public teacher of all aspects of music" to the academy (he suggested himself) and, second, by making the director of the Singakademie a paid civil servant of the king. The Singakademie, "built on the national character of German steadfastness," could then encourage "public taste for all that is serious and elevated in music," that is, German musical traditions.[57] Branching out from it would be seminars for church organists and choir directors, for schoolteachers and private music instructors. As he said to his singers in the year before the French arrived triumphant in Berlin, "let us not long for foreign treasures" or "prettify with a lascivious, ingratiating, overstuffed foreignness" what is German about us—"our steady seriousness in word and deed."[58]

The most remarkable aspect of Zelter's immodest proposal to the Prussian state was his belief that an amateur musical organization could serve as the "foundation stone" of professional, German-wide musical renewal. To

[56] "Erste Denkschrift," in Schröder, 75.
[57] Eberle, *Sing-Akademie*, 44, 46–47.
[58] Ibid., 50.

be sure, directorship of a successful amateur group was what Zelter had to offer as his credentials to be the all-German guardian of serious music, but his concept rested on more than personal ambition or love of amateurism as such. Dilettantism carried negative connotations for Zelter, perhaps stirring up his own doubts about his training as a musician and evoking images of the kind of frivolity and foreign taste he had learned to condemn.[59] In his memorandum to Hardenberg in the fall of 1803 he blamed "dilettantism" for depriving music of its "true usefulness," robbing it of its "profundity and power" and leading people to value music only as "a pleasure to pass the time." He distinguished between such foolish dabblers and "true music" lovers, those who were committed to its practice in consciousness of their Germanness. Again to Hardenberg, Zelter wrote that "artistic activities can be considered an aspect of self-development only if they are directed with seriousness to a definite purpose." "Purposeless music making" was "a time waster, quickly dissipated, without the permanence or stability" that alone gave art its ennobling quality.[60] Zelter rarely called his singers or students either dilettantes or amateurs. His music making was, he believed, directed to a serious, German purpose, and those who participated in such a project were simply "the people," the *Volk*, in essence any dedicated person.

The lovers of serious music could also be the means by which broader circles of the population felt the improving powers of music, and in perceiving this, Zelter was less a dreamer than a practical man of business. The Singakademie was a representative institution for Zelter, a model for how music should be cultivated for the benefit of society as a whole. It relied on some infusion of professional musicians, and that blending of amateurs with professionals was also crucial to Zelter's vision of musical renewal. If the professionals provided knowledge and skill, the amateurs provided community connections, organizational energy, and money. The rippling effects of this combination had already been wide. Through the high quality of its few performances and the participation of well-known singers, it had earned the respect of practicing musicians, many of whom traveled around Germany and Europe and wrote for musical journals. That Beethoven should already in 1797 have heard of the group and chosen to attend its rehearsals indicates the effectiveness of such communication. Through the amateurs—wives and daughters of high-ranking officials, bankers like Abraham Mendelssohn, booksellers like Friedrich Nicolai—the group gained local supporters, which in the case of Berlin included the Prussian king and

[59] Zelter complained that initially Fasch treated him as a "dilettante" and "not as an apprentice," and his resentment at such treatment turned him against "dilettantism" in a way that later caused him much "vexation" (Zelter, *Darstellungen seines Lebens*, 242).

[60] "Zweite Denkschrift," in Schröder, 82–83.

his advisers. In the age of dwindling court and ecclesiastical resources, local networks of amateur musicians formed a new, more diffuse kind of patronage, signing on to subscription lists for new compositions and concert series, hiring teachers, and, if they were wealthy enough, commissioning a piece or two. Zelter, probably not intentionally, had created such a network in Berlin and by 1804 seems to have understood its potential for improving musical and social life elsewhere as well.

Not that anything changed immediately. Hardenberg was impressed enough to appoint Zelter as "assessor and honorary member" of the Academy of Fine Arts, a minor recognition that gave Zelter some status. But the memoranda to Hardenberg were only the beginning of a long correspondence between Zelter and officials of the Prussian cultural establishment, twenty years' worth of prodding and pleading with them to include music on the state's agenda. Over time, piece by piece, Zelter's efforts paid off. The most important piece came in 1809, shortly after Wilhelm von Humboldt's appointment as chief of educational and ecclesiastical affairs in the Prussian Ministry of the Interior. Humboldt intended to carry out a thoroughgoing reform on all levels of the educational system as his contribution to renewing the "spiritual powers" of the physically defeated state. At Goethe's suggestion, he invited Zelter to submit some "suggestions for the improvement of music." The great avatar of *Bildung* stood ready at last to recognize music, and Zelter was, according to his loyal patron Goethe, the man who was "clear-sighted and blunt" enough to guide him.[61]

So Zelter dusted off his five-year-old Hardenberg memorandum, omitted complaints about the wretched state of musical life (petty now in the aftermath of Jena and Auerstadt), and resubmitted his original suggestions. Humboldt, who rarely showed any interest in music, proved amenable. Echoing Zelter's language in support of his suggestions, Humboldt wrote to the king that the "influence music could exert on the character and the development of the nation" had been too little recognized by the state. The "lower classes" in particular demonstrated their membership in the nation (so Zelter had said) not through philosophy or poetry but rather by their "Prussian probity and constancy, the sum of which is piety."[62] In Humboldt's rendering, music could reach this common man and integrate him into the great educational project that was the German nation. Because music was essentially a language of feeling, its "strength and completeness" could be apprehended by all human beings without special knowledge;

---

[61] Quoted by George Schünemann, "Carl Friedrich Zelter, der Begründer der preussischen Musikpflege," *Zeitung für Schulmusik* 5 (1932), in *Quellentexte zur Musikpädagogik*, ed. Walter Heise, Helmuth Hopf, and Helmut Segler (Regensburg, 1973), 15.

[62] "Vierte Denkscrift," in Schröder, 111.

music was, therefore, "a natural bond between the lower and higher classes of the nation." Like a religious service, musical performance allowed "all members of the nation to unite purely as human beings and without the accidental distinctions of society."[63] Humboldt may have expected the king to understand the unwritten message: give the people this experience of full participation in the context of culture and religion and they will not seek it in political life. Here, through music, the collective uplift of the nation could reinvigorate Prussia without opening it up to the mob. In any case, the king too proved amenable, and soon Zelter became professor of music at the Academy of Fine Arts. He was provided with a salary sufficient for him to give up his masonry and with the power to oversee musical affairs in some unspecified manner.

So busy did Zelter keep himself with this work that later musicologists have been unable to resist the metaphor of "master builder" of the Prussian state's musical institutions. Even before receiving the full state imprimatur, he had begun to admit a few outsiders, usually organists and schoolteachers, to the musical instruction he had begun for his singers. Their numbers grew steadily but informally after 1804. In 1811 he wrote again to the cultural ministry about "the condition of general singing" and proposed creating a "seminary" for "cantors, prefects, and singing teachers." A decade later the state finally provided the money for the foundation of a formal Institute for Church Music.[64] Meanwhile, in 1807 Zelter initiated a weekly gathering of instrumentalists, the Ripienschule, to provide both amateurs and students with instruction and ensemble practice sessions.[65] In 1809 he founded Germany's first *Liedertafel* or men's singing group, the precursor of the hundreds that started up in cities all over German-speaking Europe in the following decades. Dedicated to fostering "the composition and performance of new lieder and choral music," the group drew together twenty-five of his friends

---

[63] Wilhelm von Humboldt, "Immediateingabe 'Über geistliche Musik' von 14. Mai 1809," in *Lehrpläne und Richtlinien für den schulischen Musikunterricht in Deutschland vom Beginn des 19. Jahrhunderts bis in die Gegenwart: Eine Dokumentation*, ed. Eckhard Nolte (Mainz, 1975), 31–33.

[64] Already in 1815 the state had paid for the establishment of a similar institute in Breslau. Zelter oversaw its founding and first years of operation. See Sowa, *Anfänge institutioneller Musikerziehung*, 120–22.

[65] Zelter's name for his school for instrumentalists refers to the Baroque concerto style of the seventeenth and eighteenth centuries, which required not an orchestra and soloist (as in the concerto form more familiar to audiences today) but rather two instrumental ensembles, the larger of which, performing the less virtuosic music in the concerto, was called the *ripieno* (the smaller group with the soloistic, more virtuosic music was called the *concertino*). Likewise, the workaday, professional instrumentalist in an orchestra was often called a *ripienista*. Zelter was thus making clear that he was not in the business of training virtuosic violinists. On the Ripienschule itself, see Gruhn, *Geschichte der Musikerziehung*, 91; Sowa, *Anfänge institutioneller Musikerziehung*, 92.

and Singakademie members, each of whom had to be poets or composers as well as singers, and performed songs, mainly for their own enjoyment, which "resonated with the breath of German sense, earnestness, and jollity."[66] Finally, after things settled down in 1815, Zelter began to travel around German-speaking Europe—to Breslau, Königsberg, the Rhineland, Stuttgart, Hamburg, Heidelberg, Vienna, many times to Weimar, once to Switzerland. He met with musicians, investigated musical conditions, collected manuscripts for the growing Singakademie collection, listened to famous organs and new instruments, and looked into teaching methods and instructional innovations. Perhaps he introduced himself as the head of Berlin's famous Singakademie, perhaps as the musical inspector of the Prussian state, perhaps as the friend of Goethe and the composer of lieder, probably as all of these things. He never made it to Italy, much to his regret. But his traveling brief was to learn about German musical ways and in that, at least, he probably succeeded.

All this sounds like a lot of activity, yet master builder or no, there was something curiously temporary about his work, as though it amounted only to sketches of buildings rather than actual bricks and mortar. He had many students, at least two of whom (Giacomo Meyerbeer and Felix Mendelssohn) became enduringly famous, but such basic musical instruction as he offered left only a vanishing mark on his pupils as well. Rochlitz, writing Zelter's obituary for the *AMZ* in 1832, seemed hardly to have noticed it, because he mainly honored Zelter's leadership of the Singakademie, making no mention of his long years of involvement in musical institutions, bureaucracies, and educational reform. The Ripienschule provides a good example of his vision and its limitations. Born of the need to have inexpensive accompaniment for his singers, its training of instrumentalists represented an important innovation in the pursuit of public musical instruction. If he had combined it with the Singakademie's training function, Zelter could have had a conservatory within his grasp, the first in German-speaking Europe, a cornerstone indeed.[67]

But the problem with that metaphor is that it connotes intent, and Zelter never actually created a lasting institution out of the pieces he alone held together. Other states, other people, other decades oversaw the creation of conservatories in German-speaking Europe. He did petition Hardenberg in 1811 for the construction of a new building, perhaps next to the Academy of Fine Arts, into which he could expand his operations. Hardenberg never

---

[66] Schünemann, "Zelter, der Begründer," 16.
[67] Sowa, *Anfänge institutioneller Musikerziehung*, 90.

answered. Renewed fighting with France intervened, and by the time Napoleon was safely exiled to St. Helena, Zelter had reduced his request to more chairs and closet space in the academy itself. When at last constituted in 1822, the Institute for Church Music, or in its official title "the musical institute in Berlin for the promotion of church music and the training of organists and music teachers in Gymnasiums and teacher colleges," amounted to much less than a conservatory, indeed much less than the sum of Zelter's works. Its pupils—and there were rarely more than thirty—studied for only one year and included neither singers nor instrumentalists. What they got, mainly from Bernhard Klein and August Wilhelm Bach, two superb musicians whom Zelter had recruited to teach for him, was an introduction to methods of singing instruction, piano and organ instruction, and music theory. But in Zelter's lifetime, the institute had no regular teaching schedule or course outlines, indeed no institutional statutes of any kind. Only after his death did the institute become more conventionally institutional. And by then, the Ripienschule had long since ceased to exist; nor was the Singakademie itself any more in the business of training singers.

Seen from the perspective of professional musical education, Zelter's failure to establish any institution that would embody his lofty ideals in the way that Humboldt's university embodied his, is a curious one. He was a man of endless energy for teaching, traveling, investigating, collecting, and composing; moreover, he lived in a musical culture obsessed with the question of how to produce good musicians. As David Gramit has pointed out, educational reform "occupied virtually every significant writer on music," especially in the decades between 1800 and 1830; moreover, many a minor musician sought to make his mark by founding some kind of musical institute or other.[68] Several times a year throughout the first decades of its existence, the *AMZ* published critiques of the existing professional training, wretched private teaching practices, and proposals for singing schools and "institutes for aesthetic education."[69] Even writers never much concerned with musical matters joined in. The now-forgotten playwright Ernst Wagner, for instance, wanted to initiate a grand national project to establish schools of art and music "for all Germans." His imagined nation, like the nation Rochlitz had constituted in the networks of the *AMZ*, consisted of a string of institutes in fifty-one cities, one of which would be the "school city," and the others "mother cities" providing citizens to it. "Saxons, Aus-

---

[68] David Gramit, *Cultivating Music: The aspirations, interests, and limits of German musical culture, 1770–1848* (Berkeley, 2002), 95.

[69] For an exhaustive list of all these proposals and early efforts at public musical instruction between 1800 and 1843, see Sowa, *Anfänge institutioneller Musikerziehung.*

trians, Prussians, Hamburgers, and so on" would come together and realize themselves as "Germans or even more as humanity" through art and music "set forth in freedom."[70]

Utopian though this vision was, it belonged to the same intellectual and musical milieu as Zelter, and there is little in it, save the romantic exclamatory style, with which Zelter would have taken issue. And that tells us something, because for all his memorandum writing and organizational energy, which we are inclined to see as the marks of incipient professionalism, Zelter's projects failed, no less than the castles in the air of Ernst Wagner, to constitute the foundations of professional musical training in central Europe—although perhaps he never intended them to. The professional musicians could take care of themselves. Apart from suggesting to Hardenberg in 1804 that he put some effort into reinvigorating musicians' guilds (in fact six years later Hardenberg presided over the abolition of all guilds in Prussia), Zelter remained throughout his career the trainer and organizer extraordinaire of amateurs.[71] Even his vigorous efforts to improve the musical work of schoolteachers and church musicians had as its goal the improvement of the musical competence of ordinary people.

EDUCATING THE AMATEURS

Zelter's focus on such ordinary people, to the neglect of what he might have done to hasten the development of professional musical training in central Europe, brought him in contact with a motley array of musical reformers and charlatans then pushing their wares across Europe. A brief survey of these people and their ideas illuminates the broader musical context within which amateurism flourished. The first decades of the nineteenth century saw an outbreak of schemes promising everything from quick mastery of musical instruments to world peace through school choral practice. Technological changes played a role in this, with printed musical editions, many of them collections of simple concoctions intended for the not-very-gifted beginner, affordable and available without prior subscription. Advancement in the design and production of pianos was in turn responsible for their spread into more households, in Germany as in England and

---

[70] Ernst Wagner, *Reisen aus der Fremde in die Heimat* (Leipzig, 1806), 3. As Sowa points out, Wagner was a great friend of the romantic writer Jean Paul and seems to have been trying to realize Jean Paul's *Vorschule der Ästhetik* (ibid., 60–61).

[71] On Hardenberg and the Prussian Trades Edict of 1810, which tried to free the productive forces of society from corporative restrictions, see Thomas Nipperdey, *Germany from Napoleon to Bismarck*, trans. Daniel Nolan (Princeton, 1996), 36.

France.[72] But people had always been able to make music. What was also changing, as we have already seen, were the connotations of musical practice, which now connected to notions of cultivation, a cultural literacy to which a person without title or wealth could aspire. As a free market in all aspects of music took over privileged and traditional practices of music making, the possibilities for exploiting the middle order's desire to be musical grew apace.

A final element in this mixture was what social historians have identified as a new attitude toward childhood and thus to child rearing and education. The discovery of childhood brought to musical life a determination to give young children musical training, along with a fondness for publicly performing prodigies. Of course, for the advocates of serious music, children's musicality too was a serious matter. In Reichardt's *Berlinische Musikalische Zeitung*, the pedagogue and reformer Georg Christian Friedrich Schlimmbach wrote about such matters as recognizing musical talent and choosing an instrument for one's child to study (never start with the violin). Schlimmbach raised the question of whether a capacity to learn music was "inherited or acquired," only to dismiss the practical importance of musicality. All children, up and down the social scale, had some degree of musical receptivity, he asserted, which needed to be "awakened, developed, and through stimulation, use, and practice, fully realized."[73]

His position encapsulated the German Enlightenment's mixture of rationalism and humanism that came together in the Humboldtian idea of *Bildung*. Education in music was not about learning a mechanical skill but about self-realization. Nature had given man the greatest instrument of all in the voice; the capacity of speech revealed a capacity for musical expression as well. The more one sang, just as the more one used language, the more human one became. But inborn ability, no matter how great, counted for nothing in Schlimmbach's eyes without the careful labor of shaping and refining it. Within this philosophical framework, the training of the singing voice, starting in childhood, took on added significance. But so too did every question concerning musical instruction, from whether scales were important to when one should learn the rules of harmony. Binding it all together was not just the pursuit of *Bildung* but the search for community. In the words of another of Reichardt's writers, Christian Friedrich Michaelis,

---

[72] A kaleidoscopic and beautifully illustrated new account of the history of the piano is James Parakilas, with E. Douglas Bomberger et al., *Piano Roles: Three Hundred Years of Life with the Piano* (New Haven, 1999).

[73] G. C. F. Schlimmbach, "Einige Briefe über den Unterricht in der Musik," *BMZ* 1, no. 13 (1805): 49–50.

music was the most "communally useful" of the fine arts. The best proof that children or adults had developed their musical capacities came through their exercise of "taste," their capacity to distinguish among "the good, the bad, and the mediocre."[74]

In 1805 Schlimmbach and Michaelis had sounded the main issues around which discussion of musical education revolved in the decades to come: the foundational importance of singing, the possibility of self-realization, the need for simplicity in instruction, the promise of community in practice. The musical training of adult amateurs and children (other than prodigies) became entangled in first decades of the nineteenth century, more to the detriment of the children's musicality than that of their hardier parents. In north Germany especially, the more music became caught up in the intellectual currents of humanism, the more its instruction became subject to the reforming zeal of people with more philosophy than practical sense or more entrepreneurship than musicianship. As the semiofficial Prussian state overseer of musical matters, Zelter was not much of a gatekeeper. Instead, he reflected these trends, often unable to sort out the sense from the nonsense amidst the schemes clamoring for attention. In retrospect, his legacy to Prussian schoolchildren was less valuable than to amateur musicians. He allowed the dissemination of at least two fashions in the training of children that might better have been squelched or ignored, traveling to Switzerland to investigate one and sponsoring the other in its initial foray into Berlin.

As for the first, Zelter alone was not responsible for the fifty-year hold on musical-pedagogical imagination of Hans Georg Nägeli and Michael Traugott Pfeiffer's "school of choral singing." The Swiss-born Nägeli (1773–1836) was already a man of considerable reputation in the musical world. In the 1790s, he had established a music store and lending library in Zürich, later founding a publishing firm and assembling an extraordinary collection of autograph manuscripts. Through his work, he had contact with the composers of the day, including Beethoven, Weber, and Schubert; his contribution to the early-nineteenth-century reception of Bach was substantial, as we shall see in the next chapter. In 1805 Nägeli founded an Institute for Singing (*Singinstitut*) along the lines of the *Singakademie*, for which he wrote lieder, mainly settings of his own poetry.

Meanwhile, a man named Michael Traugott Pfeiffer (1775–1849), the son of a Bavarian cantor, had come to Switzerland to study, risen in the cantonal government of Aargau, and like so many others, become a devoted admirer of the pedagogue Johann Heinrich Pestalozzi. Pestalozzi's revolu-

[74] C. F. Michaelis, "Ueber die Prüfung der musikalischen Fähigkeiten," *BMZ* 1, no. 56–57 (1805): 222–26.

tionary ideas about teaching children, by allowing them to move at their own pace from sense impressions to abstract ideas, were already becoming famous—through his writings (*Leonard and Gertrude* in 1781–87 and *How Gertrude Teaches Her Children* in 1801) and a constant stream of visitors to his model schools at Burgdorf and Yverdon. Among them was Pfeiffer. In 1804 he left the civil service to start up his own Pestalozzian school where he put Pestalozzi's methods to work in the study of musical theory—an effort at disciplinary application already tried, and approved by the master himself, in the cases of geography and mathematics.[75] Pestalozzi thought enough of this musical method to ask Nägeli to compile and publish it. The project appealed to Nägeli, working on the problem of how best to combine voice, text, and instrument in German lieder, and so in 1809 the first of a spate of pedagogical pamphlets and school song collections appeared under the ponderous title *The Pestalozzian Method of Teaching Singing, as pedagogically contrived by Michael Traugott Pfeiffer and methodologically developed by Hans Georg Nägeli.*[76]

Expanded and reissued just a year later through multiple German publishing houses, the book gained influence throughout the German-speaking world and soon beyond it as well. The method it prescribed was simple, thorough, and relentless. Taking Pestalozzi's goal of simplification to extreme lengths, Pfeiffer and Nägeli had devised a system that sought to break down the complexities of musical notation and sound production into its components, introducing each to the young pupils over an extended period of time. First rhythm, then melody, then dynamics were introduced, one element at a time. For the first sixteen chapters of the book, Pfeiffer-Nägeli pupils had to stay silent as they studied, detail by detail, every aspect of rhythm and rhythmic notation. When finally allowed to open their mouths in chapter 17, they spent many more weeks singing simple thirds, or four notes in a row, over and over again. The most minute variations in dynamics then came under investigation, with the students singing *la-la-la-la* from soft to loud until the teacher was satisfied that they had achieved the proper gradations. Finally, as instruction drew to a close, they were allowed to sing such memorable phrases as "*Gesang, Gesang, Gesang, Gesang*" or, more daringly, "*Gesang erfreut das Herz*," covering a total of four different pitches.[77]

That any teacher should have attempted to put this into practice represents the triumph of theory over life. As Wilfried Gruhn has pointed out,

---

[75] Bernarr Rainbow, *The Land without Music: Musical Education in England 1800–1860 and Its Continental Antecedents* (London, 1967), 70–71.

[76] *Gesangbildungslehre nach Pestalozzischen Grundsätzen, pädagogisch begründet von Michael Traugott Pfeiffer, methodisch bearbeitet von Hans Georg Nägeli* (Zürich, 1809).

[77] The best account in English of the method is Rainbow, *Land without Music*, 76–80.

Pfeiffer's Pestalozzian method had little in common with the atmosphere Pestalozzi himself created in his model schools. At Burgdorf and Yverdon, teachers encouraged singing everywhere, outdoors, in the refectory, in the hallways between classes. The Pfeiffer-Nägeli regimen, on the other hand, forbad children from singing actual songs, either at home or at school: "premature singing of melodies" allegedly made a child's voice "unsteady and impure."[78] This marked difference in the children's musical experiences betrayed Pfeiffer and Nägeli's failure to grasp the psychology of learning that Pestalozzi had put into practice. Rather than children learning through experiences and perceptions, Pfeiffer and Nägeli aimed to control, impede, or prevent any child-led foray into musical expression—to the point, as Gruhn puts it, of creating a system "that one could call essentially anti-Pestalozzian."[79] Why Pestalozzi would then have endorsed the Pfeiffer-Nägeli system is perhaps explicable by his willingness to "be but the initiator of the Institute, and depend on others to carry out my views."[80]

But Pestalozzi, like many of his contemporaries, could also have been persuaded that this system, however tedious (the *AMZ* considered it "wholly unusable for pedagogical purposes"), still represented a major improvement over the existing situation of rote learning of chorales in impoverished Latin schools at the hands of musically inept instructors or, even more common, no musical instruction at all.[81] If it expected too little from the students, it expected even less from the instructors, providing them with lesson scripts so detailed that only the tone-deaf or illiterate could have failed to follow them. This made it well-suited to elementary school teachers who had yet to benefit from the system of better teacher training in music that Zelter had yet to institute. David Gramit has suggested that the appeal of the Pfeiffer-Nägeli method also rested on its promise to discipline the untamed child into a cultivated human through song, while reinforcing "the distinction between those from cultivated families and those of common heritage."[82]

In Prussia, right at the height of its love affair with reform and reformers, the power of the Pestalozzian imprimatur cannot be overestimated. A late convert to his educational project, Humboldt himself had come to see the congruence between Pestalozzi's vision of human development and his own, and several of his close associates (Georg Nicolovius especially) were

---

[78] Gruhn, *Geschichte der Musikerziehung*, 56–59; Rainbow, *Land without Music*, 69.

[79] Gruhn, *Geschichte der Musikerziehung*, 61.

[80] Cited in Rainbow, *Land without Music*, 70.

[81] *AMZ* 28 (1811); on musical education at the end of the eighteenth century, see Butt, *Music Education*, 166–92.

[82] Gramit, *Cultivating Music*, 109–11.

Pestalozzians of long standing. By 1810, when the Pfeiffer-Nägeli method began to be known in Prussian and north German cities, Pestalozzi was well on his way to earning the title of "spiritual father of German educational reform."[83] Nägeli appealed to the sensibilities of progressive statesmen and educators in an introduction to the manual that promised a new "age of music" in the offing, which would first take root "in the world of children." "Soon cities and villages, from throne to hovel," he wrote, "will together bring music its greatest triumphs" and create an artistic flowering comparable to "the great public life of the Greeks."[84]

Zelter's willingness to tolerate the growing use of a system so at odds with his own traditional, chorale-based methods had much to do with his closeness to the reformist circles in Berlin and his resulting susceptibility to such rhetoric. It also reflected the incoherence of his position as protector of musical quality in the Prussian state. While he wrote his memoranda and taught his students as he always had, a handful of more energetic reformers pursued the promise of Pestalozzian musical pedagogy without help or hindrance from him. The most enthusiastic advocate of the Pfeiffer-Nägeli method in Prussia, a man named Carl August Zeller, saw himself as the forward guard of troops of Pestalozzian schoolteachers. Dispatched from Switzerland to Königsberg to spread the method to all of Prussia, he produced his own version of it as a "contribution to the promotion of Prussian national education."[85] Musical emulators of Pestalozzi were thick on the ground in those days, with manuals and singing methods for schoolchildren coming off the presses at a pace of several a year.[86] Meanwhile, controversies raged over whether to use notes on a staff or various numbering devices in teaching, when and how to introduce actual songs, and whether the Lutheran chorale still had value as a teaching device.

Zelter, surely the man best placed to help an increasingly centralized school administration choose among these methods, remained absent from the fray. He was busy, of course, and preoccupied with his space problems— "all I know is that I must wait, always wait," he wrote to Goethe of his fruitless lobbying, "we all will have to wait, until our hair falls out."[87] In 1818, while waiting, he traveled to Switzerland to receive a tutorial in the

---

[83] Nipperdey, *Germany*, 44.

[84] Hans Georg Nägeli, *Pestalozzische Gesangbildungslehre nach Pfeiffers Erfindung*, 68.

[85] Zeller cited in Wilhelm Kramer, *Formen und Funktionen exemplarisher Darstellung von Musikunterricht im 19. und 20. Jahrhundert* (Wölfenbüttel, 1990), 149–51.

[86] Less dogmatic and ultimately more influential was the work of Bernard Christoph Ludwig Natorp, e.g., his *Anleitung zur Unterweisung im Singen für Volkschulen. Erster und zweiter Cursus* (1813–20; repr., Frankfurt, 1989).

[87] Quoted in Fischer-Dieskau, *Zelter*, 105.

Pestalozzian pedagogy from Nägeli himself. But he never adopted the Pfeiffer-Nägeli method, or any other innovation. Meanwhile, school music instruction became all the more wedded to one version or another of simplified singing instruction. The centrality of song to general musical education in Germany helped to create the nation in which even the smallest town had a chorus and a *Liedertafel*, church services boasted enthusiastic choirs, and many thousands of amateur singers could be mobilized for any regional choral festival, all to the astonishment and alarm of foreign visitors.[88] But it also condemned generations of school children to musical instruction of a dreary and narrow sort. Not until the reforming work of Leo Kestenberg in the second great reform period of the 1920s did musical instruction in the schools achieve what the more imaginative reformers of the 1810s and 1820s had envisioned. One of the ironies of German musical development, for which Zelter does bear some responsibility, is that in the era in which instrumental music achieved its enormous prestige among the adult musical public (thanks in part to Beethoven), primary instruction in instruments and instrumental music remained almost wholly absent from the schools and hence unavailable to all but the children of professional musicians and the cultivated elite.[89]

Zelter did exert himself to make piano instruction available to greater numbers of Prussians, although one wishes in this case he had shown a little more of the hidebound traditionalism for which he had become famous.[90] In 1821 he became enamored with one of the biggest frauds to sweep across musical Europe in the first half of the century. This music man was named Johann Bernhard Logier. Born in Kassel in 1777, he had worked as a journeyman player of wind instruments since his teenage years, most recently in Dublin. Such positions hardly offered a living, even if, like Logier, one taught piano on the side. In those early days of free-market musical instruction, when the piano was a new piece of technology, the possibilities for acquiring a number of individual pupils were good, but the possibilities for

---

[88] Lowell Mason, considered the progenitor of the American choral movement and music education, described attending a church service in Hamburg in 1837: "They were singing a Chorale—the whole congregation and sung loud. . . . The hymns were very long." In Berlin a week later, the "congregation was singing a choral as I went in—the effect was sublime and highly devotional. . . . but the organ is always very loud and all sing loud; Here was a choir of about 8 or 10 boys and as many men—the boys sang treble the men base [*sic*] and all very loud" (*A Yankee Musician in Europe: the 1837 Journals of Lowell Mason*, ed. Michael Broyles [Ann Arbor, 1990], 60, 64).

[89] David Gramit argues that this development confined choral music to "the lower term of a status binary"; in music journalism, choral music occupied "a distinctly subsidiary place" (Gramit, *Cultivating Music*, 112–13).

[90] In 1821, for instance, a group of young musicians established a new *Liedertafel* in Berlin out of frustration with Zelter's stodgy original.

profiting from the ambitions and the musical ignorance of their parents were even better. Logier realized at some point in his early twenties that he would never rise in the world teaching one child at a time, so he came up with a scheme by which he profited handsomely and through which all the amateur musical hopes of the age were reflected back on themselves, as though in a funhouse mirror.

Logier's scheme brought together the appeal of higher learning, the promise of quick results, and the magic of machinery. He established first one, then a whole series of "academies" in Dublin, in which twenty pupils in twice-weekly lessons were taught the basic scales, harmony, and counterpoint, along with mastery of the piano by means of a device of Logier's invention called the Chiroplast. His advertising brochures touted his simple harmonic teachings (no more than what students had always learned) as an innovation that would remove "the tremendous barriers which have hitherto stood in the way of general pupils procuring a scientific knowledge of music," thus enabling anyone to emulate "Corelli, Handel, Haydn, and Mozart." As for the Chiroplast, it consisted of four parts: the "Gamut board," a small board marked with note-names and resting over the keyboard; the "position frame," a contraption of wooden rails and brass rods into which the pupil inserted his or her hands; the "finger guides," two brass plates attached to the "position frame," with holes for thumbs and fingers; and the "wrist guides," brass wires running between the finger guides and the pupil's wrists. The Chiroplast was more like an instrument of torture than music, but Logier acquired a "royal patent" in 1814, installed them on the pianos in his academies, and began signing up students in droves. Well-known musicians, foremost among them Muzio Clementi, the celebrated pianist, composer, and, as it turned out, manufacturer of Chiroplasts, provided testimonials. From Dublin, Logier moved to Edinburgh, then to London itself, where the famous piano virtuoso (and fellow German expatriate) Friedrich Kalkbrenner, not averse to making money off the scheme himself, endorsed Logier and helped establish an academy on Russell Square. Logier did encounter the forces of skepticism in the form of the London Philharmonic Society, which in 1818 published a pamphlet declaring him a fake and his system a fraud. Nevertheless, twenty-one new academies and hundreds of Chiroplasts (from Clementi's Cheapside factory) later, Logier, the former flute-player in a Dublin band, had become a rich man.[91]

---

[91] A number of music histories have described this fad. Of these accounts, the most amusing is Loesser's (*Men, Women, and Pianos: A Social History* [New York, 1954], 295–301), although he claims Logier established eighty-two academies in England—the actual number was twenty-one. More scholarly accounts include Gruhn, *Geschichte der Musikerziehung*, 93–94; Sowa, *An-*

Despite these initial successes, Logier's scheme had little staying power: no matter how tolerant of keyboard bondage the academies' child-pupils may have been (most were girls, starting with Logier's own daughter), it usually became obvious within a year that they had learned little in their group lessons or had learned despite the Chiroplast. But even as the English-speaking world came to share the views of the London Philharmonic Society, the German-speaking world, led by the Prussians, succumbed to Logier's peculiar appeal. His triumphant and timely return to his homeland came at the specific request of none other than Carl Friedrich Zelter. Zelter probably learned of Logier and his methods from a series of favorable reports published in the *AMZ*, the first in 1818 by the respected writer Christian Friedrich Michaelis and the second in 1820 by the composer and violinist Louis Spohr.[92] He wrote to Logier and invited him, on behalf of the government of Prussia, to come to Berlin in person and show what his methods could do. In February 1823, six months after his arrival, sixteen of his young pupils played the piano en masse for Zelter, Minister of Education Karl Friedrich von Altenstein, A. B. Marx, and other musicians. With Zelter's approval, Logier was offered a three-year assignment in Prussia to set up academies and train schoolteachers. His work received extensive coverage in the musical press, most of it favorable, and Logier published a supplementary explanation himself, all for sale in his brother's Berlin bookstore. By 1825 he had established schools across the length and breadth of non-Austrian Germany, from Königsberg to Koblenz, from Hamburg to Munich.[93]

The question remains why such a sober group as Zelter and company should have taken up the Logier fashion as seriously as they did. Arthur Loesser suggested that the group piano lessons resembled an "infantry formation," "intoxicatingly delightful" to Prussian officialdom.[94] More likely a

---

fänge institutioneller Musikerziehung, 151–62 (with a diagram of the Chiroplast); and Wolfgang Scherer, *Klavier-Spiele: Die Psychotechnik der Klaviere im 18. und 19. Jahrhundert* (Munich, 1989), 118–33.

[92] *AMZ* 21 (1818): 893; *AMZ* 23 (1820): 527. Zelter was further spurred to action by the shenanigans of a young man named Franz Stoepel, who came to Berlin claiming to be the authorized representative of the famous Logier method. Dismissed by an unimpressed Zelter, Stoepel subsequently moved from city to city in Germany, setting up Logier-like academies for group piano lessons, minus the Chiroplast, and now claiming to have been the official Prussian representative sent to London to check out Logier's methods. He also published incessantly about his own contributions to the spread of chiroplastery. See his *Beyträge zur Würdigung der neuen Methode des gleichzeitigen Unterrichts einer Mehrzahl von Schülern im Piano-forte Spiel und der Theorie der Harmonie* (Gotha, 1823). None of his ventures were successful, and he died penniless in Paris at age forty.

[93] See Gruhn, *Geschichte der Musikerziehung*, 92.

[94] Loesser, *Men, Women, and Pianos*, 300.

source of delight, however, was Logier's updated approach to German musical tradition. Spohr, for instance, thought Logier's method of teaching harmonics embodied the best of Bach, via Kirnberger. A. B. Marx's journal published a review of Logier's work by Karl Loewe, music director and organist in Stettin. A former Singakademie member and Zelter protégé, Loewe stood even closer than Zelter to the eighteenth-century traditions of Bach and the Lutheran cantorate. Like Spohr, Loewe admired Logier's simplification of harmonization so that even musical beginners could grasp its essential rules. Like Zelter, he wanted musical instruction made more available to those who could not afford private instruction and thought that Logier's academies, with their group instruction, offered "a fundamental understanding of this most precious art to the children of less well-off parents."[95]

But an unsigned article, following upon Loewe's analysis, provided the conclusive statement of Logier's importance and made clear the extent to which Logier had become caught up in the German search for identity through music. According to this author (Marx?), Logier's recent problems in England had stemmed from the musical philistinism of the English. Thankfully, "pure love for his work and for his fatherland" had brought Logier back to Germany, "the land most suited and most dedicated to the promotion of knowledge in general, and of musical knowledge in particular." We find ourselves here in Prussia, the author continued, "in the midst of a new spiritual awakening," to which Logier's work would make an important contribution. Only Germany, it seemed, with Prussia leading the way, could appreciate such a man and his work. With his ingenuity, musical learning, and ranks of earnest pupils, he embodied the uniquely German musical spirit.[96] Logier himself, always the master of timing, did not stick around to see how long this uniquely German appreciation would last. He returned to London in 1826 and for twenty more years lived there in comfort off the profits from his chiroplastery. His schools lingered on in Prussia especially, though the Chiroplast itself soon fell out of use; by 1840 both it and Logier were all but forgotten.

THE PUBLIC ROLE OF MUSICAL AMATEURISM: THE SINGAKADEMIE'S NEW BUILDING

From the perspective of our time in which Chiroplasts are gone but a Singakademie still rehearses in Berlin, Zelter's enduring legacy was to make

---

[95] Karl Loewe, "Ueber Logiers Musik-System," *BAMZ* 2, no. 4 (26 January 1825), 25–26; no. 5 (2 February 1825), 33–34; no. 6 (9 February), 45–46; no. 8 (23 February 1825), 57–58.
[96] *BAMZ* 2, no. 8 (23 February 1825): 60.

choral singing—not piano recitals, not string quartets, not even the manly *Liedertafel*—the public face of musical amateurism. In the 1820s the group achieved its two most lasting claims to public attention—its own building, still standing, right in the midst of all the stately edifices on Unter den Linden, and its participation in the revival of the *St. Matthew Passion*. Zelter deserves full credit for the first, and some credit, as we have already seen, for the second. Both the building and the performance contributed to the emergence of musical amateurism out of the parlor into the public, where it remained as a visual and aural demonstration, constantly renewed, of Germany's musical identity.

Not Zelter, however, but the enterprising Hans Georg Nägeli of Switzerland articulated the highest expectations of musical amateurism in this decade of its growing public prominence. In 1823 and 1824, needing money to shore up his failing businesses, he left Zürich for Germany, the land (he hoped) of musical opportunity. He wished to acquire citizenship in Frankfurt am Main, so he organized a series of public lectures there in the late fall of 1823. These met with such interest that he embarked on a lecture tour of southwestern German cities and in 1826 published them with the firm of Cotta in Stuttgart.[97] The lectures provided brief histories of music and musical practices, and in their published form were dedicated, thanks to Beethoven's intervention, to Rudolph, archduke of Austria, cardinal archbishop of Olmütz, younger brother of the emperor Franz, and devoted patron of Beethoven. Rudolph seems an odd choice for the Swiss republican Nägeli, a Protestant whose many references to Luther and J. S. Bach in the text implied his expectations of a north German, Protestant readership. But Nägeli dedicated his work to Rudolph for his representative qualities: amateur pianist, composition student, "comrade in art," and "friend of the beautiful and the good." He wrote the lectures "in consideration of dilettantes," those lovers of art who were united in the "realm of art, that beautiful province of the realm of God." He also wrote in consideration of their buying power. By the time he set out on his lecture tour, the importance of paying audiences had long been clear to observers of the musical scene, but their discernment as musical consumers remained an anxiety. "Division, dissipation, stagnation, and instability" still characterized musical life, thought Nägeli, and now it was time to educate the "entire public," not just the children.[98]

While Nägeli sought to provide "the simplest possible perspective" on

[97] Hans Georg Nägeli, *Vorlesungen über Musik mit Berücksicktigung der Dilettanten*, ed. Martin Staehelin (Darmstadt, 1983), v–vii.

[98] Ibid., vi, 16, 266, x.

everything musical from philosophy to pedagogy, Hegel was delivering his own far-from-simple thoughts on art and music to large audiences in Berlin.[99] This odd couple of aesthetic educators, Hegel and Nägeli, could hardly have been more dissimilar. Hegel, as Kant before him, lived in an era of immense musical creativity, yet managed to see only a poverty of artistic imagination all around him. Also like Kant, he dismissed music as lacking in ideal—that is to say, serious or abstract—content and deemed it suitable only for satisfying his own considerable appetite for mindless entertainment. With little appreciation for the works of Beethoven, Hegel saw no possibility for the kind of artistic dominance within social life that he, like many idealists, regarded as the supreme achievement of ancient Greece. In the modern era of abstract thought, art must necessarily yield to philosophy. Nägeli diverged from such views all down the line. Art bound humanity together; it "elevated life, nourished love, and promoted the fellowship of all." The integration of poetry and music in song and the wordless beauty of instrumental music were of equal value to him. As much inclined to categorization of the arts as was Hegel, he nevertheless declined to rank them in importance, preferring to see all art as striving toward God: "even in the lesser regions" of art, he wrote, "where sensuality seduces and only emotions are nourished," art deserved attention.[100] Nägeli's criticisms of contemporary musical life did not lead him to conclude, as had Hegel, that art no longer really mattered. Instead he envisioned a future Germany in which music would be as central to the Germans as epic and tragedy had been to the Greeks.

Consequently, Nägeli's lectures, unlike Hegel's, exhorted listeners to change. He sought to persuade "dilettantes" of their importance, educate them, and then move them out in public as promoters of lasting musical values. His views on the motivations of dilettantes, from the most frivolous to the most earnest, were hardly complimentary, revealing considerable ambivalence about the very people to whom he was lecturing. He thought them ignorant, their taste in music execrable, and their susceptibility to "sensual excitation" a major factor in the "false culture" of theatrical display. Yet at the same time, he thought them perfectible, capable of "observing and enjoying," "practicing and participating" in the most demanding music, capable of something greater than they had already achieved. Art of any sort, no matter how brief or frivolous one's encounter with it, held the promise of perfectibility and "longing" toward "the ideal." By "bringing to

[99] Hegel's lectures on aesthetics took place at the University of Berlin in the winter of 1820–21, the summers of 1823 and 1826, and the winter of 1828–29. See his *Introductory Lectures on Aesthetics*, trans. Bernard Bosanquet, ed. Michael Inwood (New York, 1993), xiv.

[100] Nägeli, *Vorlesungen*, 5.

consciousness" this potential in every lover of art, Nägeli wanted to prepare a future in which music everywhere, in theater, concert hall, and church, would move people beyond the "simple" and "easy" pleasures of indulged emotion to the higher satisfaction of feeling and thought integrated in the "totality of artistic achievement." His "philosophy of art," he claimed, was "simplicity itself," but he warned his audience to beware of musical pleasure achieved without effort.[101]

For Nägeli, musical dilettantes represented the salvageable part of unenlightened humanity and the part best positioned to influence the rest. Professional musicians had to earn a living by their music and therefore lacked the ability to act disinterestedly that nineteenth-century liberals saw as essential to public life. A disinterested love of art was the essence of dilettantism, and one achieved it through the recognition that "our artistic powers" led one beyond "a life of sensation" to something more "intellectual and godly." Dilettantes became free the moment they began to practice their music, thus entering the "realm of art" and of self-realization. All of Nägeli's desiderata for musical life—more musical associations, more frequent concerts, more sacred music with or without church services, more "unrestricted public life" in which one could "live free"—reflected the emphasis he placed on the amateur's importance to a moral transformation in society as a whole.[102]

Nägeli's exhortations to musical amateurs to take a more prominent role in public life came at the same time the musical press had begun to review works for amateur pianists and report on student recitals and salon concerts. The term *Hausmusik*, referring to music played at home, did not appear in the press until 1837, in Robert Schumann's *Neue Zeitschrift für Musik*, and several decades went by before the term had any referential stability.[103] But even without a name, the phenomenon had become sufficiently widespread for alarmists like Nägeli and A. B. Marx to fear that the flash and triviality of the professional musical world were overtaking amateurism as well.[104] Publishers had the greatest success in selling easy piano versions of popular Italian arias or pieces cleverly written to make the merely competent pianist gallop up and down the keyboard like a virtuoso. In contrast, the noble but demanding sonata, brought to perfection by Haydn, Mozart, and now

---

[101] Ibid., 4–12, 16, 266, 272.

[102] Ibid., 21, 272.

[103] Nicolai Petrat, *Hausmusik des Biedermeier im Blickpunkt der zeitgenössischen musikalischen Fachpresse (1815–1848)*, Hamburger Beiträge zur Musikwissenschaft, vol. 31 (Hamburg, 1986), 24–25.

[104] *BAMZ* 1, no. 48 (1 December 1824), 415.

Beethoven, languished in the music stores. As early as 1825, one of Marx's reviewers wrote that the sonata was dead, killed off by a plague of easy-playing, easy-listening piano potpourris. By the mid-1830s, Mozart's sonatas were barely available for purchase.[105] For Nägeli and Marx, then, the struggle against musical triviality and the defense of serious music had to involve amateurs, who were too often both the consumers of bad music and the carriers of bad taste.

Marx devoted more column space to covering professional musical performances, but even from the first year of his journal, he held the leaders of amateur musicians accountable for Berlin's poor musical condition. And that meant, above all, Carl Friedrich Zelter. The Singakademie had by 1824 a nearly unassailable reputation throughout German-speaking Europe, garnering accolades from all sides and favorable reviews whenever it performed. It had behind it a quarter-century of musical participation in sacred festivities and solemn occasions, like funerals of royalty (the beloved Queen Luise in 1810), celebrations of victories (the battle of Leipzig in 1813), and return of kings (Friedrich Wilhelm III to Berlin in 1814). It had a membership in the hundreds, among them prominent citizens (the wife of the great architect Schinkel, the intendant of the royal opera, Count von Brühl), child prodigies (Fanny and Felix Mendelssohn), and retired professional singers. It enjoyed the generosity of nobility and wealthy burghers. It held a library of musical manuscripts of astonishing size and scope for an amateur organization, including the private collection of Friedrich Wilhelm II and Carl Philipp Emanuel Bach's collection of his father's scores.[106] Beethoven himself had recognized its stature when he wrote to Zelter in 1823 to offer the Singakademie a manuscript copy of the *Missa Solemnis*, in his own hand, for a mere fifty ducats.

None of this impressed Marx, whose combative attitude toward sacred cows like Zelter and his Singakademie would only have sharpened had he known that Zelter wrote back to Beethoven refusing the offer. Zelter's boneheaded dealings with Beethoven were, in any case, all of a piece with what Marx diagnosed as an aversion to innovation of any sort. Only four

---

[105] Petrat, *Hausmusik*, 71–73.

[106] The royal collection was given to the Singakademie by Friedrich Wilhelm III; C. P. E. Bach's collection was a gift from the private collector Georg Poelchau. The Singakademie sold the Poelchau collection, which included much else besides C. P. E. Bach's musical estate, to the Prussian royal library in 1854, where it survived the destruction of the Second World War and remains the foundational collection of the musical section of the state library in Berlin today (Eberle, *Sing-Akademie*, 80–81). The rest of the Singakademie library was thought for years to have been destroyed in the war, but in 1999 many of the missing manuscripts were discovered in Kiev. See Wolff, "Recovered in Kiev."

months into publishing his journal, Marx launched an attack. It began with
a respectful if routine review, not by Marx, of the Singakademie's annual
performance on Good Friday of Graun's *Tod Jesu*, praising its usual "precision and intensity" and its contribution to "the refinement of artistic taste
and the ennoblement of our sensibilities." Then Marx weighed in: "With
all due respect to the insightful author of the previous report," he declared,
"I cannot stay silent about misconduct, the like of which I have not encountered even in much smaller cities and which is utterly unworthy of
Berlin and Fasch's nobly formed academy." The performance, he continued, had been marked by "grave deformities."[107] The Singakademie, he accused, had squandered its "rich resources," doing little to "benefit its members, the public, and the progress of art." Its recent performance was a
disastrous display of "obsolete and harmful practices," from fussy pitch production, to unevenness of tempo, indifference to form, inattention to
progress in instrumentation, and an attitude on the part of Zelter that could
only be described as uninvolved and uncaring.[108]

Each of Marx's claims point to controversies concerning historical performance practice still alive to this day, and Marx was generally happy to debate with his readers on the respective merits of authenticity and
progress.[109] But on one point Marx would not budge, even several years
later when he apologized for the harshness of his 1824 review. Zelter, he insisted, had neglected the "first duty of an academy director," which was to
enlighten the public as a whole by providing "a thoughtful and purposeful
range of works in regular public performances." The Singakademie performed too infrequently—by Marx's count, three concerts in as many
years—and tended to repetition. "Year after year," he complained, Graun's
Tod Jesu took precedence over "even Handel's *Messiah*," a work of much
greater profundity. Marx drew attention to innovative performances by
other amateur singing groups—in Hamburg, Leipzig, Darmstadt, Frankfurt, Stettin, indeed all over the "republic of scholars and artists" that constituted the "German nation."[110] In Berlin itself, a choir director named
Hansmann was outperforming Zelter and his famous Singakademie: Hansmann, wrote one of Marx's reporters, had "earned the thanks of all Berliners" for his performances of new works; even the roughness of his performances was forgivable given the "deplorable circumstances" in Berlin,

---

[107] J. P. S., "Charfreitags-Musik," *BAMZ* 1, no. 17 (28 April 1824): 152; A. B. Marx, "Ueber
denselben Gegenstand," *BAMZ* 1, no. 17 (28 April 1824): 152–53.

[108] Marx, "Ueber denselben Gegenstand," 153–56.

[109] K, "Bemerkungen," *BAMZ* 1, no. 20 (19 May 1824): 178.

[110] A. B. Marx, "Ueber den Zustand der Musik in Darmstadt," *BAMZ* 4, no. 22 (30 May 1827):
173.

where "the richest and noblest powers of singing slumber unused, year after year, in the Singakademie."[111]

Nor was Marx's criticism of the Singakademie's low public profile unprecedented. In 1805 Friedrich Mann had suggested in the pages of Reichardt's *Berlinische Musikalische Zeitung* that the Singakademie seemed to have "secrecy and silence" as a "founding principle"; it strove "too little for the applause of the world" and relied too much "on the patronage of noble and powerful people."[112] Even longtime supporters like Lea Mendelssohn had developed a jaundiced view of the group. Describing Zelter's less-than-stunning performance of Handel's *Judas Maccabeus* in 1827, she echoed the 1824 correspondent: "It is heartbreaking how such vigorous, extensive resources in our city turn mountains into mice."[113] Yet Zelter, for his part, was not as somnolent as Marx and others implied. While Marx promoted Germany's musical greatness by fulminating in the musical press, Zelter pursued similar goals in another way, one that involved more bricks and mortar than pens and ink.

At least since 1811, Zelter had hoped to persuade the Prussian government to build the Singakademie its own hall next to the Academy of Fine Arts. Buildings signified permanence for Zelter, and a building for the Singakademie, especially one on the stately promenade of Unter den Linden, would secure its standing in public life, with or without performances. Practicality spoke in its favor as well. The Singakademie had always rehearsed in cold and damp places smelling of horse stalls and anatomy laboratories.[114] Performance space was equally unsatisfactory, though for different reasons. Its rare performances had lately been held in the Royal Opera House, where the acoustics and prestige were excellent but the stage was too small to accommodate all the singers.

Amateur groups everywhere faced these same difficulties. The Hamburg Gesangverein, modeled on Zelter's group, rehearsed in the back of a music store and performed anywhere it could find space.[115] Vienna, by everyone's

---

[111] A. B. Marx, "Standpunkt der Zeitung," *BAMZ* 3, no. 52 (27 December 1826): 423; Marx, "Ueber denselben Gegenstand," 153; Jex, "Korrespondenz," *BAMZ* 2, no. 16 (20 April 1825): 124; S, "Korrespondenz," *BAMZ* 1 (13 October 1824): 349.

[112] Friedrich Mann, "Feierliche Versammlungen der Berlinischen Singeakademie im Jahre 1805," *BMZ* 1, no. 19 (1805): 73.

[113] Lea Mendelssohn to Karl Klingemann, 28 December 1827, in Klingemann, *Briefwechsel*, 45.

[114] Zelter enjoyed telling an anecdote about a "peasant woman" who happened to be walking by the academy building when a rehearsal was in progress and, thinking that she was hearing an anatomical dissection underway, "clasped her head with her hands and cried out to passersby in true Brandenburger dialect, 'O dear Jesus! How the poor men suffer! It is a sin and a disgrace!'" (*AMZ* 8, no. 7 [13 November 1805]: 111).

[115] Josef Sittard, *Geschichte des Musik- und Concertwesens in Hamburg* (Altona, 1890), 295.

reckoning the most glittering musical city in German-speaking Europe, had no hall adequate for even medium-scale instrumental or choral concerts—professional or amateur—until 1870.[116] Measured solely in terms of public spaces and buildings, choral and instrumental music ranked way below operatic music for many more decades. Certainly no amateur group anywhere in central Europe had its own building, let alone one as close to the centers of power as Zelter envisioned. So despite Marx's belief that the old man had run out of ideas and energy, the master mason's plans for the public acknowledgment of music's importance were in some ways even bolder than Marx's faith in the printed word. After all, music journals had been around for years, but choral society edifices existed nowhere.

Still, by 1818 Zelter seemed further from satisfaction than ever. King Friedrich Wilhelm III's conversion of the stables of the Academy of Fine Arts into a permanent museum was underway, fitfully to be sure, and had rendered the Singakademie temporarily homeless. Despite letters aplenty from Zelter to the cultural authorities, Hardenberg himself (then the king's chief minister) declared in 1821 that there would be no return to the academy building, or to any of the land immediately around it. At the same time, he told Zelter that the king was ready to give him a plot of land "next to the moat behind the new watch building."[117] At this point, Zelter's hopes became unexpectedly caught up in those of Karl Friedrich Schinkel, who as an architect, builder, and would-be urban planner had been rising in the ranks of Prussian state service since 1810. As James Sheehan has written, Schinkel "combined a devotion to the classical style with a Schillerian faith in art's moral power and civic purpose," and by 1817 he had drawn up his own plan for a reorganization of the entire heart of official Berlin.[118] In 1819 he designed the Palace Bridge, or Schlossbrücke, which linked the island on which the royal palace stood to the westward expanse of Unter den Linden, with its growing array of stately buildings, including some of his own design.

Schinkel's ability to realize his plan was, nevertheless, limited by the king's consent, which was never more than partial over the decades of Schinkel's service to the state. The Singakademie episode illustrates the constant frustrations he faced, for the plot of land Hardenberg had described to Zelter lay right in the midst of the broad area Schinkel still hoped to transform. It was, to be sure, set back from Unter den Linden itself, be-

---

[116] Sigrid Wiesmann, "Vienna: Bastion of Conservatism," in *Music and Society: The Early Romantic Era between Revolutions, 1789–1848,* ed. Alexander Ringer (Englewood Cliffs, NJ, 1990), 91–92.

[117] Hardenberg letter, 10 June 1821, in Schröder, 24.

[118] James Sheehan, *Museums in the German Art World* (New York, 2000), 71–73.

hind and between the main university building and Schinkel's own Neue Wache, but it still represented a prime piece of official real estate, one that would be essential to any unified reorganization. In 1821, maybe at Zelter's request but more likely on his own initiative, Schinkel provided Zelter with a design for the proposed new Singakademie building, perhaps hoping that this unexpected whim of the king's, to give precious space to an amateur choral society, could still serve what was a shared vision of art's essential place in public life. In the year that followed, he drew up plans for a new art museum to be built not by the Academy of Fine Arts further down Unter den Linden but right across the canal from the proposed site for a Singakademie building, at the northern end of the palace's Lustgarten. In early 1823, the king approved the plan, and Schinkel began work on what is now known as the Altes Museum.

With its placement in a group of buildings that included the palace, the cathedral, and the arsenal, Schinkel's museum made, in Sheehan's words, "a powerful statement about the significance of art," asserting "its claim to equal status with dynasty, church, and army."[119] Music might have been part of that statement too, and perhaps in the end it was, but more by virtue of proximity than any actual involvement of Schinkel. When in 1825 the group had finally secured enough money to proceed with building plans, Zelter did not award the contract to Schinkel but to Karl Theodor Ottmer, a twenty-four-year-old architect from Braunschweig and former protégé of Zelter himself. Ottmer promised to build something at half the cost Schinkel had proposed, so in June 1825 Zelter ceremonially broke ground for the project. In November 1825, the traditional *Richtfest*, or topping-out ceremony, took place, at which all the masons, carpenters, and joiners gathered to crown the new rafters with a garland so burdened with "flowers and ribbons and gee-gaws" that it took four men to carry it from Zelter's house to the building site. As he wrote to Goethe the next day, "unfortunately, one man got drunk for the occasion, and today I'm only sorry it wasn't me."[120]

The building was completed by January 1827, but at three times the cost Ottmer had promised, mainly because of problems with boggy ground. Inexperienced and unfamiliar with the ground, Ottmer had not anticipated such problems, but Zelter, master builder and lifelong Berliner, who knew the land had been partially reclaimed by filling in an old moat, ought surely to have done so. In any case, Ottmer built something at least reminiscent of

---

[119] Ibid., 73.

[120] "Besoffen war leider nur ein Einziger und heute ärgert's ich dass ich selbst nicht der Einzig gewesen bin" (Zelter to Goethe, 26 November 1825, in Schröder, 32).

The Singakademie, Berlin. Engraving after a drawing by Klose, 1833. From *On Wings of Song: A Biography of Felix Mendelssohn* by Wilfrid Blunt (New York, 1974), by permission of the Preussische Kulturbesitz.

Schinkel's classicism—a rectangular two-story white stone building with a peaked roof, triangular architrave, and simple classical motives on the four columns at each end of the building. If the design was more squat than Schinkel's, the lines and proportions subtly less graceful, it still pleased the eye, and its opening was occasion for great celebration in April 1827. The Singakademie performed, finally, Fasch's sixteen-part mass, the composition of which had started all this singing more than thirty years earlier.

The building forced the Singakademie into the public eye, and not just because of its prominent place. The construction of the building, with its massive cost overruns, left the group with a mountain of debt and no obvious way to raise money. The leadership tried legal action, suing Ottmer for false cost estimates, but since he was already bankrupt, it got no satisfaction. Next, the Singakademie petitioned the king for an interest-free loan to pay off most of the debt, citing all the singing it had done for charity and the contributions it made to the general welfare. The king refused, not once but twice. Finally, reluctantly, the group was forced to resort to a number of measures that chipped away at the exclusivity and intimacy of its initial founding. It expanded the membership dramatically, reaching a peak of 642 members in 1842. It began to rent out the new building to lecturers and virtuosi: August Wilhelm von Schlegel lectured there in its first year of existence, Alexander von Humboldt delivered his sixteen-lecture series on the cosmos to packed audiences night after night, and Paganini performed to the usual swooning crowds in the same spring as the revival of the *St. Matthew Passion.* In 1848 it became the site for the convening of the newly elected Prussian National Assembly, though we cannot tell whether this group of liberal revolutionaries ever paid rent to the Singakademie before decamping to the Schauspielhaus several blocks away. Most important, after Zelter's death in 1832 the Singakademie finally accepted the need for more frequent public concerts, with ticket receipts going to the group itself rather than to charities in Berlin.[121]

The burden of debt made the Singakademie's increasing public prominence seem as much forced on them by financial necessity as freely chosen, but plenty of people, the outspoken Marx among them, found much that was virtuous in this necessity. "With the opening of its own impressive place," announced the *Berliner Allgemeine Musikalische Zeitung,* "the Singakademie has laid the keystone for an independent institution dedicated wholly to art," at last risking the approval of a "changeable public" for the sake of the public's own good. In finally growing up, the Singakademie must also, urged the journal, reveal to the public the great choral works it had heretofore treated as though "a secret exclusively for them to protect": "art cannot live by secrets and exclusivity"; "her admirers and worshippers must be allowed to come freely into the community" formed in its service and shaped by its greatness of "mind and spirit."[122] It was now time for the Singakademie, ensconced in its gleaming new building in the heart of Berlin, to take up the challenge of bringing art to the people, just as Alexander von Humboldt had brought science.

AMATEURISM IN PERFORMANCE: THE SINGAKADEMIE IN 1829

The 1829 performance of the *St. Matthew Passion* would seem to have emerged from such exhortations as though called forth. Yet Marx was thinking more of Fasch's sixteen-part mass than anything by Bach. In 1827 and 1828 Marx's interest in Bach focused on making available the scores of his large-scale works, for study first of all, and only then, maybe, for performance. Nor did the building inspire Felix Mendelssohn, who set off on his travels around Germany shortly after the opening celebrations, returning in September to take up private rehearsals of the *St. Matthew Passion* in his

---

[121] Eberle, *Sing-Akademie,* 77–79.
[122] A. B. Marx, "Ueber die Faschische Sing-Akademie," *BAMZ* 4, no. 10 (7 March 1827): 73–74.

living room, among an exclusive circle of friends and with no clear end in view. Eduard Devrient, on the other hand, who as one of Zelter's stable of soloists performed at least three times in the building over the next two years, must have seen its possibilities. But whether or not the building itself inspired the performance, the performance did indeed take place in this new hall and did provide, after two disappointing performances of Handel oratorios over the course of 1827 and 1828, the first and most powerful demonstration of what the Singakademie could accomplish as a public institution.

We know little about what Singakademie members thought of rehearsing and performing the *St. Matthew Passion*, except what two of those intimately involved in the project—Fanny Mendelssohn and Therese Devrient—said of their colleagues' excitement and enthusiasm. Zelter had always rehearsed more of the Singakademie's musical treasures than he allowed in performance, so the singers were familiar with at least a few of the chorales, and for years they had sung the Bach motets, which in their complexity were comparable to the most technically demanding choruses of the *St. Matthew Passion*. In 1811 Zelter had introduced them to the Kyrie from the B-minor Mass but gave it up because it was too difficult; rehearsals in 1815 of portions of the *St. Matthew Passion* had likewise petered out. Thus was it left to the foreigner and Bach novice, Gasparo Spontini, to direct the first Berlin performance of the B-minor Mass, using professional singers.

For his part, Mendelssohn placed far greater demands on the singers than had Zelter, not perhaps in sheer accuracy of singing but in the amount of music to be learned, its level of complexity, the fast pace of preparation, and the glare of publicity. The publicity, of course, was initially supplied by Marx, but as the performance drew near, other Berlin newspapers picked up on the gathering sense of excitement. Zelter wrote to Goethe two days before the performance that "you will already have seen from the paper that we are going to perform the Passion music of J. S. Bach."[123] The first performance was given to a larger audience than the Singakademie had ever before faced, and two more performances followed in quick succession, once again an unprecedented experience for these amateur singers.

Yet despite Zelter's belief that if one asked too much of them the singers would quit, they did not. Devrient, probably the least disinterested of observers, wrote of the Singakademie that it "achieved in these choral performances its most outstanding accomplishment": "whoever heard the sound of these three to four hundred highly trained amateurs, whoever experienced with what fervent zeal great music inspired them, will under-

---

[123] Zelter to Goethe, 9 March 1829, in *Goethe's Letters to Zelter, with extracts from those of Zelter to Goethe*, ed. and trans. A. D. Coleridge (London, 1892), 351; hereafter Coleridge.

stand that, with perfect leadership, perfection was achieved." Reviewers, for their part, went beyond their usual praise for the Singakademie. The reporter in the *Spenersche Zeitung* wrote that it had exceeded even its reputation for "being the best in Europe." Ludwig Rellstab, along with Marx the leading music critic in the city and at least as hard to please, wrote that "we have never heard such a perfect performance." Further, "this reporter felt again how invaluable and noble is this art"; to all who took part in the performance, "we owe the greatest thanks."[124]

As for Marx, in his relentless coverage of the performances, he spared hardly a word for the Singakademie itself, until the third time when Zelter conducted the work. This provided him with an occasion to justify all his earlier sniping, and to a lesser extent, to make up for it. Zelter had performed the greatest service yet to this work, proving, by Marx's reasoning, that with Mendelssohn's departure, the work itself would not disappear but live on among the public in its full glory. "To Herr Zelter also goes high honor," wrote Marx, "for he has shown himself ready to change his ways," "without concern for the contradiction" between today's "new paths" and "the old ones he once followed so persistently." As for the "incomparable Singakademie," wrote Marx, it had performed a work on Good Friday "worthy of the times and worthy of the people." It had fulfilled "our long-held and long-expressed wishes" for the ennoblement of musical performance in Berlin, and the good effects on the public were "unmistakable." "The future," he concluded, "will reveal the ever more important consequences" of these events.[125]

Zelter's own impressions, left to us solely in the form of his letters to Goethe, are by contrast understated and dry. He was pleased with the acclaim that his beloved Bach, his building, his pupil, and his life's work, the Singakademie, had received in the wake of the performance: "Our Bach music came off successfully yesterday, and Felix, without any fuss, held his forces well in hand. The King and the entire Court saw a closely packed house before them; I, with my score, posted myself in a small corner near the orchestra, whence I could survey my little people and the public at the same time."[126] Yet his unease with the proceedings persisted—"the music in general" was "scarcely practicable"—and he never embraced Marx's view of the Singakademie as an institution with its face turned toward the public. His reluctance to perform publicly, about which Marx was not mistaken, reflected a belief that grew stronger as the years went by, that the public

---

[124] Geck, 53.

[125] A. B. Marx, "Fünfter Bericht über die Passionsmusik nach dem Evangelium Matthäi von Johann Sebastian Bach," *BAMZ* 6, no. 16 (18 April 1829): 121.

[126] Zelter to Goethe, 12 March 1829, in Coleridge, 351.

could not love the music he loved and that even the loyal Singakademie could hardly be prevailed on to do more than come to their regular rehearsals. What had once been a desire to see the musical past animate and enrich the musical present became a dogged hanging on to traditions he himself had invented, chief among them the performance, year in and year out, of Graun's *Tod Jesu*.

His letters to Goethe in the last fifteen or so years of their lives took on the increasingly melancholy tone of one who has lived long and feels more and more left behind. Writing from Vienna in 1819, Zelter spoke of these "out-of-joint times," in which a new requiem by Cherubini "pleased everywhere" because there was "no true word in it" and "not the faintest feeling." A few years later, he suggested to Goethe the futility of building theaters for the people, which led Goethe to remark to his friend Eckermann that Zelter was "a splendid fellow," but had never really understood why he, Goethe, had devoted his "whole life to the people and their improvement."[127] Zelter's gloomy mood lifted only in his delight at young Felix, "still the head lad," as he wrote in 1824, and his "wide-awake" sister Fanny, who were "fond of me just as they find me": "even if I myself fail to do anything much, I have in any case kept my lads to it." "Any good that comes" to Felix, he wrote a year later, "I enjoy tenfold." Zelter's time may have passed; he was, as Goethe had written only a month earlier, "the last of an epoch which will not so soon return again." But Felix had seized "the age by the ears" and carried it "along with him." But while Goethe mused on a world with "railways, quick mails, steamships, and every possible kind of facility in the way of communication" and Zelter grumbled about the "nullity of the present," Felix himself had turned back to the past, to recover Bach in a way more public and more lasting than any Zelter had ever dared.[128]

---

[127] Zelter to Goethe, 29 July 1819, in Coleridge, 179; Goethe to Zelter, 11 April 1825, in Coleridge, 241; Zelter to Goethe, 19 April 1825, and editor's note, in Coleridge, 243.

[128] Zelter to Goethe, 10 December 1824, in Coleridge, 237; Zelter to Goethe, 17 March 1822, in Coleridge, 209; Goethe to Zelter, 6 June 1825, in Coleridge, 246–47; Zelter to Goethe, 1 July 1825, in Coleridge, 248; Goethe to Zelter, 30 October 1828, in Coleridge, 335.

The St. Matthew Passion

in Concert

Protestantism, Historicism, and Sacred Music

The public performance of the *St. Matthew Passion* in 1829 in Berlin, as we have seen, required a hall, a score, singers, instrumentalists, a conductor, and an audience. But to explain the logistics of how each got there does not answer two questions central to the meaning of the event: Why Bach? and Why the *St. Matthew Passion*? Eduard Devrient's memoirs described the doubts of the organizers over the appropriateness of the composer and the piece for contemporary listeners: "How will the public receive a work so utterly strange to them?" he recalled thinking. Short movements by Bach had been performed "as a curiosity and received as a piece of antiquarianism." But how, he asked, could one devote a whole evening to "Sebastian Bach, whom the public conceived as unmelodious, dry, and unintelligible?"[1]

To answer these questions takes us to the intermingling of historical consciousness and faith in progress within the music aesthetics of the era. As Dahlhaus explains, "the century of revolutions was also the century of muse-

[1] Devrient, *Meine Erinnerungen*, 46.

ums," and in it the history of music came to be seen as "a string of innovations," which would in time pass into the category of the classical, an "imaginary museum" of past innovations that still spoke to the present.[2] Mendelssohn's "great deed" in 1829 became the first public realization of such views of
past, present, and future. Its success made it possible, only six years later, for
Schumann to write that his musical "attitude" was "simple": "to recall the past
and its music with all the energy at our disposal, to draw attention to the ways
in which new artistic beauties can find sustenance at a source so pure."[3] To understand why this emerging aesthetics of historicism and progress could have
had such appeal in 1829, we need to consider one final piece of the puzzle:
how Mendelssohn's *Passion* performance invoked another spirit of the age, that
of religion and more specifically of Protestant Christianity.

Historicism, Protestantism, and progress were bound together in the reception of Bach in 1829 in ways that were self-evident to the people who
participated in the revival. We tend to regard these attitudes in isolation—
here a book on the idea of progress, there one on historic preservation,
elsewhere a book on the Prussian church union. In the 1830s the conservative theologian Ernst Wilhelm Hengstenberg predicted that the opposition
between the "two peoples" of "our time," those of faith and those of "in-
fidelity," would grow "increasingly intense and exclusive," but the *St.
Matthew Passion* in 1829 worked otherwise.[4] Those who were moved by the
music included defenders of orthodoxy like Friedrich Wilhelm III, rationalists like Abraham Mendelssohn, Catholic aesthetes like Joseph Maria von
Radowitz (then Prussian chief of artillery), and pantheists like Hengstenberg's bête noire Goethe. The variety of responses defies the efforts made
over the years to sum up its meaning in a single phrase such as "nineteenth-
century nostalgia" or "romanticization of Bach" or "art as secularized religion." There may be some truth to each of these, but the intersecting of
cultural attitudes and social developments in the 1829 reception of Bach's
Passion music remains its distinction. The ironies that such intersections
tend to produce resonate in the oft-quoted exclamation of Felix Mendelssohn to Eduard Devrient, after obtaining Zelter's permission to perform the
work publicly: "And to think that it should be an actor and a Jew who give
back to the people the greatest of the Christian works."[5]

[2] Dahlhaus, *Nineteenth-Century Music*, 247.

[3] Robert Schumann, opening statement for his *Neue Zeitschrift für Musik* in 1835, quoted in
ibid.

[4] Quoted in John Toews, *Hegelianism: The Path toward Dialectical Humanism 1805–1841* (Cambridge, 1980), 250.

[5] We have no one's word but Devrient's that Mendelssohn actually said this, but it remains a frequent feature in accounts of the performance as well as a staple of the increasingly voluminous

GERMAN PROTESTANTISM AND THE PRUSSIAN CHURCH UNION

Of all the contexts with which this "greatest of Christian works" resonated in 1829, the most difficult to recreate is the most obvious, that of the Protestant community of Berlin. Protestants made up more than 90 percent of Berlin's population at this time, but the contours of their culture remain obscure. In contrast to the many studies of Berlin's Jewish community, one of the most scrutinized groups of people in German history, the scholarship on Protestants has barely touched the history of everyday confessional life.[6] Yet the period between the Prussian defeat in 1807 and the revolutions of 1848 witnessed a close intertwining of political and ecclesiastical issues and a diverse process of religious renewal. As Christopher Clark has emphasized, this was a period of unprecedented state activism in church affairs, colliding and combining with movements of pietistic awakening, resurgent orthodoxy, and religious rationalism.[7]

Of all these developments, the most immediately important for Berlin Protestants was Friedrich Wilhelm III's announcement in 1817, in the midst of celebrations of the three-hundredth anniversary of Luther's ninety-five theses, of a union between the Lutheran and Reformed branches of Protestantism. To dramatize the event, the royal family, once divided between the king's Calvinist Protestantism and the queen's Lutheranism (she died in 1810, having never taken communion with her equally devout husband), attended a joint Reformed and Lutheran service in the royal chapel at Potsdam.[8] The union represented a curious culmination of the era of reform, which had begun after the inglorious collapse of the Prussian state in 1807. The reformers' efforts to free the state and its subjects from the deadening

---

writings on the nature, or even existence, of Mendelssohn's Jewish identity (Devrient, *Meine Erinnerungen*, 57).

[6] The foundational account of Berlin's Jews is Ludwig Geiger, *Geschichte der Juden in Berlin* (Berlin, 1871). Recent notable additions to the long historiographical tradition are Jacob Katz, *Out of the Ghetto: The Social Background of Jewish Emancipation, 1770–1870* (Cambridge, MA, 1973); and Hertz, *Jewish High Society in Old Regime Berlin*. On Protestants in Berlin, see Deborah Fleetham, "In the Shadow of Luther: The Reshaping of Protestantism in Berlin, 1815–1848" (Ph.D. diss., University of Rochester, 2001).

[7] Christopher Clark, "Confessional Policy and the Limits of State Action: Frederick William III and the Prussian Church Union 1817–40," *Historical Journal* 39, no. 4 (1996): 985–1004; Clark, "The 'Christian' State and the 'Jewish Citizen' in Nineteenth-Century Prussia," in *Protestants, Catholics and Jews in Germany, 1800–1914*, ed. Helmut Walser Smith (New York, 2001), 67–93; and Clark, *The Politics of Conversion: Missionary Protestantism and the Jews in Prussia, 1728–1941* (Oxford, 1995), esp. 83–123.

[8] Friedrich Wilhelm III's statement of 27 September 1817 to consistories, synods, and superintendents, cited in Clark, "Confessional Policy," 985.

weight of the past had at first left church affairs on the margins, but in 1812 Karl August von Hardenberg briefly turned to them. True to the diminishing fervor of reform, his nationalization of church lands and reorganization of church institutions reflected fiscal considerations more than liberalizing or religious ones. The announcement of the union by Friedrich Wilhelm III just half a decade later seemed to be an extension of this rational state management from church administration to church service, informed perhaps by the Enlightenment impulse to create harmony among all religious confessions.[9]

But the king's involvement actually departed from the reformers' secular humanism. Instead it reasserted the conservative religious principles he had articulated already in 1802 in a royal memorandum "On the Decay of Religiosity." Church and state were not separate entities, he stated then, nor was the order of liturgy a matter for individual parishes to decide for themselves. The union of 1817, fifteen years and successive crises of the state later, enforced the state's interest in all aspects of church life on the basis of the conservative notion that "the state was in some sense Christian."[10] As the ruler of the Christian state, Friedrich Wilhelm III claimed the right to shape every aspect of Christian worship, expending his never-abundant energies in the 1820s in repeated revisions of the new liturgy. The Union Church liturgy was Friedrich Wilhelm's own invented tradition, with its mingling of aspects of the German, Swedish, Huguenot, and Anglican orders of service and, most unexpectedly, its inclusion of modern arrangements of medieval Russian Orthodox chants.

Each of these aspects of the union—its reformism, its statism, and its assertion of religious orthodoxy—aroused some form of dissent among the king's citizens. The 1820s thus became a unsettled decade in the practice of Protestantism in Prussia, riven by controversies over what constituted the Protestant community and how belief enjoined the believer to act. Freethinking pastors and theologians, among them Friedrich Schleiermacher, resented—and resisted—the imposition of an administrative union from above, rather than from within the church, and regarded many aspects of the new liturgy as repulsively Roman Catholic in their distancing of clergy from congregation. "Old Lutherans" were dismayed by the Calvinist replacement of communion with a mere breaking of bread, and in some places they resisted vigorously.[11] Likewise, the "Berlin Awakening" of the 1820s opposed the union for diluting religious experience, on the one hand,

---

[9] On eighteenth-century modernizing precedents, see Nicholas Hope, *German and Scandinavian Protestantism 1700–1918* (Oxford, 1995), 314, 287–88.

[10] Clark, "The 'Christian' State," 75–77.

[11] Conflicts among Protestants are the subject of Clark, "Confessional Policy."

and threatening the traditional privileges of old regime corporate bodies, especially the aristocracy, on the other.[12] Caught in crosscurrents of enlightenment and conservatism, reform and reaction, the union did not so much polarize the Prussian Protestants as reveal them to be precisely *not* what Friedrich Wilhelm III imagined they ought to be, that is, a unified community in harmony with the interests of the state.

Heterodoxy did not amount to secularization, but the struggle over church union does draw attention to a deeper transformation in the nature of religious piety. Lucien Hölscher has argued that the meaning of communion changed decisively in the course of the eighteenth century, from a "judgment of conscience" that bound the community together in "rigorously enforced" church attendance, to a more metaphorical experience that had "lost its power of socio-political and physiological-spiritual integration." This "epochal caesura" in the history of piety signaled the emergence of a "modern piety" that was just as widespread but less "churched" than traditional piety. The nineteenth century saw belief made individual and religious experience made private.[13] Seen from this perspective, Friedrich Wilhelm III's effort at union defied transformations in devotional culture. His Union Church enjoined public religious uniformity that for Protestants, at least, had become separate from their beliefs. It embodied his own religious preferences, imposing them with "unabated tenacity" on every Prussian Protestant.[14] But because even state action could not tighten the loosening bond between piety and community, he encountered resistance from all sides and met with indifference to the point of neglect even among those who complied.

ROMANTICISM, HISTORICISM, AND THE CRISIS OF PROTESTANT CHURCH MUSIC

The travails of the Prussian union and the transformation of devotional culture are one context in which to understand the reception of Bach in the 1820s, especially his *St. Matthew Passion*. Hölscher's eighteenth-century

[12] Christopher M. Clark, "The Politics of Revival: Pietists, Aristocrats, and the State Church in Early Nineteenth-Century Prussia," in *Between Reform, Reaction, and Resistance: Studies in the History of German Conservatism from 1789 to 1945*, ed. Larry E. Jones and James N. Retallack (Providence, 1993), 31–60.

[13] Lucien Hölscher, "The Religious Divide: Piety in Nineteenth Century Germany," in Smith, *Protestants, Catholics, and Jews*, 35; Hölscher, "Die Religion des Bürgers: Bürgerliche Frömmigkeit und Protestantische Kirche im 19. Jahrhundert," *Historische Zeitschrift* 250 (1990): 595–630.

[14] Clark, "Confessional Policy," 987; and Thomas Stamm-Kuhlmann, *König in Preussens grosser Zeit: Friedrich Wilhelm III, der Melancholiker auf dem Thron* (Berlin, 1992), 477–86.

"caesura" in the history of piety fell between the first performance of the *St. Matthew Passion* in Leipzig's Thomaskirche on Good Friday in 1727 and Mendelssohn's reintroduction of it into public musical culture in the hall of the Berlin Singakademie on a Friday without special religious significance in 1829. So glaring is the absence of religious markers in the 1829 performance—no traditional religious service, no cantor, no choir, no church, no altar, no cross, not to mention the salient presence of an actor and a Jew—that the thesis of secularization has proven irresistible.[15] In his definitive history of Protestant church music, Friedrich Blume wrote that Bach's vocal music was revived not "because it was churchly"; it "was revived in a process of secularization."[16] Yet what exactly did secularization mean in such a context? Music did become caught up in fundamental changes in the relations among belief, institutions, and society. But the appearance in a concert hall of a piece of patently religious music, indeed of a Passion oratorio enacting the very core of Christian belief, may reflect the free-floating of piety to places outside traditional sacred spaces just as much as the decline of religious belief. Dahlhaus urges us to understand the romantics' religious apprehension of art not as "an offshoot of anticlericalism" but rather "as a legitimate form of religious awareness, one that typified its age in the history of human piety."[17] The fate of religious music in particular, throughout these successive phases of reform, union, and resistance in the first decades of the nineteenth century, reveals just how vexed were people's thoughts on the role of the sacred in communal life.

The classic view of Protestant church music regards the period from the death of J. S. Bach in 1750 to the three-hundredth anniversary of the Reformation in 1817 as a period of decline, followed gradually by restoration, renewal, and revitalization.[18] Ever since Philipp Spitta published his monumental biography in 1873 and 1880, the figure of Bach has shaped this entire narrative line. For Spitta, Bach was the "Protestant church composer absolute and his music *the* Protestant church music"—the "focal point towards which all the music of Germany has tended during the last three centuries" and from which "all its different lines" started "afresh," diverging

---

[15] For example, see Ingeborg Drewitz, "März 1829—oder die Säkularisierung der Künste," in *Bachtage Berlin: Vorträge 1970–1981 Sammelband*, ed. Günther Wagner (Neuhausen-Stuttgart, 1985), 201–10.

[16] Friedrich Blume, *Protestant Church Music: A History*, rev. ed., in collaboration with Ludwig Finscher, et al. (New York, 1974), 315.

[17] Dahlhaus, *Nineteenth-Century Music*, 95.

[18] By church music, scholars mean both service music and nonliturgical music with a "Protestant base." See the grand narrative in Blume, *Protestant Church Music*, 317–506; on the definition of church music, xiv.

"towards new results."[19] The neglect of Bach in the half century after his death corresponded to the period of decline in religious music; the recovery of Bach in the first decades of the nineteenth century ushered in the gradual recovery of Protestant church music, a process hastened after 1900 when the Neue Bach Gesellschaft was founded with the mission to make Bach's complete works available for practical use.

The grandeur of this narrative has faded over the past century, but what remains largely undisputed is the disintegration of the institutional arrangements that sustained Bach in his lifetime. The same period in which Hölscher has found the decline of institutional belief saw, in musical terms, the decline of the Lutheran cantoral position, the relegation of the organist to an impoverished profession, the deterioration of the chorale, the spreading silence of the congregation, the marginalization of musical training in the Latin schools, and the virtual disappearance of the trained choir of students. The Prussian Allgemeines Landrecht of 1794, enlightened absolutism's effort to create a uniform system of law, hastened the disintegration of traditional musical life by abolishing the corporate categories of cantor and organist, much as a herdsman would cull the weakest from his herd. Likewise, the guilds of town musicians, which had regulated the participation of their members in sacred music, were disappearing by the end of the century. So too went the *Kantoreien*, the societies of townsmen who sang Protestant choral music in the churches. They had begun in the time of Luther, persisted through religious warfare, schisms, and reforms, but could not survive the decline of their institutional context or the advent of competing groups like Zelter's *Singakademie* and patriotic *Liedertafeln*. Add to all that the suspicions of religious rationalists and pietists about music's distracting frivolity, and by the late eighteenth century the average German churchgoer would have experienced a service in which the word had achieved absolute dominion over music.[20]

At the same time that music languished in the Protestant churches of north Germany, secular musicians and writers helped to spread new interest in an older Italian tradition of religious music, in part to contrast its simple beauty to the "excessive liveliness" and "mechanical artifice" of contemporary sacred music. Reichardt, for instance, returned from his trips to Italy proclaiming Giovanni Pierluigi Palestrina "the greatest known composer of works in the noble, solemn church style" and calling for a renaissance of the

---

[19] Ibid., 392; Philipp Spitta, *Die Wiederbelebung protestantischer Kirchenmusik auf geschichtlicher Grundlage* (Berlin, 1882); Spitta, *Bach*, 1:i.

[20] Joyce Irwin, "German Pietists and Church Music in the Baroque Age," *Church History* 54 (1985): 29–40.

"true church music" of the past.[21] For Ludwig Tieck also, "true church music" consisted of purely choral music, unaccompanied by instruments (in Italian: *a capella*, literally, in the style of the chapel or choir).[22] For Tieck's friend Wackenroder, such music was "the noblest and most exalted" of music, even the simplest chord of which "causes an upheaval in our entire souls." For Herder, unaccompanied sung words, "freed from the struck string or the narrow pipe," resounded "freely in the heavens," "in one tone harmoniously all tones."[23]

The appeal, then, of a cappella church music lay in its evocation of lost times and sublime, almost inaccessible emotions. The vogue for it among both musicians and writers signals the increasing presence in the educated elite of two intertwined attitudes—first, the consciousness of the past as separate, different, cut off from the present but still accessible through study and reflection, and second, the rejection of religious rationalism. Historicism and romanticism, as historians have usually identified such attitudes, became the dominant families of ideas shaping the Bach revival, but we often forget that they shaped, first of all, a sustained discussion about religious music, without which the *St. Matthew Passion* of 1829 might not have taken place or would at least have been differently received. Those who wrote about the decline of religious music from some earlier period of glory contributed to what Reinhart Koselleck has called a new "semantics of historical time." Modernity definitively arrived, said Koselleck, when anticipation of the future was no longer bounded by past experiences, and a "disciplined obsession with the past" took the place of the "authority of remembrance." Or as Goethe put it, the end of the eighteenth century was "an era of dispersion and loss," one in which people no longer took for granted the continuance of past into future. By 1800, concludes Koselleck, it became possible "to conceive the past as something that was fundamentally 'other.'"[24] Thus the otherness of early church music was what made it attractive, in contrast to the dispiriting tones of contemporary church compositions.

The romantics themselves—Tieck and Wackenroder, Herder and the Schlegels—had no interest in musical practices in the actual churches in Protestant Germany, but together with writers like Reichardt they dissem-

[21] Reichardt quoted in Charlton, 352; *Musik in Geschichte und Gegenwart*, 2nd ed., s.v. "Zeitschriften," 2257.

[22] Charlton, 352–53.

[23] Excerpts from Wilhelm Heinrich Wackenroder, *Phantasien über die Kunst für Freunde der Kunst,* and Herder, *Kalligone,* in Lippman, *Musical Aesthetics: Reader,* 16, 18, 40.

[24] Koselleck, *Futures Past,* 246–59.

inated an aesthetic sensibility about how music could stimulate religious feelings in the listener.[25] Publicly active musicians, often sharing the romantics' belief in the transcendent power of music, went further and sought to understand its implications for music in church and society. The wretched state of performance in churches, the poor quality of new compositions for the church, and the decline of religious feeling itself seemed all of a piece with the superficial, trivial, and just plain bad music in operas and concert rooms, against which musical writers from Reichardt to Rochlitz to Marx had fulminated from the beginning. They declared the crisis of church music a matter of concern for any serious-minded person, and they embarked on an effort to combat both bad music and lost faith by rescuing the religious music of the past while improving its counterparts in the present. Rochlitz, for instance, intrigued by Herder's findings on the folk traditions surrounding St. Caecilia, regretted that Germans, especially educated, refined Germans, increasingly neglected "religious songs" as incompatible with "the spirit of the age." Enlightened people had become "completely incapable" of rescuing sacred music because they were filled "not only with indifference but with a positive distaste" for religion and all that sustained it. "The churches remain empty," he observed, "and the theaters are full."[26]

This same image cropped up in Reichardt's *Berlinische Musikalische Zeitung*, where Georg Christian Friedrich Schlimmbach, a cantor (hence music educator) in Berlin, published a lengthy examination of church music's decline. Like Rochlitz, Schlimmbach was an educated man, fond of tossing Greek and Latin quotations into his texts, but at the same time concerned that churches had lost the attendance of workers and peasants as well as educated people. Only one out of every twelve people went to church services anymore, he claimed, and the situation was worse in the countryside. "Civilized people" used to put considerable effort into "making the church service beautiful," but now "we are in love only with ourselves." Enlightenment had degenerated into a "fashionable toy," and churchmen hid their own neglect of the church service behind claims that music profaned it by exciting only superficial and irrational emotion. Such attitudes in turn led to services so spare and intellectual as to drive people away, es-

---

[25] For an illuminating discussion of the persistence and pervasiveness of such attitudes, see Albert L. Blackwell, *The Sacred in Music* (Louisville, KY, 1999). On the influence on Zelter of romantics like Wackenroder and Friedrich Schleiermacher, see Fischer-Dieskau, *Carl Friedrich Zelter*, 44.

[26] Friedrich Rochlitz, "Feyer des Andenken der heiligen Caecilia," *AMZ* 6, no. 8 (23 November 1803): 117–29.

pecially "the large portion of men who work," for whom the Sabbath was the only day to enjoy the beauties and morally uplifting power of true church music.[27]

Zelter, too, found it impossible to disentangle the decline in church music from a more general proliferation of superficial taste and popular disdain for serious music. In his several petitions to the Prussian government from 1804 to 1811, he claimed that a "rising sauciness" marked the times— Zelter used the word *Petulanz*, of French origin, like the contemporary malaise he observed. "The inferior [in art] is raised up, and the great is cast aside," with the result that "serious, one might even say, religious" music lay "uncultivated in these modern times." "Nothing interesting or healing," no "edification and emotion," could be found in churches, only "much that is cold and dirty," "a bungler at the organ," and "pitiful voices, deforming and dismembering the noble, elevated chorale." Music, declared Zelter, had abandoned the church for the theater, and to the "disdain and horror of philosophers and moralists," it had become a "luxury good," plied by "flute players and dancers" in the "chambers of the wealthy."[28]

Finally, E. T. A. Hoffmann, the most influential of early nineteenth-century music critics, contributed a diatribe on these ills titled "Old and New Church Music," published in the *Allgemeine Musikalische Zeitung* in 1814. "Genuinely enlightened music lovers," he wrote, were entirely justified in thinking that "works for the church" had declined in the past twenty years of "unparalleled frivolity." "As though governed by demonic forces," people were "held spellbound within their miserable, blinkered world." They "turned against all that was noble, true, and sacred," the "divine spark" was extinguished, and "the cold tongues of fool's fire that flared up in the hopeless desolation could never kindle that inner glow from which in everlasting incandescence true works of art arise."[29] Against a sinister background worthy of his tales, Hoffmann sketched the process of artistic change and development, in which both the artistic integrity of the past and its separation from the present became clear.

But unlike Winckelmann and other creators of the modern historical consciousness, Hoffmann found no timeless musical ideal among the ancients by which to assess current distress. In the confusion of overlapping attitudes of rationalism, *Sturm und Drang*, neoclassicism, and romanticism, music provided a way to make generational distinctions. Winckelmann had

---

[27] G. W. F. Schlimmbach, "Ideen und Vorschläge zur Verbesserung des Kirchenmusikwesens," *BMZ* 1, no. 59 (1805): 231; no. 60 (1805): 235–36.

[28] Zelter to Hardenberg, 1 June 1802; "Erste Denkschrift," 28 September 1803; "Zweite Denkschrift," n.d., in Schröder, 69, 78, 84–86.

[29] E. T. A. Hoffmann, "Old and New Church Music," in Charlton, 2, 353–54.

nothing to say about music; Goethe and Zelter had awkward and unsatisfactory exchanges on what music must have sounded like in ancient Greece; and Hoffmann firmly denied that the history of music owed anything of significance to the ancients. But for Hoffmann and his generation of romantics, the apparent lack of importance of music in the classical era took nothing away from its more recent, and ultimately its universal, significance. Music, declared Hoffmann, arose "directly from man's spiritual nature"; its "sound audibly expresses an awareness of the highest and the holiest, of the spiritual power which rekindles the spark of life in the whole of nature." An "expression of the total plenitude of existence, a paean to the Creator," music and singing "could not be the property of the ancient world, in which sensual embodiment was all." Only in Christendom could and did the "seedlings" of musical expression "sprout splendidly and bear blossom and fruit in luxuriant abundance." And even then only with the advent of Palestrina in the sixteenth century were "the sacred wonders of music" revealed "in their most essential form"; with him "began what is indisputably the most glorious period in church music (and hence in music in general)."[30]

This era lasted through "our deeply intellectual Sebastian Bach" but petered out afterward, with a few exceptions, into "empty ostentation" and "increasing instrumental display." Hoffmann acknowledged the possibility that the most recent instrumental music had, spiritually at least, taken the place of church music. A few years earlier, his now-famous review of Beethoven's Fifth Symphony had spoken of Beethoven's instrumental music unveiling "before us the realm of the mighty and the immeasurable," unlocking "the wonderful realm of the infinite," and setting "in motion the machinery of awe, of fear, of terror, of pain" that awakens "the infinite yearning which is the essence of romanticism."[31] But now four years later, Hoffmann took no pleasure in this historical progression. "Enfeeblement and sickly sweetness" had overcome art, and the times "when Christianity still shone forth in all its glory seem to have vanished from the earth forever." It might still be possible for a young composer to "search his soul and confirm that he possesses the spirit of truth and piety." But by and large, the standard set by the "truly sacred music of former times" could no longer be met, and "many an otherwise excellent composer has disgraced himself as soon as he set about composing a church work."[32]

The question, of course, was what was to be done, and here Hoffmann

---

[30] Ibid., 355–57.
[31] E. T. A. Hoffmann, "Review of Beethoven's Fifth Symphony," in Charlton, 238.
[32] E. T. A. Hoffmann, "Old and New Church Music," in Charlton, 370–72.

offered only hope, and not much of that either. "The prevailing spirit of the age forever drives us on and on," he wrote, and "the vanished figures will never return" in earthly joy. Only a heightened awareness of the past held any promise of recovery, "for truth is eternal, imperishable," and "the great masters live on in spirit," if only we can learn to hear them "through the seething clamor of frenzied activity that has broken over us."[33] The indecision in his and other writings over which was more urgent, saving music or saving religion, proved ultimately paralyzing. Zelter, Schlimmbach, and Rochlitz alike attempted to finesse the possible conflict between these two goals by arguing that both could be fulfilled simultaneously. Churches could be full, Rochlitz thought, of music and of people, if only churchmen would understand the importance of appealing to the whole human being, a creature who was aesthetic and sensual as well as intellectual.[34] Schlimmbach wishfully claimed that all problems, musical and religious, could be solved at once by combating "fashion mongering and voluptuousness, frivolity and coquetry" with the "true and noble character" of music restored to now-silent churches. Moreover, he thought, if people's "love of the beautiful and the good" could be reawakened in churches, then music could exercise its powerful influence on the "cultivation of the entire nation."[35]

What Schlimmbach really wanted was for the state to take a more active role in overseeing church musical affairs. As did, of course, Zelter, with his plan for a musical inspectorate that he kept submitting to Prussian state officials. The progress of Zelter's appeals over the course of 1804 reveals much about this intersection of art and religion in the years before full-scale state reform. Zelter's memoranda took the disparate musings of romantics and humanists on the significance of art and attempted to distill them into a coherent plan for state action. After his first memorandum to Hardenberg had achieved only a polite demur, Zelter sought the advice of Goethe and Schiller. Both told him to tone down his indignation at bungling organists and emphasize instead, in Schiller's words, "the ecclesiastical and political side." "Generally," advised Goethe, "you should dwell more upon the advantages which religion and morals would derive . . . and less upon those which Art has to expect." Schiller agreed: "It seems to me an extremely happy circumstance," he wrote, "that the interest of art just now meets such an external want." Yet even if the rulers of the state should be interested, he observed, few felt that same urgency about art as they did about religion.

[33] Ibid., 376.

[34] Friedrich Rochlitz, "Feyer des Andenken der heiligen Caecilia," *AMZ* 6, no. 8 (23 November 1803): 117–29.

[35] G. W. F. Schlimmbach, "Verbesserung des Kirchenmusikwesens," *BMZ* 1, no. 60 (1805), 235; no. 59 (1805): 232.

Zelter should present the Berlin Singakademie as the "instrument lying ready to hand" for "coming to the aid of religion," not art.[36]

Schiller and Goethe both recognized religion as the business of the state, in part because religion bridged the gap between "the cultivated and the uncultivated," encouraging "higher feelings" in both, especially in the latter. For people still living in the powerful wake of the French Revolution, and shortly to be engulfed by a second wave of French aggression, the social question impinged on aesthetic debates. For Schiller especially, the aesthetic, social, and political needs of man had to converge if humanity was to achieve a state of freedom and full development. In Zelter's petition, which Goethe supported mainly to help Zelter make his own life a little easier, Schiller saw the seeds of genuine change in the right direction. The time was ripe for Berlin, which had once "in the dark days of superstition" lit "the torch of rational religious freedom," now to win "another glory without forfeiting the first": "now let Berlin add warmth to the light, and ennoble Protestantism, of which it is destined to be the metropolis." "Something," he thought, had to be done "for spirituality and morals," especially in Protestant countries, and he recommended that Zelter go talk to Schleiermacher.[37]

So Zelter took the advice of these mighty Germans and began his petitions by downplaying the importance of the Singakademie ("only an experiment") and pressing instead the needs of public church singing, "the most important branch of the musical arts," now lying "in complete stagnation and unholy corruption." Invoking the example of "the great Luther," who along with "the greatest German artists and men" had once been a choir boy, Zelter claimed that he could bring the common people, with their "Prussian probity and constancy, the sum of which is piety," back into the "empty churches." He needed only a state musical authority, with himself as director of the Singakademie at its head, and a general revival of church and community—through choirs, town music-making, and daily musical practices—would follow. The "development of the nation" depended on such measures, he argued. They would preserve "the German nation in its most essential characteristics of constancy and seriousness."[38]

As we have seen, Hardenberg did admit Zelter to a marginal status in the Academy of Fine Arts, and five years later, after another round of petitions, Humboldt's interest in "the effectiveness of music in raising the level of the church service and enhancing national education" led to Zelter's appoint-

---

[36] Goethe to Zelter, 13 July 1804; Schiller to Zelter, 16 July 1804, in Coleridge, 23–25.
[37] Ibid.
[38] "Fünfte Denkschrift," 14 August 1804, in Schröder, 109–13.

ment as a professor of music at the Academy of Fine Arts. Friedrich Wilhelm III approved this appointment on the grounds of the "particular importance" of encouraging an "uplifting church music."[39] Out of these negotiations, an Institute for Church Music emerged, first in Breslau and later in Berlin, but these were limited undertakings, providing musical instruction for only a handful of teachers and church musicians. In music as in church matters, poor finances, "haphazard patronage," too many churches, and ill-paid, little-respected officeholders were the main impediments to improvement.[40] No belated instruction in counterpoint and chorale accompaniment was going to make any difference to all that.

Moreover, after 1817 the ability of musicians like Zelter to improve church music diminished even further with Friedrich Wilhelm III's abrupt imposition of church union on a baffled and uncooperative population. The "colossal muddle" of the union introduced, as we have seen, the monarch's new liturgy, which included an eccentric set of requirements for service music. Friedrich Wilhelm's taste, like that of his romantic contemporaries, tended toward the music of Palestrina's era and even earlier. During his exile from Prussia after the defeats of 1806, he had heard church music in the Russian military encampments and had become enamored of the male-voice, a cappella sound of the Russian Orthodox service, so reminiscent of Gregorian chant and so distant from the instrumental chamber music he is said to have detested since childhood. Friedrich Wilhelm's new service rites of 1817, 1821, and 1822 broke with contemporary church music, such as it was, as well as with the entire Protestant musical tradition that originated with Luther. He retained only fragments of the original Lutheran sung liturgy, reduced congregational participation to a mere three hymns, and called for much of the liturgy to be sung between priest and a capella male choir, with the priest facing the altar throughout. Even if they put aside their distaste for the Catholic ritualistic coloration of the proceeding, congregations had to deal with the fact that the king's liturgy required the kind of highly trained choir that had not existed in German Protestant churches for many decades. Moreover, his prohibition on women singing in any but the hymns made even more unlikely the remote possibility that Prussia's impoverished parishes would be able to muster the musical forces necessary to put this peculiar effort at historical reconstruction into practice.

The Union Church thus provided no solution to the deepening crisis of Protestant church music. By the time Marx embarked on his career as a

---

[39] Friedrich Wilhelm to Humboldt, 17 May 1809, in Schröder, 124.
[40] Hope, *German and Scandinavian Protestantism*, 314, 342–44.

music journalist in Berlin, the union had been in place and under revision for nearly seven years, a new wave of pietist awakening had begun, and according to no less an observer than Heinrich Heine, the ongoing controversies over the king's hobby horse were the talk of the town.[41] But the musical consequences of disarray at the highest institutional levels were persistent stagnation at the lowest, in the churches themselves. Some localities did manage to muster adequate musical forces, but in Marx's view, Berlin was not among them. In 1827, distressed at the "so utterly pathetic condition" of church choirs in Berlin with their "screeching descants, fantastically hooting altos, dandified tenors, and blockheaded beer basses," he wondered that the "new church order" had done so little to improve the situation.[42]

On the other side of Germany in Heidelberg, an amateur musician and collector of old musical manuscripts, Anton Friedrich Justus Thibaut, still thought that the Prussian union represented the best hope for musical reform in Germany. He had set down his own diagnosis of what was wrong with church and contemporary music in a polemical tract published in 1825 and soon widely read across German-speaking Europe. Thibaut was not the average musical amateur. He was one of Germany's most distinguished legal theorists, a professor of law who had held appointments at Kiel, Jena, and now Heidelberg, and the author of heavy tomes of legal history with titles like *The System of Pandekt Law* and *A Theory of the Logical Exegesis of Roman Law*. He had gained national attention in 1814 when he published a collection of essays calling for the construction of a single national law code for all Germans. The legal historicist Savigny attacked Thibaut for this, and perhaps all the commotion helped drive him into the calmer realm of aesthetic experience. Certainly, when a decade later he published his tract, called simply *Purity in Music*, he urged readers to appreciate the "solemn reflection" occasioned by "the setting sun" or "the song of nightingales on a spring evening or the sighing of the wind in the trees," or the "simply beauty" of sacred plainsong "chastely rendered by a choir in a devotional spirit."[43]

But *Purity in Music*, which appeared in 1825, involved Thibaut in the second great controversy of his life, for reasons the reverse of those that got him into trouble earlier. Whereas Savigny had taken him to task for undermining historically sanctioned legal custom, his opponents in the musical uproar over his tract (especially Hans Georg Nägeli of Switzerland) attacked

[41] Ibid., 346.
[42] A. B. Marx, "Beschwerde," *BAMZ* 3, no. 25 (20 June 1827): 193.
[43] Thibaut, *Reinheit*, 103–4.

him for too great an attachment to old music.[44] Thibaut did indeed find little to praise in contemporary musical life, starting with church music.
Churches, he argued, had opened themselves up to the "foolish vagaries of
fashion" and "pride of modern times." Because of his interest in Italian Renaissance sacred music, scholars have routinely associated him with the Cae-
cilian movement, an effort mainly of German Catholics to reform Catholic
church music. But Thibaut's criticisms and praise crossed confessional lines.
The only bright spots he saw in all of Europe were a few Russian orthodox
churches, the Moravian churches of the Herrenhüter movement, and the
Sistine chapel, in each of which church leaders had managed to hold on to
authentic musical traditions, so Thibaut thought. Everywhere else he found
only the frills and trills of organists' egotism. Church leaders needed to "re-
trace their steps" and, "dismissing all sectarian spirit," restore to purity the
original melodies of the past.[45]

SACRED MUSIC IN SECULAR SETTINGS

Thibaut's hopes that Friedrich Wilhelm III's church reform would be
good for music were, in any case, disappointed. From the perspective of
music history, the king's obsessions only exacerbated the inability of
churches to support performance and innovation in musical life. While a
generation of church composers and choirmasters engaged in a fruitless effort to produce the kind of music the king would like, the most important
developments in the history of music, church and otherwise, took place in
amateur organizations, opera houses, and concert halls.[46] This trend was
long in the making. In the late eighteenth century, groups like the Singakademie and concerts like Reichardt's *Concerts spirituels* had tried to com-
pensate for the poor quality of church music by taking sacred music out of
churches and into secular public spaces. Reichardt believed that concerts of
sacred music could do the moral work of church services, and Zelter described the Singakademie as a means to "preserve until the arrival of more

---

[44] Marx found the tone of such attacks intemperate; see his review of *Der Streit zwischen der alten
und neuen Musick, enthaltend Nägeli's Beurtheilung der Schrift: Die Reinheit der Tonkunst, BAMZ* 4, no.
28 (11 July 1827): 219–22.

[45] Thibaut, *Reinheit*, 6–7, 18–19, 13, 7, 9, 14–15.

[46] The situation of church music outside of Prussia was different, but non-Prussian Protestantism made few contributions either to the restoration of the Lutheran musical tradition or to the
improvement of church musical conditions in general. An important exception was Bernhard
Christoph Natorp, pastor in Münster and enthusiastic Pestalozzian. Natorp pioneered nineteenth-
century efforts to restore the Lutheran sung liturgy, publishing a book in 1817, *Über den Gesang in
den Kirchen der Protestanten*, which argued that the liturgy was an art form that should not be left to
the whims of the clergy. In his manuals he tried to teach people basic church musical know-how
(collect, response, litany, and so on).

propitious times a branch of music that in its seriousness and religious tendencies remains wholly neglected in our times."[47]

But the process of cutting sacred music loose from liturgy changed both it and people's attitudes toward it. People like Zelter and Reichardt contributed to what Lydia Goehr has called a "change in the dominant conception [of music] around 1800." This "modern way of thinking about music" understood it "in terms of the production, performance, and preservation of works," rather than the practice of a craft shaped by the needs of church or court or whatever occasions the music merely adorned.[48] Seeing a musical work as something intrinsically, not functionally, valuable underlay the transformations in musical life we have already observed, from the growth of music journalism to the spread of musical amateurism to the decline of guilds and the rise of a musical marketplace. To regard sacred music as worthy of performance and preservation, indifferent to the needs of a worship service, required a shift in cultural meaning just as jarring as the idea of regarding purely instrumental music as valuable. By 1835, when Franz Liszt called for the establishment of "an assembly to be held every five years for religious, dramatic, and symphonic music, by which all the works that are considered best in these three categories shall be ceremonially performed" and then placed in a "musical museum," the idea of performing and preserving religious works, just like other musical works, had become commonplace, as had the entire notion of musical preservation.[49] In 1804, when Zelter put forward the Singakademie as just such a museum, both ideas— the essential congruity among all serious music and their worthiness to be heard again and again—were still new.

But the trouble with leaving the cultivation of sacred music to the free market was the predictable lack of adequate financial support and the somewhat less predictable objections on religious and aesthetic grounds. As to the first, few subscription concerts could attract sufficient audiences for programs consisting of sacred music, however inspiring the romantic writers may have found some of it. Advocates of serious music regularly ranked the sacred cantata and oratorio with the symphony as "occupying the highest rank" among potential concert music, but those responsible for making a concert into a paying event knew that adaptations of opera scores and visits of virtuosi—both dubious propositions to the serious crowd—produced a happier audience.[50] Publishers rarely published sacred music, except in the anodyne form of sentimental song collections, some of a quasi-religious

[47] Zelter to Hardenberg, 1 June 1802, in Schröder, 69.
[48] Goehr, *Imaginary Museum*, 203.
[49] Liszt cited in Goehr, *Imaginary Museum*, 205.
[50] See Gramit, *Cultivating Music*, 125–60.

character. In 1808 when Beethoven attempted to sell his Mass in C, the Leipzig publisher Breitkopf & Härtel told him that there was simply "no demand for church works."[51] Aware of Beethoven's problems in bringing this work to the public, E. T. A. Hoffmann regretted that "the excellent Fasch," "a master of the old tradition" and a composer of "profound works," was "so little regarded by the feckless multitude" that his sixteen-part mass was never published. He urged publishers to make broadly available the works of the "early masters."[52]

The aesthetic and religious objections to turning over sacred music to a secular public proved just as vexing. Even Hoffmann balked at the notion of sacred music being performed in public venues. In this he agreed with Friedrich Wilhelm III himself, who in 1803 had forbidden public concerts to charge entrance fees in churches and in 1806 followed this up with a ban on using churches for concerts, indeed for anything but private prayer and public worship. Friedrich Wilhelm promulgated these measures in the spirit of ejecting the moneylenders from the temple, and Hoffmann too declared ticketed concerts in churches "utterly unworthy and contrary to all Christian piety," mainly for their effect of creating class distinctions between different levels of ticket buyers. Such objections summon up images of prima donnas singing songs of passion in the sacred precincts. In reality, of course, to the extent that churches did serve as concert venues, oratorio rather than opera made up the program. Schlimmbach for one, writing shortly after the ban took effect, objected to the notion that an oratorio could defile a sacred space. His editor Reichardt added a footnote rebuking those "esteemed theologians" who had lately forbidden a local choir director to perform his annual oratorio concert in Berlin's Nicolaikirche. Both Schlimmbach and Reichardt pointed out that impoverished churches depended on the income from such musically and ethically worthy events to keep afloat.[53]

And if not in a church, then where? Was it really appropriate to perform sacred music *outside* a church? Hoffmann thought not. Acoustically speaking, he argued, the older music composed to be heard in a church simply sounded better there, resonating as the composer had intended. In fact, sacred music heard in concert performances seemed to him an altogether bad idea: "music intended for worship is meaningless when played separately," he insisted, "because such music is *worship itself* and thus seems like a mass celebrated in a concert or a sermon preached in a theatre." It was all very well for Wackenroder to describe his art-loving monk, the fictional Joseph

---

[51] Charlton, 325.
[52] E. T. A. Hoffmann, "Old and New Church Music," in Charlton, 360–61, 376.
[53] G. W. F. Schlimmbach, "Verbesserung des Kirchenmusikwesens," *BMZ* 1, no. 59 (1805): 233.

von Berglinger, listening to music "with precisely the same reverence as if he were in church—just as still and motionless, his eyes cast down to the floor."[54] Hoffmann doubted that was possible. A concert audience would be "distracted in a thousand ways" from the devotional spirit that serious music should induce, hence "the revival of early works in the concert-hall in no way compensates for their disappearance from the church." Speaking of what he considered the greatest, perhaps the only great, piece of contemporary sacred music, "the profound and incomparably magnificent Requiem by Mozart," he famously declared that "the Requiem performed in a concert-hall is not the same music—it is like a saint appearing at a ball!"[55]

For all the panache of Hoffmann's juxtapositions of the sacred and the profane, no obvious way out of this dilemma of preserving church music without the traditional institutional support of the church presented itself. Music was not like painting or sculpture, requiring only space and light for its preservation and effect. As Hoffmann's essay suggested, music needed to be heard to be appreciated. Already in 1802, Johann Nikolaus Forkel had made the same point: "The most effective means of promoting a lively preservation of musical artworks is undoubtedly the public performance of them in front of large audiences."[56] That required not only space and light but published scores and groups of highly trained people. It also required at least the possibility of repetition, since, as Kant had so unkindly pointed out, the effect of music on the mind was transitory, leaving behind nothing "for reflection." Kant, to be sure, thought music existed only for enjoyment, and hence repetition produced "weariness" and boredom. But Goethe too, although more optimistically, described music as an "art of the moment." In his final letter to Zelter, written days before his death, he held out the hope that Zelter had been able to create "a series of consecutive moments," which would be "always a kind of eternity."[57] Certainly, Hoffmann and his contemporaries were hard pressed to come up with anything secular that might preserve church music the way the cyclical rhythm of the church calendar had done as a matter of course. Hoffmann thought something like a sacralization of secular groups might prove workable: he praised the "admirable institution of choral societies" for preventing the "complete decline of singing," adding that if such groups were to have "any real influence on church music, they should not remain private undertakings but should be established and maintained in some religious form by the state." He recommended that the groups at least rehearse "in sanctified places and

[54] Wackenroder cited in Dahlhaus, *Nineteenth-Century Music*, 94.
[55] Hoffmann, "Old and New Church Music," in Charlton, 374–75.
[56] Forkel, *Bachs Leben*, 22.
[57] Goethe to Zelter, 11 March 1832, cited in Eberle, *Sing-Akademie*, 116.

thus make conservatories of them," as in Italy where they had produced "the great composers of earlier times."[58]

The Prussian state and monarch were no more ready to embark on some scheme to reconstitute the Italian Renaissance church culture in Protestant Germany than they were, more plausibly, to reinvigorate the moribund musical legacy of Luther. But Zelter and his fellow directors of amateur choral societies did gradually create something else, more secular than sacred, more private than public or state sponsored, but enough of a mixture of all those qualities to serve the multiple purposes implied by the notion of preserving church music. The key to this achievement was the humble vehicle of the weekly group meeting. To start with the Berlin Singakademie itself, acknowledged even in its own time as the prototype of the serious singing society, its mission to preserve "sacred and serious music" always put more emphasis on the rehearsal than the performance.[59] All the early memories and records of the group concern rehearsals—attendance books, detailed accounts of when and where they were held, records of what they sang. By contrast, its earliest performances received scant mention, looming large only in later histories of the group, which assume the primacy of performance. Zelter's first contribution to the running of the Singakademie, after all, had been to institute more rehearsal time, and not because he felt the urgency of some upcoming performance. His next contribution was to secure semipermanent rehearsal space for the group, to which he clung for the next twenty years, come storm and winter, drafts and leaks, war, occupation, and renovation, leaving only when ordered to do so but with the promise of his own building to come. And Zelter continued to see the new building as a guaranteed, permanent practice room, with the added benefit of being rentable to other groups and speakers for actual performances.

As time went on and the Singakademie grew, it did accumulate a record of performances. But the first paragraph of its belated statutes of 1816, a quarter century after the group's founding, specified that its purpose remained the "practical study of musical works for the edification of its members" and only "seldom" for public performance.[60] Moreover, it always rehearsed far more pieces than it performed—a simple fact that many have noted but few explained. To take the most relevant example, Zelter introduced a few choruses from the *St. Matthew Passion* into rehearsal already in May 1815, with no intention of bringing them to public performance, ever. This inexplicable gesture, this habit that the outsider just does not get, re-

---

[58] Hoffmann, "Old and New Church Music," in Charlton, 375.

[59] 1816 Statutes of the Singakademie, reprinted in Werner Bollert, ed., *Sing-Akademie zu Berlin: Festschrift zum 175jährigen Bestehen* (Berlin, 1967), 64.

[60] Bollert, *Sing-Akademie zu Berlin*, 64.

veals much about Zelter's world. Adolf Bernhard Marx did not get it either, but Marx lived more comfortably in the public sphere than did Zelter and reflected changes in expectations about the public's right of access to cultural treasures.[61] Marx found Zelter selfish and neglectful, like a hoarder jealously guarding his secret piles of treasure and oblivious to the starving multitudes around him. People needed to hear this music, Marx thought, and Zelter had a public obligation to perform. But Zelter did allow people to attend rehearsals and listen as much as they wanted. Beethoven went to Singakademie rehearsals, as did Schiller and many visitors to and from Berlin (never Goethe, despite repeated invitations from Zelter); the rehearsal attendance books recorded them all. The point is simply this: if the purpose of the Singakademie was to preserve a certain kind of neglected music until better times arrived, then the weekly and sometimes twice-weekly rehearsals, not the magnificent collection of musical manuscripts and emphatically not the few-and-far-between performances, were the museum in which the works lived on.

Nor was the Singakademie unique in its attention to the weekly routine of rehearsals. Thibaut's influential tract *Purity in Music* placed the regular practice of choral societies at the center of musical reform. The best societies, he thought, gathered solely "for the enjoyment of musical classics, with a view to the edification and refinement of the mind." Attention to the music rather than "eating and drinking" was required, as was regular attendance and a large musical library of old works. But performance was neither necessary nor desirable, and on this point Thibaut proved more explicit than Zelter. Choral societies should "devote their best energies to those masterpieces that take us aside from worldly ways," he suggested, thus "a constant appearance in public" would be "as paradoxical a proceeding as to invite educated and uneducated alike, without distinction of persons, to listen to the recital of a profoundly conceived poem." Life had taught him that "privacy, except for a few intimate friends," was as essential to choral societies as to individuals, because it made possible "that calm and even temper essential to a serious passion for music."[62]

More than preparation for performance, more than an imaginary museum of sacred musical works, rehearsals also spoke to the transformation of devotional culture and the diffusion of religious experience out of the church. Church attendance declined, but middle-class Protestants continued to say prayers at the dinner table and at bedtime, to read the Bible with

---

[61] On how this shift in expectations affected art museums, see Sheehan, *Museums in the German Art World,* esp. 43–82.

[62] Thibaut, *Reinheit,* 172–81.

their children, and to celebrate religious festivals.[63] They volunteered in charitable associations and, with similar consciousness of moral propriety, joined choral societies. The practice of sacred music at choral rehearsals was suggestive of the religious sensibility that infused secular associational life. The regular nature of rehearsal was also suggestive of devotional practice and of the church choir, although the rehearsals were not confined to service music and antedated mixed-sex church choirs.[64]

We might speak of devotion to art, but to go a step further and describe these secular organizations as constituting a religion of art would obscure the extent to which most remained explicitly Christian, their public pronouncements filled with Christian piety. The Singakademie described itself as an "art association for sacred and serious music," but the sacred outweighed the secular. During Zelter's directorship, the only serious music without sacred text the group rehearsed was a setting of Goethe's *Faust*, composed by Prince Radziwill, one of the Singakademie's most devoted patrons. In Hamburg a similar choral society first appeared in 1819, founded by the composer Louise Reichardt, daughter of Johann Friedrich Reichardt and herself a former member of the Berlin Singakademie. Founded in wake of the Reformation tercentenary, the Hamburg Gesangverein described itself as dedicated to the "communal practice of religious singing."[65] Choral societies in Leipzig, Weimar, Dresden, Cassel, Lübeck, Frankfurt, and beyond into the Catholic areas of Bavaria and the Hapsburg Empire expressed similar dedication. As Thibaut concluded, choral societies allowed one to practice "the words of Luther, 'Music is a fair and glorious gift from God, and I would not for the world renounce my humble share of it.' "[66]

Performances did have a role to play in the culture of choral singing as it developed in German-speaking Europe, though Berlin, thanks to Zelter, did not take a leading role. Starting in 1810, the first of what would become a German-wide practice of regional music festivals took place in Frankenhausen in Thuringia, organized by the local cantor G. F. Bischoff. In 1804 Bischoff had put together a choir of some eighty singers to perform Haydn's *Creation* with the Gotha court orchestra, and the excitement of this performance led him, some six years later, to try for something even bigger.

[63] See the articles cited in note 13 above, and Lucien Hölscher, "Säkularisierungsprozesse im deutschen Protestantismus des 19. Jahrhunderts," in *Bürger in der Gesellschaft der Neuzeit*, ed. Hans-Jürgen Puhle (Göttingen, 1991), esp. p. 250.

[64] When the American choir director Lowell Mason visited Germany in 1837, he was impressed by the force of congregational singing; the choirs, which he found to be small but loud, were all male. Mason, *A Yankee Musician in Europe*, 64, 71.

[65] Its full title was the Gesangverein der Freunde religiösen Gesangs; see Josef Sittard, *Geschichte des Musik- und Concertwesens in Hamburg* (Altona, 1890), 290–95.

[66] Thibaut, *Reinheit*, 194.

He asked Louis Spohr, admired as a violinist and composer, to direct the two-day festival, with a chorus and orchestra each of over a hundred members, amateur and professional.[67] The *Creation* was the highlight of the first day; several pieces by Spohr and Beethoven's Fifth Symphony the program of the second day. More festivals followed in Frankenhausen and elsewhere. In 1818 the first of what became the most prestigious of these events, the Lower Rhine Festival, took place in Elberfeld, again with Spohr as director and with a large orchestra and a huge chorus, all drawn from the region.

The increasing size, frequency, and geographical reach of these events, which continued unabated throughout the nineteenth century, left no important German composer or musician untouched, though some (like Mendelssohn) showed more enthusiasm and sense of duty toward them than others (Wagner). Given that the centerpiece of each festival was the performance of a big choral work, often newly commissioned, and that all depended on the participation of choral societies, these festivals do demonstrate that under certain circumstances a performance could become the raison d'être of a choral society, at least temporarily. They helped shape a new musical public, drawn to the excitement of these large events; contemporary enthusiasts, like Hans Georg Nägeli, who organized massive oratorio performances, saw them as educational.[68] But the religious aura of local choral activities became attenuated in these gigantic occasions, despite the fact that virtually all the choral works performed were religious in nature. These were not big-tent revival meetings or open-air masses as much as regional musical events, each one intent on upstaging the previous one. They had political and national overtones as well, and provided a public demonstration of what democratically organized groups like the choral societies could achieve.[69]

But they also contrasted dramatically to the usual practices of choral societies not on the road. At home, a choral society would perform only on the holy days of the church year, heightening the quasi-religious experience already available at regular rehearsals. For both the Berlin Singakademie and the Hamburg Gesangverein, only the high solemnity of Good Friday provided enough of an occasion to force a public performance out of them. The Berlin Singakademie, moreover, always performed the same piece, Carl Heinrich Graun's Passion oratorio of 1755, *Der Tod Jesu* (The Death of Jesus). This tradition began in 1801 and ended only in 1884, by which time the group had performed it seventy-two times, more than any other musi-

---

[67] Louis Spohr, *The Musical Journeys*, trans. and ed. Henry Pleasants (Norman, OK, 1961), 79.

[68] See, for instance, Cecilia Porter, "The New Public and the Reordering of the Musical Establishment: The Lower Rhine Music Festivals, 1818–67," *19th-Century Music* 3 (1979–80): 211–24.

[69] See especially Raynor, *Social History of Music*, 89–91.

cal work.[70] Other performances—at royal funerals, at charitable benefit concerts, at the king's return from exile—also had a quasi-religious aura, which the exclusively sacred music they sang reinforced. When Zelter finally built a performance space neither too sacred to admit a paying audience nor too secular to preclude religious awe, his ambitions for it, as we have seen, remained restricted to the occasional oratorio, notably the disappointing performance of *Judas Maccabeus* in 1827.

But if the upheaval in Protestant church life contributed to the flourishing of religious music in new, more secular settings, it had the further unintended consequence of encouraging an intensely historical approach to the question of religious music. The commercial market for music tells us something of this dual phenomenon of secularism and historicism. Whereas in 1808, as we have seen, the publishers Breitkopf & Härtel declared there to be no market in religious music, by the 1820s publishers were recognizing that a major market of music buyers existed in the amateur singing groups "spreading across all of Germany." They began scrambling to provide them with the kind of music they liked to sing, what came to be called the "classics" of church and oratorio music. With new church music in short supply and low demand, bringing older works into circulation was more commercially attractive than commissioning new ones, even though it required editing and adaptation. At this time also, the notion of a musical classic had greater resonance among amateur groups than among professional musicians and music directors. Amateur musical associations, like their counterparts in local history or archeology, shared a mission to preserve the creations of the past; this mission spread to public concerts only when Mendelssohn, steeped in the tradition of the Berlin Singakademie, took over the Leipzig Gewandhaus Orchestra in 1835. But already in 1826, the firm Trautwein in Berlin published seven volumes of "classical works of old and new church music" for use by singing groups, including excerpts from Handel's oratorios and Mozart's Requiem, along with one Bach motet.

Thibaut characterized the "recourse to forgotten treasures" as an expression of "disgust with the rubbish" people heard in public concerts. He "devoutly hoped" that more amateur musical societies, dedicated to the musical past, would be "established universally." "Stricken with poverty and narrowness of spirit," music had little of the appreciation of its past found among the other arts, which had long since learned "not only to live in the present, but to make the works of all ages one's own."[71] Marx too wanted to

---

[70] Only the Mozart Requiem came close in frequency of performance.
[71] Thibaut, *Reinheit,* 58.

provide amateur musicians "with correct and well-laid-out voice parts" of "consistently worthy and indeed often exemplary" works from the past.[72] Although his self-appointed role as champion of the still-living Beethoven made him initially indifferent to musical historicism, no one who considered himself a Hegelian, as Marx did, could entirely neglect historical study. In a tribute to Reichardt, Marx wrote of the need to "direct the lively well-springs of the past into the flow of the present." "The spirit, the life of mankind is all a single whole, building upon itself through all times," he continued, and "the task of the human spirit," "the key to our own immortality," is "to see the unified forward flow of life by combining many historical viewpoints."[73]

This was not the usual stuff of musical journalism. But it informed Marx's understanding of the greatness of Beethoven, and it allowed him to see the contribution of older religious music to the present. Marx told a history of musical development in which music evolved from serving religion (thesis) to serving court and Mammon (antithesis) to finally realizing its essential character when artists like Beethoven created compositions complete in themselves, existing for music alone, not to aid in worship or entertain and adorn. But Marx was not willing to leave the matter of religious music to lie in the dustbin of history. For one thing, religion itself, though musically bereft, seemed to be recovering rapidly from its period of eclipse in the age of rationalism, or so Marx thought. People today were "more inclined to religious things," he wrote in 1827, and indeed Marx was surrounded by people who not only were religiously aware but debated and mobilized around religious issues.[74] Orthodoxy and pietism, neither of which showed any particular interest in church music, asserted themselves in consistories and communities, and the tradition of enlightened Protestantism survived at the University of Berlin, where its "greatest theoretical exponents," Hegel and Schleiermacher, both tried to create a synthesis of theology and philosophy, faith and reason.[75]

Enlightened Protestantism was the religious milieu in which both Marx and Thibaut dwelt; it was the milieu most articulate on the nature of sacred music, past and present. Both Schleiermacher and Hegel, for instance, discussed music at length in their lectures on aesthetics, delivered over the

---

[72] See the review by Marx of "Klassische Werke älterer und neuerer Kirchenmusik in ausgesetzten Chorstimmen," *BAMZ* 3, no. 51 (20 December 1826): 409; and of "Kirchengesänge der berühmtesten ältern italienischen Meister," *BAMZ* 4, no. 22 (30 May 1827): 169.

[73] A. B. Marx, "Allerlei," *BAMZ* 1, no. 27 (8 July 1824): 245.

[74] A. B. Marx, "Beschwerde," *BAMZ* 3, no. 25 (20 June 1827): 193; Sheehan, *German History*, 555.

[75] Sheehan, *German History*, 562.

course of the 1820s.[76] Schleiermacher considered music a powerful influence on a person's capacity for inner thought: "To that same extent that
people have music, so too will we find a definite movement toward reflection, a definite rise in consciousness."[77] Hegel too thought music made
"perceptible the inwardness of the inner," but in Schleiermacher this quality of musical experience constituted a richly sensual reiteration of religious
experience. Musical experience too was one of immediacy and intimate in-
vasiveness, of both awareness of self and loss of self, of complexity and sub-
tlety beyond the power of language to describe, and of autonomy beyond
purpose or usefulness. "What the word made clear," lectured Schleiermacher, "music must make alive."[78]

Whether or not Marx heard any of these lectures, he later accounted
for his own conversion to Christianity as a kind of enactment of Schleiermacher's understanding of the close affinity between musical and religious
apprehension. His Jewish father, whom he compared to Abraham
Mendelssohn, was "wholly indifferent to any kind of religion whatsoever."
In contrast, Marx found himself "led from an acquaintance with Mozart's
Requiem and then with Handel's *Messiah*, which first brought me to the
study of the Bible, and from there to the most intense inclination toward
Christianity and indeed to Lutheranism." What drew him to Christianity,
as he described his belief, was "less unconditional faith" than enduring
fascination with the "poetic sublimity and deep wisdom of this book of
books," and what kept him there was the realization of this sublimity in
music.[79]

Moved by whatever cause to a greater critical engagement with religious
music, Marx came up with a historical scheme that divided it into two
streams of development. All religious music, he suggested, followed the
model of either Palestrina or Handel, Catholicism or Protestantism: either
religion as mystery, closed to all but the initiated, or religion as clarity, "the
open declaration of belief by the unified Christian community."[80] Marx associated Palestrina with the "purely Catholic" tendency to separate people

---

[76] Schleiermacher in 1819 and again in 1825, Hegel in 1820–21, 1823, 1826, and 1828–29. See
Schleiermacher, *Vorlesungen über die Aesthetik*, ed. Carl Lommatzsch (1842; repr., Berlin 1974), 366–
429; and Hegel, *Aesthetics*, introduction.

[77] Schleiermacher, *Vorlesungen*, 426.

[78] Albert Blackwell, "Schleiermacher on Musical Experience and Religious Experience: 'What
hath Vienna to do with Jerusalem,'" in *Friedrich Schleiermacher and the Founding of the University of
Berlin: The Study of Religion as a Scientific Discipline*, ed. Herbert Richardson, Schleiermacher Studies and Translations 5 (Lewiston, 1991), 121–39; Blackwell, *Sacred in Music*, 210.

[79] Marx, *Meine Erinnerungen*, 8–9.

[80] A. B. Marx, review of *Charinomos: Beiträge zur allgemeinen Theorie und Geschichte der schönen
Künste von Karl Seidel*, *BAMZ* 3, no. 9 (1 March 1826): 68

from direct religious experience, thus removing music to an unreachable sacred realm; his choruses "never served individual expression but were rather an effort musically to create heavenly speech." The Protestant chorale, on the other hand, developed as an expression of the "spontaneous devotion of the people"; it enabled the people to "express their religious beliefs clearly and collectively."[81]

Marx did not fully develop his ideas about the history of sacred music until later, nor did he ever make an unequivocal argument for the superiority of Protestant music, of Handel over Palestrina, of the chorale over the plainchant. He was too subtle a music critic, too ecumenical a music lover, and too engaged an advocate of serious music altogether ever to dismiss the Catholic legacy of sacred music; moreover, his historicism provided a framework to embrace the entire range of sacred musical composition, even Jewish sacred music, which he wrote about briefly in 1824.[82] When he wrote about Beethoven, Marx may have been a Hegelian, seeing in musical history a process of struggle, overcoming, and transcendence. But when he wrote about sacred music, he tended to be more of a Herderian, finding variety, change, and equal closeness to God. Thibaut too, like Marx an intellectual combining nationalist conviction and Protestant faith with catholic taste, wished only for music of authenticity and "purity." People should be "many-sided," he wrote, and "thank God for providing them with all forms of beauty," which "stir, purify, and ennoble the heart and soul of man in all kinds of ways." For both men, the more music became available for study and for performance, private or public, amateur or professional, the greater the musical and moral improvement of society. As Thibaut wrote, "I would never grow old in spirit if a kind destiny were to preserve for me throughout my life an unimpaired enjoyment of fine music."[83]

Still, in their calls for a renewed appreciation of the sacred music of the past, Thibaut and Marx were preaching to the choir, or at least to the growing numbers of amateur musicians and music lovers of central Europe. By 1826 the intellectual climate for serious and sacred music showed every sign of receptivity to sacred music like that of Bach. Yet as late as 1826 no plans existed in Germany, Switzerland, Denmark, England, or anywhere else in Protestant or musical Europe to perform Bach's sacred vocal works in public. Mendelssohn and Devrient together changed that, suddenly, brilliantly, and in a blaze of publicity (thanks to Marx). As Friedrich Blume wrote

---

[81] *BAMZ* 1 (1824): 301.
[82] *BAMZ* 1, no. 1 (7 January 1824): 5–6.
[83] Thibaut, *Reinheit*, 149–50, 193.

many years ago and not quite accurately, "a younger generation entered upon the scene" and "for no discernible reason suddenly displayed a spontaneous fervor for Bach's music."[84] To understand how that happened and why it took so long, we need to turn at last to where Bach had been all those years.

BACH AND THE GERMAN PUBLIC

In addition to its yearly ritual of performing Graun's *Tod Jesu*, the Singakademie performed a surprising variety of other works in its infrequent public appearances—works by Graun and Mozart, Fasch and Zelter most often, but also works by Handel, Haydn, Palestrina, Benevoli, and others. Of all the composers whose works they rehearsed, the only major one whose works they never performed publicly before 1829 was, in fact, Johann Sebastian Bach. That Bach should have lingered so long after his death in the shadowy regions of esoterica, exerting an enormous influence on music theorists and a significant one on composers but largely unknown to the musical public, has no simple explanation.[85] This persistent public obscurity, long after the romantics, Thibaut, and others had demanded to hear more of the music of Palestrina and long after music journalists had begun to debate the future of church music, reveals the unevenness of any transformation in cultural attitudes. The new aesthetics that regarded the autonomous musical work as worthy of preservation and performance did not definitively arrive like Napoleon's armies. In Goehr's unfixed chronology, "things had begun to change in significant ways in the 1770s (if not before), numerous changes occurred around 1800, and many if not all the changes stabilized during the course of the nineteenth century."[86]

Trying to pin down a date for Bach's emergence from esoteric into public knowledge proves equally difficult. By any measure, it was a slow, protracted process. Bach's public debut at the Berlin Singakademie in 1829 was certainly, as Hugo Ricmann wrote in 1901, a milestone in this process, but at the same time it was a milestone encountered well into the journey: forty-five years after C. P. E. Bach had performed the Credo of the B-minor Mass to acclaim in Hamburg; thirty-five years after Fasch had begun rehearsals of Bach motets; twenty-six years after both the *Well-Tempered Clavier* and the *Art of the Fugue* had become readily available in published

---

[84] Blume, "Bach in the Romantic Era," 298.

[85] Martin Zenck, "Reinterpreting Bach in the Nineteenth and Twentieth Centuries," in *The Cambridge Companion to Bach*, ed. John Butt (New York, 1997), 226.

[86] Goehr, *Imaginary Museum*, 206.

form and the Leipzig firm of Hoffmeister & Kühnel had embarked on the publication of Bach's complete keyboard works; twenty-seven years after Forkel had published his biography, in which he called for more public performances of Bach's works; fifteen years after Hoffmann had urged people to listen to "the great masters" of old church music; and fourteen years after Zelter led the Singakademie in rehearsals of the *St. Matthew Passion* choruses.[87]

One might call the 1829 performance the climax of this slow revival, but such a characterization suggests more momentum in the process than existed. Consider the case of Zelter, who in the eyes of his contemporaries was a Bach *Kenner* of unmatched devotion, more knowledgeable even than the distinguished Herr Professor Forkel, Bach's commissioned biographer.[88] For many of these decades, Zelter alone had the scores and singers to undertake a major public performance of Bach's vocal works, yet he did not. Devrient's account of pounding on Zelter's door dramatizes this decades-old reluctance. To explain it requires understanding not just why so great an admirer of Bach's music would shy away from performing it but also why he and many of his contemporaries showed no such hesitation in performing the works of other equally bygone composers.

The story of Bach's posthumous fate—his "death and resurrection" in Albert Schweitzer's memorable phrase or, in Christoph Wolff's, "a tale of posthumous success unique in the history of music"—has been so often told that we need only review it here with particular attention to the difficulties involved in bringing his large-scale vocal works to public attention.[89] Friedrich Blume once wrote that "for the most part there was in fact nothing of Bach's work to be forgotten because it had never been really known,"

---

[87] *New Bach Reader*, 485.

[88] Erwin R. Jacobi, "C. F. Zelters kritische Beleuchtung von J. N. Forkels Buch über J. S. Bach, aufgrund neu aufgefundener Manuscripte," in *International Musicological Society: Report of the Eleventh Congress 1972*, vol. 2 (Copenhagen, 1974), 462–66.

[89] Albert Schweitzer, *J. S. Bach*, 2 vols., trans. Ernest Newman (New York, 1966), 1:222–65; *New Bach Reader*, 486. To provide a full accounting of the reception of Bach after his death is practically to write a history of music after 1750. Michael Heinemann and Hans-Joachim Hinrichsen have attempted something close to that in their three-volume, multi-authored survey: Michael Heinemann and Hans-Joachim Hinrichsen, eds., *Bach und die Nachwelt*, 3 vols. (Laaber, 1997–2000). Other recent accounts, which mainly summarize the findings of the massive Heinemann-Hinrichsen undertaking, include Martin Geck, *Bach: Leben und Werk* (Reinbek bei Hamburg, 2000), 11–42; Arno Forchert, *Johann Sebastian Bach und seine Zeit* (Laaber, 2000), 250–62; Forchert, "Reception and Revival," in *Oxford Composer Companions: J. S. Bach*, ed. Malcolm Boyd (New York, 1999), 384–407; and Martin Zenck, "Bach Reception: Some Concepts and Parameters," in Butt, *Cambridge Companion to Bach*, 218–25. Still useful is Gerhard Herz, translated as "Johann Sebastian Bach in the Age of Rationalism and Early Romanticism," in his *Essays on J. S. Bach*, Studies in Musicology 73 (Ann Arbor, 1985), 1–124.

and while few today would entirely agree, it remains the case that in Bach's circumstances, fame of a modern sort did not exist.[90] No elevated notion of the musical work enjoined the preservation of compositions churned out with greater and lesser skill by musicians in church and town; only a tiny number of Bach's staggering number of compositions was available to the public during his lifetime or immediately after his death. The publicity that disseminates an individual's reputation was not available to those who practiced music outside of court culture, and even at court, musical reputations were meant to promote the fame and glory of the prince. Musical celebrity adhered to a very few, but Bach's chance at it came and went in 1717, when an organ contest at the court in Dresden with the keyboard virtuoso Louis Marchand of Paris never took place because Marchand declined to show.

The incident became famous only later, in the changed context of literary culture. There it gathered patriotic significance: Bach's obituary writers, Johann Friedrich Agricola and his son Carl Philipp Emanuel Bach, used it to condemn court culture itself, so besotted with things French that the Saxon king was ready to offer the less worthy Marchand "a highly paid post in the Royal service," so corrupt that "a certain servant" managed to cheat Bach even of a gift the king had intended to bestow on him. "Strange fate," they exclaimed, that "a Frenchman voluntarily abandons a permanent salary offered to him," and "the German . . . cannot even obtain possession of the one special gift intended for him by the favor of the King."[91] But that minor piece of attention came later; the musical press of the early eighteenth century was small and transitory, and within it, Bach virtually escaped detection.[92] To have reported on what was played in a church the previous Sunday, however monumental the piece or grand the church, would have required a transgression of the boundaries within which the public sphere sought to pursue learning in a disinterested space, free from the corporate privileges and narrow concerns of church, prince, and townsmen.

Whatever might be said about Bach's own participation in this new public sphere, the large vocal works that today count among his greatest

---

[90] Friedrich Blume, *Two Centuries of Bach: An Account of Changing Taste*, trans. Stanley Godman (New York, 1950), 24.

[91] *New Bach Reader*, 301.

[92] The exceptions all concerned his keyboard work and were positive, even glowing (*New Bach Reader*, 309–54). Christoph Wolff considers the criticism Bach encountered in the music press to be inconsequential, especially the infamous article by his former student Scheibe in *Critischer Musikus* in 1737, which characterized his pieces as lacking the "natural element" and marked by a "turgid and confused style" that darkened their "beauty by an excess of art." What other scholars have considered a devastating rejection of Bach by a younger generation of musicians and critics, Wolff would have us regard as criticism that was, at most, annoying to Bach but "not particularly severe." See *New Bach Reader*, 337–38, and *Bach: The Learned Musician*, 431–31.

achievements did not belong in it, could not attract the attention, critical or adulatory, of its denizens, and were, in short, not public works at all in the modern sense.[93] Christoph Wolff does characterize the circumstances in which Bach wrote his "great Passion," the *St. Matthew*, as his first opportunity for a "showcase performance," but one cannot transpose that phrase into a modern context without losing sight of its historical predecessor—a church service on Good Friday in a smallish German city.[94] There was no advance buzz, no sold-out house, no people crowding into a hall just to hear the music, and no post-performance acclaim of the sort that makes history, that is, the sort written down. There was only a reprimand from the city council for Bach's failure to do the work the council wanted him to do and a unanimous decision to reduce further his small annual income. "The authorities are odd and little interested in music," wrote Bach in despair, and "I must live amid almost continual vexation, envy, and persecution."[95] The virtuosic efforts of generations of Bach scholars have likewise turned up nothing more than a few stray remarks on the phenomenon of large-scale Passion music by one Christian Gerber, the gist of which was to comment on how much all the listeners disliked it: "God save us, my children! It's just as if one were at an Opera comedy," exclaimed "an old widow of the nobility." Gerber wrote his account three years after the first performance of the *St. Matthew Passion*, and scholars today now believe it possible these remarks did not even concern that work.[96]

After Bach's death, knowledge of his art was passed on mainly outside the scope of the eighteenth-century public sphere. Yes, some of his music was published, but a 1756 edition of his monumental *Art of the Fugue*, prefaced by a notable critic, Friedrich Wilhelm Marpurg, and recommended by the even more notable Mattheson, sold only thirty copies. Music theorists

[93] Christoph Wolff's biography of Bach, published on the 250th anniversary of Bach's death, stresses Bach's participation in the most forward-looking intellectual trends of his day; Wolff's Bach is truly the Newton of music (as admirers then and later called him). John Butt has suggested that this picture of Bach idealizes and modernizes him: Wolff has too readily dismissed evidence of the "unmodern, pre-Enlightened, non-liberal Bach." See John Butt, "The Saint Johann Sebastian Passion," *New Republic* (July 10 and 17, 2000): 33–38.

[94] Wolff, *Bach: The Learned Musician*, 294.

[95] Documents on the city council minutes and Bach's letter to Erdmann are in *New Bach Reader*, 144–45, 151–52. This unhappy period in Bach's life has been the source of much controversy among scholars, with some arguing that the council was really not as narrow minded as its minutes would indicate and others taking the opposite view. In the midst of debates on what was appropriate behavior in early eighteenth century town politics, we should not lose sight of the fact that no evidence exists suggesting that Bach's employers appreciated his musical output in these years: for the church alone the *St. John Passion*, the *St. Matthew Passion*, the *Magnificat*, and more than two hundred church cantatas. And yet the town council complained that "the cantor does nothing."

[96] *New Bach Reader*, 326–27.

like Marpurg and the Bach student Johann Philipp Kirnberger were engaged with Bach's works, but, learned and respected though they were,
their subject was arcane and their reading public tiny, even by eighteenth
century standards.[97] Published editions of a few Bach cantatas and his four-
part chorales came out in the 1760s; already by the 1770s they were difficult
to come by, in effect out of print.

A lively traffic in Bach manuscripts, copied from originals in the possession of his sons and students, represented another means of transmission,
this one several steps removed from public access. Men like Baron Gottfried
van Swieten, an Austrian diplomat and musical connoisseur of the highest
order, loom large in this story. Haydn, Mozart, and Beethoven learned
much of Bach from van Swieten, but in the case of a man like that, we are
back in the exclusive circles of court culture, slightly more penetrable by
the end of the eighteenth century but still a social space requiring an entrance ticket that was hard to come by, whether through high birth or musical genius.[98] Van Swieten belongs in the world of early modern collectors,
whose rolls consisted of social equals and experts (scientists, in the case of
natural history collecting; professional musicians, in the case of musical
manuscripts), but not the general public.[99] Within this world, manuscript
copies of the *Well-Tempered Clavier* circulated more freely than any other
work, even the published ones, though often in partial or garbled form. In
1807 the leader of the English Bach revival, organist Samuel Wesley, described the copy C. P. E. Bach himself had given to Charles Burney in the
1770s as so "miserably mangled and mutilated" in its version of the preludes
"that had I not met them in such a collection as that of the learned and
highly illuminated Doctor Burney, I verily believe that I should have exclaimed, 'An Enemy hath done this.'"[100]

Finally, the sons and students of Bach became teachers themselves, and
through a Bach-infused pedagogy they spread knowledge of his keyboard
music—from Wilhelm Friedemann Bach to Sara Itzig Levy to Lea Men-

---

[97] See Thomas Christensen, "Bach among the Theorists," in *Bach Perspectives*, vol. 3, *Creative
Responses to Bach from Mozart to Hindemith*, ed. Michael Marissen (Lincoln, NE, 1998), 23–46.

[98] See especially Ludwig Finscher, "Bach's Posthumous Role in Music History," in Marissen,
Bach Perspectives, 9–15.

[99] See, for example, Krysztof Pomian, *Collectors and Curiosities: Paris and Vienna, 1500–1800*
(Cambridge, MA, 1990); Paula Findlen, *Possessing Nature: Museums, Collecting, and Scientific Culture
in Early Modern Italy* (Berkeley, 1994); and Susan Pearce, *On Collecting: An Investigation into Collecting
in the European Tradition* (New York, 1995). As we have seen, Mendelssohn's great aunt Sara Itzig
Levy, was an important collector of Bach manuscripts, and her father Abraham Mendelssohn did
some collecting himself, purchasing Bach manuscripts in Hamburg in 1805 (he later gave them to
Zelter and the Singakademie). See Todd, *Mendelssohn*, 30–31.

[100] Peter Williams, ed., *The Wesley Bach Letters* (London, 1988), 4.

delssohn, from Christian Gottlob Neefe (a self-taught student of Bach, via C. P. E. Bach's and Marpurg's treatises) to Beethoven. Altogether, the picture that has emerged over the past decades of renewed scholarly attention to Bach's posthumous fate depicts a dispersed and small group of individuals who shared their knowledge of this "Orpheus of the Germans" (Schubart) "with whom we can certainly defy foreign nations" (Scheibe) but lacked both the means and the desire to extend this knowledge to a larger, nonspecialist public, either through popular writing or performance.[101]

This picture began to change around 1800, first through writing and only second and much later through performance. In the last decades of the eighteenth century, music journalists and scholars began to find more and more occasions to discuss Bach or invoke his memory. Ludwig Finscher has implied that historians of Bach's reception have placed undue emphasis on this "verbal evidence," with its "advantage of being delivered in print," to the neglect of composers and compositional influences, but there are defensible reasons for emphasizing such writing, especially if the question one wants to answer concerns the emergence of Bach into public consciousness.[102] Reading and writing, not musical compositions, defined the early public sphere, and to be able to detect Bach's presence in the work of another composer required musical expertise that was not then common knowledge, nor is it now. Considering the music that people actually heard throughout the latter part of the eighteenth century, Bach was indeed hidden in plain view, most literally in the works C. P. E. Bach performed in Hamburg, which were not infrequently those of the father passed off as those of the son.[103] The possibility exists that Hamburgers had heard at least parts of the St. *Matthew Passion* half a century before Berliners, but in the absence of copyright laws and firm views on the inviolability of the original musical work, composers borrowed freely from one another's compositions. Handel pilfered his own and other's work, and C. P. E. Bach need not even have felt a twinge of conscience—in him, as contemporaries liked to observe, the father lived on.

The increasing frequency of references in print to Sebastian Bach by the end of the eighteenth century amounted to a major step into public knowledge. This attitudinal change parallels similar ones toward historical objects. The collecting of objects shifted from an essentially private activity of "wealthy or educated individuals" to a collective and public effort that involved both the "performance of ownership" and the "production of his-

---

[101] Christian Friedrich Daniel Schubart's and Scheibe's comments are in *New Bach Reader*, 369, 332.

[102] Finscher, "Bach's Posthumous Role," 4–5.

[103] Herz, *Essays on J. S. Bach*, 31.

torical knowledge" for the public as a whole.[104] Just so did such writers as Gerber and Forkel produce compendia of musical knowledge, adding a sense of urgency to enlightenment by asserting its national importance, aestheticizing the national while nationalizing the musical.[105] Bach emerged gradually in this print context. Gerber included him in his *Lexikon*, with praise for his pedagogy, harmony, and organ playing, by which "in 1717 he saved the honor of his nation against the most famous French organist of the time, Marchand."[106] Still, Bach was one among many admirable men in Gerber's telling, nor did the structure of a biographical dictionary allow Gerber to draw more attention to Bach than many other musicians. In 1796 Reichardt wrote with reserve and admiration of Bach as a "great artist" who exceeded even "the best and deepest of the Italians" in developing "all the possibilities of our harmony." By 1798, Rochlitz was calling him the "patriarch of German music," the "Albrecht Dürer of German music," the sun "from whom all true musical wisdom emanated"—and put his picture on the cover of the first bound volume of the *Allgemeine Musikalische Zeitung*.[107]

FORKEL, ZELTER, AND THE BACH LEGACY

But more decisive than these remarks, still few and scattered, was the publication in 1802 of Forkel's full-length biography of Bach, long in preparation and, as we have already seen, unambiguous in its tone of patriotic urgency. No scholar considers this first Bach biography anything but a landmark: its preeminence among written testimonies to Bach at the turn of the century reflects Forkel's mastery of sources uniquely available to him, especially his contact with Bach's sons, Wilhelm Friedemann and Carl Philipp Emanuel.[108] Less familiar are the circumstances under which Forkel wrote the biography in a matter of months in 1802, after having let decades go by since he first conceived of the work and corresponded with the sons. Forkel had always intended to integrate his Bach research into his unfinished general history of music, the first volume of which had come out in 1788 and the second, which reached only to the sixteenth century, in 1801. But as a scholar, Forkel suffered from the tendency—not uncommon in an

---

[104] Crane, *Collecting and Historical Consciousness*, 64–65.

[105] These developments were considered in chapter 2.

[106] Gerber, *Historisch-Biographisches Lexikon*, 87.

[107] Reichardt in *New Bach Reader*, 373; Rochlitz, *AMZ* 1, no. 8 (21 November 1798): 115; *AMZ* 2, no. 5 (30 October 1799): 103.

[108] For an overview of Forkel's contribution to Bach research, see Hans Joachim Hinrichsen, "Johann Nikolaus Forkel und die Anfänge der Bach-Forschung," in Heinemann and Hinrichsen, eds., *Bach und die Nachwelt*, I: 193–254.

era rushing to produce grand syntheses—to pursue many big projects simultaneously, which then competed for his limited time and wandering attention. So few fellow music historians did he have, he seemed to believe no one else could do the work. As his total history of all music everywhere dragged along, new projects began to distract him—a complete bibliography of writings on music, the editing for publication of "monuments" of music, starting far back with early church music. There is no telling how long he might have lingered on the latter project: he ultimately gave it up in discouragement when the French seized and melted the copper-engraved plates after their victory at Jena in 1806. His letters indicate that he also devoted a great deal of time to hunting down and capturing musical manuscripts of Bach and his children, and this passion, had it not been for the actions of a publisher in Leipzig, could well have remained a semiprivate one in the established tradition of genteel and scholarly collectors.

In 1801, however, the Leipzig firm of Hoffmeister & Kühnel (the predecessor of C. F. Peters) decided to tap into the growing European market of music teachers and amateur keyboard players by publishing an edition—in small monthly installments—of Bach's inventions, fantasias, suites, preludes, and fugues under the grand title of *Oeuvres complettes de Jean Sebastien Bach*.[109] When the plan was far advanced, the firm wrote to ask Forkel's opinion of it, and Forkel, put out at not having been asked to edit it, jumped into action to save his Sebastian from an incompetent display of his genius. Over the next several years, he showered Hoffmeister and Kühnel with warnings on the pitfalls they faced in producing "sensible" versions of the works. They must not print too many of Bach's early works, for "like every other man, Bach had to start out as a bungler before he could become a master."[110] They must beware of the many "miserable, ill-chosen, and ill-kept" collections of Bach manuscripts scattered about: "you will find hardly two or three among a great many organists, cantors, etc. who really know what the nature of their presumed treasure really is." They must be knowledgeable in their indications of ornamentations, about which "Seb. Bach was so conscientious."[111] If they did not do all this and more, then "such classic works as those of S. Bach," the "most classic of all German com-

---

[109] George B. Stauffer, ed., *The Forkel-Hoffmeister & Kühnel Correspondence: A Document of the Early 19th-Century Bach Revival*, trans. Arthur Mendel and George B. Stauffer (New York, 1990), 123; hereafter *Forkel-Hoffmeister*.

[110] Forkel was at his most wrong in his judgments on Bach's alleged juvenilia, because he assumed (as did Zelter) that the more elaborate a piece, the earlier it must be, for perfection came in the process of retrieving the essence from ill-considered elaboration. See Arthur Mendel, introduction to *Forkel-Hoffmeister*, xxv–xxvi.

[111] The editor, according to Forkel, "obviously knows neither the nature of the ornaments customarily introduced in the music of the Bach school nor the signs used to indicate them." Forkel to

posers," would be misunderstood and dismissed as unimportant, a "public scandal" would ensue, the "whole venture will miscarry," and "neither you nor the German nation will be honored by it."[112]

By early 1802 Forkel had issued so many dire predictions of failure, along with a threat to send his opinions "as a true musical patriot" to various journals, that Hoffmeister and Kühnel offered to publish a short essay by him as introduction to one or more of the volumes. Forkel demurred, claiming reluctance to "take responsibility before the public" in "the dissemination of Bach's works." But he indicated willingness to publish a "little essay" for the public's enlightenment "on the life and works of J. S. Bach."[113] Yet the task grew in its execution, and by the time he completed it, Forkel wanted his "little essay" printed on expensive paper, with a high-quality engraving of Bach, and translated into French, English, and Russian. Everything must be "done in proper fashion," he wrote to the publishers, so that the book would be "read by people of quality" and not be "thrown aside as common stuff."[114]

Such increasing ambition to reach as influential a part of the reading public as possible indicates that saving Bach had incrementally turned into publicizing Bach, as though neither could be achieved without the other. Like his contemporaries, the founders of historical associations and museums, Forkel had come to believe that preservation of the past required participation of the public, a connection not evident to earlier generations of collectors—or Bach initiates. His biography, in which he presented Bach in categories anyone could grasp (the Clavier Player, the Organist, the Composer, the Teacher, the Man, the Genius), marked the emergence of Bach from the private cult of his followers into the public world. The outspokenly national tone of his Bach portrait also reflected his dual imperatives of saving and publicizing, rather than some "tide of nationalism . . . running high."[115] Forkel's insistent patriotic refrain—from an opening dedication to the "patriotic admirers of true musical art" to a closing exhortation for "the Fatherland [to] be proud of him, and, yes, worthy of him too," "this man, the greatest musical poet and musical orator who has ever lived or will ever live," this "German"—made forceful claim to broad public attention. As he

---

Hoffmeister and Kühnel, 4 May, 26 October, and 4 December 1801, in *Forkel-Hoffmeister*, 3, 5, 11–13.

[112] Forkel to Hoffmeister & Kühnel, 4 May 1801, in *Forkel-Hoffmeister*, 5.

[113] Forkel to Hoffmeister & Kühnel, 15 February 1802, in *Forkel-Hoffmeister*, 22–25.

[114] Forkel to Hoffmeister & Kühnel, 5 March, 18 June, 16 July, and 19 July 1802, in *Forkel-Hoffmeister*, 29, 37, 41, 43.

[115] Mendel, introduction to *Forkel-Hoffmeister*, xxiv.

repeatedly argued, not just musicians, not just art, but the nation needed Bach.[116] At the same time, Forkel remained actively engaged in his publishers' efforts to sell Bach's music and biography outside German-speaking Europe, and he considered his own patriotic effusions neither unseemly nor likely to dampen foreign sales.[117] The appeal of Bach may have been universal, as Forkel did believe, but meanwhile it could only help the cause of saving and publicizing Bach to emphasize his Germanness—to give him an identity, a national identity, the kind that the literate European public increasingly regarded as essential. Still, Forkel's efforts to nationalize Bach did not take hold right away. Writing to Kühnel several years later, in the face of wartime hardships and lagging sales, he hoped that "better times and circumstances" would prove Bach's works "the most substantial of wares." He himself stood ever ready "to remind the public of its national musical treasure," but "under such circumstances as obtain today we should be preaching to deaf ears."[118]

But hard times did not entirely account for the biography's inability to spark a more full-blown Bach revival, nor did the skeptical reception of the work on the part of critics like Reichardt, who found this "one-sided modern panegyric" "unnecessary," since Bach already had plenty of admirers and Handel was more in need of rescue.[119] Reichardt's criticism raises the question of whether the incompleteness of Forkel's portrait of Bach also limited its public impact. As Reichardt implied, the biography simply provided a fuller account of the Bach his admirers already knew, the Bach of the keyboard, not the composer of the vocal works, of which Forkel knew little and had heard less. Just as his publishers' "complete works" consisted only of keyboard compositions, so too were Forkel's estimations of Bach's "dwarfing all other musicians from the height of his superiority" based only on some of his output. And on just such partial knowledge had Triest's "Remarks on the Development of the Art of Music in Germany," published the year before in Rochlitz's journal, understood Bach in the terms already established by the musical theorists Marpurg and Kirnberger, that is, the "greatest law-giver of harmony who has ever lived." For Triest, Bach

---

[116] Forkel, *Bachs Leben*, 18, 21–22, 137.

[117] See especially his letters to Hoffmeister and Kühnel of 16 July, 23 December, and 4 February 1803, in *Forkel-Hoffmeister*, 41, 67, 71–73.

[118] Forkel to Kühnel, 20 June 1808, in *Forkel-Hoffmeister*, 89.

[119] J. F. Reichardt, "Einige Anmerkungen zu Forkels Schrift: Ueber Joh. Sebast. Bach," *BMZ* 2, no. 38 (1806): 149–50. Other reviewers were more friendly: see, e.g., J. G. K. Spazier, *Zeitung für die elegante Welt,* 5 February 1803; F. Rochlitz, *AMZ* 5 (23 February 1803). On Forkel's interest in his reception, see *Forkel-Hoffmeister*, 63, 67, 114.

was a scientist, with a "spirit like Newton's," and also the master of "mysteries . . . which one may not approach without a sacred awe."[120] This sense of the sacred was itself secular. Neither Triest nor Forkel defined Bach by his composition of church or religious music, though both knew well the details of his employment and, in Forkel's case, had a more or less complete list of his compositions.

The question of which Bach went public speaks directly to the problem of performance and the broader public dissemination it underwrote. In his preface, Forkel had written that public performances were the "most effective means to promote a lively preservation of musical artworks," yet he advised against them in the case of Bach. The Bach he knew intimately, the Bach of the keyboard, was not suited to intervals between opera acts or subscription concert potpourris. Only "a few people" were competent to perform his works; the public was not yet ready to *hear* them, only to *see* them in published form.[121] Even in so musically sophisticated a person as Forkel, print culture still defined the public sphere; performance could only muddle the process of enlightenment his biography had initiated. The publication and wide dissemination of works like the *Well-Tempered Clavier* in these years hardly changed this picture. Most people regarded them as something to be studied not performed, or rather performed only in semiprivate settings like Baron Van Swieten's Sunday afternoon reading sessions or, some twenty years later, the Mendelssohn family's Sunday concerts and Goethe's home recitals. Mozart transcribed Bach's keyboard fugues for string ensemble and added his own modern preludes to make the works more appropriate for listening, and later composers "enhanced" Bach's music by adding new parts to the scores "almost as a matter of course."[122] The Catholic cleric and traveling organ virtuoso Georg Josef (Abbé) Vogler, who wrote about the organ for the musical press and liked to alarm listeners with thunderous sound effects he achieved by playing the organ with his elbows, newly harmonized a number of Bach chorales for publication. Although many musicians derided his alterations, others, like his student Carl Maria von Weber, admired them for making Bach modern.[123]

---

[120] Triest, "Bemerkungen über die Ausbildung der Tonkunst in Deutschland im achtzehnten Jahrhundert," *AMZ* 3 (1800/1801). See also the brief discussion in chapter 3. Donald Mintz's classic article "Some Aspects of the Revival of Bach" (*Musical Quarterly* 40 [April 1954]: 201–21) gives Triest precedence over Forkel in bringing Bach out into public view. See also Bernd Sponheuer, "Reconstructing Ideal Types of the 'German' in Music," in Applegate and Potter, *Music and German National Identity*, 48–52.

[121] Forkel, *Bachs Leben*, 22–24.

[122] George B. Stauffer, "Changing Issues of Performance Practice," in *Cambridge Companion to Bach*, 205–7.

[123] Herz, *Essays on Bach*, 89; Christensen, "Bach among the Theorists," 34–35.

But even had Forkel known the vocal works better, it is doubtful he would have recommended their public performance. Published scores were hardly available—the motets in 1802, a few chorale settings in 1804, the Magnificat in 1811, the promise of the B-minor Mass in 1817 not fulfilled until 1833 and 1845, a cantata or two (spectacular commercial failures) in the 1820s, the *St. Matthew Passion* and the *St. John Passion* in 1830. One could talk about availability of manuscripts, delving into all those questions of authenticity and dispersal that drove Forkel to write his biography in the first place. But such a discussion of technicalities obscures the basic problem, which was the near extinction of the German Protestant culture of sacred choral music over the course of the eighteenth century, a decline that had reached its nadir around 1800, just as Forkel sought to bring Bach to the public. Influential clerics and leaders (including the king of Prussia) were trying, as we have seen, to ban anything resembling a concert from churches, and other ecclesiastical problems precluded the possibility of Bach's own musical milieu serving as the site of his revival. Few churches had choirs capable of singing a Bach chorale, let alone a cantata or motet, even had they access to the scores. The supply of organists was slightly better, with pupils of Bach and pupils of his pupils scattered across Thuringia, Saxony, and Prussia. For choral singing, Leipzig was practically alone in its preservation, albeit often interrupted, of a continuous Bach tradition.

But people did not travel to Leipzig in the late eighteenth century just to hear the Thomasschule choir, the reputation of which is mainly a by-product of a Bach revival in full swing much later in the nineteenth century. Rochlitz's anecdote of Cantor Doles treating Mozart to a performance of the double-chorus motet *Singet dem Herrn ein neues Lied* frames the event as a "surprise"—not, in other words, what Mozart had come to Leipzig to experience. Whether or not this was strictly true, the story in its frequent repetition after 1800 served its tellers—like Zelter to Goethe—as the paradigm of what they saw as the rediscovery of Bach.[124] Mozart's astonished delight, his romantic-religious response ("now his whole soul seemed to be in his ears"), and his demand to see more of this unfamiliar Bach all suggested the recasting of Bach from rational harmonist to transcendent and spiritual dramatist. Yet even in this epiphany, Mozart appeared as much student as listener: he pored over the musical manuscripts ("sacred relics"), "with the parts all around him—in both hands, on his knees, and on the chairs next to

---

[124] Rochlitz published the anecdote first in the *Allgemeine Musikalische Zeitung* in 1798, then again in his *Für Freunde der Tonkunst*; Zelter wrote to Goethe of it, and so it spread, cropping up regularly in the belletristic press, contributing to the growing cult of genius. A. B. Marx used it at the beginning of his final musical summation, *Die Musik des neunzehnten Jahrhunderts und ihre Pflege* (Leipzig, 1873), 14.

him," not getting up again "until he had looked through everything of Sebastian Bach's that was there."[125]

School choirs like the Thomasschule, never very securely funded, were not in any case a vehicle suited to the requirements of early nineteenth century musical publicity. No clever marketer of choral singing had yet dared to put boy singers in white ruffs and burgundy robes and take them on concert tours. Child prodigies were, of course, a familiar feature of the new concert scene, but they came only singly or in sibling pairs and their virtuosity tended to the instrumental. But Zelter's adult singers could have performed Bach. Considering them brings us back to his attitudes toward the performance of Bach's choral works and reveals that in his handling of the Bach legacy, the would-be forward-looking public servant Zelter adhered almost entirely to the old model of Bach initiate. He was well acquainted with surviving students like Kirnberger and had had some contact at least with C. P. E. and W. F. Bach. He was inclined to regard Bach's work as the foundation of musical pedagogy, certainly of a very high order, but not as the repertoire of modern performance. He was a rationalist to the brink of irreligiosity. And he was proprietorial about his own knowledge of Bach to the brink of secrecy. Such knowledge could be shared with other knowledgeable ones and passed on to carefully groomed students, but it could not be shared with the public as a whole, particularly not in the form of public performance. Donald Mintz once speculated that Zelter felt himself "personally and exclusively in contact with what he regarded as the greatest spirit of any age" and might have been "reluctant to violate this experience by undertaking public performance."[126]

At the same time, and only in apparent contradiction to that attitude, Zelter shared the view that Bach could only appear in public in modern dress, that is, after well-chosen alterations had been made. He had his orchestral students of the Ripienschule practice Bach clavier fugues set for string quartet and, not just for convenience of performance, made all sorts of other alterations to the music of this master he admired so deeply.[127] Bach, he suggested in a much-quoted letter to Goethe, was "despite all his originality a son of his country and of his age"—that is, too receptive to cultural influences from France. But, pronounced Zelter, "one can separate him from this foreign element; it comes off like thin froth, and the shining contents lie immediately beneath." Of his own rearrangements, his "heart told him" that "old Bach nods approval." Perhaps his heart also made him

[125] Friedrich Rochlitz, "Verbürgte Anekdoten aus Mozarts Leben," *AMZ* 1, no. 8 (21 November 1798): 116–17.

[126] Mintz, "Some Aspects," 214.

[127] Eberle, *Sing-Akademie*, 82–86.

doubt, because Zelter insisted on the private ("solely for my own pleasure") and privileged ("not *everyone* may do so") nature of these skimming exercises. In response to Goethe's demand that he specify just what he meant by this "French froth," Zelter could say only, after months of delay in answering, that it was "like ether, everywhere present yet untouchable."[128]

One cannot help but think that with friends like these Bach hardly needed enemies to keep his vocal works unheard and unappreciated, but he had enemies as well, or at least vocal detractors. Reichardt set the tone in the 1790s, reflecting a generational rejection of the musico-religious aesthetic embodied in the cantatas, Passions, and (to a lesser extent) the motets. The vocal works, wrote Reichardt, were "full of invention" and even expression, yet they lacked "genuine good taste" and "hardly maintain their currency."[129] Bach's love of word-painting, using descending musical lines to depict tears or rising ones to depict climbing, struck Reichardt as antiquated and naïve, likewise the elaborate contrapuntal textures and the *basso continuo*, long thought outmoded. And for the rising generation of romantics, who sought transcendence in the simplest echoes of a harmonic universe, Bach's settings of religious texts seemed heavy and earthbound.

Yet one senses as much ignorance as clashing taste in the judgments of Reichardt and others coming after him. Zelter, more deeply acquainted with the great vocal works of Bach than anyone, and a published author to boot, had nothing to say about them in print.[130] Had Bach found in this period a public advocate of his vocal works, one who knew their full range and wrote with the erudition of a Forkel or the conviction and eloquence of a Hoffmann, the romantic apprehension of music could have discovered an unending abundance of awe, sublimity, and emotional intensity in a *St. Matthew Passion*. But at the time he wrote "Old and New Religious Music," Hoffmann knew of Bach's vocal composition only in the instance of a short, two-movement mass, probably not even by Bach at all but by his distant cousin Johann Ludwig Bach.[131]

Thibaut followed his legal colleague closely in his high opinion of Palestrina and his dismissive opinion of Bach, who failed his litmus tests for simplicity, grandeur, and of course "purity." Bach had his moments, Thibaut acknowledged, but he inclined to "florid part-writing," indifferent to "the requirements of ordinary people." Bach was, in short, unperformable, his

---

[128] The exchange, which took place in 1827, is cited in full in Herz, *Essays on Bach*, 95.

[129] *New Bach Reader*, 373.

[130] By 1815 he had published a well-received biography of Fasch, which Forkel cited several times to his publishers as a model for what the Bach biography ought to look like, and he contributed a number of articles to the *AMZ*, among others.

[131] Hoffmann, "Old and New Church Music," 360n28.

music "composed by mere ingenuity" as "a sort of mathematical exercise without any life." Even after young Felix Mendelssohn visited Thibaut in Heidelberg in 1826 and told him about the *St. Matthew Passion*, Thibaut remained unimpressed. After all, Thibaut had already admonished composers for promiscuously mixing the three "pure" musical styles of church, oratorio, and opera. Bach's Passions, with their blending of chorale (first style), chorus (second), and solo recitative and aria (third), could not please this categorical legalist. In any such mixture, Thibaut had written, "passion" and "eccentricity" prevailed, neither of which belonged in music any more than "cramp in a healthy body."[132]

HANDEL VERSUS BACH

But there was more to this strange failure of appreciation than Thibaut's categorical aesthetic or Zelter's inclination to hoarding. Musical judgments in the early nineteenth century, like judgments in general, tended to be comparative. As these writers and musicians became caught up in the construction of their imaginary museum filled with the great works of great past masters, they wrote increasingly about the comparative strengths of these composers arrayed before them: Palestrina and Pergolesi; the elder Bach and the younger Bachs; Handel, Hasse, and Graun; Mozart, Haydn, and Gluck. But no comparison was more common or more fiercely argued than that between Bach and Handel.[133] Because of the frequency of this linkage in the late eighteenth and early nineteenth centuries, the history of their reception can be seen as a single narrative in which judgments of one shaped those of the other. The foundational exchanges in the Handel–Bach debate took place in the 1780s, after the publication of Charles Burney's biography of Handel on the occasion of his centenary. Burney became so carried away that he claimed Handel superior to Bach even in his organ playing and keyboard compositions. This provoked C. P. E. Bach himself, under the cloak of anonymity, to compose a lengthy and patriotic rebuttal ("an Englishman can have no clear conception of the true and essential qualities of an organist and must therefore not set himself up to be a judge of great organists") published in Friedrich Nicolai's *Allgemeine Deutsche Bibliothek*.[134]

German literary culture thus joined the fray, in this instance more on patriotic than musical grounds. In any case, Bach's vindication in German eyes

---

[132] Thibaut, *Reinheit*, 11, 17, 37, 25.

[133] Archibald T. Davison, *Bach and Handel: The Consummation of the Baroque in Music* (Cambridge, MA: Harvard University Press, 1951), 9.

[134] C. P. E. Bach, "Excerpt from a Letter of February 27, 1788, Written at ———," *New Bach Reader*, 400–409.

took place only on the field of keyboard music. In vocal competition, he was not even a contender, nor did his son attempt a defense. As a composer of large numbers of operas and oratorios, Handel was an international figure during his lifetime and enduringly famous after his death, public and visible in all the ways and places—courts and cities, opera houses, concert halls, and newspaper notices—that Bach was not. Music writers routinely compared Bach's inability to write for the voice with Handel's mastery. Bach, wrote Reichardt, had lacked "the truthfulness and the deep feeling for expression which inspired Handel," and without them he was only "more learned and more diligent."[135] This was faint praise indeed, but consistent with long-held views of Bach as master of musical intricacy, a man of science and effort rather than feeling. Handel, on the other hand, was regarded as a musical dramatist of extraordinary capacity, the composer of works magnificent to hear, to feel, and to contemplate.

The performance history of the oratorios shows how effortlessly Handel fit into the emerging culture of middle-class concerts and amateur singing groups. The oratorios had never ceased to be performed in England, and from the 1770s on could be heard in Germany as well, in more public settings than the occasional airing of Bach's motets in Leipzig. Hamburg audiences heard *Messiah* repeatedly, as well as *Alexander's Feast*, the coronation anthems, and *Judas Maccabeus*; C. P. E. Bach participated in the Handel choral movement not the Bach one, for the simple reason that there was none.[136] In Leipzig, Hiller's enthusiasm for Handel and lack of it for Bach were also well known—Zelter accused him of filling his singers "with horror at the crudities of that Sebastian."[137] In 1788 Mozart reorchestrated *Messiah*; this version was heard often over the next decades and was much discussed and admired. By the second decade of the nineteenth century, Handel had already become, in Gerhard Herz's phrase, "the mainstay of German vocal concerts" and soon of the large-scale choral festivals as well.[138] In Berlin, Zelter led the Singakademie in performances of Handel's works, which became more frequent in the 1820s. Concertgoing Berliners had, in other words, heard much more of Handel by 1829 than they had of Bach, and once again, Zelter seems to have found nothing amiss in that situation.

Handel became, then, an actual obstacle to the appreciation of Bach's large choral works, in practical as well as intellectual terms. Because Handel's scores were so easily obtained, the music so easily learned and so

---

[135] From his 1782 publication *Musikalisches Kunstmagazin*, cited in Herz, *Essays on Bach*, 27.

[136] Sittard, *Musik- und Concertwesens in Hamburg*, 110–12.

[137] Coleridge, 298.

[138] Herz, *Essays on Bach*, 75.

quickly familiar, and the sheer number of oratorios so vast, his very existence undermined the urge to explore the musical past more broadly, especially on the part of amateur choral societies. And not only that, Handel was also serious and German. Music writers concerned about frivolity and foreignness in musical life could only rejoice in Handel's spreading popularity and wonder at the national treasure he represented. Writers of the late eighteenth century forgave and forgot all Handel's Englishness, translated the texts, and made him a shining light of German genius in foreign lands. Cramer's *Magazin der Musik*, a Hamburg periodical well placed to recover Handel's Germanness, described his *Messiah* as so great that "the human spirit could hardly grasp it"; it required many hearings to experience its range and depth of feeling.[139] Rochlitz, the Leipziger, was the rare exception in praising both Handel and Bach as choral composers. Yet here too were nuances of disapproval. Handel remained "as accessible and popular as an artist can be, that is, without becoming vulgar and common," while Bach, "who neither wanted to nor *could* deny his deep learnedness" and wrote with more complexity, was "rich in artistry" but likely "to leave nonmusicians cold."[140] Goethe, for his part, confided to Zelter that he was "strangely attracted to Handel," and Thibaut considered him the equal of Palestrina, "soaring above the clouds" with his "splendid powers."[141]

And until he began to realize the significance of Bach's choral works around 1827, even Marx could find nothing but praise for the seriousness of Handel's nonoperatic compositions. Of course no one performed them well. Zelter and the Singakademie sang *Messiah* with precision, but the tempi were all wrong; noble choruses were rushed and sprightly ones dragged. Worst of all, Zelter presented only excerpts from this "great totality," this "complete effort in pursuit of the highest and noblest." The appreciation of "old art treasures" required that "all powers," "not just a third of the Singakademie but all academies, choirs, and orchestras" of Berlin and "all capable dilettantes," unite to make a performance "as great as the work itself." Only then could "the greatest work of music once again live, in Germany, where it belongs."[142] But five years later, Marx called Bach's *St. Matthew Passion* the "greatest and holiest musical work of all people" and the "greatest work of our greatest master." In the end, at least from Marx's perspective, Handel had just warmed up the crowd.

[139] Cramer, *Musik* 1 (1788–89): 441, 557, 560.

[140] Rochlitz, "Feyer des Andenkens der heiligen Caecilia," *AMZ* 6, no. 8 (23 November 1803): 125.

[141] Goethe to Zelter, 8 March 1824. in Coleridge, 227; Thibaut, *Reinheit*, 30, 96.

[142] A. B. Marx, *BAMZ* 1, no. 50 (8 December 1824): 427; no. 51 (15 December 1824): 439.

GRAUN VERSUS BACH

Before turning at the last to the work that finally enabled the whole of Bach to emerge in public life, one last obstacle to his performance deserves mention. In Berlin of the 1820s, the place and time most musically and intellectually prepared to perform Bach, one religious choral work had become enshrined in public consciousness through repeated, annual performances. It was not the *St. Matthew Passion*; it was not, as Marx hoped in 1824, Handel's *Messiah* or anything else by him or Haydn or Mozart. It was, rather, Carl Heinrich Graun's Passion music of 1755, *Der Tod Jesu*, a work now so obscure as to be inaccessible except in well-stocked music libraries. In 1824, while Marx was defending *Messiah* against its despoilers and the score of the *St. Matthew Passion* lay unused in Zelter's library, the Berlin public went to hear *Tod Jesu*, this "Prussian national art treasure," for the sixty-ninth and seventieth times, "with their usual interest and to their equal edification."[143] Since 1801, Zelter's Singakademie had been responsible for at least twenty of those performances. For the bulk of the public who knew nothing of its other musical interests, the Singakademie simply was the group that appeared every year, in different churches, performing *Tod Jesu* on Good Friday.

As even the prickly pair of Thibaut and Marx acknowledged, Graun was at worst harmless. "Graun had not Handel's genius," wrote Thibaut, "but the devotional and childlike spirit of his *Tod Jesu* will and must render it immortal, like Handel's *Messiah*."[144] The passion oratorio showed the same emotive vocal style of Handel's writing but was shorter than his oratorios, written for church rather than concert performance, and in every way undemanding, thus well suited to amateur performance. *Tod Jesu* had, moreover, a peremptory claim on public recognition in Prussia. Graun had been Friedrich II's longest-serving kapellmeister and a composer of secular cantatas, operas, ballet music, instrumental music, and sacred music, all long admired for, among other virtues, the "the purity and clarity of his harmony" and "the agreeable melody."[145] Graun composed *Tod Jesu* in 1754, performing it during Holy Week at Berlin's Domkirche in 1755 to the acclaim he knew well. By trick of fate, the publishers Breitkopf & Härtel obtained rights to its publication just as they introduced their newly improved movable type, thus making reproduction of it affordable and rapid for decades to

---

[143] *BAMZ* 1, no. 17 (28 April 1824): 151.

[144] Thibaut, *Reinheit*, 151.

[145] Gerber from his *Lexikon*, cited in Howard Serwer, preface to *Tod Jesu*, by Carl Heinrich Graun, ed. Howard Serwer (Madison, 1975), viii.

come. Bach's Passions, by contrast, existed only in manuscript form, barely legible to even the most experienced musicians and inaccessible to all but a privileged few. *Tod Jesu* maintained a simplicity of orchestration and vocal writing throughout, a homogenizing means for Graun to create a "uniform stylistic territory and a uniform realm of sonorities."[146] Compared only to the size and musical complexity of the *St. Matthew Passion*, without reference to any other of its remarkable qualities, *Tod Jesu* was easy listening, middlebrow music at its most ingratiating.

No wonder, then, that Marx found it so grating. Its inoffensive and universally well-liked melodiousness drove him in 1824 to his denunciation of Zelter, who mangled *Messiah* yet managed year after year to bring forth *Tod Jesu* to a lulled public. In dealing with *Tod Jesu* itself, Marx argued against a public who regarded it as a timeless classic, safe in its excellence from changing fashion and fickle taste. For Marx, Graun and his librettist Ramler represented an antiquated aesthetic with nothing more to say, musically or ethically. "The times are long gone," he wrote, "when we granted the highest glory to suffering alone—such a narrow, weak view of the death of Jesus belongs only to the unenlightened." "We may and must feel deeply his sorrows, agony, and death," he continued, "our souls must cry in anguish and with him die a little, but then we may and must rise up with the enlightened and gather his light with our eyes." This hopeful conjugation of the philosophy of enlightenment with the theology of resurrection represented Marx's effort to integrate Hegel and Handel. *Messiah*, not *Tod Jesu*, spoke to the Christian of 1824: neither Graun's theology nor his music could compare to it or—all evidence to the contrary notwithstanding—"inspire" a modern audience.[147]

One can perhaps explain Marx's disparagement of *Tod Jesu*, which contradicted both his support for performances of serious music and his injunction to learn from the past, as a frustrated response to Zelter's musical immobility. Certainly he later apologized, more to Zelter than to Graun or his admirers. But the judgment also pointed to a tension between the influence of Herder and Hegel on Marx's criticism. Marx's view of the needs of his times crept into his assessment of sacred music of the past, and over time his viewpoint redounded increasingly to the benefit of Bach over any other composer of religious works. One of the most pressing needs of the time, so it seemed, was to rescue Bach, especially the religious Bach, from the ignorance of the public. Historical relativism had its critical limits, and he confronted them as he became aware of Bach in his compositional entirety.

---

[146] Herz, *Essays on Bach*, 51–65.
[147] *BAMZ* 1, no. 27 (28 April 1824): 153.

The question of Marx's conversion to Bach is thus at the same time the question of a musical classic and how it is made.[148] In 1824, Graun's *Tod Jesu* held that status for the Berlin public, and the *St. Matthew Passion* did not. Today the situation is close to being the reverse, less because people find Graun trivial than because they do not know him, perform him, or listen to him at all. But Marx's growing interest in Bach reflected something stronger than a desire to add more music to the repertoire. As Marx came to believe, Bach's work, in contrast to Graun's, spoke to the present and was important in some essential way that Graun's never could be. Thus did Herder and Hegel meet in the recovery of Bach.

THE *ST. MATTHEW PASSION* IN 1829

The first indication that Marx's thoughts were turning to Bach in this way came in 1827, when he welcomed the publication of Handel's oratorio *Joshua*. Marx explained that Handel's frequent use of Old Testament subjects for his oratorios reflected the pragmatic nature of his English public, seeking "practical wisdom, edification, and satisfying resolutions" for their everyday lives. But "the true meaning of the religious and the holy" lay not "in outward events but in the indwelling idea, in the conceptual thoughts of Christianity." "It is truly remarkable," he went on, "that we find this very perception fully realized in one of Handel's contemporaries, that is, in Sebastian Bach." The sudden, almost hidden reference to Bach is startling, unheralded in any way. "In his great double-chorus Passion [the *St. Matthew*]," Marx continued, "the Jewish people and every individual are fully portrayed," yet "Bach has raised the holiness in Christianity and especially in the person of Jesus above the purely human drama." Handel's *Joshua* now suffered by comparison.[149] Less than a year later, as Mendelssohn immersed himself in the *St. Matthew Passion*, Marx called it the "sun of a new day into the fog of our times."[150] It remains, then, to consider contemporary responses to it not as the project of a young composer and an ambitious journalist, not as the performance of a local singing society and its master, but as a musical and philosophical masterpiece.

Bach's *St. Matthew Passion* has been called a "drama of epic grandeur," the "noblest, most inspired musical treatment of the story of the crucifixion of Christ." This description, which appears on the cover of the Dover edition of the score, reprinted most recently in 1990, reveals how fundamental

---

[148] For an overview of this term, see Ludwig Fischer, "Zum Begriff der Klassik in der Musik," *Der Musikwissenschaft* 2 (1966): 9–34.

[149] *BAMZ* 4, no. 3 (17 January 1827): 20–21; 4, no. 4 (24 January 1827): 27–28.

[150] *BAMZ* 5, no. 13 (27 March 1828): 97.

the 1829 performance and its immediate reception were to all subsequent views of the work. With their emphasis on its dramatic character, its size and seriousness, and its revelation of Bach's Christian faith, these words stand in direct descent from the first descriptions of the work from Marx and others. They come down to us through the figure of Julius Rietz, brother of Eduard Rietz, Mendelssohn's friend, concertmaster, and violin soloist at the 1829 performance. Julius and Eduard together undertook the task of making copies of voice and instrumental parts for the performers, and Julius went on to become the editor of the 1856 Bach-Gesellschaft edition of the *St. Matthew Passion*, which the Dover edition reprinted with a slightly updated adaptation of its accompanying text.

To understand what the work meant in 1829 is thus to understand, with the kind of double vision Marx would have appreciated, something of both their times and ours, indebted as we remain to their initial work of interpretation. As listeners or performers today, we do not experience the sheer surprise of their response. Fanny Mendelssohn, we recall, wrote that even the Singakademie members "marveled, gaped, admired" and expressed "astonishment that they of all people should have had so little knowledge that such a work even existed." But since much of their reaction seems, like the music, very familiar to us, the struggle now is to place their reactions in an 1829 context. To take one example, in his first article after the performance, Marx filled the front page of his journal with two measures from the *Passion*. These two measures, which come right after the death of Jesus and in which both choirs together sing the text of Matthew 27:54, "Wahrlich dieser ist Gottes Sohn gewesen" (Truly this was the Son of God), are arguably the most important ten seconds of the entire work, and in the opinion of one recent commentator, the most beautiful two measures in all of Bach's music, maybe in all music. Why, though, did Marx reprint them? He did not comment on them, as though this musical moment spoke for itself, and we are left wondering how to disentangle judgments that seem so universally valid from those that reflect the limiting work of his or our own cultural horizon.

Part of the explanation for the contemporary sound of these 1829 reviews is that they have little to say about the performers, the acoustics of the hall, the balance of voices and instruments, or other particulars that characterized the majority of nineteenth-century concert reviews. Marx even suggested that it would be a sacrilege to review this concert as though it were comparable to the general run of musical events. It was, he wrote in his article after the first performance, a "religious celebration," something one could perhaps "repeat but never report upon."[151] He mentioned

---

[151] *BAMZ* 6, no. 11 (14 March 1829): 82.

Mendelssohn, Devrient, and Heinrich Stümer, the tenor who sang the part of the Evangelist, only in order to declare them worthy in their artistry of so great a work. Almost every commentator spoke of the large size and enthusiasm of the audience and about the public demands for more performances, but even these comments spoke, as we shall see shortly, to questions of theology more than of taste or reportage. The dearth of commentary on the living participants in the performance made all the more prominent the commentary on the past—on Bach, on his music, and on the biblical text and events themselves. The responses to the 1829 *St. Matthew Passion* thus represent an exemplary moment of historical consciousness in action. The central paradox of this "remarkable event" lay in the presentness of the past or, in Marx's words, in the circumstance that this work "was performed again for the first time."[152]

Of course, one can make too much of this. At one level all Marx meant was that the work had not been heard since its first performance in 1729 (which we now know was neither its first performance nor its last before 1829). But something beyond the prosaic moved many commentators as they struggled to come to terms with the simultaneous novelty and antiquity of this work. The ideal of self-cultivation, which informed the way the Germans attending the performance understood new experiences, held that the study of history taught one also about oneself, because how the works of man changed over time revealed what it meant to be human. What sort of an artwork was this, how did it fit into the scheme of human creations, what difference did it make that it had once existed and was heard again, and what did it mean that Bach, whom they had slotted into history differently, was its composer? These were not the ordinary kind of questions shaping musical commentary, but the *St. Matthew Passion* raised them in people's minds, even in determined skeptics like Ludwig Rellstab and Rahel Varnhagen.

Nor were they questions to which one easily found answers, and several commentators resorted to a formulation that sounds hackneyed but was not in that context—the experience of hearing this music, many wrote, was indescribable. "It is impossible for me to speak of the work itself and its effect," wrote Marx, "already the first chorus leads all listeners to forget the music they had heard before, to forget all means of musical judgment they had once used."[153] As we have already seen, he thought only a lifetime of listening would produce full understanding, and as if to prove his point,

---

[152] *AMZ* 31 (24 March 1829): 234; "Mittwoch, am 11 Mäz 1829, ist dieses Werk zum ersten Mal wieder aufgeführt worden"; *BAMZ* 6, no. 11 (14 March 1829): 79.

[153] "Zweiter Bericht," *BAMZ* 6, no. 11 (14 March 1829): 82.

Ludwig Rellstab went to all three performances, altering the tone of his reviews from indulgent skepticism ("an artistic event of the highest importance," even if "we hesitate to call this absolutely the greatest work German art ever produced") to "greater and greater astonishment and wonder."[154] Goethe, who did not hear it, nevertheless sensed these limitations of language when he congratulated Zelter for his description of "that which is almost impossible to represent." Then he reached for a comparison: it must have been "like the inner apprehension I had recently in seeing again the works of Mantegna, . . . art in its most complete form, the possible and the impossible already fully alive, but still not yet all developed; were it not so, then it would not be what it is here, not so venerable, not so firm in foundation or rich in hope."[155]

Marx similarly tried to capture the *St. Matthew Passion* by offering a comparison, in his case to the Strasbourg Cathedral, a comparison E. T. A. Hoffmann had already made a decade or so earlier. "Bach's music," Hoffmann had written, "bears the same relationship to that of the early Italians as the cathedral in Strasbourg to St. Peter's in Rome": "I see in Bach's eight-part motets the wonderfully bold, romantic structure of the Cathedral rising proudly and gloriously in the air, with all its fantastic ornaments artfully blended into the whole."[156] In both these cases, Goethe proved the inescapable presence. His "Hymn to the Strasbourg Cathedral" of 1772, with its appropriation of the Gothic for modern sensibilities, was already a classic text by the time Hoffmann wrote down his "random thoughts" in the second decade of the nineteenth century. By the third decade, Marx did not even have to refer to the essay by name, just to say that Goethe had "taught us to see" the Strasbourg Cathedral, as we must now "see" the *St. Matthew Passion*—the "richest of artistic creations ultimately so simple in the combined effect of all its parts."[157] He returned to the comparison several times over the course of his reports on the performances. Just as the cathedral "inspired the highest wonder on first glimpse, and all details disappear," so too the *St. Matthew Passion*; and again like the cathedral, only gradually did the presence of "that same holy spirit, in such profundity, in such sublimity, existing even in the smallest part" make itself felt to the listener.[158]

But perhaps the most lasting and generalized effect of these efforts to find language to describe this music was the transformation of Bach from composer, organist, and pedagogue into something greater, something that re-

---

[154] Ludwig Rellstab in the *Vossische Zeitung*, 13 and 29 March 1829, reprinted in Geck, 51, 53.
[155] Goethe to Zelter, 28 March 1929, in Geck, 46.
[156] Hoffmann, "Extremely Random Thoughts," in Charlton, 104.
[157] A. B. Marx, "Erster Bericht," *BAMZ* 6, no. 10 (7 March 1829): 77.
[158] A. B. Marx, "Dritter Bericht," *BAMZ* 6, no. 12 (21 March 1829): 89.

moved him from the list of great musicians, German or otherwise, and placed him among philosophers, poets, and prophets, seekers of truth about God and humanity. Johann Wilhelm Loebell, in his letter to Ludwig Tieck, described hearing Bach's work as "entering into a new and hitherto un-known world of artistic creation," which the "whole pack of so-called ex-perts" had missed entirely in their characterization of Bach as "austere" and dry. He was, on the contrary, "stern" and "above all serious, but in such a way that in the midst of all the seriousness of his subject, in the midst of deep suffering, lamentation, distress, remorse, and repentance, the bright-ness and joy of existence at its most wondrous breaks forth." "I have to tell you," continued Loebell, "that I believe I have at last found, after long searching, the composer who can be compared to Shakespeare." Bach was the "most dramatic, the most epic, the most lyrical" of composers; "many times the instinctive cry of the deepest feeling can be heard, the irresistible bursting through of the suffering heart, expressed in music like to nature it-self, and yet even in this is art and intention."

Joseph Maria von Radowitz, a musically gifted member of the court cir-cle and later a diplomat, also compared Bach to Shakespeare, as incompara-ble figures like no other. Bach, he wrote, was also like Shakespeare in that he was not simply Christian, a term too limiting—"or rather Christianity is in his works, like every other element of existence." Radowitz, like Rell-stab, went to all three performances, and by his own account thought at length about the work: "In it one finds," he wrote, "the whole world; the creation is in it, as is the central point of world history, as are we ourselves in our barren present." Bach's work contained "the whole of humanity, the whole of life, the whole world," he wrote two years later, and "that pre-cisely is the unique character of his music, that it is never marked by some-thing determinate or single but represents instead everything all together." "What music," he exclaimed, "this profundity, this richness, this wondrous power and loftiness cannot be praised enough": "the gentlest and most ten-der, the deepest and most sublime, all is together."[159]

Commentators acknowledged that their understanding of Bach had changed because of the unexpected drama and beauty of the music itself, both qualities, as Devrient said, that "no one had expected from old Bach."[160] Rellstab admired the choruses for their grandeur—"Sind Blitzen, sind Donner in Wolken verschwunden" was "indescribably magnificent." Writing in advance of the first performance, Friedrich von Raumer, a pro-fessor of history at the University of Berlin and member of the Sin-

---

[159] Loebell to Tieck and excerpts from Radowitz, *Fragmentary Musings*, in Geck, 46, 50.
[160] Devrient, *Meine Erinnerungen*, 62.

gakademie, promised that "those who hold the opinion that Sebastian Bach produced more artful pieces than artistic masterpieces" would learn otherwise: Bach delivered "a message of such simplicity, sweetness, and inner emotion that only one who has been completely corrupted by our current meaningless frippery will fail to be moved by this."[161] Johann Theodor Mosewius, the leader of the Breslau Singakademie and no stranger to Bach, rushed to Berlin on reading the first reports of the performance, arriving in time to hear the third performance on Good Friday. This work, he later recalled, "so significantly different from all his others," "seized one unawares with its power and greatness, its lyricism and drama."[162]

But people could not separate the music, however much it "seized" them, from the content, what Loebell called the *Stoff*, of the work. Reading through all the reactions, one comes, finally, to the most basic of conclusions. What people overwhelmingly responded to in the *St. Matthew Passion* was Bach's musical rendering of the "drama of the sacrifice of Jesus," in other words, the religion. Their responses were aesthetic, pious, philosophical, skeptical, secular, sectarian, and patriotic, in varying combinations. All, however, were marked by an intense religious awareness and, to go further, fascination with what Bach's music revealed about this most familiar narrative. Participating in the performance, as listener or performer, seems to have been, indeed, a revelation. "The impression of the whole," wrote Johann Philipp Samuel Schmidt, the Berlin correspondent of the Leipzig *Allgemeine Musikalische Zeitung*, "was an astonishment that transported the listeners and took them unawares, astonishment at the unforeseen greatness and profundity of this sublime work, so full of genuine religiosity and soulful feeling."[163]

Marx took this to mean that people had been ready to hear the religious Bach. The appearance of the *St. Matthew Passion* in 1829 was a "sign" that the days of "fashion-mongering and vanity," and of "enervation and hopelessness" on the part of true music lovers, were over, and "a new and higher period of music" had arrived. Since Bach's death, Gluck had "opened the halls of world history," Mozart had "led us into an ever sweeter and closer relationship to our inner life," Haydn had "honored the Creator in the joy of his Creation," and Beethoven, finally, had "led us back out of society in order to sound again the deepest secrets of nature that lay in his kindred spirit," liberating people from the "yoke of complete egoism." Only now could "Bach's song of the sacrifice of Jesus again be taken up and under-

---

[161] The article, which appeared in the daily *Spenerschen Zeitung*, was reprinted by Marx in *BAMZ* 6, no. 11 (14 March 1829): 80.

[162] Mosewius, in Geck, 48.

[163] *AMZ* 31 (1829): 234.

stood": "So have world history and art history developed to a higher union of a life made conscious of itself in the idea of our religion."[164] The sense of Marx's remarks can be easily lost in the undergrowth of his concepts, but his overall purpose was to ensure the reception of Bach's religious message in a more complicated and secular—a more modern—world. He understood the gulf that separated Leipzig's Thomaskirche in 1729 and the Singakademie on Unter den Linden in 1829, but he did not regard it as impassable: as Bach served religion, "so must we follow him on his way to the altar, if we are to grasp his work and its greatness completely." The contemporary performances of the *St. Matthew Passion* would "open up the gates to a long-closed temple," calling people "not to a festival of art but to a solemn religious celebration."[165]

But a religious celebration not "closed off" in a church, as several observers noted, in muted acknowledgment of changed times. Rellstab went so far as to recommend against any future performances of the *St. Matthew Passion* in churches, where he thought the words would not be audible. Marx, with similar reservations, had something more world-historical in mind. "We recognize the wisest, most beautiful providence in the gradual disappearance of the Bachian spirit" over the course of the eighteenth century, he explained. Now people could receive his music and his ideas differently and, as Marx thought, more fully than before. The spirit of Bach and of Christianity lived again, not just in churches "but in all aspects of life."[166]

Even so, both Marx and some of the better-informed reviewers thought it necessary to provide some explanation for the structure of the *St. Matthew Passion*, with its unfamiliar combination of texts known and unknown (biblical and traditional German chorale texts, on the one hand, and the poetry of the long-forgotten Picander on the other) and musical styles drawn from liturgy, oratorio, and opera. Thibaut was not alone in finding this combination odd, even inappropriate, and his contemporaries had experienced dramatic sacred music only in the form of the more straightforward oratorio. Their ignorance of the tradition of singing the Passion of Jesus according to each of the four Gospels in the course of Holy Week, a tradition that reached back into the early Middle Ages and had continued across the divide of the Reformation in both Protestant and Catholic services, is perhaps not as surprising as it at first seems. Even before Friedrich Wilhelm III's church union, Protestant Germany had abandoned many of its musical

---

[164] A. B. Marx, "Bekanntmachung," *BAMZ* 6, no. 9 (28 February 1829): 66–67.
[165] Marx, "Erster Bericht," 73.
[166] Marx, "Bekanntmachung," 66–67.

traditions, replacing them with a simplified, more "enlightened" structure of readings, prayers, and preaching. By 1829 some restoration efforts were nevertheless underway, without the king's blessing. Around the time of the *St. Matthew Passion* performances, the Berlin Cathedral adopted the new, restorationist liturgical agenda that Schleiermacher had championed, and a new hymnal appeared, restoring many of the old hymn texts and melodies. But in the realm of liturgical music, such efforts hardly went beyond hymns. The more far-reaching historical scholarship, which in the course of the nineteenth century reconstructed older traditions, had yet to be written.[167]

People who attended the performances in 1829 had the guidance of a textbook prepared by Zelter, with a brief explanatory introduction.[168] The "epic-didactic" form of the *Passion*, which combined "the sung words of the Gospel with nonliturgical devotional words in order to sanctify the end of Holy Week through a recapitulation of the suffering of Jesus," had fallen completely out of custom since the mid-eighteenth century, he wrote. But, with the rationalist's preference for classical antecedents, he recommended that audiences regard it as a kind of "historical link" between the chorus of ancient Greek tragedy and the modern church cantata. Like the Greek chorus (an idea he and Goethe had discussed), Passion music gave voice to the community, who could thus participate in, empathize with, and comment on the tragic events unfolding in front of them. The complicated interplay among chorus and solo, storytelling and contemplation, explained Zelter, served Bach's purpose of "devotion and uplifting of the spirit into the certainty of existence and immortality." The end result, in Marx's much longer explanation, was "the most moving intermixture of past and present."[169]

For many commentators, the aspect of the *St. Matthew Passion* for which they reserved their highest praise was not Bach's rendering of the Passion music tradition but his setting of the Gospel text, especially in the recitative of the Evangelist and Jesus. According to Marx, composers such as Gluck,

---

[167] Most important of these was Philipp Spitta's Bach biography, with the first historical explanation of Passion music: see Spitta, *Bach*, 2:477–569. On Spitta himself, see Wolfgang Sandberger, *Das Bach-Bild Philipp Spittas: Ein Beitrag zur Geschichte der Bach-Rezeption im 19. Jahrhundert* (Stuttgart, 1997), esp. 98–114. Landmarks in music scholarship before Spitta included the Erlangen edition of Luther's music in 1833, Raphael Kiesewetter's *History of European and Western Music* in 1834, and August Carl von Winterfeld's *Protestant Church Singing and Its Relationship to the Art of Composition* in 1843.

[168] *Passionsmusik von Johann Sebastian Bach, nach dem Evangelium Matthai, cap. 26 und 27*, ed. Carl Friedrich Zelter (Berlin, 1829). Marx also reprinted Zelter's brief introduction to the text in *BAMZ* 6, no. 11 (14 March 1829): 81–82.

[169] Marx, "Erster Bericht," 75.

Handel, Mozart, Haydn, and Beethoven, all of whom the audience knew better than Bach, had either composed "conventional and unremarkable" recitative or none at all, reserving their "deepest, most expressive music" for arias. But "in Bach's recitative, each word was so illuminated" that "not a single note could be altered without diminishing the whole." "In this recitative alone," wrote Marx, "we grasp the words of Jesus and feel in our hearts that Bach alone among all composers was worthy to set them forth." Through him, we "learn them anew."[170] Rellstab, who wished Mendelssohn had left out even more arias from the performance than he did, felt nothing but wonder at Bach's setting of the Gospel text itself. "The eternal, great, and endlessly amazing power and sublimity of the work, which defies all passage of time," lay in Bach's "treatment of the Evangelist's words themselves."[171]

The intense scholarly interest in historical Christianity that marked this era and culminated in 1835 with the publication of a *Life of Jesus* by a leading Young Hegelian, David Friedrich Strauss, worked its influence on listeners.[172] Rellstab found it particularly remarkable that Bach had "dared, as no other composer," to set to music the words of Jesus. Marx addressed an entire review, his third one, to a question that he said many were asking, about whether it was appropriate for a person (Devrient, in this case) to portray Jesus. He welcomed evidence that the music had reached people's religious consciousness and defended the dramatic portrayal of Jesus with Johann Hemling's recent scholarly discussion of the image of Jesus. Rellstab also approved of Bach's portrayal of Jesus, the "highest of all assignments," undertaken with "inexhaustible invention," "simplicity of means and a richness of expression." Bach's musical language expressed "rising inspiration" as the story drew to its terrible climax with Jesus's words on the cross. "With indescribable depth of understanding and out of the most intimately pious feeling," wrote Rellstab, Bach had "created music that penetrates our shuddering hearts with the irresistible power of sublime sadness."[173]

The importance of Bach's setting of the Gospel text to listeners in 1829 points us, in turn, to the specifically Protestant aspect of this reception. This was, as we have seen, a society caught up in another kind of historical con-

[170] Ibid., 77.

[171] Geck, 51, 53.

[172] Marx, "Dritter Bericht," 80; on Strauss, see Horton Harris, *David Friedrich Strauss and His Theology* (Cambridge, 1973); and Marilyn Chapin Massey, *Christ Unmasked: The Meaning of the Life of Jesus in German Politics* (Chapel Hill, 1983). On the theology of the young Hegelians, see Toews, *Hegelianism.*

[173] Rellstab in Geck, 52.

sciousness as well, that of the Protestant Reformation. Commemorations had begun in 1817 with tercentenary celebrations. These had brought with them the "colossal muddle" of the Prussian church union and the devastating political fallout of the Wartburg Festival, both forces still dominating the political and religious milieu of Berlin in 1829. But commemorating, and with it reshaping the place of Protestantism in the modern world, did not end there. People like Schleiermacher, another (unfortunately silent) member of the audience in 1829, were already looking ahead to 1830 and the tercentenary of the Augsburg Confession, the defining doctrinal statement of the Lutheran Church, and pressing forward with the restoration of traditional liturgical elements to the union-reformed services.[174] People thus heard the *St. Matthew Passion* in the context of heightened consciousness of their Protestantism, and many drew attention to Bach's inspired illumination of what was most essential to it.

And that, for most commentators, consisted of two things, the word of the Gospel and the community of worshippers. To be sure, those who wrote of the emotional intensity Bach had achieved in the *Passion* might seem to have had affinities with the Pietist movement, then in the midst of the reawakening of the 1820s. But there is little evidence that Pietism as a movement influenced the reception of Bach in 1829. People in the 1820s knew, for instance, that Bach himself had not been a Pietist but an orthodox Lutheran, and in any case the Pietist movement had over the past century paid little or no attention to Bach or to church music. Critics like Rellstab, who wanted all the arias excised, found precisely the pietistic aspects of Picander's poetry antiquated and unappealing. Radowitz, who ultimately preferred the austerity of Palestrina to Bach's Passions, "could not conceal" that he found "this biblical opera, with its swirling winds of emotions turning the soul inside out like a glove, both theologically and musically objectionable."[175] For those who did admire the emotionality of the *St. Matthew Passion*, it would perhaps be better to speak of the individualization of worship and the diffusion of religious romanticism rather than of a specific pietistic influence.

More prominent in the public response in 1829 was wonder at the mag-

---

[174] Schleiermacher's formulation "What the word made clear, music must make alive" might seem a fitting description of the *St. Matthew Passion*, but the remark in fact came from his *Christmas Eve* dialogue of 1805, which Albert Blackwell calls the "most musical of his written works" (Blackwell, "Schleiermacher on Musical Experience," 138). Martin Geck was unable to find any reference to hearing the *St. Matthew Passion* in Schleiermacher's writings, other than a note in his diary on 11 March 1829: "Noon with Wiegand. Passion music. Later with Luise" (Geck, 49).

[175] Radowitz in Geck, 50.

nificence with which Bach had set the language of Luther's German translation of the Bible—another epochal event, the three-hundredth anniversary of which had just been celebrated. This took the listeners of 1829 to
the heart of the Reformation, with its insistence on faith alone, mediated
through the reading of scripture. "What power lies in his absolute adher-
ence to the words of the Bible," wrote Marx, "and the returns on this faith-
fulness to the word are riches the equal of which can be found in no other
musical work." Rellstab believed that the music had been "lifted ever higher
by the power and gravity of the words," and his concern, referred to above,
that the *St. Matthew Passion* not be performed in the large echoing space of,
for instance, the Prussian monarchy's favorite Garnisonkirche further reflected his belief that "the most important part of the work" lay in the word
of the Bible. Another commentator thought that Bach had resolved the
tension between tones and word that went back to the beginning of music,
allowing each complete autonomy and perfect dependence. The *St.
Matthew Passion* was an exegesis on the passage from the Gospel according to
John, "God is the Word." As one listened, "eighteen hundred years disappeared," and the listeners felt themselves to be in the immediate presence of
"Jesus, his disciples, the high priests, and the people."[176]

But it was left to a twenty-year-old newcomer to public life, Felix
Mendelssohn's friend Johann Gustav Droysen, to make the most explicit
link between the *Passion* and the Protestant reformation. Droysen, who later
became an immensely influential historian, Prussian liberal, and theorist of
historical thinking, claimed that "Bach's Passion music" had given back
Berliners a sense of their evangelical origins in a lost time when everyone
"diligently read the Bible, diligently listened to the preacher, and during
Holy Week, held themselves apart from the noise and bustle of the world in
order to read the scripture in the quiet circle of the family and think over
the sufferings of Christ and of the redemption." As this image suggested,
the reading of scripture was a communal as well as individual practice, and
in Droysen's account of the *St. Matthew Passion*, scripture and community
played equal roles in defining its essential Protestantism. Bach had created
the "music of the free, evangelical belief of those who trusted in God," not
"of a forgotten and impossibly distant time" and not (implicitly referring to
Palestrina and other Italians) "of a Catholic cathedral, cloudy with incense
and incomprehensible ritual." Fifty years before Spitta wrote of the "deep
congregational feeling" that lay at the heart of Bach's Passion music and

---

[176] Marx, "Erster Bericht," 76; Rellstab in Geck, 52–53; B., "Grosse Passion von Johann Sebastian Bach," *BAMZ* 12 (21 March 1829): 93.

called the *St. Matthew Passion* itself "in a remarkable degree a popular work," Droysen asserted that it belonged "not to art and its history alone but much more, as art should, to the community, to the people."[177]

As for Marx, he too found the theological content of the work in the "founding of our religion through the covenant of the New Testament and the self-sacrifice of Jesus for the redemption of mankind" and, just as important, in the "reflections and feelings of the community," witnessing the sufferings of Jesus and understanding their meaning. The message of the new covenant and redemption, he thought, could also be found in Handel's *Messiah*, but the sense of the communal participation in these "great events" could only be found in the *St. Matthew Passion.*[178] "Through his presentation of the community," argued Marx, "we know not only what happened but we see and experience its endurance"; "the religion itself" found "its fulfillment" in Bach's music.[179]

Perhaps responding to this, commentators in 1829 tended to refer to the audience in active terms, as participants rather than passive auditors. Loebell described the "quite extraordinary and unexpected participation of the public"; Rellstab could think of no other performance of serious music that had excited such "enthusiastic participation" on the part of the public, and Marx wrote of "the most general and liveliest participation of the whole public" in this work which had "from its first reappearance in Berlin penetrated deeply into all hearts."[180] The use of such language emphasized the religious and Protestant nature of this secular concert, just as Fanny Mendelssohn had described the atmosphere in the Singakademie building at the first performance as "like a church": "the deepest stillness, the most solemn devotion overcame the gathering, interrupted only by the occasional involuntary cries of deeply moved feeling."[181] For Marx, the twelve chorales that Bach inserted among the Passion narrative and arias accounted for the work's evocation of religious community, even in a secular setting.[182]

---

[177] Johann Gustav Droysen, "Ueber die Passions-Musik von Johann Sebastian Bach," reprinted from the *Berliner Konversationsblatt* in *BAMZ* 6, no. 13 (28 March 1829): 98–99; Spitta, *Bach*, 2:567, 570.

[178] It is worth pointing out the obvious, that the text for which Handel composed *Messiah* came from the King James version of the Bible. Translated into German by Klopstock to fit Handel's music, the German text owed much to Luther's translation, but the relationship between the music and the German language of Luther was not as close, as direct, or (as Marx would have said) as perfect as it was in Bach's *St. Matthew Passion.*

[179] Marx, "Erster Bericht," 73.

[180] Loebell and Rellstab in Geck, 46, 51; Marx, "Dritter Bericht," 89.

[181] Fanny Mendelssohn to Karl Klingemann, 22 March 1829, in Hensel, 239.

[182] Jeffrey Sposato provides a full accounting of the Mendelssohn cuts and possible reasons for them. In the case of the chorales, Mendelssohn removed five, including two of the recurrences of the melody of "Haupt voll Blut und Wunden." Sposato believes that Mendelssohn was motivated

Like collective prayers, hymns were moments in a service when the group spoke in one voice, and congregational hymn singing had always been a distinctive part of Protestant services. But music pedagogues had for years been chipping away at the traditional use of church chorales as a means of elementary music instruction. Friedrich Wilhelm's new service order for the Union Church, in which congregational singing was all but obliterated, drew the venerable Lutheran hymn into further controversy. By 1829, then, the chorale no longer held the automatic place in German culture that it once had; instead, it had become the object of both conscious consideration and heated defense, neither of which could replace the lost aura Droysen so lamented. Nevertheless, the presence of the chorales in concert struck people as something extraordinary and significant, in Droysen's account a call to recover piety and community, to re-enchant the world.

For indeed, their presence in Bach's *St. Matthew Passion* was something extraordinary, even in his time and even in ours. To take the most important example, the melody bound to the text "O Haupt voll Blut und Wunden" (O sacred head, sore wounded) forms a motivic thread running through the *St. Matthew Passion.* Theologian Jaroslav Pelikan calls this chorale the "most intriguing musically, as well as the most complex theologically" of all the "themes and variations" Bach pursued in his Passions. The melody appears six times in the course of the *St. Matthew Passion* (Mendelssohn included four of these), each time with a different text or a different stanza of the "Blut und Wunden" text, each time in a different key, with a different theological message. It returns for the last time in "ultimate simplicity" at the moment of his death, and by this time, as Pelikan believes, "anyone who has listened carefully and repeatedly to the Saint Matthew Passion, especially with a score in hand and a lifetime of memories of the chorales, must surely feel that Bach has exhausted all the possibilities, musical as well as theological, in this Lenten motif." Medieval in origin, the "Blut und Wunden" text had moved from Latin into German, from Catholicism into Lutheran and then Reformed Protestantism. Pelikan considers it "the most beloved Lenten chorale in German Protestantism," with its "conception of salvation and atonement" expressing "the mainstream of Continental Protestant spirituality."[183] The participants of 1829, regardless of whether they attended church regularly or were Protestant or Catholic, probably knew this melody and knew most of the texts Bach used with it in

---

by the need he perceived to keep the initial performance of this unknown work at a length the audience would find reasonable and to emphasize textual and melodic material that it might recognize, e.g. Gospel and well-known chorale texts and melodies. See Sposato, "The Price of Assimilation," 73–131.

[183] Jaroslav Pelikan, *Bach among the Theologians* (Philadelphia: Fortress, 1986), 79–88.

the *St. Matthew Passion*. Graun's *Tod Jesu*, so familiar to this audience through its frequent performances, used the melody, with new text written by Graun's librettist Ramler.

As they listened to Bach's successive harmonizations and textualizations of the melody in 1829, its first nineteenth-century audience thus may have felt that same combination of familiarity and uncanny newness that struck them when hearing the Gospel text. Droysen's account of the *St. Matthew Passion* used the chorale to evoke a scene from a German Protestant past he was fast mythologizing: "Back then on Good Friday there was complete and solemn quiet in the city, and the streets were free of traffic, the market empty, and all the bells summoned people to church. One heard a devotional sermon on Christ and God's mercy, and took communion with one's own, with one's community, and all worshipped and sang together, O Haupt voll Blut und Wunden." "That," wrote Droysen, "is the essence of our evangelical confession."[184]

But he did not end there, turning in conclusion to the most resonant contemporary meaning of the performance. "We cannot fail to recognize," he wrote to Berliners, "that Bach's music, the true essence and witness of our evangelical faith, came to life again in our city, the very countenance of our Prussian Fatherland." "Prussia," declared the future historian of a Prussian-led Germany, "is the land of Protestantism." "Born through the labor pains of the Reformation," it "grew to adulthood" during the Thirty Years War, becoming finally today the "homeland" of the "message of the Scriptures," its "great and unceasing champion." Droysen's rhetoric evoked both the religious wars of the distant past and the Napoleonic wars of the recent past; it also placed an explicitly Protestant face on the German national movement. "The time has come," he wrote, to restore this religion to where it belongs, as the "central point and purpose of our lives and the life of the state." And in the most explicit political appropriation of Bach in 1829, he claimed Bach's music in order to bring "courage and strength" to a larger restoration.[185]

Droysen's rhetorical excess was that of a young man who had missed out on thrilling patriotic action during the "wars of liberation" from the French. Like so many of his generation, his ardor went along with a sense that the chance for some greater German achievement had been lost in 1815, irretrievably so given the repressive political atmosphere of Metternichian Europe. Droysen's views on the national mission of Protestant Prussia were also more insistent than those of most of his contemporaries; in the

---

[184] Droysen, "Passions-musik," 98–99.
[185] Ibid.

1820s, the Protestant triumphalist strand of German nationalism had hardly separated itself from the vague whole of German national consciousness. Cultural differences along confessional lines remained muted, even as the "treasure trove" of historical works, as Thibaut called it, was becoming accessible to all and, thus thrust into the public sphere, increasingly open to debate and divisions of all kinds.[186]

Droysen's belief in Bach's embodiment of something essentially German spoke to a broader consensus, across confessional lines. Marx, of course, thought that Bach belonged especially to Germany and that through him Germans would know themselves better. For Friedrich von Raumer, the performance had been "a celebration of this great work of art of our Fatherland." For an anonymous correspondent in Marx's journal, it would push Germans "finally to recognize the worth of their Fatherland" and "no longer look for the seat of the Muses in foreign lands."[187] Thus in 1829 did Bach and his *St. Matthew Passion* join the public world, lending themselves to the construction of the German nation and becoming as essential to its self-conscious culture as Rhenish castles, Gothic cathedrals, and Weimar sages.

---

[186] On the significance of the "confessional divide" among Protestants, Catholics, and Jews in Germany, see Chris Clark and Helmut Smith, "The Fate of Nathan," in Smith, *Protestants, Catholics and Jews*, 3–32.

[187] B., "Grosse Passion," 93; Raumer in Geck, 139.

6

The history of the 1829 performance of Bach's *St. Matthew Passion* amounts
to something more than a case study in cultural appreciation. Bach's masterpiece is too great and the specific circumstances of its recovery too unusual
to allow us to see the 1829 performance as typical in any obvious sense of
the word. Neither the nineteenth nor any other century had many like
Felix Mendelssohn with the intelligence, vision, and musical gifts sufficient
to the challenge of this music. Nor does the *St. Matthew Passion* stand
merely as one among many other Passions, by Bach or others; it was and remains a work of such grandeur and intensity that one can only marvel at the
apparent inability of Bach's contemporaries and immediately subsequent
generations to acknowledge it. As for Bach, as Goethe remarked, he allows
us to hear all of creation, "as if the eternal harmony were conversing with
itself."[1] He stands at once as the father and foundation of all German music

---

[1] This indeed is how Klaus Eidsam concludes his provocative, anti-scholarly biography of
Bach—he "binds us to the universe" (Er verbindet uns mit dem All) (*Das wahre Leben des Johann Sebastian Bach* [Munich, 1999], 382).

(Wagner), the fifth evangelist, "rather an ocean than a brook [*ein Bach*]" (Beethoven), a "manifestation of God, clear but unclarifiable" (Zelter), the Newton, the Dürer, and the Shakespeare of music, and none or all of these things and more. There is, in any case, something extraordinary about this encounter between Mendelssohn and Bach in the music of the *St. Matthew Passion*, and reading the contemporary accounts, one feels that those who heard the fruits of this collaboration in 1829 sensed it as such. Something of this sense has spilled over into accounts of it ever since, from Blume's characterization of it as "a miracle" to Dahlhaus's dubbing it a "music-historical great deed."

One could, of course, compare this particular episode in Bach's reception to hundreds of others, contrasting the use of keyboard works to cantatas, the relatively rare performances of chamber music to frequent ones of organ music. One could consider the variations on the theme of admiration for Bach as expressed by Mendelssohn, Schumann, Brahms, Wagner, Mahler, Widor, Busoni, Schoenberg, and countless others. In such varied contexts, the 1829 performance shrinks in significance, becoming at most an episode in the romantic reception of Bach, characterized (allegedly) by unnecessary cuts, unfortunate instrument substitutions, and inappropriate tempi. Given the temper of the times, some group, sooner or later, was going to perform the piece, and what does it matter whether it was Mendelssohn in 1829 or Mosewius in 1830 or Spohr in 1832? Musicologists today recognize this event, of course, but they point to recent scholarship that shows it not to have been such a milestone, and therefore perhaps not as important to the history of the reception of Bach as the manuscript copying services of the Breitkopf firm in Leipzig during the second half of the eighteenth century.[2]

Yet one pays a price for goring sacred cows. If we decide that this event was noteworthy but not amazing, then we begin also to lose sight of the historical changes that separated Leipzigers of 1727 from Berliners of 1829. This book has emphasized the importance of Mendelssohn's revival in order to dramatize these changes. It does not attempt to contribute to our understanding of how Bach was regarded in his own time, but it has argued that the profound appreciation of him and of his Passion music in Berlin in 1829 depended on richly intertwined developments in human endeavors as distinct as journalism, publishing, association formation, aesthetic philosophy, history writing, pedagogy, religious practice, and, of course, nation building. None of these activities came to an end in 1829; all, in their continuing play, helped to define the culture of German nationhood for generations to

[2] Wolff, *Bach: The Learned Musician*, 463.

come. So while the 1829 performances were the end of nothing and not precisely the beginning of anything, they nevertheless stand as a culmination. For stargazers, this is the point at which the celestial body crosses the meridian of the observer, thus reaching the highest point above the observer's horizon. For cultural historians, this must mean the moment when many things came into full effect, all working together to create something remarkable. When, three years later, the famous violinist and composer Louis Spohr directed the *St. Matthew Passion* in Kassel, only thirty people attended, and the press barely took notice. To be sure, the performance had fallen afoul of a major brouhaha between court and town, and Spohr himself complained to a friend of living in a "veritable Siberia of art."[3] But the moment of culmination had passed, in both time and place, and with it, some magic that resists analysis.

But much also remained, and in the paths followed by those who had shaped the 1829 performance, we see the extent to which their experiences in 1829 informed their later contributions to German cultural life. These contributions varied widely, but a common context drew them together and made them pieces of a coherent undertaking: the project—or perhaps better, the culture—of nation building. Enough has been said so far to convey something of the diffuse and various nature of nation building in German-speaking central Europe in the nineteenth century. Nationally minded people of this era did not make neat distinctions between the cultural content of nationhood and its political implications; to believe that Germany existed as a cultural reality was also to believe in a set of political ideals—autonomy or self-government chief among them—as well as in a political goal of unified statehood.[4] Still, given that this was a highly articulated society, not all nationally minded people were political publicists, even if most were members of an educated elite. People expressed their consciousness of their nationality in different ways, lawyers as lawyers, philologists as philologists, and musicians as musicians. But whatever one's profession, participating in the culture of nationhood took place in public. The community of the nation in which people believed and which people helped to create (belief and creation being indistinguishable) was a living one. Underlying it, for lawyers and musicians alike, was the common commitment to *Bildung*, that full flowering of self that drew its seeker into a community of common purpose and enjoined a secularized mission to educate and enlighten others. As Brian Vick writes, "the apparatus of the public sphere" served as the "locus of identity," and the nation that people

[3] Geck, 111–13.
[4] See especially Vick, *Defining Germany*, 16, 22–23, 205–8.

envisioned had to be made real through action, infused with life and raised to a conscious level of experience.[5]

From such a perspective, the performances of 1829 become a paradigm of the German nation. If the nation had to be performed to exist, then for those passing moments in the spring of 1829 and in the minds of those in attendance, the community defined by German nationhood did exist. After the concerts were over, we lose sight of such consciousness, because written declarations of national intentions did not accompany every new musical initiative. Still, the next half-century brought more evidence of institutional consolidation around the idea of a distinctively German music within the broader stream of European musical development. That German music had developed over a long time and continued to form a vibrant part of educated high culture helped, in turn, to define German nationhood altogether. That process of musical consolidation was an aspect of German nation building, and it did not end in the political events of 1871. Its significance lies in the accumulation of nationally inflected musical experiences, in small towns and major cities, among amateurs and professionals, in study, practice, and performance. The people and institutions involved in Mendelssohn's and Bach's *St. Matthew Passion* of 1829 were, to be sure, a tiny minority of musically active Germans, but to follow them is still to see the variety of ways that people made a nation.

The Berlin Singakademie gained in prestige from the 1829 performances, which confirmed its place as the premier choral society in Germany and the model for many more such groups throughout the German states. The years that followed saw significant increases in the numbers of public appearances of the group—ten public concerts in 1830 alone, the majority performances of Handel oratorios. The substantial debt from the new building, rather than post-*Passion* euphoria, was probably the greater factor in determining the hectic schedule. Nor was Zelter, now over seventy years old and suffering badly from arthritis, quite up to it. Fanny Mendelssohn thought even the third performance of the *St. Matthew Passion*, on Good Friday in 1829, showed signs of his decrepitude ("Zelter's almost continually incorrect accompaniment"; "Zelter conducted only when it occurred to him").[6] The music critic Ludwig Rellstab urged him to retire, comparing the Singakademie to a "splendid army going into the field under the command of an ancient general."[7] Goethe's last letter to Zelter, written in the same week that Rellstab published his remarks, struck an oddly similar theme, joking

[5] Ibid., 206.

[6] Fanny to Felix Mendelssohn, 18 April 1829, in Citron, *Letters of Fanny Hensel*, 25–26.

[7] Ludwig Rellstab, review of Messiah performance, *Iris im Gebiete der Tonkunst* 3, no. 10 (10 March 1832).

about fossils accumulating around them and implicitly contrasting Zelter and himself to the vibrancy of youth and art.[8] Goethe died a few days later, Zelter in two months.

By choosing as his successor not Mendelssohn, who at his father's urging made a formal application for the position, but Carl Friedrich Rungenhagen, Zelter's assistant since 1815 and a prolific composer of easy vocal works in all genres, the Singakademie confirmed its collective sense of itself as a well-regulated, conservative, and still essentially private group.[9] Zelter had been Fasch's assistant and succeeded him upon his death; Rungenhagen (whom Fanny called a "fat donkey") had patiently followed Zelter's lead for nearly two decades.[10] After Rungenhagen's death in 1851, he too was succeeded by his assistant and longtime member of the group, Eduard Grell. Under Rungenhagen and even more so under Grell, the Singakademie held to its original aesthetic and ethical orientation: unaccompanied sacred music in the first place and accompanied choral works on religious themes in the second. A brief effort to replace the annual Good Friday performance of Graun's *Tod Jesu* with the *St. Matthew Passion* met with royal displeasure, and so the Singakademie continued for fifty more years to give it pride of place. To be sure, the group performed the *St. Matthew Passion* occasionally and extended its mastery of Bach's vocal compositions to include the difficult B-minor Mass (first performed in 1834–35, not again until 1856), the *St. John Passion*, and the Christmas Oratorio. Over the years, it performed Haydn's *Creation* frequently, his *Seasons* infrequently, a great deal of Handel, some Mendelssohn, and a little Beethoven (the *Missa Solemnis*, which the audience so disliked in 1836 that it took another sixty-three years before it became a regular offering). Not until 1886 did the group perform Brahms's *German Requiem*, nearly twenty years after the work had premiered in Bremen to enormous acclaim and had become a staple of the repertoire of every other German choral society.

The failure to appoint Mendelssohn, the slowness to perform Brahms, and the reluctance to give up Graun reflected the consistent lack of emphasis the Singakademie placed on contributing to concert life and, closely related, an obliviousness, at least on the part of a succession of directors, to the nature of their national prestige and the expectations other Germans had of them. Still, their aversion to public performances did not mean that the Singakademie made no contribution to the cultural work of the nation,

[8] Letter of 11 March 1832, quoted in Fischer-Dieskau, *Zelter*, 190.

[9] Devrient wrote that Rungenhagen's supporters admitted the public "on sufferance only"; they "were free to stay away": Wm. A. Little, "Mendelssohn and the Berlin Singakademie: The Composer at the Crossroads," in Todd, *Mendelssohn and His World*, 81.

[10] Fanny to Felix Mendelssohn, 15 January 1838, in Citron, *Letters of Fanny Hensel*, 539.

but it made its contribution a curious, almost unintended one. The case of the Singakademie suggests, first, that the preservation of certain works of the past involved a greater variety of activities than just concerts and publications, to which historians have usually looked, and second, that nation building did not necessarily involve the work of individuals intent on a nationalizing mission. Cultural canons, so essential to the formation of a collective sense of what a nation consists of culturally, come about in many ways. Zelter saw his amateur singers as exemplary members of their society, whose music making of the highest ethical and artistic standards counteracted the passivity and superficiality of contemporary concert audiences. In this he adhered closely to the notion of *Bildung*'s moral, external mission, beyond mere self-cultivation. And he thought such activity sufficient to preserve the musical legacy of the past, a body of work he valued for an inseparable mixture of reasons—spiritual, musico-aesthetic, and national-patriotic. A half century later, in the context of an ever more expansive concert scene, Eduard Grell wanted mainly to yank the Singakademie back from its debt-induced drift toward public performance and restore its commitment to individual moral and musical self-improvement. Grell was motivated by a concern, Thibaut-like, for purity in music and disliked the way concerts favored masterworks, virtuosity, and performative perfection over the vocal writing of what he thought had been simpler times.

Only in the 1880s, with the advent of a new director (Georg Schumann) and the founding of the Berlin Philharmonic, did the Singakademie finally take on a more prominent role in the concert life of Berlin, performing frequently with the new orchestra. It survived throughout the twentieth century, at more or less the size it achieved in the Second Empire, sang Brahms's *German Requiem* on April 14, 1945, in the ruins of the Berlin Philharmonic Hall, and finally moved to the western sector of divided Berlin, taking up rehearsal quarters in Scharoun's new Philharmonic Hall. In its pamphlets and other accounts of itself since the war, the events of 1829 have become the defining point of its existence—"now as before," stated the commemorative work written on its 175th anniversary, "the performances of Bach remain at its core."[11]

Yet, as we have seen, the group was not founded with such performances in mind. Nor did any of the men and women who served as its directors and board members in its first half-century of existence make the decisive move toward the first performance in 1829. Those qualified and earnest people, all growing old in the service of serious music, acted rather as the backdrop for a younger generation of musicians and musical activists. The

[11] Bollert, *Sing-Akademie zu Berlin*, 20.

moving forces behind the 1829 performances were not Zelter (at the age of seventy) or his assistant director Rungenhagen (fifty-one) but Felix Mendelssohn (then twenty), Eduard Devrient (twenty-eight), Adolf Bernhard Marx (thirty-four), and Eduard Rietz (twenty-eight), with the participation and encouragement of Mendelssohn's intellectual and musical circle, including Fanny Mendelssohn (twenty-three), violinist Ferdinand David (nineteen), cellist Julius Rietz (sixteen), philology student Johann Gustav Droysen (twenty-one), and theology students Julius Schubring and Albert Baur (both twenty-three). None of these people, with the possible exception of Marx, wanted a public break with Zelter's leadership of the Berlin Bach tradition, but all had a more dynamic sense of what musical historicism could accomplish in the service of national culture. They shared Zelter's sense of old music's moralizing role in public culture. But they wanted to integrate the public performance of old music into a progressive, expansive musical culture that included new music as well, and they thought that better music and a more inclusive national community would be the result.[12] Several of these participants went on to make significant, sometimes defining, contributions to the historical and musical practice of nineteenth-century Germany. Their lifelong efforts to bring the past into an active relationship with the present, thus shaping the future of German culture, began with that great event of 1829 and continued in the euphoria of its achievement.

To look, then, at their subsequent careers is to see the national consciousness of the nineteenth century in action. Hegel was certainly an influence on a number of these young people, steeped as they were in the intellectual life of Berlin. Mendelssohn heard his lectures on aesthetics and entertained him in his home. Devrient too, like many Berliners, had attended a few lectures, probably to see what all the fuss was about. Marx had developed a kind of Hegelian music criticism in the pages of the *Berliner Allgemeine Musikalische Zeitung*. Droysen, Schubring, and Baur were all students at the University of Berlin and to various degrees students of Hegel.[13] In any case, this collection of people, drawn together by friendship with Mendelssohn and love of music, shared the desire of many educated Ger-

[12] Toews, "Memory and Gender," 735–36. Vick too emphasizes the inclusive, rather than exclusive, implications of the ideas of nationhood based on the foundation of Bildung (Vick, *Defining Germany*, 212).

[13] A biographer of Droysen describes his "more than typical interest" in Hegel (Robert Southard, *Droysen and the Prussian School of History* [Lexington, KY, 1994], 13). Schubring called himself "an unconditional Schleiermachian." Schleiermacher was Hegel's great rival at the University of Berlin in the 1820s, offering an alternative theology and rival lectures on philosophy and aesthetics as well. See Toews, *Hegelianism*, esp. 30–67. On Schubring, see his "Reminiscences of Felix Mendelssohn-Bartholdy," in Todd, *Mendelssohn and His World*, 227.

mans to translate their consciousness of the past into progress in the present. Hegel had written gloomily of knowledge bringing with it a kind of passivity. His "owl of Minerva" took flight only at dusk, when the grays of philosophical understanding indicated that "life has already grown old," beyond rejuvenation.[14] Yet this generation believed that they had not just recognized Bach's great creation but indeed rejuvenated it and, especially in Marx's estimation, brought it back into the progressive movement toward improvement in moral life and the creation of national community.

The life's work of those who participated in this musical event worked to analogous ends. Julius Rietz, the much younger brother of Mendelssohn's concertmaster and violin teacher Eduard Rietz, had the distinguished career, closely linked to that of Mendelssohn, which early death had denied to his brother. Julius served as Mendelssohn's assistant and then successor in musical directorships in Düsseldorf, at the Lower Rhine Festival, and eventually, after Mendelssohn's early death, of Leipzig's Gewandhaus orchestra. He helped to form the Bach Gesellschaft in 1850, a pathbreaking organization in the effort to translate historical understanding into national patrimony. Rietz served as its secretary from 1855 to 1860 and edited its enduringly important editions of the B-minor Mass and the *St. Matthew Passion* itself. Ferdinand David, the young violin prodigy who had played in the *Passion* performance, joined Mendelssohn again as his concertmaster at the Gewandhaus and head of the violin department at the new conservatory; he also published the first practical edition of Bach's unaccompanied violin works. Through his violin etudes and transcriptions of historical works for the violin, he exemplified what musical historicism could achieve in practical terms for both pedagogy and performance.

At some distance from music itself yet still within the spirit of the 1829 Bach revival, Johann Gustav Droysen turned already in 1831 to open political activism. Of all the 1829 participants, Droysen illustrates best the intertwining of cultural and political elements in the culture of nation building. In the wake of the July Revolution in Paris, he wanted to found a political journal that would link historical inquiry with political advocacy and thus to realize his vision of a "spiritual national unity and personality," formed in the medium of public opinion.[15] Several schemes failed, but after his appointment to the University of Kiel, he turned to the tangled history of the duchies of Schleswig and Holstein, a topic with great political import for liberal nationalists like Droysen. With the Schleswig-Holstein question much on his mind, he was elected to the Frankfurt National Parliament in

[14] Quoted in Southard, *Droysen*, 15.
[15] Ibid., 11; Vick, *Defining Germany*, 40.

1848–49, where he served on the constitutional committee and advocated Prussian leadership of a national German state. The Prussian king's refusal of the German constitutional monarchy in 1849 disappointed but did not derail him. In the 1850s and 1860s, he developed his influential ideas on historical method and Prussia's national mission, never abandoning his efforts to "remedy the sad derangement of our political and social affairs" and find "the right course to a happier future" through a "genuinely historical point of view."[16]

The work of Devrient, Marx, and Mendelssohn showed the application of this kind of thinking to the arts, specifically to the creation of a national community for the cultivation and improvement of the arts. Devrient was nearing the peak of his operatic career in 1829, and though important roles continued to come his way, he overtaxed his voice and stopped singing altogether in 1838. From then until his retirement in 1870, he turned from opera to spoken drama, first as an actor and then as a theater director in Dresden and finally Karlsruhe. This final role, which he held for more than half his professional life, defined Devrient in the eyes of his contemporaries. Through his leadership in German-wide theater associations, his exemplary theater directing, and his prolific writings on German theatrical history and practice, he became as important to nation building in his field as Droysen or Mendelssohn were in theirs. His four-volume history of German theater and his ten volumes of essays on drama and dramaturgy remained indispensable guides well into the twentieth century, and his work in bringing formal theatrical training into existence still has resonance, especially his ideas about using both improvisation and education to "bring the individual character of the talent freely into its own."[17]

Devrient's writings and theatrical practice embodied the nineteenth-century faith in the usefulness of historical understanding to nation building, progress, and new art works. He championed both the revival of old works and the production of new ones. With his son, he worked on new translations of Shakespeare, and in Karlsruhe especially he promoted the new works of Richard Wagner, whom he had first met in Dresden. Consulting closely with Hermann Levi, Devrient brought *Tannhäuser* to the stage no fewer than forty-two times during his stay in Karlsruhe, made sure the *Mastersingers of Nuremberg* appeared there within months of its premier in 1868, and altogether presided over ninety-four Wagnerian productions. His importance to Wagner in their Dresden period was probably consider-

---

[16] Quoted in Sheehan, *German History*, 844.

[17] Only actors, he wrote in 1846, were "still left to develop in the wild." See Gerhard Ebert, "Vorwort zu 'Improvisation und Schauspielkunst,'" part of *100 Jahre Schauspielschule Berlin*, http://www.berlinerschauspielschule.de/impro_vorwort.htm.

able, though Wagner was, in his usual fashion, loathe to acknowledge either it or Devrient's work in making Germans aware of Wagner.[18] Devrient did share something fundamental with Wagner, and that was a belief that Germans needed and deserved better aesthetic experiences, if they were to realize fully their potential as a people.[19]

Adolf Bernhard Marx had also not said all he had to say—about music, aesthetic experience, or the German nation—by 1829. The *Berliner Allgemeine Musikalische Zeitung* did not prove the lasting vehicle for his musical work, as the Leipzig *Allgemeine Musikalische Zeitung* had been for Rochlitz. At the end of 1830 he produced his last edition and bade farewell to his readers with a final statement of his "hope in the [indivisible] progress of art and of the German people." Like Droysen and other liberal nationalists of the period, Marx believed that only "unlimited freedom of opinion" could insure such progress; people had to have the independence to make up their own minds, in art as in political life.[20] Only then, as he had long argued in his editorializing, could Germans know themselves as well as others. Leaving behind journalism to preside over musical studies at the University of Berlin, Marx spent the next decades publishing influential works on music theory and composition. He became the first to name and analyze the sonata form. He also worked in a number of ways to promote progressive reforms in music education, often arguing, as he had before, that the great works of the past could be a "living memory" in the service of a "new flowering" of art.[21] His writings on music helped to make technical knowledge of music more accessible to the lay musical public, and in that sense they served the broader purpose of building an inclusive national community through aesthetic improvement.

Marx's most comprehensive effort to place music "in its larger relation to mankind" was a book published in 1855 called *The Music of the Nineteenth Century, and Its Culture*, in which he sought to account for "the nature of art" itself. The years had not diminished his sense of urgency or idealism about *Bildung*, aesthetic experience, and progress. Musical learning could "purify [the learner's] feelings and inclinations without depriving them of their originality or individuality." Without musical and artistic culture,

---

[18] Wagner did publish a scathing review of Devrient's *Recollections of Felix Mendelssohn Bartholdy*, which he took as an occasion to mock the failure of Mendelssohn ("Fortune's darling") to write an opera, and to castigate Devrient for his vulgar use of the German language and pronounce him not as smart as everyone thought. See Richard Wagner, "Eduard Devrient," in *Art and Politics*, trans. William Ashton Ellis (Lincoln, NE, 1996), 275–88.

[19] For a balanced discussion of Wagner's national thinking, see Hannu Salmi, *Imagined Germany: Richard Wagner's National Utopia* (New York, 1999).

[20] A. B. Marx, "Abschied des Redakteurs," *BAMZ* 7, no. 52 (24 December 1830): 414–16.

[21] Ibid.

mankind would "come to a standstill, and relinquish the ideal to which we once aspired."[22] A decade later, in his guide to the performance of Beethoven's piano compositions, he wrote that art offered an alternative to "our workaday lives" and "lifeless industries"; it offered "the promise of another life infused with imperishable fragrance, the life of inner feeling, higher contemplation, great achievements," of "justice and freedom and the well-being of people and nations."[23]

Marx's liberal hope for a springtime of all peoples was undiminished in this passage written in 1863. Indeed, Marx seemed to grow more hopeful about human progress as the years went by. "Since the days of those artists whom we call our 'classics,'" he wrote in *Music of the Nineteenth Century*, "ever since the time of Beethoven, the last of them," talented people had "constantly opened new roads" in keyboard, vocal, and orchestral works, and "the 'opera of the future' has been proclaimed." Events like the 1829 Bach revival, he suggested, had made such progress possible. Echoing a comment of Fanny Mendelssohn's a quarter century earlier, that "the Passion has been given to the public, and has become the property of all," he wrote:

> The creations of our forefathers are now no longer known only to the learned, nor lie dormant in rare and inaccessible libraries; they have again come to life, like those grains of wheat which after four thousand years' concealment in the hands of Egyptian mummies were sown in our soil and brought forth fruit. . . . The past is no longer a hidden treasure, but has become the property of our times.[24]

Both Fanny Mendelssohn Hensel and Felix Mendelssohn, whose lives subsequent to the Bach revival are better known, also remained true to its spirit. In the case of Fanny, the adoption of a narrative of disappointment and thwarted hopes has proven irresistible for most of her modern admirers. In it, this remarkably talented musician faced the opposition of both father and brother to her potentially brilliant musical career and so retreated into domesticity, the only vocation these two villains found acceptable for a woman of her class. As Marion Kimber has remarked, in the course of undermining the evidential and ideological foundations of such a narrative, "here is a woman who was largely happy in her personal life, was wealthy enough to enjoy travel, art, and music, and had sufficient leisure time to pro-

---

[22] Marx, *Musik*, 12, 16.
[23] A. B. Marx, *Anleitung zum Vortrag Beethovenscher Klavierwerke* (Berlin, 1863), 3–4.
[24] Marx, *Musik*, 1–2.

duce over four hundred compositions—where is the 'story'?"[25] There is, of course, a story, but as Kimber argues, it was not so much one of oppressive male relatives and an uncomprehending society as of powerful social conventions shaping the conditions within which she could exert herself musically. For Fanny, such conventions placed limits on her development as a musician and composer but did not prevent her either from enjoying a close musical partnership with her brother or from pursuing ceaseless musical activities, often in company with the most celebrated musicians of her time.

Bach was a constant presence in this musical life, both before and after 1829, and consequently a presence in Fanny's life as a whole, since music, especially German music, constituted an intimate and essential part of her identity. She practiced and performed Bach throughout her life, usually in the context of her family's musical salon, which she took over in the 1830s, managing an ambitious program of biweekly, semiprivate performances. As leadership in the Bach revival passed out of Zelter's Berlin, she remained closely in touch with its participants through Felix and musical friends like Franz Hauser, an opera singer and vocal teacher who became one of the most important collectors of Bach manuscripts. She named her child Sebastian, she performed newly discovered cantatas at her Sunday musicales, and on her travels she, like Felix before her, served as an ambassador of German musical culture and the Bach movement. In 1840 she wrote to Felix from Rome that she had "had to play the Concerto in D-minor at least a dozen times" and "they're wild with delight over it."[26] She referred to, among others, the young Frenchman Charles Gounod, who was studying in Rome and, to his surprise, learning about German as well as Italian music. Gounod's memories of Fanny, as Fanny's of him, show how people of the nineteenth century made nationality the basis of their cosmopolitanism, thinking nationally even if living and working internationally. Fanny was "a musician beyond comparison," he wrote, and when she sat at the piano "I was brought to the knowledge of a mass of the chief works of German music of which I was completely ignorant at that time, among others a number of pieces by Johann Sebastian Bach . . . and several Mendelssohn compositions which were, also, a revelation to me from an unknown world."[27] That the *Passion* performances generated all this is certainly debatable, yet 1829, the year of both the performances and of her marriage, with its ambiguous mixture of musical fulfillment and retreat, stayed close to her

[25] Kimber, " 'Suppression' of Fanny Mendelssohn," 120.

[26] Fanny to Felix Mendelssohn, 10 May 1840, in Citron, *Letters of Fanny Hensel*, 291.

[27] Charles Gounod, *An Autobiography*, trans. Annette E. Crocker (New York, 1970), 125.

Felix Mendelssohn Bartholdy. Drawing by Wilhelm Schadow, 1834. By permission of the Bildarchiv Preussischer Kulturbesitz / Art Resource, NY.

consciousness throughout her life. In the view of one historian who has studied her life, it shaped her musical output and her identity altogether as a musician, a Protestant, and a German.[28]

Turning finally to Felix Mendelssohn, so many aspects of the musical culture in which he flourished anticipated, duplicated, and reinforced his work in reviving the *St. Matthew Passion* that it can seem not a remarkably

[28] Toews, "Memory and Gender," 727.

innovative action at all but a product of the zeitgeist, with Mendelssohn merely swimming with the historicist tide. In the words of Susanna Grossmann-Vendrey, the author of the definitive work on his musical historicism, Mendelssohn was "through his origins and the influences of his youth predestined for the cultivation of the music of the past."[29] Richard Wagner chose to regard his historical interests that way and worse. The gist of his accusation in "Jewishness in Music," the immediately notorious essay on Meyerbeer and Mendelssohn published three years after the latter's death, was that Jews in their ongoing emancipation and assimilation could only hope to imitate art, not create it as it must be created, out of the deepest wellsprings of national life. Later, in his 1869 essay on conducting, he returned to the same theme. Mendelssohn, so celebrated in his time as the genius of modern conducting, had never in fact achieved greatness as a conductor, for he suffered from "that peculiar sense of constraint," that "gnawing inward pain," which arose from striving too hard after a true national belonging that he, as a Jew, could never spontaneously express.[30] Seen from a Wagnerian perspective, then, Mendelssohn's involvement with Bach revealed the essence of his nature—his thirst for public acclaim, his great technical gifts, his personal charm, his parasitical reliance on the genuine artistry of others, his lack of authentic national identity.

About the only insight one can take away from Wagner's analysis is that, in Leon Botstein's words, his "struggle for self-definition" reflected his "intense lifelong preoccupation with Felix Mendelssohn."[31] One can go along with Wagner only to the extent of agreeing that Mendelssohn's lifelong preoccupation with Johann Sebastian Bach did reflect something of his national origins and education, his ambitions and his aesthetic and moral values, in short, his struggle for self-definition.[32] In Mendelssohn's personal and professional history, the cultivation of Bach was always linked to his efforts to realize the German-Jewish-Christian symbiosis that was his fraught and ambiguous inheritance. Mendelssohn was not a person who wrote

[29] Grossmann-Vendrey, *Vergangenheit*, 221.

[30] Richard Wagner, "On Conducting," in *Art and Politics*, 341. Three contrasting yet illuminating discussions of this overworked topic may be found in Bryan Magee, *The Tristan Chord: Wagner and Philosophy* (New York, 2000), 249–52; Eric Werner, *Mendelssohn: Leben und Werk in neuer Sicht* (Zurich, 1980), 366–76; and Leon Botstein, "The Aesthetics of Assimilation and Affirmation: Reconstructing the Career of Felix Mendelssohn," in Todd, *Mendelssohn and His World*, 5–42.

[31] Botstein, "Aesthetics of Assimilation," 9–10. "Intense lifelong preoccupation" is perhaps too strong a characterization of the occasional, quickly passing attention Wagner bestowed on Mendelssohn in the vast corpus of his writings.

[32] For a recent summation of Mendelssohn's "Bach reception," see Wolfgang Dinglinger, "Aspekte der Bach-Rezeption Mendelssohns," in Heinemann and Hinrichsen, eds., *Bach und die Nachwelt*, I: 378–420.

much about music: in 1837, in response to a request from a baffled Droysen that he explain Beethoven's Ninth Symphony to him, Mendelssohn replied that "it is altogether difficult to speak about music; you must above all hear it."[33] His biographers have thus had to piece together his views of particular composers or pieces or performances from the rich trove of letters he left behind, numbering in the thousands, from the letters and reports of others, and from the ample evidence of his actions—as composer, conductor, organizer, and teacher. In the past decades of admiring reengagement with this composer, so nearly relegated to an undeserved obscurity, an image has gradually emerged of a person more conscious of his Jewish heritage than once thought, more profoundly committed to his Christianity than once assumed, more attuned to the needs of the national culture that he was helping to shape, and more courageous, original, and suffering than once asserted. In general, the postwar Mendelssohn is a person with a vision of what music could achieve, for Germany and for humanity, that bears little resemblance to Wagner's characterization of him as someone who gave the cultivated middle classes "the consolation of a little pleasing and elegant entertainment amid the shifting and turmoil of the times."[34] Mendelssohn certainly recognized the shifts and the turmoil, as his letters frequently show. But he hoped nevertheless that music making of the sort he promoted—the "cause for which I stand," as he wrote to his brother Paul—would do some of the difficult work of improving people.

The *St. Matthew Passion* performances of 1829 began the process of realizing that vision. In one way or another, they presaged all of his future work. His various official positions—director of the Lower Rhenish Festival and other musical festivals, music director in Düsseldorf, director of Leipzig's Gewandhaus Orchestra and founding director of the Leipzig Music Conservatory, kapellmeister to the king of Saxony, musical director to the king of Prussia—and his guest conducting abroad, especially in England, appealed to him because of the opportunities they afforded to shape the musical sensibilities of Germany and Europe through carefully crafted public concerts. Over the years, he reassembled the elements of the 1829 performances many times over, striving to strike a balance between broad participation and high stan-

---

[33] He continued that he too found the choral movement hard to grasp, and concluded that "when with such a great master this is the case, then the fault must lie with us." He also speculated that very few musical organizations, and none in Berlin, where Droysen had heard it, were capable of a decent performance of it. See Droysen to Mendelssohn, 28 October 1837; Mendelssohn to Droysen, 14 December 1837, in *"Ein tief gegründet Herz": Der Briefwechsel Felix Mendelssohn-Bartholdys mit Johann Gustav Droysen*, ed. Carl Wehmer (Heidelberg, 1859), 46, 49. See also the discussion in Botstein, "Aesthetics of Assimilation," 30–31.

[34] The latter view being, not surprisingly, that of Wagner; cited in Botstein, "Aesthetics of Assimilation," 24.

dards of musicianship, between the music of the past and new creation, and between the particular claims of different nations and religions and the universal claims of a common humanity. He did not convince everyone that such balancing acts were necessary. Berlioz, who took delight in playing the outrageous jokester to what he took to be Mendelssohn's high-minded sobriety, wrote that he was "a little too fond of the dead."[35] And Mendelssohn's letters are, of course, frequently eloquent on the failings of this or that musical situation, the inadequacy of rehearsal time or space, or the recalcitrance of officialdom. But the essential thing remained constant—to set into motion a process of musical improvement which would continue without his constant urging and which would work, finally, to communicate universal values of enlightenment and ethical community.

His compositions expressed this same cultural project. Especially in the large-scale choral works *St. Paul* in 1836 and *Elijah* in 1847, he realized, to tremendous acclaim in his time, the recovery of the oratorio as an art form that could still speak seriously to a large public. One can hear in them both the creative appropriation of Bach and Handel and, more distant but still audible, the refusal to allow Judaism to drop out of the story of modern humanity. The oratorios, despite their narratives of conversion and fulfillment, resist the triumphalism of Christian supersession of Judaism, seeking instead to emphasize the commonality of Judeo-Christian suffering and faith.[36] As in the *St. Matthew Passion*, neither the Christian essence of Mendelssohn's religious works nor their rootedness in a consciously German musical heritage contradicted the universal import of both music and text. A man of, in Michael P. Steinberg's phrase, "multiple cultural consciousness," Mendelssohn himself tried throughout his life to reconcile what others experienced only as oppositional.[37]

---

[35] Hector Berlioz, *Memoirs of Hector Berlioz, from 1803–1865*, trans. Ernest Newman (New York, 1966), 279.

[36] Sposato's "The Price of Assimilation" is the most sustained scholarly effort to assess the extent to which Mendelssohn's oratorios depicted Jews sympathetically or not. Sposato argues that Mendelssohn eventually, and not before presenting significantly anti-Judaic images in his early oratorios, settled on a "strategy of dual perspective," in effect allowing the audience to retain their negative view of Jews while distancing himself from such conclusions (Sposato, "Price of Assimilation," 485). Despite Sposato's careful analyses of the oratorios, this argument ultimately relies on unprovable speculations about how the audience might have responded to the works. See also Botstein, "Aesthetics of Assimilation," 25; Martin Staehelin, "*Elijah*, Johann Sebastian Bach, and the New Covenant: On the Aria 'Es ist genug' in Felix Mendelssohn-Bartholdy's Oratorio *Elijah*," in Todd, *Mendelssohn and His World*, 121–35.

[37] Michael P. Steinberg, "Mendelssohn and Judaism," in Peter Mercer-Taylor, ed., *The Cambridge Companion to Mendelssohn* (New York, 2004), 40. Steinberg's article represents an intervention in an ongoing debate about the legacy of Eric Werner's Mendelssohn scholarship, which in its day was pathbreaking in insisting on the importance of Judaism in Mendelssohn's life. Since then, scholars, especially Jeffrey Sposato, have found many errors, most of them tendentious, in the evidence

It is easy enough to find all Mendelssohn's own credo, especially his belief in "the power of music as a peaceful instrument of human solidarity and love of God and nature," either irrelevant, disingenuous, or risible.[38] In his own time and with gathering effect after it, the hope that art could improve people or liberalize nations gave way to more ironic or exclusionary views of both art and nations. And Mendelssohn himself found it difficult to sustain, this work of trying to lead people to a place they did not think they needed to go. Despite the admiration and affection he inspired and despite the acclaim with which all his musical projects were greeted, he remained painfully aware of how "little remain[ed]" when a concert was over, how "depressing, flighty and evanescent" were musical performances. He experienced the dispersal of childhood friends and the disappointment of youthful hopes with a combination of gloomy resignation and nagging guilt: "I often doubt myself," he wrote to Droysen in 1844, "and feel responsible for all of it, for being insufferable and unbearable and unfeeling, and who knows what else—the worst thoughts one can have of oneself." At age thirty-seven, shortly before his death, he wrote to Droysen again, in an effort to console his old friend on the death of his wife. "If only you could really work again, if only you had an occupation like that of a craftsman or a doctor or a preacher," he wrote, not very consolingly. "I have always envied them, because they are really necessary to people and they really help others, so they can always work, regardless of how they feel on the inside. But in such times as yours now, to write a book or a symphony, to deliver a lecture or lead a concert, it all comes to nothing."[39]

Yet if the effect of music seemed to him at times so fleeting as to be meaningless, and if the capacity to create music was a poor defense against the injuries of time and mortality, he also believed, perhaps contradictorily, that the essence of music could be renewal. A sentence later, he urged

---

Werner used to support his "new view" of Mendelssohn. See especially the exchange in *Musical Quarterly*: Jeffrey Sposato, "Creative Writing: The [Self-] Identification of Mendelssohn as Jew," *Musical Quarterly* 82 (1998): 190–209; Leon Botstein, "Mendelssohn and the Jews," *Musical Quarterly* 82 (1998): 210–19; Peter Ward Jones, "Letter to the Editor," *Musical Quarterly* 83 (1999): 27–30; Michael P. Steinberg, "Mendelssohn's Music and German-Jewish Culture: An Intervention," *Musical Quarterly* 83 (1999): 31–44; Leon Botstein, "Mendelssohn, Werner, and the Jews: A Final Word," *Musical Quarterly* 83 (1999): 45–50; and Jeffrey S. Sposato, "Mendelssohn, *Paulus*, and the Jews: A Response to Leon Botstein and Michael Steinberg," *Musical Quarterly* 83 (1999), 280–91. See also Marian Wilson Kimber, "The Composer as Other: Gender and Race in the Biography of Felix Mendelssohn," in John Michael Cooper and Julie D. Prandi, *The Mendelssohns: Their Music in History* (New York, 2002), 335–52.

[38] Botstein, "Aesthetics of Assimilation," 35–36.

[39] Felix to Paul Mendelssohn, 29 October 1837, in *Briefe aus den Jahren 1830–1847*, ed. Rudolf Elvers (Frankfurt, 1984), 2:155–57. Mendelssohn to Droysen, 19 January 1844 and 5 April 1847, in Wehmer, *Briefwechsel Droysen*, 85, 104.

Droysen to find among his musician friends in Kiel someone who would play Bach's choral prelude "Schmücke Dich, O liebe Seele" for him, for "such music would give you joy."[40] Mendelssohn had just returned from Berlin, where he had hoped to see Droysen, and had found everything there "so changed on the outside and inside" that "nearly everything that in our time there seemed fresh and young is now disappeared, desolated, decayed, and worsened." But only "nearly everything," he emphasized. And if we recall that the bygone time Mendelssohn evoked in this passage was precisely the time of the *St. Matthew Passion* performances of 1829, then perhaps we can find some echo of it in his next lines: "I found still, thank God, that the best things have not disappeared, but rather remain eternally renewed, even in death. . . . For the best things do not fall like dead leaves from the trees, God alone knows why, but they do not fall."[41]

The progress of the Bach movement, consisting as it did of many different strands of activity, is more difficult to follow than the careers of individuals, even prolific and many-faceted ones like Mendelssohn's.[42] Performances, publications, and scholarship increasingly converged in the decades following 1829 to transform Bach from an esoteric to a familiar figure. His newly discovered familiarity derived from the incontrovertible fact of his Germanness, a quality that the performances of 1829 had established perhaps even more decisively than his musical genius. As we have seen, the thirty decades before 1829 had seen growing agreement about who were the "classics" of German music; but national histories, like national identity, have never been static entities, unchanging once established. For German nationalists especially, many possible national histories competed for preem-

---

[40] "Deck Thyself, My Soul, with Gladness," BWV 654. Robert Schumann remembered Mendelssohn saying of this work, "If life had deprived you of hope and faith, then this single chorale would replenish you with both" (*Schumann on Music: A Selection from the Writings*, trans. and ed. Henry Pleasants [New York, 1965], 93). Mendelssohn also played this choral prelude at the organ concert that took place in 1840 in the Thomaskirche in Leipzig to celebrate the dedication of a monument to Bach, newly erected outside the church. Mendelssohn had restored the organ in the church and organized a series of concerts, the profits from which went toward building the monument.

[41] Mendelssohn to Droysen, 5 April 1847, in Wehmer, *Briefwechsel Droysen*, 104–5.

[42] See especially Bodo Bischoff, "Das Bach-Bild Robert Schumanns," in Heinemann and Hinrichsen, eds., *Bach und die Nachwelt*, I: 421–499; Michael Heinemann and Hans-Joachim Hinrichsen, "Der 'deutsche' Bach," in Heinemann and Hinrichsen, eds., *Bach und die Nachwelt*, II: 11–30; and Hans-Joachim Hinrichsen, "Die Bach-Gesamtausgabe und die Kontroversen um die Aufführungspraxis der Vokalwerke," in Heinemann and Hinrichsen, eds., *Bach und die Nachwelt*, II: 227–98.

inence in the nineteenth century, and a host of potential national heroes emerged out of the fog of the past—the well-meaning if befuddled King Ludwig of Bavaria assembled a whole hall of them at his German Valhalla rather than settling on just one or two.[43]

Bach's emergence into the forefront of German musical heroes happened more gradually and unevenly than Beethoven's, who was a German hero even in his lifetime.[44] In 1836 Schumann went off in search of Bach's grave in Leipzig, and finding neither it nor any marker of his having once lived there, wondered at this "still insufficiently appreciated" great man. In 1837 he wrote that it was high time that "the German nation" decided to gather the lost, forgotten, and hidden-away treasures of Bach into a publicly available collection. In 1840 Richard Wagner, writing for a Parisian music journal, described Bach's Passions as embodying "the whole essence, the whole spirit of the German nation," "products of the heart and habits of the German people." In 1843 Mendelssohn was finally able to erect a monument to Bach, and in 1848, in the midst of that Prussian-sponsored national cultural project, the completion of the Cologne Cathedral, Franz Brendel once again compared Bach's music to the Strasbourg Cathedral, as great German art, often misunderstood, ever striving toward heaven. In 1850 the Bach Gesellschaft called the publication of all his works the "highest duty of the nation." In 1865, again Wagner, in his much-read essay "What Is German," called Bach "music's wonder man," "unfathomably great," embodying "the history of the German spirit's inmost life throughout the gruesome century of the German people's complete extinction." Finally in 1873 Philipp Spitta's landmark biography of Bach identified him as having "purely and thoroughly German" roots, the "grandeur" of his personality clinging deeply "to the soil of German life and nature."[45] By the time of the foundation of the German Empire of 1871, then, Bach had become a "national symbolic figure," comparable to Goethe, Beethoven, or Schleiermacher as the embodiment of all that was, in Wilhelm Dilthey's phrase, "great and wondrous" in German development.[46] By the end of the nineteenth century, Hans von Bülow's remark about the three B's of German music (Bach, Beethoven, and Brahms) had become commonplace wis-

[43] On the multiplicity of national histories, see Vick, *Defining Germany*, 48–78.

[44] See especially Bauer, *Wie Beethoven auf den Sockel Kam*; David Dennis, *Beethoven and German Politics* (New Haven, 1996), 1–31; Estaban Buch, *Beethoven's Ninth*, trans. Richard Miller (Chicago, 2003), 111–32; Scott Burnham, *Beethoven Hero* (Princeton, 1995).

[45] Pleasants, *Schumann on Music*, 93, 147; *Neue Zeitschrift für Musik* 15 (1848): 104, 213–14; Wagner, "On German Music," in *Pilgrimage to Beethoven*, trans. William Ashton Ellis (Lincoln, NE, 1994), 94; Brendel cited in Sandberger, *Bach-Bild*, 72–73; Richard Wagner, "What Is German," in *Art and Politics*, 162; Spitta, *Bach*, 1:1, i.

[46] Quoted in Sandberger, *Bach-Bild*, 205.

dom about German national identity itself, and the special musical mission of Germans to the world had become inconceivable without Bach as its elder statesman.

Because the aura of Bach took so long to gather, its history before and after 1829 is far from obvious. Considering only the *St. Matthew Passion*, Mendelssohn's recovery of it inspired a number of choral directors already linked to the Singakademie through former membership or professional circles, and the following decades saw about forty performances in a limited set of north German cities. Johann Theodor Mosewius in Breslau, Louis Spohr in Kassel, and Karl Sämann in Königsberg were responsible for most of those outside Berlin. Mendelssohn himself did not again direct a performance of the *St. Matthew Passion* until 1841, when he brought it back to Leipzig and the Thomaskirche for the first time since Bach's death. Carl Ferdinand Becker announced the great event in Schumann's *Neue Zeitschrift für Musik*, with words drawn directly from Marx's series of articles in 1829—a "high festival of religion and art," the "highest flight" to "edification and exaltation" out of our "benumbing, deafening present," and so on. Yet the article expended fewer words praising Bach and his Passion music than describing Mendelssohn's feat of 1829, when "like Pygmalion, he breathed warm, vigorous life into this precious but dead stone."[47] Bach's return to Berlin in 1829 had meanwhile become legend, and every participant in it, from the opera singers to the young second concertmaster David, still glowed with the lingering glory of that time.In the more Catholic cities of Munich, Vienna, and—to a lesser degree—Frankfurt and Dresden, performances also took place, without repetition or advance buzz. The Hamburg Gesangverein, modeled on the Berlin Singakademie, began to rehearse the work in 1831 but did not produce a full performance until 1862. After 1870 (and renamed the Singakademie), however, it performed it every other year, with a devotion rivaled only by the Berlin Singakademie.

Meanwhile, immediately after the 1829 performances, the Berlin firm of Schlesinger had published the full score of the *Passion* under the editorship of Marx. In 1834 Marx also produced a piano-vocal score, adding and changing notes and ignoring or altering phrasings and dynamic markings.[48] The Marx editions of the *St. Matthew Passion* served for the next twenty years, over the course of which editions of other Bach works also became available in piecemeal fashion and occasional performances took place here and there. But these years were decisive for Bach's posthumous fate in ways

---

[47] *Neue Zeitschrift für Musik* 8 (1841): 99–100.

[48] Barbara David Wright, "Johann Sebastian Bach's 'Matthaus-Passion': A Performance History, 1829–1854" (Ph.D. diss., University of Michigan, 1983), 363.

less obvious than the dwindling number of performances and the few publications of his work would suggest. In retrospect, they were a time of preparation, of gathering scattered manuscripts, authenticating them, making copies, and compiling lists, all activities that led to the vast project of Bach recovery announced in Leipzig in July 1850 to mark the hundredth anniversary of the composer's death. The twenty-four founding members of the Bach Gesellschaft set themselves the task of publishing a complete critical edition of Bach's works. The idea for such an ambitious undertaking originated with Mendelssohn and his circle in the 1830s, and its founding members included all the musicians and scholars with whom he had worked closely over the past thirty years: Franz Hauser, Moritz Hauptmann, Julius Rietz, Ignaz Moscheles, Johann Mosewius, and Robert Schumann. The new organization was, then, another culmination of Mendelssohn's labors, this one grander in conception if less dramatic in immediate impact than the performances of 1829.[49] In 1856, under Julius Rietz, it brought out its edition of the *St. Matthew Passion*, an editorial achievement of lasting value. Its work continued until 1900, at which point the original Bach Gesellschaft dissolved, its task completed.

The general public awareness of Bach in the meantime expanded steadily, and actual performances of his works—as the case of Hamburg illustrated—became frequent and regular. In the same period, knowledge of Bach and his works increased dramatically because of the publication in 1873 and 1880 of Philipp Spitta's two-volume biography. This was a work of scholarship so thorough in its exploration of sources, so confident and persuasive in its dating of musical compositions, and so gigantic in scope that subsequent generations of Bach scholars, even when presenting major challenges to such matters as compositional dating or authenticity, seemed merely to be nibbling at its edges. Its immense reach stretched from Bach genealogical investigations going back generations (a 180-page prelude to the biography proper that a number of contemporary reviewers begged to be excused from reading) to a thorough accounting of major and minor works. The *St. Matthew Passion* alone, quite apart from a full treatment of the whole German Passion tradition, required thirty-two dense pages.[50] Just as the efforts of the Bach Gesellschaft dwarfed those of similar societies devoted to Handel, Heinrich Schütz, or Palestrina, so too did Spitta's biography exceed by any measure—length, thoroughness of research, breadth of

---

[49] On the importance of the work of a longtime Mendelssohn friend, the opera singer Franz Hauser, to the collecting and cataloguing of Bach's works, see Jorgenson, *Franz Xavier Hauser*, esp. 95–121.

[50] The unabridged English edition came out in 1889 and has been reprinted often since. On contemporary responses, see Sandberger, *Bach-Bild*, 78–87.

investigation, depth of analysis—the biographies of Mozart, Beethoven, Handel, and others that were written around the same time. Even for those who may secretly not have cared for his music at all, Bach had become, thanks to Spitta, a figure of proportions so immense and profundity so proven that he could not be ignored.

But that Bach should have become the "most famous among the many unknown German musicians," as Klaus Eidsam mischievously put it, attests to more than the extraordinary diligence of his admirers and brings us again to the question of his national significance.[51] It has become yet another cliché among the many that have attached themselves over the years to Bach that the reverence his work came to enjoy in the nineteenth century was simply due to inexorable forces like the "rise of nationalism," "nationalistic passions," and "tide of nationalism running high."[52] Certainly the national significance that Bach accrued from the 1770s on has been the major focus of this book's account of the background to the 1829 performances. We have seen the ways that Bach became the cynosure of the nationalizing consciousness of men like Rochlitz and Reichardt, Forkel and Marx. The contemporary accounts of the *St. Matthew Passion* of 1829 contained persistent currents of national awareness, flowing in and among responses to the religious, musical, and dramatic aspects of the work. Yet at the same time we must understand this nationalizing of Bach as neither inexorable nor one-dimensional. Once begun, it continued, but in contexts that must be understood if we are to take the measure of his place in national imaginings.

Just as important to bear in mind, Bach's posthumous movement from obscurity into fame did not follow the same trajectory as that of the coalescence of German states into a national union and is thus only in some vague way the pendant of nation-state building. Although this might seem an obvious point, it needs emphasis. The frequent mention of the term "nationalism" in conjunction with Bach in the nineteenth century leads to the assumption that the Bach movement somehow drew its momentum from its association with German national unification, with gymnastic associations and shooting clubs, with veterans of the wars against Napoleon and student organizations, with liberal politicians, parliamentarians, and ambitious kings. This was not, I think, the case. Just as nationalism became attached to incompatible political agendas, so too did many of the cultural movements of the eighteenth and nineteenth century in German-speaking Europe, the Bach movement among them, develop nationalizing agendas without all

---

[51] Eidsam, *Das wahre Leben*, 7.

[52] Joseph Kerman, "How We Got into Analysis, and How to Get Out," *Critical Inquiry* 7 (1980): 314–15; Hans Lenneberg, *Witnesses and Scholars: Studies in Musical Biography* (New York, 1988), 85; *New Bach Reader*, 418.

meaning or wanting the same thing by them. We might look at nationalism, as some of its theorists have suggested, as an emergent cognitive model for educated Europeans, a way of ordering experience, of looking at the world and making sense of one's place and identity in it—in the words of one, a mode of "vision and division of the world."[53] Carl Dahlhaus has written to similar effect that in the nineteenth century "nationalism was seen as a means, not a hindrance, to universality," and the "strong national tint" evident in Weber, Chopin, and Mussorgsky was not "necessarily an obstacle to international recognition; indeed, it was almost always the vehicle."[54] As we have seen already in the case of Forkel, he intended the national inflection he gave to Bach as a means of enhancing his book's—and Bach's—appeal to a German-speaking audience and to a foreign one.

The existence of national characteristics helps explain the deep appreciation of Bach's compositions in the face of a general incomprehension and even dislike, the repeated performance of his works in the face of a concert scene focused primarily on new compositions, and the untiring effort to make sense of Bach in the face of a patchy historical record and an incomplete understanding of his musical predecessors. All this required a conviction that the man and his music were worth the great effort involved, that both could speak to the present and help point the way to the future. To provide Bach with a distinctly national coloration aided in all these tasks, even if it feels to our late modern sensibilities like an act of historical misappropriation. But cultivating the German Bach never was intended merely to soften people up for political union, just as making Bach part, indeed the founder, of a national music tradition was not an end in itself. For all those who contributed to Bach's emergence as a "national symbolic figure," his music mattered more than his national identity, not that the choice would have made any sense to them. The national designation identified the man and his music, and it need hardly be said that Bach gave more to the category of German or German music than either gave to him. At the same time, the national designation provided an arc of historical continuity, by which the past enriched both present and future. As Schumann wrote of Mendelssohn's efforts to construct a Bach monument, the future "would give us credit for this as a sign of the enlightened artistic sensibility of our own era . . . [for it] binds all artists and friends of art," from Bach's time, through Mozart's and Beethoven's, and into the future.[55]

Yet the cultivation of Bach under the sign of the German nation also

---

[53] Pierre Bourdieu and Loïc J. D. Wacquant, *An Invitation to Reflexive Sociology* (Chicago, 1992), 12.

[54] Dahlhaus, *Nineteenth-Century Music*, 37.

[55] Cited in Grossmann-Vendrey, *Vergangenheit*, 151.

created problems that did not prove so easily resolvable as the matter of his sheer importance. Chief among these was the confessional question. The nineteenth century, in Germany as elsewhere, was in Thomas Nipperdey's phrase "alive with the fight over Christianity and modernity."[56] Religious communities, whether Protestant, Catholic, or Jewish, had to find new places within changing structures of state power and negotiate new relationships to social groups in flux between countryside and city, old trades and new. Everything about religious life came under the pressure generated by the great transformations of the nineteenth century. Schisms and new forms of cooperation developed within and among the officially recognized churches. Religious belief itself underwent all sorts of modification, from intense revivalism to loss of it altogether, marked overall by a trend toward a more individualized, more privately experienced kind of piety.[57]

Added to this was the equally vexed national question, for how one hoped to see the German nation-state take shape depended in many cases on what religion one confessed. Just as church establishments and church members had to come to terms with national identities in the nineteenth century, so too did nationalists need to come to terms with the universalism of Christian belief. Declaring Protestantism to be essentially German, and therefore (illogically, but satisfyingly) claiming Germany to be essentially Protestant, was only one way to resolve the tension between religious and national identities. Needless to say, it did not work for those who were German and Catholic or German and Jewish or even German and more Calvinist than Lutheran.[58] Church music became caught up in all of this. Indeed, the more Germans spoke and wrote and thought of themselves as the people of music, and the more they sought confirmation of this in their past, the more important it became to place the enormous legacy of church music into the stream of Germany's emergence as a national group. And where church music came in, so too, inevitably, did Bach.

But as the previous chapter explained, the church establishment itself, for a variety of reasons, proved to be the missing champion in the Bach revival. This was, of course, only to be expected in the case of the Catholic Church in Germany, for what little was known of Bach, especially the chorale settings that lingered on in Protestant churches, ill served though they were by organists and congregation, spoke to his essentially Protestant character.

---

[56] Nipperdey, *Germany*, 356.

[57] See the collection of articles concerning many aspects of these changes, with an emphasis on relations among the religious communities, in Smith, *Protestants, Catholics and Jews*.

[58] The most thorough treatment of these vexed issues is Wolfgang Altgeld, *Katholizismus, Protestantismus, Judentum: Über religiös-begründete Gegensätze und nationalreligiöse Ideen in der Geschichte des deutschen Nationalismus* (Mainz, 1992).

Had he not served north German Protestants all his life, in court and town? And despite the B-minor Mass, little known and harder to grasp, was he not chiefly the author of those peculiar accretions of Protestant piety, the musical Passions?

Yet Protestantism—Old Lutheran, Reformed, or newly Unionized—proved no more eager to embrace its faithful servant. In one of the few convergences of Protestant and Catholic reform in this era of increasing confessional confrontation, church music in both confessions suffered under the tyranny of the a cappella aesthetic. Caecilianism in the Catholic Church found its Protestant counterpart in the officially sanctioned efforts of men like Carl von Winterfeld to promote the plainer, more ethereal music of composers like Palestrina and the "Prussian Palestrina" Johannes Eccard for use in Protestant worship. "We may rightly call Eccard's compositions *churchly*," wrote Winterfeld in 1847, "because they correspond to the capabilities and the viewpoint of the community, whereas those of Bach are animated by individual, narrow artistic purposes and have their origins in the effort to depict particular, uniquely colored emotions, which can never bear the stamp of *churchly* no matter how spiritually and worthily they are composed." As for the *St. Matthew Passion* in particular, Winterfeld found it wholly inappropriate for liturgical use, because its "extraordinary impact on the emotions of the listener, even the means by which this is achieved, exclude the miraculous work of the church and take the place of worship itself."[59]

In Winterfeld's critique, we can hear echoes of Thibaut's concern for purity in music in 1825, Wackenroder's "heartfelt outpourings" in 1799, and even the "God save us, my children! It's just as if one were at an Opera comedy" of the woman upon hearing the Passion music for the first time in 1729. Romantic aesthetics had somehow converged with a variant of liturgical puritanism to produce a ban upon Bach. Churches were, in any case, in no financial position to muster the resources necessary to study or perform works of such musical complexity.

So the movement to recover Bach for nineteenth-century men and women developed outside of religious institutions, although not in the absence of religious belief. The Singakademie and its many imitators were part of a process historians now call reconfessionalization, by which reli-

---

[59] Cited in Sandberger, *Bach-Bild*, 99–100; Winterfeld's most influential works were *Johannes Pierluigi von Palestrina, seine Werke und deren Bedeutung für die Geschichte der Tonkunst* (Breslau, 1832) and *Der evangelische Kirchengesang und sein Verhältniss zur Kunst des Tonsatzes*, 3 vols. (Leipzig, 1843–47). On the broader context for Winterfeld's work, see James Garratt, *Palestrina and the German Romantic Imagination: Interpreting Historicism in Nineteenth-Century Music* (New York, 2002).

gious practices and beliefs adjusted themselves to modernity, loosening their connection to established churches and developing a more private devotional culture apart from institutions.[60] They practiced in secular spaces and had a wholly secular organizational structure. They performed sometimes in churches and sometimes not—the setting hardly mattered, for the religious sensibility that pervaded their activities was adaptable, institutionally unhitched, and well channeled into alternative organizational forms and places.

The fact that Bach's music initially spread outside church and state establishments made it more widely known across confessional lines than might otherwise have been the case—indeed made it more accessible to the culture of nationhood than a strictly Protestant Bach would have been in the period before 1871. It was, to be sure, harder to get mainly Catholic musical organizations interested in performing Bach, or audiences in listening to him. Schelble, director of the Catholic Caecilien Verein in Frankfurt, brought the *St. Matthew Passion* to a Catholic audience already at the end of 1829, but he could not persuade his group to make it a regular part of its repertoire. Mendelssohn had to give up his efforts to get his chorus in Düsseldorf to perform the work, or indeed much else by Bach; and Franz Hauser, himself a German-speaking Catholic from Bohemia, had only minor success in creating a demand for Bach in Munich. The *St. Matthew Passion* never made it into the regular repertoire of the Lower Rhine Music Festival, which relied as much on Catholic as Protestant participants, but then again, it never made it into the choral festival circuit anywhere, in north or south Germany, nor did the *St. John Passion*, the B-minor Mass, or any of Bach's cantatas. These mass popular events all favored the more easily performed oratorios of Handel and Mendelssohn, with Beethoven's Ninth a more likely choice for extra effort than anything by Bach. The confessional divide was thus real enough, but not impenetrable or all-determining and certainly not an obstacle to Bach's gathering national significance. In the case of Bach, Catholics and Jews, as well as Protestants, cared enough about his music to regard it as an essential part of the national patrimony.

This situation thus shaped the exact dimensions of Bach's national identity as it emerged in these years. Protestant he certainly was, but not in the same way as Luther or the hero-general of the Thirty Years War, Gustavus Adolphus, who became the focus of a large, exclusively Protestant popular organization in these same years.[61] Bach's ability to transcend confessional

---

[60] See the discussion in chapter 5 and Hölscher, "Religious Divide," 33–47.

[61] Kevin Cramer, "The Cult of Gustavus Adolphus: Protestant Identity and German Nationalism," in Smith, *Protestants, Catholics, and Jews*, 97–120.

divisions was all of a piece with the confessionally indifferent nature of musical culture itself, never so divided along religious lines as were other aspects of national life. Mendelssohn, the converted Jew who was a devout Lutheran, was feted as a musical leader all across Germany, not just in the Protestant parts—that is, until Wagner's rise and with it his efforts to cut the Jewish Mendelssohn down to musical insignificance. Franz Hauser, the Bohemian Catholic opera singer and Bach enthusiast, held positions in Prague, Dresden, Kassel, Frankfurt, Vienna, Berlin, Leipzig, and Breslau before settling in Munich, where he too eventually fell afoul of Wagnerian opposition. One could multiply such examples across the spectrum of performing musicians, all pursuing that essential element of nineteenth-century progress, the career open to talent, in a context that was often international in geographical scope but strongly national in cultural identifications. Confessional indifference also marked the attitudes toward composers, past or contemporary. The Catholic Palestrina, like the Protestant Bach, had admirers in all religious groups. People lined up on the sides of the Brahms-Wagner divide without caring whether one or the other was Catholic or Protestant. Wagner, born in Protestant Leipzig, eventually settled in Catholic Bavaria; Brahms, born in Protestant Hamburg, ended up in Catholic Vienna.

The essential ambiguity of the German musical tradition's confessional identity even meant that the political borders of 1871, which embodied the solution to the German question more favored by Protestant than Catholic Germans, did not change what people regarded as "German music." The nation-state that finally emerged in 1871 had, after all, failed to encompass the German musical heritage, though few people were literal-minded enough to ask whether Mozart or Haydn or Beethoven himself must now be considered an Austrian musician and not a German one at all. Indeed, the notable feature of music and German national identity after 1871 was the continuity of established ways of talking and thinking about German music across what one might expect to be a momentous divide. The musical nation that discussions of the past decades had done much to consolidate was not reconfigured by political unification nor made suddenly Protestant, just as its consolidation before 1871 had not been precluded by political fragmentation nor irreconcilably divided by confessional identities.

But these are broad generalizations. All did not remain unchanged for either the image of Bach or the performance of his music after 1871, and for the immediate cause of this shift, which slowly but definitely distanced his choral works from the Mendelssohnian performances of 1829, we must not look to the wars of Bismarck but return to the writings of Spitta. The hallmark of Spitta's great Bach biography of 1873–80 was his effort to reestablish Bach as the Protestant church composer without whom Protestant church music could hardly be conceived, let alone practiced. After some forty years of sustained reengagement of German musical culture with the composer and some seventy years of more than passing acquaintance, Spitta now insisted that Bach's Protestantism and his Germanness were essentially the same thing. His precursor was Droysen, whose reviews of the 1829 *St. Matthew Passion* (which Spitta probably had not read) had made the same argument and whose influential work on historicism and biography directly informed Spitta's historical method.[62]

Spitta asserted throughout, though with particular intensity in the case of the *St. Matthew Passion*, that Bach's genius was rooted in his "inheritance from a long race of artists," the Bach family, who were themselves the particular representatives of "a tradition founded in an unbroken intimacy with the life of the people," that is, the tradition of Protestant church music stretching back to Luther. In Bach, the "feelings, deeds, and thoughts" of the German people had become "an innate and inseparable part of his being," and in "the works of his creation" were to be found "the highest outcome of an essentially national art, whose origin lies in the period of the Reformation." Bach was both culmination and restoration: in the case of the *St. Matthew Passion* especially, he had taken "a form of art as vacuous as the Passion had become" and given it back "all the dignity and mastery of the German genius." He had made it "to a remarkable degree a popular work," whose character did "not rest solely on its connection with certain national aspects of thought, or in the faithful preservation of church traditions that had grown dear," but in the music as a whole, which for "all its profundity, breadth, and wealth and in spite of all the art lavished upon it" never betrays "the lucidity and simplicity which are its essence."[63]

Thus did Spitta refute Winterfeld and the scandalized church ladies and lay the groundwork for the return of Bach's music to the Protestant churches. At the same time he recovered "the almost forgotten centuries" of Germany's "own musical history," of which Bach was the culmination, and represented them as the musical parallel to Germany's history. Spitta was the counterpart then, in music-historical scholarship, to the Prussian school of historiography, of which Droysen was the great representative. The travails of the eighteenth century, when in Bach's sons "we may mark the decay of that power which had culminated after several centuries of growth, and which utterly disappeared in their posterity," paralleled the disarray of the Holy Roman Empire and the German states. The recovery of

[62] Sandberger, *Bach-Bild*, 13–14.
[63] Spitta, *Bach*, 2:504, 567; 3:278.

the German nation's "connection with Bach" and his works—"like a precious seed which bursts the soil at last to be garnered in perennial sheaves"—accompanied that nation's spiritual and political consolidation. "Henceforth," declared Spitta, "it will not be possible that Bach should be forgotten so long as the German people exist." Yet Spitta did not present this Protestant Bach for a Protestant German people in the spirit of crude triumphalism so derided by Nietzsche in his untimely meditations of that same decade. His was still an inclusive vision of Bach and of the German nation, in which he emphasized the importance of leading people to an understanding of this Protestant Germany, not excluding them from it.[64] It was, he concluded the duty of "each in his degree" to work such "that the spirit of the great man may be more widely understood and loved."[65]

Spitta wanted Bach back in churches as well as concert halls, an effort already begun in the 1840s by Mosewius, the Breslau music director who had long ago rushed to Berlin just in time to hear the third performance of the *St. Matthew Passion* in 1829.[66] What his biography achieved most immediately, however, was an intensification in the cultivation of Bach's vocal works in the German choral movement, the *St. Matthew Passion* especially. As we saw earlier, the Hamburg Singakademie performed it more than twenty-five times in the period between the publication of Spitta's biography and the foundation in 1900 of the Neue Bachgesellschaft (New Bach Society), explicitly dedicated to making Bach's works more available for practical use, especially in churches. The Berlin Singakademie abandoned its century-long devotion to Graun's *Tod Jesu* once and for all and took up the *St. Matthew Passion* as its Good Friday musical offering. By the time Alfred Heuss sat down to write a new interpretation of the work in 1908, he could refer to its "unique place in contemporary musical performance," so regular in performances throughout Germany that people "could scarcely imagine" Good Friday and Easter without it. Indeed so close had the association become between the "dilettante choruses" and the Good Friday worship that Heuss felt it urgently necessary to separate the work and the liturgy once again. The *St. Matthew Passion* was "so great and so completely full of meaning in itself" that it existed as a pure work of art, independent of time and place. The increasingly inartistic and routinized performances were slowly but surely ruining it for German audiences; what it needed was

---

[64] Vick makes a similar point about the 1848 nationalists (*Defining Germany*, 212).

[65] Spitta, *Bach*, 3:278.

[66] Mosewius's writings included *Johann Sebastian Bach in seinen Kirchen-Cantaten und Choralgesängen* (Berlin, 1845), and *Johann Sebastian Bachs Matthäuspassion musikalishc und ästhetisch dargestellt* (Berlin, 1852); Sandberger, *Bach-Bild*, 103.

a space and a prolonged time of its own, comparable, wrote Heuss, to what Wagner had created for his works at Bayreuth.[67]

Heuss, like Spitta before him or Winterfeld or Marx or anyone else writing on Bach with more or less complete knowledge of his sacred compositions, struggled—as did Bach himself in all likelihood—to balance the demands of his art with the constrictions of established religious practices. For all the regret in the writings of a Mosewius or a Spitta that Bach had somehow escaped the sacred confines of church life, the fact that his music had spread in the nineteenth century outside of them secured his place in German national life. For this, Mendelssohn and his generation were more responsible than any other individual or group of Bach admirers. Heuss described Mendelssohn's performances of 1829 as "an event of lasting significance," and for reasons not so dissimilar, we can agree. Mendelssohn made the reconciliation of competing and conflicting elements in the unstable mixture that was German national culture seem possible and even easy. He made it possible to imagine that the broad participation of the talented and the merely enthusiastic, the amateur and the professional, could gradually involve everyone in the cultural life of the nation. He made it possible to imagine that there could be a flourishing secular culture in Germany that embraced Protestantism, Catholicism, and even Judaism. He made it possible to imagine that the German present and future could be nourished by the past, even one known only in fragments. He made it possible to imagine a German nation defined by confidence in its cultural riches and dedicated to cultivating them in concert with the other nations of Europe. In the 1829 *St. Matthew Passion*, perhaps he thought such integration had begun.

---

[67] Alfred Heuss, *Johann Sebastian Bachs Matthäuspassion* (Leipzig, 1909), 3–4. On Heuss and the Neue Bach-Gesellschaft, see Sven Hiemke, "Bach-Deutungen im Umfeld der Kirchenmusikalischen Erneuerungsbewegung," in Heinemann and Hinrichsen, *Bach und die Nachwelt*, III: 65–75.

BIBLIOGRAPHY

PERIODICAL SOURCES

Allgemeine Musikalische Zeitung
Berlin: Eine Zeitschrift für Freunde der schönen Künste, des Geschmacks und der Moden
Berliner Allgemeine Musikalische Zeitung
Berliner Schnellpost für Literatur, Theater und Geselligkeit
Berlinische Musikalische Zeitung
Berlinisches Archiv der Zeit und ihres Geschmacks
Caecilia: Ein Taschenbuch für Freunde der Tonkunst
Eutonia, eine hauptsächlich paedagogische Musik-Zeitschrift
Iris im Gebiete der Tonkunst
Journal der Tonkunst
Magazin der Musik (1783–84; *Musik* 1788–89)
Musikalisch-kritische Bibliothek
Musikalische Korrespondenz der Teutschen Filharmonischen Gesellschaft
Musikalische Monathsschrift
Musikalische Realzeitung
Musikalischer Almanach
Musikalisches Kunstmagazin
Neue Zeitschrift für Musik
Zeitung für Theater und Musik zur Unterhaltung gebildeter, unbefangener Leser

PRINTED PRIMARY SOURCES

Arnold, J. K. F. *Musikalische Dialogen, oder Philosophische Unterredungen berühmter Gelehrten, Dichter und Tonkünstler über den Kunstgeschmack in der Musik.* Altenburg, 1805.
Baker, Nancy Kovaleff, and Thomas Christensen, eds. *Aesthetics and the Art of Musical*

Composition in the German Enlightenment: Selected Writings of Johann Georg Sulzer and Heinrich Christoph Koch. Cambridge, 1995.

Berg, Conrad. *Ideen zu einer rationallen Lehrmethode für Musiklehrer überhaupt mit bes. Anwendung auf das Clavierspiel.* Mainz, 1826.

Berlioz, Hector. *Memoirs of Hector Berlioz, from 1803–1865.* Trans. Ernest Newman. New York, 1966.

Blum, Carl. *Die Musik: Anleitung, sich die nöthigen Kenntnisse zu verschaffen, um über alle Gegenstände der Musik richtige Urtheile fällen zu können; Handbuch für Freunde und Liebhaber dieser Kunst.* Berlin, 1830.

Burney, Charles. *The Present State of Music in Germany, the Netherlands, and United Provinces; or, the journal of a tour through those countries, undertaken to collect materials for a general history of music.* 2 vols. London, 1775.

Citron, Marcia J., ed. and trans. *The Letters of Fanny Hensel to Felix Mendelssohn.* New York, 1987.

Coleridge, A. D., ed. and trans. *Goethe's Letters to Zelter, with extracts from those of Zelter to Goethe.* London, 1892.

D'Aubigny von Engelbrunner, Nina. *Briefe an Natalie über den Gesang als Beförderung der häuslichen Glückseligkeit und des geselligen Vernügens: Ein Handbuch für Freunde des Gesanges, die sich selbst, oder für Mütter und Erzieherinnen, die ihre Zöglinge für diese Kunst bilden wollen.* Leipzig, 1803.

David, Hans T., and Arthur Mendel, eds. *The New Bach Reader: A Life of Johann Sebastian Bach in Letters and Documents.* Revised and enlarged by Christoph Wolff. New York, 1998.

Devrient, Eduard. *Dramatische und Dramaturgische Schriften.* Vol. 10, *Meine Erinnerungen an Felix Mendelssohn Bartholdy und seine Briefe an mich.* Leipzig, 1869.

Devrient, Therese. *Jugenderinnerungen.* Stuttgart, 1905.

Dorn, Heinrich. *Aus meinem Leben: Musikalische Skizzen.* Vol. 1, *Erinnerung an einen Jugendfreund: Eine musikalische Reise und zwei neue Opern; Ritter Gasparo Spontini.* Berlin, 1870.

Dronke, Ernst. *Berlin.* 1846. Reprint, Berlin, 1953.

Eckardt, Julius, ed. *Ferdinand David und die Familie Mendelssohn-Bartholdy.* Leipzig, 1888.

Elvers, Rudolf, ed. *Felix Mendelssohn: A Life in Letters.* Trans. Craig Tomlinson. New York, 1986.

Forkel, Johann Nikolaus. *Über Johann Sebastian Bachs Leben, Kunst und Kunstwerke.* Ed. Claudia Maria Knispel. 1802. Reprint, Berlin, 2000.

Freytag, Gustav. *Bilder aus der deutschen Vergangenheit.* 10th ed. 4 vols. Leipzig, 1876.

Geck, Martin. *Die Wiederentdeckung der Matthäuspassion im 19. Jahrhundert: Die zeitgenössischen Dokumente und ihre ideengeschichtliche Deutung.* Regensburg, 1967.

Gerber, Ernst Ludwig. *Historisch-Biographisches Lexikon der Tonkünstler.* Ed. Othmar Wessely. 1790–92. Reprint, Graz, 1977.

———. *Neues Historisch-Biographisches Lexikon der Tonkünstler.* Ed. Othmar Wessely. 1812–14. Reprint, Graz, 1967.

Gilbert, Felix, ed. *Bankiers, Künstler, und Gelehrte: Unveröffentliche Briefe der Familie Mendelssohn aus dem 19. Jahrhundert.* Tübingen, 1975.

Gounod, Charles. *An Autobiography.* Trans. Annette E. Crocker. New York, 1970.

Bibliography

Graun, Carl Heinrich. *Tod Jesu.* Ed. Howard Serwer. Madison, 1975.

Grimm, Jacob, and Wilhelm Grimm. *Deutsches Wörterbuch.* 10 vols. Leipzig, 1854.

Hegel, G. W. F. *Introductory Lectures on Aesthetics.* Ed. Michael Inwood. Trans. Bernard Bosanquet. New York, 1993.

Heine, Heinrich. *Sämtliche Werke.* Vol. 8. Ed. Otto Lachmann. Leipzig, 1913.

Heinemann, Michael, and Hans-Joachim Hinrichsen, eds. *Bach und die Nachwelt.* 3 vols. Laaber, 1997–2000.

Heise, Walter, Helmuth Hopf, and Helmut Segler, eds. *Quellentexte zur Musikpädagogik.* Regensburg, 1973.

Hendrie, Gerald, ed. *Mendelssohn's Rediscovery of Bach: A Humanities Foundation Course.* Bletchley, UK, 1971.

Hensel, Sebastian. *Die Familie Mendelssohn 1729–1847.* 1879. Reprint, Frankfurt am Main, 1995.

Heuss, Alfred. *Johann Sebastian Bachs Matthäuspassion.* Leipzig, 1909.

Hiller, Ferdinand. *Mendelssohn: Letters and Recollections.* Trans. M. E. von Glehn. New York, 1972.

Hiller, Johann Adam. *Anweisung zum musikalisch-richtigen Gesange.* Leipzig, 1774.

——. *Anweisung zur Singekunst in der deutschen und italienischen Sprache.* Leipzig, 1773.

——. *Musikalisches Handbuch für die Liebhaber des Gesanges und Claviers.* Leipzig, 1773.

Hoffmann, E. T. A. *E. T. A. Hoffmann's Musical Writings: Kreisleriana, The Poet and the Composer, Music Criticism.* Ed. David Charlton. Trans. Martyn Clarke. Cambridge, 1989.

——. *Leben und Werk in Briefen, Selbstzeugnissen und Zeitdokumenten.* Ed. Klaus Günzel. Düsseldorf, 1979.

Kalkbrenner, Christian. *Kurzer Abriss der Geschichte der Tonkunst, zum Vergnuegen der Liebhaber der Musik.* Berlin, 1792.

Kleist, Heinrich von. "St Cecilia or the Power of Music." In *The Marquise of O—and Other Stories,* trans. David Luke and Nigel Reeves. London, 1978.

Klingemann, Karl, Jr., ed. *Felix Mendelssohn-Bartholdys Briefwechsel mit Legationsrat Karl Klingemann in London.* Essen, 1909.

Koch, Heinrich Christoph. *Kurzgefasstes Handwörterbuch der Musik für praktische Tonkünstler und für Dilettanten.* Leipzig, 1807.

——. *Musikalisches Lexikon, welches die theoretische und praktische Tonkunst, encyclopaedisch bearbeitet, alle alten und neuen Kunstwörter erklärt, und die alten und neuen Instrumente beschrieben, enthält.* 1802. Reprint, Hildesheim, 1964.

Kocher, Conrad. *Die Tonkunst in der Kirche, oder Ideen zu einem allgemeinen, vierstimmigen Choral und einem Figural-Gesang für einen kleineren Chor, nebst Ansichten über den Zweck der Kunst im Allgemeinen.* Stuttgart, 1823.

Krause, Karl Christian Freidrich. *Darstellungen aus der Geschichte der Musik, nebst vorbereitenden Lehren aus der Theorie der Musik.* Göttingen, 1827.

Krohn, Barthold Nicolaus. *Neues Hamburgisches Gesangbuch zum öffentlichen Gottesdienste und zur häuslichen Andacht ausgefertiget von dem Hamburgischen Ministerio.* Hamburg, 1787.

Ledebur, Carl Freiherr von. *Tonkünstler Lexicon Berlins.* Berlin, 1861.

Lippman, Edward, ed. *Musical Aesthetics: A Historical Reader.* Stuyvesant, NY, 1988.

Mattheson, Johann. *Das Neu-Eröffnete Orchestre* . . . . 1713. Reprint, Hildesheim, 1993.

Marx, Adolf Bernhard. *Anleitung zum Vortrag Beethovenscher Klavierwerke.* Berlin, 1863.

———. *Erinnerungen aus meinem Leben.* Berlin, 1865.

———. *Die Musik des neunzehnten Jahrhunderts und ihre Pflege: Methode der Musik.* Leipzig, 1873.

———. "Zur Beurtheilung Hoffmanns als Musiker." In *E. T. A. Hoffmanns Leben und Nachlass.* Ed. Julius Eduard Hitzig. Vol. 3. 3rd ed. Stuttgart, 1839.

Mason, Lowell. *A Yankee Musician in Europe: The 1837 Journals of Lowell Mason.* Ed. Michael Broyles. Ann Arbor, 1990.

Mendelssohn, Felix. *Briefe.* Ed. Rudolf Elvers. Frankfurt am Main, 1984.

Michaelis, C. F. *Kathechismus der Musik, oder kurze und fassliche Erläuterung der wichtigsten, die Tonkunst betreffenden Begriffe und Grundsätze, nebst einer allgemeinen Einleitung in die Kunst, das Pianoforte zu spielen.* Leipzig, 1819.

———. *Kathechismus über J. B. Logier's System der Musikwissenschaft und der musikalischen Composition, Inbegriff des sogeannten Generalbasses, als Leitfaden zum Unterricht.* Leipzig, 1828.

Mosewius, Johann Theodor. *Johann Sebastian Bach in seinen Kirchen-Cantaten und Choralgesängen.* Berlin, 1845.

———. *Johann Sebastian Bachs Matthäuspassion musikalish und ästhetisch dargestellt.* Berlin, 1852.

Nägeli, Hans Georg. *Die Individual-Bildung: Sieben Aufsätze über Solo-Gesangbildung.* Ed. Arnold Geering. Zurich, 1978.

———. *Johann Sebastian Bach.* Ed. Günter Birkner. Zurich, 1974.

———. *Von Bach zu Beethoven: Aus den Vorlesungen über Musik.* Ed. Willi Reich. Basel, 1946.

———. *Vorlesungen über Musik mit Berücksicktigung der Dilettanten.* Ed. Martin Staehelin. 1826. Reprint, Darmstadt, 1983.

Natorp, B. C. L. *Anleitung zur Unterweisung im Singen für Volkschulen. Erster und zweiter Cursus.* 1813. Reprint, Frankfurt am Main, 1989.

Nichols, Roger, ed. *Mendelssohn Remembered.* London, 1997.

Nolte, Eckhard. *Lehrpläne und Richtlinien für den schulischen Musikunterricht in Deutschland vom Beginn des 19. Jahrhunderts bis in die Gegenwart: Eine Dokumentation.* Mainz, 1975.

Pfeiffer, Michael Traugott, and Hans Georg Nägeli. *Gesangbildungslehre nach Pestalozzischen Grundsätzen, pädagogisch begründet von Michael Traugott Pfeiffer, methodisch bearbeitet von Hans Georg Nägeli.* Zürich, 1809.

Pleasants, Henry, ed. and trans. *Schumann on Music: A Selection from the Writings.* New York, 1965.

Reichardt, Johann Friedrich. *Beleuchtung der vertrauten Briefe über Frankreich.* Berlin, 1804.

———. *Briefe, die Musik betreffend.* Ed. Grita Herre and Walther Siegmund-Schultze. Leipzig, 1976.

———. *Ueber die Pflichten des Ripien-Violinisten.* Berlin, 1776.

Rellstab, Ludwig. *Henriette, oder die schöne Sängerin.* Leipzig, 1826.

———. *Ludwig Berger: Ein Denkmal (1777–1839).* Berlin, 1846.

———. *Ueber mein Verhältniss als Kritiker zu Herrn Spontini als Komponisten und*

Generalmusik-Direktor in Berlin, nebst einem vergnüglichen Anhange: Ein Beitrag zur Kunst-und Tagesgeschichte. Leipzig, 1827.

Rochlitz, Friedrich. *Für Freunde der Tonkunst.* 4 vols. Leipzig, 1825.

Schiller, Friedrich. *On the Aesthetic Education of Man in a Series of Letters.* Trans. and ed. Elizabeth Wilkinson and L. A. Willoughby. Oxford, 1967.

Schleiermacher, Friedrich. *On Religion: Speeches to Its Cultured Despisers.* Ed. and trans. Richard Crouter. New York, 1988.

——. *Vorlesungen über die Aesthetik.* Ed. Carl Lommatzsch. 1842. Reprint, Berlin, 1974.

Schröder, Cornelia. *Carl Friedrich Zelter und die Akademie: Dokumente und Briefe zur Entstehung der Musik-Sektion in der Preussischen Akademie der Künste.* Berlin, 1959.

Schubring, Julius, ed. *Briefwechsel zwischen Felix Mendelssohn-Bartholdy und Julius Schubring, zugleich ein Beitrag zur Geschichte des Oratoriums.* Leipzig, 1892.

Senner, Wayne M., Robin Wallace, and William Meredith, eds. *The Critical Reception of Beethoven's Compositions.* Lincoln, NE, 1999.

Spitta, Philipp. *Johann Sebastian Bach: His Work and Influence on the Music of Germany, 1685–1750.* 2 vols. Trans. Clara Bell and J. A. Fuller-Maitland. New York, 1951.

——. *Die Wiederbelebung protestantischer Kirchenmusik auf geschichtlicher Grundlage.* Berlin, 1882.

Spohr, Louis. *The Musical Journeys.* Ed. and trans. Henry Pleasants. Norman, OK, 1961.

Stauffer, George B., ed. *The Forkel-Hoffmeister & Kühnel Correspondence: A Document of the Early 19th-Century Bach Revival.* Trans. Arthur Mendel and George B. Stauffer. New York, 1990.

Stoepel, Franz. *Beyträge zur Würdigung der neuen Methode des gleichzeitigen Unterrichts einer Mehrzahl von Schülern im Piano-forte Spiel und der Theorie der Harmonie.* Gotha, 1823.

——. *Freimütige Worte: Ein Beitrag zur Beurtheilung der Schrift "System der Musik-Wissenschaft und der praktischen Composition" von J. B. Logier.* Munich, 1827.

——. *Grundzüge der Geschichte der modernen Musik, nach den besten Quellen bearbeitet, mit Vorwort von Gottfried Weber.* Berlin, 1821.

——. *Neues System der Harmonie-Lehre und des Unterrichts im Pianoforte-Spiel.* Frankfurt am Main, 1825.

Thibaut, Anton Friedrich Justus. *Über die Reinheit der Tonkunst.* Heidelberg, 1825.

Varnhagen von Ense, Rahel. *Rahel: Ein Buch des Andenkens für ihre Freunde.* Berlin, 1834.

Wagner, Ernst. *Reisen aus der Fremde in die Heimat.* Leipzig, 1806.

Wagner, Richard. *Art and Politics.* Trans. William Ashton Ellis. Lincoln, NE, 1996.

——. *Pilgrimage to Beethoven.* Trans. William Ashton Ellis. Lincoln, NE, 1994.

Weber, Carl Maria von. *Writings on Music.* Ed. John Warrack. Trans. Martin Cooper. New York, 1981.

Wehmer, Carl, ed. *"Ein tief gegründet Herz": Der Briefwechsel Felix Mendelssohn-Bartholdys mit Johann Gustav Droysen.* Heidelberg, 1859.

Weissweiler, Eva, ed. *"Die Musik will gar nicht rutschen ohne Dich": Fanny und Felix Mendelssohn Briefwechsel 1821 bis 1846.* Berlin, 1997.

Williams, Peter, ed. *The Wesley Bach Letters.* Facsimile reprint of the first printed edition. London, 1988.

Winterfeld, Carl. *Der evangelische Kirchengesang und sein Verhältniss zur Kunst des Tonsatzes.* 3 vols. Leipzig, 1843–47.

————. *Johannes Pierluigi von Palestrina, seine Werke und deren Bedeutung für die Geschichte der Tonkunst*. Breslau, 1832.

Wolf, Georg Friedrich. *Kurzer aber deutlicher Unterricht im Klavierspielen*. Göttingen, 1783.

Zelter, Karl Friedrich. *Darstellungen seines Lebens*. Ed. Johann-Wolfgang Schottländer. Weimar, 1931.

————. *Selbstdarstellung*. Ed. Willi Reich. Zurich, 1955.

————, ed. *Passionsmusik von Johann Sebastian Bach, nach dem Evangelium Matthai, cap. 26 und 27*. Berlin, 1829.

SECONDARY SOURCES

Allen, Warren Dwight. *Philosophies of Music History: A Study of General Histories of Music 1600–1960*. New York, 1962.

Altgeld, Wolfgang. *Katholizismus, Protestantismus, Judentum: Über religiös-begründete Gegensätze und nationalreligiöse Ideen in der Geschichte des deutschen Nationalismus*. Mainz, 1992.

Altmann, Alexander. *Moses Mendelssohn: A Biographical Study*. Birmingham, AL, 1973.

Anderson, Benedict. *Imagined Communities: Reflections on the Origin and Spread of Nationalism*. Rev. ed. London, 1991.

Applegate, Celia. "How German Is It? Nationalism and the Idea of Serious Music in the Early Nineteenth Century." *19th-Century Music* 21, no. 3 (spring 1998): 274–96.

Applegate, Celia, and Pamela Potter, eds. *Music and German National Identity*. Chicago, 2002.

Avineri, Shlomo. "Hegel and Nationalism." *Review of Politics* 24 (October 1962): 461–484.

Bauer, Elisabeth Eleonore. *Wie Beethoven auf den Sockel Kam: Die Entstehung eines musikalischen Mythos*. Stuttgart, 1992.

Baumann, Gerhart. "Goethe: 'Über den Dilettantismus.' " *Euphorion: Zeitschrift für Literaturgeschichte* 46 (1952): 349–69.

Beaufils, Marcel. *Comment l'Allemagne est devenue musicienne*. Paris, 1983.

Beiser, Frederick C. *Enlightenment, Revolution, and Romanticism: The Genesis of Modern German Political Thought 1790–1800*. Cambridge, MA, 1992.

Bell-Villada, Gene H. *Art for Art's Sake and Literary Life: How Politics and Markets Helped Shape the Ideology and Culture of Aestheticism 1790–1990*. Lincoln, NE, 1998.

Bigler, Robert M. *The Politics of German Protestantism: The Rise of the Protestant Church Elite in Prussia, 1815–1848*. Berkeley, 1972.

Birke, Adolf M., and Lothar Kettenacker. *Bürgertum, Adel, und Monarchie: Wandel der Lebensformen im Zeitalter des bürgerlichen Nationalismus*. Munich, 1989.

Birtsch, Günter. *Patriotismus*. Hamburg, 1991.

Blackall, Eric. *The Emergence of German as Literary Language, 1700–1775*. Cambridge, 1959.

Blackbourn, David. *The Fontana History of Germany 1780–1918: The Long Nineteenth Century*. London, 1997.

Blackwell, Albert L. *The Sacred in Music*. Louisville, KY, 1999.

Blomert, Reinhard, Helmut Kuzmics, and Annette Treibel, eds. *Transformationen des Wir-Gefühls: Studien zum nationalen Habitus*. Frankfurt am Main, 1993.

Blount, Wilfrid. *On Wings of Song: A Biography of Felix Mendelssohn*. London, 1974.

Blume, Friedrich. "Bach in the Romantic Era." *Musical Quarterly* 50 (1964): 290–306.

——. *Protestant Church Music: A History*. Rev. ed. in collaboration with Ludwig Finscher et al. New York, 1974.

——. *Two Centuries of Bach: An Account of Changing Taste*. Trans. Stanley Godman. New York, 1950.

Blumenberg, Hans. *Matthäuspassion*. Frankfurt am Main, 1988.

Bollert, Werner, ed. *Sing-Akademie zu Berlin: Festschrift zum 175 jährigen Bestehen*. Berlin, 1967.

Botstein, Leon. "Listening through Reading: Musical Literacy and the Concert Audience." *19th-Century Music* 16 (1992): 129–45.

——. "Mendelssohn and the Jews." *Musical Quarterly* 82 (1998): 210–19.

——. "Mendelssohn, Werner, and the Jews: A Final Word." *Musical Quarterly* 83 (1999): 45–50.

Bourdieu, Pierre, and Loïc J. D. Wacquant. *An Invitation to Reflexive Sociology*. Chicago, 1992.

Boyd, Malcolm, ed. *Oxford Composer Companions: J. S. Bach*. New York, 1999.

Boyle, Nicholas. *Goethe: The Poet and the Age*. New York, 1992.

Bruckner-Bigenwald, Martha. *Die Anfänge der Leipziger Allgemeinen Musikalischen Zeitung*. Hilversum, 1965.

Burnham, Scott. "Criticism, Faith, and the *Idee*: A. B. Marx's Early Reception of Beethoven." *19th-Century Music* 13 (spring 1990): 183–92.

Butt, John. *Music Education and the Art of Performance in the German Baroque*. Cambridge, 1994.

——. "The Saint Johann Sebastian Passion." *New Republic* (10 & 17 July 2000): 33–38.

——, ed. *The Cambridge Companion to Bach*. Cambridge, 1997.

Carse, Adam. *The Orchestra from Beethoven to Berlioz*. Cambridge, 1948.

Cassirer, Ernst. *Kant's Life and Thought*. Trans. James Haden. New Haven, 1981.

——. *The Philosophy of the Enlightenment*. Trans. Fritz C. A. Koelln and James P. Pettegrove. Princeton, 1951.

Caygill, Howard. *Art of Judgement*. Cambridge, MA, 1989.

Chytry, Josef. *The Aesthetic State: A Quest in Modern German Thought*. Berkeley, 1989.

Clark, Christopher. "Confessional Policy and the Limits of State Action: Frederick William III and the Prussian Church Union 1817–40." *Historical Journal* 39 (1996): 985–1004.

——. *The Politics of Conversion: Missionary Protestantism and the Jews in Prussia, 1728–1941*. Oxford, 1995.

——. "The Politics of Revival: Pietists, Aristocrats, and the State Church in Early Nineteenth-Century Prussia." In *Between Reform, Reaction, and Resistance: Studies in the History of German Conservatism from 1789 to 1945*, ed. Larry E. Jones and James N. Retallack. Providence, 1993.

Clements, Keith. *Friedrich Schleiermacher: Pioneer of Modern Theology*. London: Collins Liturgical Publications, 1987.

Crane, Susan. *Collecting and Historical Consciousness in Early Nineteenth-Century Germany*. Ithaca, NY, 2000.

Dahlhaus, Carl. *Between Romanticism and Modernism*. Trans. Mary Whittall. Berkeley, 1980.

——. *The Esthetics of Music*. Trans. William Austin. New York, 1982.

——. *Foundations of Music History*. Trans. J. B. Robinson. New York, 1983.

——. *The Idea of Absolute Music*. Trans. Roger Lustig. Chicago, 1989.

——. *Nineteenth-Century Music*. Trans. J. Bradford Robinson. Berkeley, 1989.

——, ed. *Das Problem Mendelssohn*. Regensburg, 1974.

——. *Realism in Nineteenth-Century Music*. Trans. Mary Whittall. New York, 1982.

——, ed. *Studien zur Musikgeschichte Berlins im frühen 19. Jahrhundert*. Regensburg, 1980.

——. "Zur Entstehung der romantischen Bach-Deutung." *Bach-Jahrbuch* 64 (1978): 192–210.

Dann, Otto. "Die Anfänge politischer Vereinsbildung in Deutschland." In *Soziale Bewegung und politische Verfassung: Beiträge zur Geschichte der modernen Welt,* ed. Ulrich Engelhardt, Volker Sellin, and Horst Stuke. Stuttgart, 1976.

——. *Nation und Nationalismus in Deutschland 1770–1990*. Munich, 1993.

Daverio, John. *Nineteenth-century Music and the German Romantic Ideology*. New York, 1993.

Davison, Archibald. *Bach and Handel: The Consummation of the Baroque in Music*. Cambridge, MA, 1951.

Dülmen, Richard van. *The Society of the Enlightenment: The Rise of the Middle Class and Enlightenment Culture in Germany*. Trans. Anthony Williams. New York, 1992.

Eberle, Gottfried. *200 Jahre Sing-Akademie zu Berlin*. Berlin, 1991.

Ebert, Gerhard. "Vorwort zu 'Improvisation und Schauspielkunst,'" part of *100 Jahre Schauspielschule Berlin*. http://www.berlinerschauspielschule.de/impro_vorwort.htm.

Ehinger, Hans. *E. T. A. Hoffmann als Musiker und Musikschriftsteller*. Cologne, 1954.

——. *Friedrich Rochlitz als Musikschriftsteller*. Leipzig, 1929.

Eidsam, Klaus. *Das wahre Leben des Johann Sebastian Bach*. Munich, 1999.

Engel, Hans. *Musik und Gesellschaft: Baustein zu einer Musiksoziologie*. Berlin, 1960.

Engelhardt, Ulrich. *Bildungsbürgertum: Begriffs- und Dogmengeschichte eines Etiketts*. Stuttgart, 1986.

Fellerer, Karl Gustav. *Studien zur Musik des 19. Jahrhunderts*. Vol. 2, *Kirchenmusik im 19. Jahrhundert*. Regensburg, 1985.

——. *Studien zur Musik des 19. Jahrhunderts*. Vol. 3, *Romantik und Akademismus*. Regensburg, 1987.

Findlen, Paula. *Possessing Nature: Museums, Collecting, and Scientific Culture in Early Modern Italy*. Berkeley, 1994.

Fischer, Ludwig. "Zum Begriff der Klassik in der Musik." *Der Musikwissenschaft* 2 (1966): 9–34.

Fischer-Dieskau, Dietrich. *Carl Friedrich Zelter und das Berliner Musikleben seiner Zeit*. Berlin, 1997.

Flaherty, Gloria. *Opera in the Development of German Critical Thought*. Princeton, 1978.

Fleetham, Deborah. "In the Shadow of Luther: The Reshaping of Protestantism in Berlin, 1815–1848." Ph.D. diss., University of Rochester, 2001.

Forchert, Arno. *Johann Sebastian Bach und seine Zeit*. Laaber, 2000.

Frei, Walter. *Johann Sebastian Bach in den Wandlungen der Europäischen Geistesgeschichte, dargestellt am Schlusschor der Matthäus-Passion*. Wiesbaden, 1986.

Gadamer, Hans-Georg. *Truth and Method*. Ed. Garrett Barden and John Cumming. New York, 1975.

Bibliography

Garland, Henry, and Mary Garland. *The Oxford Companion to German Literature*. 2nd ed. New York, 1986.

Garratt, James. *Palestrina and the German Romantic Imagination: Interpreting Historicism in Nineteenth-century Music*. New York, 2002.

Gawthrop, Richard. *Pietism and the Making of Eighteenth-Century Prussia*. Cambridge, 1993.

Geck, Martin. *Bach: Leben und Werk*. Reinbek bei Hamburg, 2000.

Geiger, Ludwig. *Geschichte der Juden in Berlin*. Berlin, 1871.

Gellner, Ernest. *Nations and Nationalism*. Ithaca, NY, 1983.

Gerth, Hans H. *Bürgerliche Intelligenz um 1800: Zur Soziologie des deutschen Frühliberalismus*. 1935. Reprint, Göttingen, 1976.

Giesen, Bernhard. *Intellectuals and the Nation: Collective Identity in a German Axial Age*. Trans. Nicholas Levis and Amos Weisz. New York, 1998.

Goehr, Lydia. *The Imaginary Museum of Musical Works: An Essay in the Philosophy of Music*. Oxford, 1992.

Gorrell, Lorraine. *The Nineteenth-Century German Lied*. Portland, OR, 1993.

Goslich, Ilse. "Zelter und seine Verleger: Eine biographisch-bibliographische Studie." *Jahrbuch der Sammlung Kippenberg* 7 (1927/28): 67–101.

Gramit, David. *Cultivating Music: The Aspirations, Interests, and Limits of German Musical Culture, 1770–1848*. Berkeley, 2002.

Grossmann-Vendrey, Susanna. *Felix Mendelssohn Bartholdy und die Musik der Vergangenheit*. Regensburg, 1969.

Gruhn, Wilfried. *Geschichte der Musikerziehung: Eine Kultur- und Sozialgeschichte vom Gesangunterricht der Aufklärungspädagogik zu ästhetisch-kultureller Bildung*. Hofheim, 1993.

Habermas, Jürgen. *Structural Transformation of the Public Sphere: An Inquiry into a Category of Bourgeois Society*. Trans. Thomas Burger and Frederick Lawrence. Cambridge, MA, 1989.

Hampe, Theodor. *Die fahrenden Leute in der deutschen Vergangenheit*. Leipzig, 1902.

Harris, Horton. *David Friedrich Strauss and His Theology*. Cambridge, 1973.

Hase, Oskar von. *Breitkopf und Härtel: Gedenkschrift und Arbeitsbericht*. 5th ed. Wiesbaden, 1968.

Hecker, Max. "Tagebuchauszug an Zelters Tod." *Jahrbuch der Sammlung Kippenberg* 7 (1927/28): 112–15.

Hein, Dieter, and Andreas Schulz. *Bürgerkultur im 19. Jahrhundert: Bildung, Kunst und Lebenswelt*. Munich, 1996.

Heister, Hanns-Werner. *Das Konzert: Theorie einer Kulturform*. 2 vols. Wilhelmshaven, 1983.

Herrmann, Ulrich, ed. *Volk-Nation-Vaterland*. Hamburg, 1996.

Herrnstein Smith, Barbara. *Contingencies of Value: Alternative Perspectives for Critical Theory*. Cambridge, MA, 1988.

Hertz, Deborah. *Jewish High Society in Old Regime Berlin*. New Haven, 1988.

Herz, Gerhard. *Essays on J. S. Bach*. Studies in Musicology, no. 73. Ann Arbor, 1985.

Hohendahl, Peter Uwe. *Building a National Literature: The Case of Germany, 1830–1870*. Trans. Renate Baron Franciscono. Ithaca, NY, 1989.

Bibliography

Höcker, Karla. *Hauskonzerte in Berlin*. Berlin, 1970.

Hölscher, Lucien. "Die Religion des Bürgers: Bürgerliche Frömmigkeit und Protestantische Kirche im 19. Jahrhundert." *Historische Zeitschrift* 250 (1990): 595–630.

———. "Säkularisierungsprozesse im deutschen Protestantismus des 19. Jahrhunderts." In *Bürger in der Gesellschaft der Neuzeit*, ed. Hans-Jürgen Puhle. Göttingen, 1991.

Hope, Nicholas. *German and Scandinavian Protestantism 1700–1918*. Oxford, 1995.

Irwin, Joyce. "German Pietists and Church Music in the Baroque Age." *Church History* 54 (1985): 29–40.

Jacobi, Erwin R. "C. F. Zelters kritische Beleuchtung von J. N. Forkels Buch über J. S. Bach, aufgrund neu aufgefundener Manuskripte." In *International Musicological Society: Report of the Eleventh Congress 1972*, 2:462–66. Copenhagen, 1974.

Jeismann, Michael. *Das Vaterland der Feinde: Studien zum nationalen Feindbegriff und Selbstverständnis in Deutschland und Frankreich 1792–1918*. Stuttgart, 1992.

Johnson, James. *Listening in Paris: A Cultural History*. Berkeley, 1995.

Johnston, Otto W. *The Myth of a Nation—Literature and Politics in Prussia under Napoleon*. Columbia, SC, 1989.

Jones, Peter Ward. "Letter to the Editor." *Musical Quarterly* 83 (1999): 27–30.

Jorgenson, Dale A. *The Life and Legacy of Franz Xaver Hauser: A Forgotten Leader in the Nineteenth-Century Bach Movement*. Carbondale, IL, 1996.

Katz, Jacob. *Out of the Ghetto: The Social Background of Jewish Emancipation, 1770–1870*. Cambridge, MA, 1973.

Kerman, Joseph. "How We Got into Analysis, and How to Get Out." *Critical Inquiry* 7 (winter 1980): 311–31.

Kimber, Marian Wilson. "The 'Suppression' of Fanny Mendelssohn: Rethinking Feminist Biography." *19th-Century Music* 26 (summer 2002): 113–29.

Knudsen, Jonathan. *Justus Möser and the German Enlightenment*. Cambridge, 1986.

Kocka, Jürgen, ed. *Bildungsbürgertum im 19. Jahrhundert*. Vol. 4, *Politischer Einfluss und gesellschaftliche Formation*. Stuttgart, 1989.

———, ed. *Bürger und Bürgerlichkeit im 19. Jahrhundert*. Göttingen, 1987.

Kocka, Jürgen, and Allan Mitchell, eds. *Bourgeois Society in Nineteenth-Century Europe*. Providence, RI, 1993.

Koopmann, Helmut. "Dilettantismus: Bemerkungen zu einem Phänomen der Goethezeit." In *Studien zur Goethezeit: Festschrift für Lieselotte Blumenthal*. ed. Helmut Holtzhauer and Bernhard Zeller. Weimar, 1968.

Koselleck, Reinhart. *Futures Past: On the Semantics of Historical Time*. Trans. Keith Tribe. Cambridge, MA, 1985.

———. *Preussen zwischen Reform und Revolution*. Stuttgart, 1989.

———, ed. *Geschichtliche Grundbegriffe*. 8 vols. Stuttgart, 1992.

Kramer, Wilhelm. *Formen und Funktionen exemplarisher Darstellung von Musikunterricht im 19. und 20. Jahrhundert*. Wölfenbüttel, 1990.

La Vopa, Anthony. *Grace, Talent, and Merit: Poor Students, Clerical Careers, and Professional Ideology in Eighteenth-Century Germany*. Cambridge, 1988.

Laven, David, and Lucy Riall. *Napoleon's Legacy: Problems of Government in Restoration Europe*. New York, 2000.

Lawford-Hinrichsen, Irene. *Music Publishing and Patronage: C. F. Peters 1800 to the Holocaust*. Kenton, UK, 2000.

Lenneberg, Hans. *Witnesses and Scholars: Studies in Musical Biography*. New York, 1988.

Levinger, Matthew. *Enlightened Nationalism: The Transformation of Prussian Political Culture, 1806–1848*. New York, 2000.

Lindemann, Mary. *Patriots and Paupers: Hamburg, 1712–1830*. New York, 1990.

Lippman, Edward. *A History of Western Musical Aesthetics*. Lincoln, NE, 1992.

Loesser, Arthur. *Men, Women, and Pianos: A Social History*. New York, 1954.

Lowenstein, Steven M. *The Berlin Jewish Community: Enlightenment, Family, and Crisis, 1770–1830*. New York, 1994.

Magee, Bryan. *The Tristan Chord: Wagner and Philosophy*. New York, 2000.

Marissen, Michael. *Lutheranism, Anti-Judaism, and Bach's St. John Passion*. With an annotated literal translation of the libretto. New York, 1998.

——. "Religious Aims in Mendelssohn's 1829 Berlin Singakademie Performances of Bach's St. Matthew Passion." *Musical Quarterly* 77 (1993): 718–26.

——, ed. *Bach Perspectives*. Vol. 3, *Creative Responses to Bach from Mozart to Hindemith*. Lincoln, NE, 1998.

Massey, Marilyn Chapin. *Christ Unmasked: The Meaning of the Life of Jesus in German Politics*. Chapel Hill, NC, 1983.

Mayer, Andreas. " 'Gluck'sches Gestöhn' und 'welsches Larifari': Anna Milder, Franz Schubert und der deutsch-italienische Opernkrieg." *Archiv für Musikwissenschaft* 52 (1995): 171–204.

McClelland, Charles. *State, Society, and University in Germany, 1700–1914*. New York, 1980.

Meinecke, Friedrich. *Cosmopolitanism and the National State*. Trans. Robert B. Kimber. Princeton, 1970.

Menhennet, Alan. *Order and Freedom: Literature and Society in Germany from 1720–1805*. New York, 1973.

Mercer-Taylor, Peter, ed. *The Cambridge Companion to Mendelssohn*. New York, 2004.

Mintz, Donald. "Some Aspects of the Revival of Bach." *Musical Quarterly* 40 (April 1954): 201–21.

Mommsen, Wolfgang J. *Imperial Germany, 1867–1918: Politics, Culture, and Society in an Authoritarian State*. Trans. Richard Deveson. London, 1995.

Moran, Daniel. *Toward the Century of Words: Johann Cotta and the Politics of the Public Realm in Germany, 1795–1832*. Berkeley, 1990.

Morrow, Mary Sue. *German Music Criticism in the Late Eighteenth Century: Aesthetic Issues in Instrumental Music*. New York, 1997.

——. "Of Unity and Passion: The Aesthetics of Concert Criticism in Early 19th Century Vienna." *19th-Century Music* 13 (spring 1990): 193–209.

Moser, Hans Joachim. *Heinrich Schütz: A Short Account of His Life and Works*. Trans. and ed. Derek McCulloch. New York, 1967.

Nipperdey, Thomas. *Germany from Napoleon to Bismarck*. Trans. Daniel Nolan. Princeton, 1996.

Nowak, Adolf. *Hegels Musikaesthetik*. Regensburg, 1971.

Parakilas, James, with E. Douglas Bomberger et al. *Piano Roles: Three Hundred Years of Life with the Piano*. New Haven, 1999.

Pearce, Susan. *On Collecting: An Investigation into Collecting in the European Tradition*. New York, 1995.

Pederson, Sanna. "A. B. Marx, Berlin Concert Life, and German National Identity." *19th-Century Music* 18, no. 2 (fall 1994): 87–104.

Peiser, Karl. *Johann Adam Hiller: Ein Beitrag zur Musikgeschichte des 18. Jahrhunderts.* Leipzig, 1894.

Pelikan, Jaroslav. *Bach among the Theologians.* Philadelphia, 1986.

Pendle, Karin, ed. *Women and Music: A History.* Bloomington, 1991.

Petersen, Christian. "Die Teutschübende Gesellschaft in Hamburg." *Zeitschrift des Vereins für hamburgische Geschichte* 2 (1847): 533–64.

Petrat, Nicolai. *Hausmusik des Biedermeier im Blickpunkt der zeitgenössischen musikalischen Fachpresse (1815–1848).* Hamburger Beiträge zur Musikwissenschaft, vol. 31. Hamburg, 1986.

Pfeiffer, Harald. *Heidelberger Musikleben in der ersten Hälfte des 19. Jahrhunderts.* Heidelberg, 1989.

Pomian, Krysztof. *Collectors and Curiosities: Paris and Vienna, 1500–1800.* Cambridge, MA, 1990.

Porter, Cecilia. "The New Public and the Reordering of the Musical Establishment: The Lower Rhine Music Festivals, 1818–67." *19th-Century Music* 3 (1979–80): 211–24.

Potter, Pamela M. *Most German of the Arts: Musicology and Society from the Weimar Republic to the End of Hitler's Reich.* New Haven, 1998.

Rainbow, Bernarr. *The Land without Music: Musical Education in England 1800–1860 and Its Continental Antecedents.* London, 1967.

Radcliffe, Philip. *Mendelssohn.* Rev. ed. by Peter Ward Jones. New York, 2000.

Raynor, Henry. *A Social History of Music, from the Middle Ages to Beethoven.* London, 1972.

Reed, T. J. *The Classical Center: Goethe and Weimar 1775–1832.* London, 1980.

Rehm, Jürgen. *Zur Musikrezeption im vormärzlichen Berlin: Die Präsentation bürgerlichen Selbstverständnisses und biedermeierlicher Kunstanschauung in den Musikkritiken Ludwig Rellstabs.* Hildesheim, 1983.

Reich, Nancy B. *Clara Schumann: The Artist and the Woman.* Ithaca, NY, 1985.

Reimer, Erich. *Die Hofmusik in Deutschland, 1500–1800: Wandlungen einer Institution.* Wilhelmshaven, 1991.

———. "Nationalbewusstsein und Musikgeschichtsschreibung in Deutschland, 1800–1850." *Die Musikforschung* 46 (1993): 17–24.

———. "Repertoirebildung und Kanonisierung. Zur Vorgeschichte des Klassikbegriffs (1800–1835)." *Archiv für Musikwissenschaft* 43 (1986): 241–58.

Richardson, Herbert, ed. *Friedrich Schleiermacher and the Founding of the University of Berlin: The Study of Religion as a Scientific Discipline.* Schleiermacher Studies and Translations 5. Lewiston, 1991.

Richter, Arnd. *Mendelssohn: Leben, Werke, Dokumente.* Mainz: Schott, 1994.

Rieger, Eva, ed. *Frau und Musik.* Kassel, 1990.

Riemann, Hugo. *Geschichte der Musik seit Beethoven, 1800–1900.* Berlin, 1901.

Ringer, Alexander. *Music and Society: The Early Romantic Era between Revolutions, 1789–1848.* Englewood Cliffs, NJ, 1990.

Rosen, Charles. *The Romantic Generation.* Cambridge, MA, 1995.

Salmen, Walter. *Das Konzert: Eine Kulturgeschichte.* Munich, 1988.

———, ed. *The Social Status of the Professional Musician from the Middle Ages to the 19th Century.* Trans. Herbert Kaufman and Barbara Reisner. New York, 1983.

Bibliography

Sandberger, Wolfgang. *Das Bach-Bild Philipp Spittas: Ein Beitrag zur Geschichte der Bach-Rezeption im 19. Jahrhundert.* Stuttgart, 1997.

Schaper, Eva. *Studies in Kant's Aesthetics.* Edinburgh, 1979.

Scherer, Wolfgang. *Klavier-Spiele: Die Psychotechnik der Klaviere im 18. und 19. Jahrhundert.* Munich, 1989.

Schleuning, Peter. *Der Bürger erhebt sich: Geschichte der deutschen Musik im 18. Jahrhundert.* Stuttgart, 2000.

Schmidt, Christian Martin, ed. *Felix Mendelssohn Bartholdy: Kongress-Bericht Berlin 1994.* Leipzig, 1997.

Schmitt-Thomas, Reinhold. *Die Entwicklung der deutschen Konzertkritik im Spiegel der Leipziger Allgemeinen Musikalischen Zeitung (1798–1848).* Frankfurt am Main, 1969.

Schoeps, Julius H. "1786–1871: Ringen um Reform und Emanzipation." In *Juden in Berlin, 1671–1945: Ein Lesebuch,* ed. Annegret Ehmann. Berlin, 1988.

Schoolfield, George. *The Figure of the Musician in German Literature.* Chapel Hill, NC, 1956.

Schottländer, Johann-Wolfgang. "Zelters Beziehungen zu den Komponisten seiner Zeit." *Jahrbuch der Sammlung Kippenberg* 8 (1930): 134–248.

Schrenk, Oswald. *Berlin und die Musik: Zweihundert Jahre Musikleben einer Stadt, 1740–1940.* Berlin, 1940.

Schulte-Sasse, Jochen. "The Prestige of the Artist under Conditions of Modernity." *Cultural Critique,* no. 12 (spring 1989): 83–100.

Schulze, Hagen. *The Course of German Nationalism, from Frederick the Great to Bismarck, 1763–1867.* Trans. Sarah Hanbury-Tenison. Cambridge, 1991.

Schünemann, Georg. "Die Bachpflege der Berliner Singakademie." *Bach-Jahrbuch* 25 (1928): 138–71.

———. *Carl Friedrich Zelter: Der Begründer der preussischen Musikpflege.* Berlin, 1932.

———. *Carl Friedrich Zelter: Der Mensch und sein Werk.* Berlin, 1937.

———. *Die Singakademie zu Berlin 1791–1941.* Regensburg, 1941.

Schweitzer, Albert. *J. S. Bach.* 2 vols. Trans. Ernest Newman. New York, 1966.

Sheehan, James J. *German History, 1770–1866.* New York, 1989.

———. *Museums in the German Art World.* New York, 2000.

Simms, Brendan. *The Impact of Napoleon: Prussian High Politics, Foreign Policy and the Crisis of the Executive, 1797–1806.* New York, 1997.

Sittard, Josef. *Geschichte des Musik- und Concertwesens in Hamburg.* Altona, 1890.

Smend, Friedrich. "Bachs Matthäus-Passion: Untersuchungen zur Geschichte des Werkes bis 1750." *Bach Jahrbuch* 25 (1928): 1–95.

———. *Goethes Verhältnis zu Bach.* Berlin, 1955.

Smith, Helmut Walser, ed. *Protestants, Catholics and Jews in Germany, 1800–1914.* New York, 2001.

Solie, Ruth, ed. *Musicology and Difference: Gender and Sexuality in Music Scholarship.* Berkeley, 1993.

Sorkin, David. *Moses Mendelssohn and the Religious Enlightenment.* Berkeley, 1996.

———. *The Transformation of German Jewry, 1780–1840.* New York, 1987.

———. "Wilhelm von Humboldt: The Theory and Practice of Self-Formation (*Bildung*), 1791–1810." *Journal of the History of Ideas* 44 (January–March 1983): 55–74.

Sösemann, Bernd, ed. *Gemeingeist und Bürgersinn: Die preussischen Reformen.* Berlin, 1993.

Southard, Robert. *Droysen and the Prussian School of History*. Lexington, KY, 1994.

Sowa, Georg. *Anfänge institutioneller Musikerziehung in Deutschland (1800–1843)*. Regensburg, 1973.

Spaethling, Robert. *Music and Mozart in the Life of Goethe*. Columbia, SC, 1987.

Sponheuer, Bernd. "Das Bach-Bild Hans Georg Nägelis und die Entstehung der musikalischen Autonomieästhetik." *Die Musikforschung* 39 (1986): 107–23.

——. *Musik als Kunst und Nicht-Kunst: Untersuchungen zur Dichotonomie von 'hoher' und 'niederer' Musik im musikästhetishcen Denken zwischen Kant und Hanslick*. Kassel, 1987.

——. "Reconstructing Ideal Types of the 'German' in Music." In Applegate and Potter, *Music and German National Identity*, 36–57.

Sposato, Jeffrey Stuart. "Creative Writing: The [Self-] Identification of Mendelssohn as Jew." *Musical Quarterly* 82 (1998): 190–209.

——. "Mendelssohn, *Paulus*, and the Jews: A Response to Leon Botstein and Michael Steinberg." *Musical Quarterly* 83 (1999): 280–91.

——. "The Price of Assimilation: The Oratorios of Felix Mendelssohn and the Nineteenth-Century Anti-Semitic Tradition." Ph.D diss., Brandeis University, 2000.

Stadelmann, Rudolf, and Wolfram Fischer. *Die Bildungswelt des deutschen Handwerkers um 1800: Studien zur Soziologie des Kleinbürgers im Zeitalter Goethes*. Berlin, 1955.

Stamm-Kuhlmann, Thomas. *König in Preussens grosser Zeit: Friedrich Wilhelm III, der Melancholiker auf dem Thron*. Berlin, 1992.

Swafford, Jan. *Johannes Brahms: A Biography*. New York, 1997.

Sweet, Paul R. *Wilhelm von Humboldt: A Biography*. 2 Vols. Columbus, OH, 1978.

Tadday, Ulrich. *Die Anfänge des Musikfeuilletons: Der kommunikative Gebrauchswert musikalischer Bildung in Deutschland um 1800*. Stuttgart, 1993.

Todd, R. Larry. *Mendelssohn: A Life in Music*. New York, 2003.

——, ed. *Mendelssohn and His World*. Princeton, 1991.

——, ed. *Mendelssohn Studies*. New York, 1992.

——. *Mendelssohn's Musical Education: A Study and Edition of His Exercises in Composition*. Cambridge, 1983.

Toews, John. *Hegelianism: The Path toward Dialectical Humanism 1805–1841*. Cambridge, 1980.

——. "Memory and Gender in the Remaking of Fanny Mendelssohn's Musical Identity: The Chorale in *Das Jahr*." *Musical Quarterly* 77 (1993): 727–48

Townsend, Mary Lee. *Forbidden Laughter: Popular Humor and the Limits of Repression in Nineteenth-Century Prussia*. Ann Arbor, 1992.

Vaget, Hans Rudolf. *Dilettantismus und Meistershaft. Zum Problem des Dilettantismus bei Goethe: Praxis, Theorie, Zeitkritik*. Munich, 1971.

Van Orden, Kate. *Music and the Cultures of Print*. New York, 2000.

Victor, Walther. *Carl Friedrich Zelter und seine Freundschaft mit Goethe*. Berlin, 1970.

Vierhaus, Rudolf. *Deutschland im 18. Jahrhundert: Politische Verfassung, soziales Gefüge, geistige Bewegungen*. Göttingen, 1987.

Wagner, Günther, ed. *Bachtage Berlin: Vorträge 1970 bis 1981 Sammelband*. Neuhausen-Stuttgart, 1985.

Walker, Mack. *German Home Towns: Community, State, and General Estate 1648–1871*. Ithaca, NY, 1971.

Wallace, Robin. *Beethoven's Critics: Aesthetic Dilemmas and Resolutions during the Composer's Lifetime.* New York, 1986.

Ward, Albert. *Book Production, Fiction, and the German Reading Public, 1740–1800.* Oxford, 1974.

Warnke, Martin. *The Court Artist: On the Ancestry of the Modern Artist.* Trans. David McLintock. Cambridge, 1993.

Weber, William. *Music and the Middle Class: The Social Structure of Concert Life in London, Paris, and Vienna.* London, 1975.

——. *The Rise of Musical Classics in Eighteenth-Century England: A Study in Canon, Ritual, and Ideology.* Oxford, 1992.

Weiner, Marc. *Richard Wagner and the Anti-Semitic Imagination.* Lincoln, NE, 1995.

Weissmann, Adolf. *Berlin als Musikstadt: Geschichte der Oper und des Konzerts von 1740 bis 1911.* Berlin, 1911.

Werner, Eric. *Mendelssohn: Leben und Werk in neuer Sicht.* Zurich: Atlantis, 1980.

Wilcox, John. "The Beginnings of *l'art pour l'art.*" *Journal of Aesthetics and Art Criticism* 2 (1953): 360–77.

Wiora, Walter, ed. *Die Ausbreitung des Historismus über die Musik.* Regensburg, 1969.

Wolff, Christoph. *Bach: Essays on His Life and Music.* Cambridge, MA, 1991.

——. *Johann Sebastian Bach: The Learned Musician.* New York, 2000.

——. "The Kantor, the Kapellmeister and the Musical Scholar: Remarks on the History and Performance of Bach's Mass in B Minor." Trans. Mary Whittall. Liner notes to J. S. Bach, Mass in B Minor, compact disc, Dorian Recordings DOR-90253 I, II, 1985.

——. "Recovered in Kiev: Bach et al. A Preliminary Report on the Music Collection of the Berlin Sing-Akademie." *Notes: Quarterly Journal of the Music Library Association* 58 (December 2001): 259–71.

Wollny, Peter. "Sara Levy and the Making of Musical Taste in Berlin." *Musical Quarterly* 77 (1993): 651–88.

Wolschke, Martin. *Von der Stadtpfeiferei zu Lehrlingskapelle und Sinfonieorchester.* Regensburg, 1981.

Woodmansee, Martha. *The Author, Art, and the Market: Rereading the History of Aesthetics.* New York, 1994.

Wright, Barbara David. "Johann Sebastian Bach's 'Matthäus-Passion': A Performance History, 1829–1854." Ph.D. diss., University of Michigan, 1983.

Zimmer, Hasko. *Auf dem Altar des Vaterlands: Religion und Patriotismus in der deutschen Kriegslyrik des 19. Jahrhunderts.* Frankfurt am Main, 1971.

Ziolkowski, Theodore. *German Romanticism and Its Institutions.* Princeton, 1990.

INDEX